GENESIS

GENESIS

From
Creation
to a
Nation

KEN FLEMING

ECS
MINISTRIES
The Word to the World

Emmaus College Press

Genesis: From Creation to a Nation
Ken Fleming

Copyright © 2005 ECS Ministries

ISBN 1-59387-012-4

First Edition 2005

Published by:
Emmaus College Press
(A Division of ECS Ministries)
P.O. Box 1028
Dubuque, IA   52004-1028
www.ecsministries.org

Printed in the United States of America

Contents

Contents

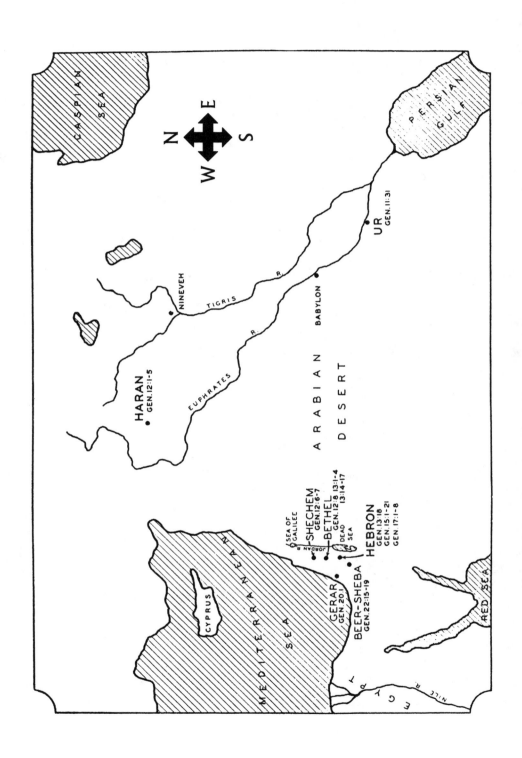

Introduction

The Importance of the Book of Genesis

God's revelation to man begins with the book of Genesis, which means that the importance of Genesis for us can hardly be overstated. It contains the truth about the origin of all things and is the key to understanding all that has happened in the subsequent history of the world. But more than that, it provides a foundation for all the great truth about God and His ways that are progressively revealed in the Bible. Genesis helps us to understand the meaning of history, and in particular, of God's purposes that are being worked out, especially in His relationship to people.

Genesis is important for us because it answers many of life's biggest questions. Where did we come from? Why are we here? What is the nature of man? What is wrong with our world? What is our future, and the future of the world?

Because it is foundational to our understanding of God's truth, Genesis is *a book of theology*. It records the creation of all things, especially the formation of planet Earth and the early history of its people. It spans the first 3000 years of human history, from the creation of Adam to the death of Joseph. In this sense, it is *a book of history*. Finally, it is a book full of narrative about people in their relationships with God and with one other. It is, therefore, *a book of insight* into human life and relations.

All the other books of the Old Testament are closely connected with the book of Genesis as the history of God's people unfolds. In referring to Genesis the way they do, they clearly show that it is not a collection of folk tales but the history of real people and events. The first great people of Genesis are called *ancients,* such as Adam and Noah (chapters 1-11).

After the Flood, the key characters are termed *patriarchs*. They were Abraham, Isaac, and Jacob, the latter being referred to in twenty of the Old Testament books and eleven of the New. The descendants of the patriarchs formed the nation Israel, whose very existence would be inexplicable without the Genesis record.

In the New Testament there are more than two hundred quotations or references to Genesis. Interestingly, more than one hundred of them refer to passages in the first eleven chapters—the chapters most under attack by skeptics.

Every one of these references treats Genesis as an actual historical record, so we can be confident that the record is true.

The word *genesis* means "beginnings" or "origins." It is a fitting title because the book reveals the origin of the universe with its galaxies and solar systems. It describes the beginning of all life forms and human life in particular. We learn also the beginnings of man's relationship with God and the origin of evil. We find there the beginnings of agriculture, trade, music, cities, government, nations, and religion. And we discover how God's chosen people, Israel, came into being and grew through the period of the patriarchs.

Moses, the Author of the Book of Genesis

The human author of Genesis was Moses, the leader of the people of Israel during their exodus from Egypt and subsequent journey and wanderings in the wilderness. The Lord Jesus Himself attributed the first five books of the Bible (which includes Genesis) to Moses. When Jesus spoke to the disciples on the Emmaus Road, it is recorded, "And beginning *at Moses* and all the Prophets, He expounded to them in all *the Scriptures* the things concerning Himself" (Luke 24:27, emphasis added). Then later that same resurrection day, Jesus said to His disciples in the upper room, "These are the words which I spoke to you while I was still with you, that all things must be fulfilled which were written in *the Law of Moses* and the Prophets and the Psalms concerning Me" (Luke 24:44, emphasis added). While there has been much controversy over the identity of the human author of Genesis by liberal scholars who do not believe in the inspiration of Scripture, conservative scholars do not doubt that it was, indeed, Moses.

The Data Moses Used to Write Genesis

How did Moses come to know the vast amount of data he recorded in Genesis? While it is true that all Scripture was given by inspiration of God, there are several ways in which the material was gathered by its human authors. One way they received it was by direct revelation from God, either audibly or visibly. Many Bible writers, such as the prophet Isaiah, heard God's voice or saw visions. When they wrote what they heard and saw, it became part of the Holy Writings. Another way by which they received it was as witnesses, either watching something happen or from the verbal testimony of others. Moses observed the crossing of the Red Sea and we read what he saw in the book of Exodus. A third way in which revelation came was from written records of the past that were selected, edited, and arranged. The two books of Chronicles were put together in this way from court records. The Holy Spirit overruled by guiding and guarding the process so that the Scriptures were written exactly as God intended.

Regarding the data for the book of Genesis, it seems most probable that much of the material came to Moses from written records left by his forefathers.

Some of these no doubt came from sources prior to the Flood and were preserved and handed on by Noah. The godly line of Shem would have continued to preserve these records. Then, family heads added to them as they were passed from one generation to the next. Abraham would have brought them with him to Canaan. Each of the patriarchs must have recorded God's revelations to them and the major events in their lives. When Jacob moved to Egypt, he would have brought them with him. In Egypt, Joseph would likely have collected all available historical material and established family archives during the years of the embryonic nation's development there.

With the fulfillment of God's original promises still in process, it would have been extremely important for His people to have in their possession all the ancient records. These would probably have been in the form of clay tablets. Moses, with his clear understanding of God's purpose for the emerging nation to return to the Promised Land, would have had them close to hand when the time came. He would also have had the oral family history passed down from Abraham, Isaac, Jacob, Judah, and Levi. Using his intellectual capacity and the educational training he received in Egypt, Moses compiled and edited the narratives to compile the book of Genesis under the infallible direction of the Spirit of God.

Circumstances Surrounding the Writing of Genesis

Genesis was most probably written after Moses led the two million Hebrews out of Egypt while they were journeying in the wilderness. He was God's chosen man to lead the people of Israel to the Promised Land. Their departure from Egypt was the most dramatic historical event since the scattering of the nations at Babel. It began when God sent ten significant plagues on Egypt, climaxing with the death of all the firstborn who were not protected by the blood of the Passover sacrifice. The Israelites then escaped from Egypt, crossed the Red Sea, and turned around to watch the destruction of Pharaoh's army beneath the waves (Exodus 3-15). This event was followed by their journey to Mount Sinai and God's dramatic presentation of the Ten Commandments there, most likely around 1445 BC (Exodus 16-20).

Their wilderness experience was a critical point in the history of the people of Israel. Their Egyptian enemies were destroyed, but many other enemies and three hundred miles of wilderness stood between them and the land that had been promised them. For the Israelites, the most severe tests were still to come. They needed confirmation that the God who had led them out into the wilderness would be with them and would fulfill His promises to bring them safely to the Promised Land. They needed encouragement to face the trials that would come, like hunger, thirst, and military attack. For the next thirty-eight years until they reached Canaan, desert life presented many challenges, both to two million restless and impatient people and to Moses' ability to lead them.

Moses' Reasons for Writing

In all probability, therefore, Moses had the needs of the Israelites in mind when he wrote the five books of the Law, of which Genesis is the first. The public reading of Genesis to the Israelites in the wilderness would have had a huge impact on them in several ways.

First, it would confirm in their minds that the God of creation was greater than the Egyptian gods that they had seen defeated at the Red Sea (Exodus 14-15). He was greater than the gods of the Amalekites, demonstrated by their early victory over them (Exodus 17:8-13). They could be confident that He would help them to victory over other hostile peoples through whom they must pass and over the Canaanite nations in the future as well.

Second, it would confirm that God was accomplishing His own purpose in history by forming them, as Abraham's descendants, into a nation. They could experience the events of their developing nationhood as part the fulfillment of God's promises.

Third, it would confirm the promises God had made with Adam, Noah, and Abraham. When they saw the initial promises about the nation being fulfilled before their eyes, they would be assured that God would faithfully fulfill the remainder. The covenant promises looked forward to a coming Messiah who would triumph over Satan and save His people. Ultimately, all the nations of the earth would be blessed (Genesis 12:1-3). When the Israelites learned the Genesis story, especially of their own destiny according to God's covenant, they were to take courage and put their trust in God.

The Structure of Genesis

Genesis is best seen as arranged around the repeated use of the key phrase "These are the generations of" (sometimes translated slightly differently) which Moses used to introduce the section that followed. The sections are often called the *toledoth* sections because the Hebrew word for "generations" is *toledoth*. Thus, the section beginning "This is the *toledoth* of Adam" (5:10) means that a new section is beginning which explains what became of Adam. The phrase occurs eleven times beginning with its use in Genesis 2:4 (see also 5:1, 6:9, 10:1, 11:10, 11:27, 25:12, 25:19, 36:1. 36:9, and 37:2).

The first chapter records the creation of the heavens and the earth, laying the foundation for the eleven divisions, making twelve well-defined sections in all. For the most part, the eleven divisions mark a new beginning in the narrative. They then show the effect of sin on what God had designed, followed by a demonstration of God's grace that gave new hope for the future. The twelve sections are carefully designed to develop the basic theme of Genesis, that is, the creation of God's world and the formation of a nation within it through which all other nations would be blessed.

The Profit in Understanding Genesis

You will be greatly rewarded by understanding what God reveals in the book of Genesis. The rest of God's Word will come alive as you connect the patriarchs in Genesis with the ongoing story that emerges out of what God began through them. You will grasp the significance of many avenues of history that start in Genesis and flow through the Exodus from Egypt, the conquest of Canaan, the rise and fall of Israel's monarchy, and that nation's exile into Mesopotamia. The story will culminate in the New Testament narrative of the Messiah, the Lord Jesus, the growth of the early church, and the hope of Christ's return to rule.

A study of Genesis will make doctrinal truths come alive as well. You will be introduced to themes such as God's holiness, the tragic effects of sin on the whole world, the promise of redemption and the blood sacrifices that foreshadowed it, and the coming of Jesus Christ the Redeemer and the prophecies that foretold it. You will learn of the character of the Triune God, His ways of revealing Himself to man, and His intervention in man's affairs.

The third facet of the Bible that will come alive to you in Genesis is how it mirrors human experience in our failures and successes, in our struggles to overcome the effects of sin, and in our daily walk with God by faith. In these ways, a serious study of Genesis will touch our minds, our hearts, and our actions.

The Toledoth
Sections Of Genesis

Prologue   Creation of the heavens and the earth (1:1 – 2:3)

   1.   What became of the heavens and the earth (2:4 – 4:26)

   2.   What became of Adam (5:1 – 6:8)

   3.   What became of Noah (6:9 – 9:29)

   4.   What became of Shem, Ham, and Japheth (10:1 – 11:9)

   5.   What became of Shem (11:10 – 26)

   6.   What became of Terah (11:27 – 25:11)

   7.   What became of Ishmael (25:12 – 18)

   8.   What became of Isaac (25:19 – 35:29)

   9.   What became of Esau (36:1 – 8)

 10.   What became of Esau - part 2 (36:9 – 37:1)

 11.   What became of Jacob (37:2 – 50:26)

The Creation

The book of Genesis contains God's first revelation to us. In Genesis, we learn the beginning of God's major purposes in relation to people and the early development of those purposes. Chapter 1 is an introduction to Genesis. It explains how everything in the world of time and space came into being. We are to understand it as an historical account of how God created the universe in seven days. God wants us to know that it was not by mere chance that the universe came into existence, but by His infinite wisdom and almighty power. More specifically, chapter 1 focuses on the origin of our planet with all its physical features and life forms. Finally, and most importantly, it explains the origin of man. Knowing how man came into being is vitally important, because we cannot properly understand our destiny unless we first understand our origins. Genesis begins with a comprehensive statement about the origin of all things. The first verse contains only ten words and is simple in form, yet it is majestic and profound in its meaning and significance. Think of it! "In the beginning God created the heavens and the earth" (v. 1). The foundation of all the truth that God has revealed in the Bible is in this verse. Every word and phrase is significant. We will look at them one by one.

In The Beginning, God (v. 1)

The primary focus is on God, who is both the Creator and Origin of everything else that exists. Before anything existed, God was there. He is eternal. He is identified by the name *God*. In the original Hebrew the word is *Elohim*, a plural name that indicates His sovereign majesty. A few commentators have suggested that the plurality of the name is connected with the triune nature of God. However that may be, the main point is that the one true God, Elohim, is revealed as the omniscient and omnipotent Creator of the universe, whose majestic name complements His awesome power.

"In the beginning" is the time notation, referring to the time when God first acted to create the universe that is described in the rest of the chapter. Prior to this point, nothing material existed. Only God was there. The Psalmist says, "Before the mountains were brought forth, or ever You had formed the earth and the world, even from everlasting to everlasting, You are God" (Ps. 90:2). Although we can be confident that it was God who originated all creation, there is no indication anywhere in the Bible as to when the beginning of creation took place.

Theories about the Age of the Earth

There are two major theories among believers as to when "the beginning" was. Many are of the opinion that the earth and the universe are very old, perhaps as old as four billion years. Their belief is called the *old earth theory.* Some old earth theorists think that earth and its life forms were created perfect at that time and subsequently suffered a catastrophe which left it in chaos. They believe that out of that chaos, God, at a much later date, formed the world as we know it. Other old earth theorists believe that God created the whole universe at a very early date by means of natural processes. After the original creation of matter, the formation of stars and planets took place naturally, over time, and life forms appeared and became increasingly complex by the process of evolution. They link the days of creation in Genesis chapter 1 with the periods of this extended evolutionary process. However, the radio metric methods of dating that they use are quite unreliable and based on unproved assumptions. The fossil record is also unreliable and does not support the theory of the evolution of biological life.

Many other evangelicals accept the theory of a *young earth* which, they assert, was created no more than ten thousand years ago. They do not see any break between the first two verses in Genesis. They believe that God specifically created life forms as we know them within a literal seven-day period, and they reject the theory of evolution. Although they are aware that the shortened time duration of this theory is at variance with most modern scientific opinion, they base their understanding on a literal interpretation of Genesis 1:1-2. They are also encouraged by much scientific exploration. Discoveries have been made in the last fifty years that provide enormous amounts of geological evidence in many different parts of the world to substantiate their view of a young earth. The idea is also consistent with the accurate and full genealogical evidence in the Bible. The author of this study believes that Genesis 1 is best understood in the light of the young earth theory, taking the Word of God literally. The reader should carefully consider the evidence and be ready to answer inevitable questions in this area (1 Pet. 3:15).

Two clear passages of Scripture may help. The first is the statement of God to Moses included in the Ten Commandments. "For in six days the LORD made the heavens and the earth, the sea and all that is in them, and rested the seventh day" (Ex. 20:11). Moses (the writer of Genesis) and the children of Israel whom he was addressing at Sinai would certainly have understood that everything that exists was made in those six literal days. The second passage is a statement made by the Lord Jesus Christ that, before the creation week in which God made man, there was no other (that is, former) creation. He said, "From the *beginning* of creation, God made them male and female" (Mark

10:6, emphasis added). The fact that the Lord referred to man's creation on the sixth day as "the beginning of creation" does not leave room for the days of creation week to be geological ages.

Created the Heavens and the Earth (v. 1)

Another important word here is the verb *created*. Since nothing existed before creation, we can say that God created the heavens and the earth out of nothing. The word "created" is only used in the Bible in connection with God, for only God can create something out of nothing. People can make or form things from existing material, but they cannot create them from nothing. When God created, He powerfully called the universe into existence. The writer of Hebrews supports this when he said, "By faith we understand that the worlds were framed by the word of God, so that the things which are seen were not made of things which are visible" (Heb. 11:3). Paul, too, spoke of the God who "calls those things which do not exist as though they did" (Rom. 4:17).

The final phrase in the momentous statement of verse 1 is concerned with what God created: "the heavens and the earth." It is a common literary phrase meaning the whole universe and everything in it. Just as the expression *day and night* means "all the time," the expression *heaven and earth* stands for the whole cosmos. When the six days of creation were finished, the same phrase is used again to define everything that God had created: "This is the history of the heavens and the earth when they were created" (2:4).

Refuting False Ideas

The truth of the first verse in the Bible refutes a number of false ideas that have grown in the minds of men down through history. It refutes *atheism,* for it assumes the existence of God. It refutes *polytheism,* for the verb "created" is singular, indicating that the Hebrews believed in one God. It refutes *materialism,* which teaches that matter is eternal. Matter cannot be eternal, for God created it. It refutes *pantheism;* the idea that everything is God, for God is clearly distinct from His creation. It refutes *naturalism,* the concept that all things in existence have appeared naturally, for it teaches that God is the Creator of all that exists. Genesis 1:1 becomes for us the foundation of revealed truth. Our view of the God of creation will affect our understanding of all truth.

The Earth was without Form and Void (v. 2)

Verse 2 seems to present a stark contrast to verse 1. "The earth was without form, and void; and darkness was on the face of the deep." Notice that the focus shifts from the universe in verse 1 to the earth in verse 2, because the earth was to become the habitat for mankind, God's special creation. No other part of creation receives such attention. The condition of the earth is described as "without form and void" or "formless and empty." There is no separation or break between the first two verses. They are closely connected with the word

"And" as is properly reflected in many translations, such as the King James Version and the New American Standard Bible.

The Gap Theory

The meaning of verse 2 has been the subject of a great deal of discussion by commentators. Their debate centers on the meaning of the phrase "without form, and void." Many have concluded that these words describe a condition of chaos which occurred in a supposed large "gap" of time between the original creation described in Genesis 1:1 and a re-creation described in Genesis 1:3-31. Proponents of the *gap theory* believe that God created the world out of a condition of chaos and darkness. They posit that after God created a perfect earth, something catastrophic happened to bring the world to a dark and formless state.

It is short step for the gap theorist to assume that if Genesis 1:2 describes chaos in the world of that time, it might have been caused by the events surrounding the fall of Satan. They link Genesis 1:2 with two biblical passages that are poetic laments over the fall of the kings of two ancient city-states, Babylon and Tyre (see Isa. 14:12-15 and Ezek. 28:12-17). Most evangelical commentators believe that, beyond the immediate reference to the contemporary kings, these passages also allude the fall of Satan. However, even if they do picture the fall of Satan, there is no indication in either passage as to when that may have occurred. Gap theorists also argue that the grammatical text in Genesis 1:2 should read "and the earth *became* [instead of "was"] formless and empty" (emphasis added). If they are correct, it would support their theory, but most textual scholars agree that there is little grammatical reason for this interpretation.

The "Not Yet" State

It seems much better to accept the text as it is written: that the earth *was* formless and empty at that time, without any suggestion that it was in a negative state of chaos due to catastrophe or divine judgment. The initial act of creation was to create the basic elements and was, as yet, incomplete. The formlessness and emptiness describe the state of transition of the earth just before God began His work to prepare it for the well being of man.

There is a connection between the words "formless and empty" and the verses that follow. Out of formlessness, God produced the *form* of geographical and geological structure of the earth; addressing the emptiness, He introduced the *fullness* of living beings to fill it. The formlessness of earth at that point might be illustrated by a lump of clay in the hands of a potter just before he begins to mold it and give it form. He might also describe it as empty, but having formed it he will also fill it, so that its purpose can be realized. "Formless and empty" depict the condition of the earth in its "not yet" or incomplete state before God called it "good." It pictures the uninhabitable earth that God proceeded to make habitable for man. The formlessness anticipated the future purpose of God. Isaiah the prophet used similar language to describe it: "Thus says the LORD, Who created the heavens, Who is God, Who formed the earth and made it, Who has established it, and Who did not create it in vain, Who formed it to be inhabited" (Isa. 45:18). The word *vain* is the same Hebrew word as "formless" in Genesis 1:2.

Darkness Was on the Face of the Deep (v. 2)

Verse 2 goes on to say that "darkness was on the face of the deep." Some have taken the word *darkness* to symbolize sin and to support the idea that there was an ominous and chaotic state over the world at that time. In Scripture, however, darkness does not always symbolize sin. God said, "I am the LORD and there is no other. I form the light and create darkness" (Isa. 45:6-7). Even the oft-repeated phrase in Genesis 1, "the evening and the morning," includes the idea of darkness and does not imply an evil state. Psalm 104:20 says of God: "You make darkness, and it is night." So the basic idea of Genesis 1:2 seems to be that the formless earth was awaiting form, the empty earth was awaiting filling, and the dark earth was awaiting illumination.

The Spirit of God "Hovering" (v. 2)

The final phrase in verse 2 is associated with the six days of creation that immediately follow. "And the Spirit of God was hovering over the face of the waters." Evidently the earth was entirely covered with water, and the Spirit of God was the divine agent who would accomplish the work. He is described here as "hovering over" as He participated in, energized, and protected the creation activity. We learn here, too, that more than one person of the Godhead was involved in the creation process: Job 26:13 says, "By His Spirit He adorned the heavens," and Colossians 1:16 declares, speaking of God the Son, "For by Him all things were created that are in heaven and that are on the earth."
We have learned three important things about God in these first two verses.

- *His eternal existence,* before anything material existed, "In the beginning God."
- *His future purpose,* anticipated in the formless and empty earth.
- *His active presence,* revealed in the reference to His Spirit.

For believers today, God's existence, purpose, and presence are vital to our relationship with Him: we can find confidence in His eternal existence; we can find hope in His purposes for the future; and we can find encouragement from the active presence and power of His Holy Spirit.

The Seven Days of Creation

The creative acts of God took place in six remarkable days. On the seventh day He rested. If one takes the "young earth" position, all of God's activity in

Genesis 1:1-3 would have taken place on the first day. For the purposes of outline, however, we have structured the work of the seven days of creation beginning with verse 3. The first six days are explained in a pattern of four parts. The first part of the pattern is a *creative word* from God as He commands something to appear, e.g., "Then God said, "Let there be light" (v. 3; see also verses 6, 9, 14, 20, and 24). The second part is a statement about the *immediate effect* of what God said, e.g., "And there was light" (v. 3; see also verses 7, 9, 15, 21, and 24). The third part is *God's evaluation* that His creative act was "good" (v. 4; see also verses 12, 18, 21, 25, and 31). And the fourth part is the *ordered numbering* of each day, e.g., "So the evening and the morning were the first day" (v. 5; see also verses 8, 13, 19, 23, and 31).

Days: Literal, Symbolic, or Literary?

Before we consider the progress of each day, we need to give some thought as to whether these days were *literal days* of twenty-four hours, *symbolic days* that refer to extended ages of time, or *literary day*s used as a literary device to describe creation, however it might have occurred. Because the generally-accepted theory of evolution requires millions of years for the development of species, the so-called *day-age* theory was offered as an explanation to accommodate that need. In this theory, the days of creation are viewed as successive ages of evolutionary time. However, there are strong objections that make it impossible to accept both the biblical text and the demands of evolutionary geology. Some of the major objections are as follows:

- The order of the creation days does not match the order of the fossil record in the rocks from which the day-age proponents get their theory.
- Day-age theorists teach that animals existed and died before the appearance of man. This contradicts the doctrine that death resulted as a judgment of man's sin (Rom. 5:12).
- The days described in Genesis 1 are clearly literal days of twenty-four hours, described as they are with an evening and a morning.
- The normal understanding of Exodus 20:8-11 suggests that the sabbath twenty-four hour day was instituted on the model of the seventh twenty-four hour day of creation week. To refer to the days as simply a literary device seems unsatisfactory to this author because it does not explain what the days actually were. It sidesteps the issue by not coming to any conclusion as to whether they were literal or symbolic days.

Forming and Filling

We have already noted an interesting connection between the phrase "formless and empty" in verse 2 and the activity of the rest of the week. The first three days have to do with the creation of form and order out of the formlessness of verse 2. The second three days have to do with the creation of fullness and harmony to rectify the emptiness. Not only is this true, but there is a striking correspondence between Days One, Two, and Three and Days Four, Five, and Six:

- Light that was created on Day One corresponds to "lights" (sun, moon, and stars) that were created on Day Four (vv. 3, 14).
- Sea and sky that were created on Day Two correspond to fish to fill the sea and birds to fill the sky on Day Five (vv. 6, 20).
- Fertile earth that was created on Day Three corresponds to animals and man with which God filled the earth on Day Six (vv. 11, 24-26).

We can see that out of the formlessness God brought about perfect order, and out of the emptiness He brought about abundant fullness. The following chart makes this plain. God's plan was perfect then, and it is a comfort to know that He still delights in order.

The Formless Earth was Formed and the Empty Earth was Filled

Days of Forming	Days of Filling
Day 1. Light and Darkness (v. 3)	**Day 4**. The Sun, Moon, and Stars (v. 14)
Day 2. Sea and Sky (v. 6)	**Day 5**. Fish (sea) and Birds (sky) (v. 20)
Day 3. Dry Land & Fertile Earth (v. 11)	**Day 6**. Animals and Man (vv. 24-26)

Note several more features of the creation days. The first three are marked by a separation of some kind:

- On Day One, God separated the light from the darkness (v. 4).
- On Day Two, the waters suspended in the clouds were separated from the waters on the surface (v. 7).
- On Day Three, the surface waters (seas) were separated from the dry land (v. 9).

Then also note that both sets of three in the chart begin with light on Days One and Four and end with a double creation on Days Three and Six. So God set out to create the universe in a very orderly way, not haphazardly. Another thing worth noticing is the majesty of creation by decree. Each act of God begins with "Then God said...." God simply spoke, and it was done.

The First Day: Light Created (vv. 3-5)

"Then God said, 'Let there be light,' and there was light." These are the first recorded words of God. The original literal text is more powerful than our translation; it says something like "Light be, and light was." We cannot explain all that is involved here or exactly what the light was. Anything beyond what is written is beyond our full understanding. This is the literal way to read the

Bible, accepting intellectually what we do understand and accepting by faith all that we do not understand. We do know that the light was visible and that it was not the light of the sun, which was created later (v. 16).

"And God saw the light, that it was good." God saw that it was beneficial for man, who would soon be created. It may be that the earth, as yet unformed and covered with water, began to rotate on its axis with the light on one side. In that way, the light was separated from the darkness as day is separated from night. From that time, on there was a regular succession of days and nights. God divided the light from the darkness and called the light *Day* and the darkness *Night*. The word "day" indicates a period of light, but we understand the last word of verse 5 to include the evening too, incorporating the full twenty-four hour day.

Scripture emphasizes the importance of light as a symbol of spiritual light. In the writings of the apostle John, God Himself is called Light (1 John 1:5-8). John referred to Jesus as "the true Light that gives light to every man coming into the world" (John 1:9). Jesus referred to Himself as Light: "Light has come into the world, and men loved darkness rather than light, because their deeds were evil" (John 3:19). He also said, "I am the light of the world. He who follows Me shall not walk in darkness, but have the light of life" (John 8:12). Following Christ the Light keeps God's people enlightened. Paul used this passage in Genesis to illustrate the light that God has put within the believer: "God who commanded light to shine out of darkness ... has shone in our hearts to give the light of the knowledge of the glory of God in the face of Jesus Christ" (2 Cor. 4:6).

The Second Day: The Firmament Dividing the Waters (vv. 6-8)

On the second day, God said, "Let there be a firmament in the midst of the waters, and let it divide the waters from the waters" (v. 6). Prior to this declaration, water covered the earth. It may be supposed that a thick blanket of vapor or fog rested on the water. On this day God placed a *firmament* (expanse) between the liquid water covering the earth and the water that was "above the firmament." Thus there was a space between the ocean waters and the water-filled clouds above. We call this space *air,* which is essential for all living forms on earth. Some have suggested that the water above was opaque, like clouds today. Others say that it was a canopy of vapor or ice crystals that would have allowed much more light to shine through. Still others think that it might have been rings of ice crystals similar to the rings surrounding the planet Saturn. The second or third of these theories seem more plausible because both would have let light shine through.

Again, we are made aware of the division between the water below and the water above, just as there was a division between the light and the darkness in verse 4. God created the domain and then controlled it by making a division in it. How often God makes divisions and distinctions! We Christians should also make distinctions between things that differ, as, for example, the difference between true religion and false religion (James 1:26-27).

God then named the expanse *Heaven* (v. 8). The Bible speaks of heaven in three ways:

- It is the place where the Lord Jesus Christ is seated at the right hand of God (Heb. 9:24).

- It is the space where the sun, moon, stars, and planets revolve in their orbits (Isa. 13:10).

- It is the atmosphere in which the clouds are suspended.

It is, of course, the atmospheric heaven that is referred to in Genesis 1. "So the evening and the morning were the second day" (v. 8).

The Third Day: Land, Seas, and Plants (vv. 9-13)

On the third day God said, "'Let the dry land appear,' and it was so" (v. 9). Again, there was an act of separation: the dry land was separated from the waters below. Landmass appeared for the first time. Nothing indicates the shape of the landmass in its original form, but it is possible that it was one large continent. We must assume that the complex makeup of rocks, minerals, geological features, and soils were all created on this day.

The Psalmist spoke of the "foundation of the earth" (Ps. 102:25) that was laid at this time. According to Genesis 10:25, the earth, or landmass, was divided in the days of Peleg. That division may have resulted in the continents similar to their form today. God called the dry land *Earth* and the gathering together of the waters He called *Seas*.

At this point the emphasis begins to shift from bringing form and order to the formless physical earth to bringing life and fullness to the empty earth. God spoke for the third time on the third day of creation: "Let the earth bring forth grass, the herb that yields seed, and the fruit tree that yields fruit" (v. 11). Each of the tens of thousands of forms of vegetation was created and grouped under the general categories of grasses, herbs, and trees. Each variety was "according to its kind" (v. 11), meaning that each was deliberately and separately created. The different kinds of vegetation did not evolve one by one from simpler forms; God created tens of thousands of species individually, all on the same day.

Within each kind of vegetation God placed the ability to reproduce itself by means of seed, according to its built-in genetic code. God created the power of fertility for all vegetation. Notice that each shrub and tree was created mature. This maturity included the appearance of age and the capacity to produce seed. If you can imagine a nurseryman planting hundreds of thousands of shrubs and trees in one day, you may have an idea of the magnitude of what God did on the third day of creation. It seems probable that there was not just one of each kind, but many.

When God had completed this task, He "saw that it was good" (v. 12). What an amazing sight it must have been, when God spoke into existence the earth's green carpet of plants and trees!

The Fourth Day: Sun, Moon, and Stars (vv. 14-19)

On the fourth day of that momentous week God created the heavenly bodies that give light to earth. He said, "Let there be lights in the firmament of the heavens." These included all the planets and stars. The firmament of the heavens in verse 14 is obviously not the same firmament as was created on the second day that separated the waters above from the waters below (v. 6). The firmament in verse 14 is the sphere where the moon, planets, and stars exist. We refer to it as outer space.

God cites four purposes for creating the star-filled heavens. All of them relate to people on earth. "Lights ... to divide the day from the night; and let them be for signs and seasons, and for days and years." First, the lights were to divide the day from the night. Again, note the separation, as there had been on the first, second, and third days (vv. 4, 6, 9). The continuing succession of days and nights make this clearly evident. Second, they were for days and years. Ever since the creation week, man has used the sun and the moon to measure time. Third, the lights would be for signs, which are marks or indications of something meaningful. For example, the plague of flies was a "sign" to Pharaoh of God's omnipotence (Ex. 8:22-24). God said that the heavenly bodies would be meaningful signs. The fourth purpose for creating the stars was for seasons that would indicate the time for a specific thing to happen. The word is used of the appointed time when Isaac was to be born to Abraham and Sarah (cf. 17:21; 18:14; 21:2).

God created the stars and placed them where He wanted them (Ps. 8:3). He also named them (Ps. 147:4; Isa. 40:26). Since God created them for signs and seasons, it may well be that they had some significance for man in connection with His plan of salvation. There is evidence in the names of major stars and star groupings that God intended them to visually indicate His purpose regarding the suffering and glory of His Son. If so, the signs in the heavens were quickly corrupted into the pseudo-science of pagan and occult astrology.

Light itself was created on the first day, but the generators of light were created on the fourth. They were set in the expanse of the heavens. From the perspective of being viewed from earth, the "greater lights" are the sun and moon (v. 16). They are not greater in size compared with other celestial bodies— far from it—but to us on earth they are the largest and brightest heavenly bodies. The sun was to rule the day and the moon was to rule the night. Then "God saw that it was good. So the evening and the morning were the fourth day" (vv. 18-19). No star in all the heavens was out of place. What an awesome God we have!

The Fifth Day: Birds and Fish (vv. 20-23)

By this time, all the necessary requirements to sustain life were in place. Though vegetable life was already created, conscious life (as the Hebrews viewed fish, birds, animals, and man) did not yet exist. The word "living creature" is also translated "living soul" in many places and carries the idea of conscious life.

On the fifth day, fish and birds were called into being by the direct command of God. "Let the waters abound with an abundance of living creatures and let birds fly above the earth" (v. 20). What God did was radically different from the evolutionary idea that a stray blob of protoplasm responded to some discharge of electricity on a primeval ocean and produced life. As Psalm 33:9 says of God, "He spoke, and it was done." When He said, "Let birds fly," suddenly the sky teemed with thousands of varieties in all the splendor of their plumage. Just as remarkably, the sea was filled with fish of every sort, size, shape, and color.

Special attention is given to the "great sea creatures" (v. 21). These would include what we call dragons, whales, and sea monsters, most of which are extinct now. Early pagans regarded them as gods, one of which was the Canaanite god *Lotan* (Hebrew *Leviathan*). This part of the creation story would assure the Israelites in the wilderness that the great sea creatures were not gods at all. They were merely creations of the one true God. The fish and birds were created "according to their kind" with a fixed DNA program for each. This allowed for variation within the species (size, color, etc), but not for change from one species to another.

The section concludes with a blessing from God saying, "Be fruitful and multiply" (vv. 22-23). The blessing gave the Israelites in Moses' day assurance of the perfection of all creation. Everything in nature was in balance and functioned according to a divine design.

The Sixth Day: Animals and Man (vv. 24-31)

God spoke on the sixth day saying, "Let the earth bring forth the living creature according to its kind: cattle and creeping thing and beast of the earth" (v. 24). These three categories of living creatures (literally "living souls," as in verse 20) were to inhabit the land. The term *cattle* probably equates to domestic animals, *creeping things*, to small animals, insects, small reptiles, and the like, and *beasts*, to wild animals. They were all made simultaneously as is evident from the fact that the three categories are listed in opposite order in verses 24 and 25.

God was pleased and satisfied with His animal creation and declared it to be "good" (v. 25). Now, at last, the earth and its environment were ready for *people*.

"All things bright and beautiful, all creatures great and small.

All things wise and wonderful, the Lord God made them all.

Each little flower that opens, each little bird that sings,

He made their glowing colors, He made their tiny wings....

He gave us eyes to see them, and lips that we might tell

How great is God Almighty, Who has made all things well."

– C. F. Alexander

The Creation of Human Beings (vv. 26–31)

The climax of the narrative toward which the whole chapter is leading is the creation of man. God made humans very different from animals, and He treats their creation in much more detail and with considerably more emphasis. Notice God's personal involvement in verse 26: "Then God said, 'Let Us make man.'" Contrast this with the less personal description of the creation of animals in verse 24 where He said, "Let the earth bring forth the living creature." God took special interest in people.

Notice, also, the phrase "Let Us make man," which has both a plural pronoun and a plural verb. The use of plurals has been taken by some to mean that there was more than one God at work, or that God worked together with angels in the creative process. These ideas are clearly wrong. It is best to understand that these plurals were used in Hebrew to indicate the majesty of God, just as we noted the use of the plural word for God in Genesis 1:1. It is possible that there may also be a hint of the triune God in the plurals, but they mainly point to the majesty of God.

In the language in verse 26, it does seem as if the members of the Godhead were communicating with one another. However, the development of the great truth of the Trinity will only be fully unfolded in the New Testament. Here, perhaps, we see it in seed form.

Man Created in the Image of God

Three times the text states that man, unlike other creatures, was made in the image of God (vv. 26-27). God specially designed man to reflect His own spiritual nature. Just as Roman coins were stamped with Caesar's image, so the image of God was "stamped" on man. This means that human beings, unlike animals, share some of God's attributes. These attributes include truth, wisdom, love, holiness, justice, personality, and symbolic speech. God gave man moral sensitivity, conscience, and the ability to think abstractly. Man, because he is created in the image of God, is a thinking being, a moral being, and a dignified being. Unlike animals, man is composed of soul and spirit as well as body. God made man with the capacity for loving Him, for worshipping Him, and for spiritual fellowship with Him.

God's Purposes in Creating Man (vv. 26-28)

The next thing we learn is that God's purpose in creating man was to make him ruler over creation. Humans were to have "dominion over the fish of the sea, over the birds of the air, and over every living thing that moves on the earth." Two verses later, man is told to "subdue it," indicating that he was to gain mastery over the earth and explore its secrets.

In addition, man was given the capacity to produce life and, in doing so, to imitate God who created life. Note that God created only two kinds of people in relation to sexuality: male and female. When it says "God created man," the word *man* is a generic term referring to both male and female. The word "man" is properly translated in this way hundreds of times in Scripture. We should not let the modern pressure for political correctness and inclusive language rob us of its proper use.

God instructed the man and the woman saying, "Be fruitful and multiply." This was part of their blessing from God. In Genesis, to be blessed means to be enriched and to be fertile. However, the bearing of children is not only a blessing—it is also a tremendous responsibility. A man and a woman are capable of producing a living soul. In bearing children, parents share in God's work of creating life. It is worth mentioning that God's command to be fruitful has not been rescinded.

Instructions Concerning Food (vv. 29–31)

God continued to speak to the man and the woman He had made, telling them that their food was to be "every herb that yields seed … and every tree whose fruit yields seed." From these verses we conclude that before sin entered into the world, both man and animals were vegetarian in diet. Later, after the Flood, God modified His instructions to include the eating of meat (9:3), but in the beginning it was not so. We are not told when animals began to have fangs and claws and to eat other animals. Perhaps it was part of the curse.

Finally, at the conclusion of the sixth day, God saw "everything that He had made, and indeed it was very good." Isaac Watts, the great hymn writer, expresses this sentiment in "I sing the mighty power of God":

I sing the goodness of the Lord that filled the earth with food,

He formed the creatures with His Word and then pronounced them good.

Lord, how Thy wonders are displayed, wher'ere I turn my eye,

If I survey the ground I tread or gaze upon the sky.

In Conclusion

God had spoken, and it was done. The world He created was perfect, filled with innumerable plants and trees with their flowers and fruit. Above and within the vegetation, the thousands of varieties of birds sang and soared. Among them and under them, the fantastic variety of animals and insects roamed. Among all these creatures, God placed one pair of human beings who could understand some of the eternal wisdom that had brought it all into being.

For the believer, to consider the creative acts of God described in the first chapter of Genesis is to understand something of the omnipotence of the Mighty God. From nothing, He brought into being the heavens and the earth. From formlessness, He brought about His perfect design and form. From emptiness, He filled the seas with fish, the sky with birds, and the land with creatures of every description. The Psalmist was right in saying, "The heavens declare the glory of God; and the firmament shows His handiwork" (Ps. 19:1). He crowned His handiwork with the creation of man, made in His image, and declared it all "very good."

Whether we try to comprehend the enormity of the whole animal creation or the complexity of one tiny ant, we should respond in worship to God for His creative wisdom and power. Like the twenty-four elders in heaven we can say, "You are worthy, O Lord, to receive glory and honor and power; For You created all things, and by Your will they exist and were created" (Rev. 4:11).

Adam and Eve in the Garden of Eden

The second chapter of Genesis provides much more detail about certain aspects of the six days of creation. The theme of chapter 2 is man and woman, who were God's crown of creation and the particular focus of His attention. We learn how God formed each of them with a special creative act, of the special garden God planted for them as their dwelling place, and of their responsibility to serve Him and to cultivate the garden. Most importantly, we are told of the commandment that God held them accountable to obey.

The Harmony of Chapters One and Two

Critics have assumed that Genesis 2 is a separate and different tradition of the creation story. It is true that there are stylistic differences. Chapter 1 comprises terse sentences, while chapter 2 has a more flowing style. Chapter 1 uses the term God, indicating His power and majesty. Chapter 2 uses the term LORD (Jehovah) God, which is His covenant name, emphasizing His relationship with His people. The first chapter is in strict chronological order and ends with the creation of the first two humans; the second concentrates on further details about man's creation, his being placed in a garden called Eden, and the formation of the first woman from one of his ribs. These differences in the two chapters do not mean that they are two separate Creation stories; rather, the added details in chapter 2 enrich the account given in chapter 1. They prepare us for the problems that will be caused by man's disobedience recorded in chapter 3.

We can be sure that both chapters 1 and 2 of Genesis are part of one harmonious account from the comment of Christ in Matthew 19:4 and 5. In speaking of marriage, He said, "Have you not read that He who made them at the beginning 'made them male and female'?" quoting from Genesis 1:27. He immediately went on to quote Genesis 2:24, saying, "For this reason a man shall leave his father and mother, and be joined to his wife, and the two shall become one flesh." So, in one continuous sentence, the Lord quotes from both Genesis 1 and 2, from which we infer that they were both from the same context.

As you read Genesis 2, you will observe that there are several clearly defined topics. These are linked with God's preparation and provision for the first humans. We shall consider these one by one. However, the first three verses cover the conclusion to the creation week described in chapter 1.

The Seventh Day of Creation (vv. 1-3)

The seventh day emphasizes the twin themes of completion and rest. God was pleased that the work was "finished," "ended," and "done." There is heavy emphasis on these completion words, which occur four times in the first two verses. When God declared the work finished, He put the lie to the whole theory of evolution which states that lower forms of life are continually evolving into higher forms. Not so! God completed His work, and it was finished. The second theme related to the seventh day is that "God ... rested from all His work." God did not rest because He was tired, but because He was satisfied. God enjoyed what He had made and celebrated His accomplishment by ceasing from creative activity.

The Sabbath

God's rest on the seventh day was later linked with the Sabbath when God instituted it for His people at Mount Sinai. "Remember the Sabbath day, to keep it holy.... For in six days the LORD made the heavens and the earth, the sea, and all that is in them, and rested the seventh day. Therefore the Lord blessed the Sabbath day and hallowed it" (Ex. 20:8-11). This was the fourth of the Ten Commandments given to Israel. God had already prepared His people for the concept of Sabbath rest by giving them manna on six days and not on the seventh. At that time Moses explained, "This is what the LORD has said, 'Tomorrow is a Sabbath rest, a holy Sabbath to the LORD.'... So the people rested on the seventh day" (Ex. 16:23-30). Thus the Sabbath became a distinct Hebrew institution. It was to be a sign of Israel's allegiance to God (Ex. 31:12-17).

God's work of creation was finished with the day of rest. But God very soon began another great work—the work of redemption. He sent His Son to complete that work (John 4:34). On the cross Jesus announced that His redeeming work was finished with His cry of victory (John 19:30). The next day was the Sabbath, and He rested on it in Joseph's tomb until the glorious resurrection morning when His finished work was demonstrated. A new age dawned. Now He rests in heaven from His work of redemption. After offering Himself as a once-for-all sacrifice for sin, He sat down at the right hand of God (Heb. 1:3; 10:12). Now, believers can enter into that rest (Heb. 4:9-10) by ceasing to work for salvation, simply trusting in Christ and His finished work. Jesus promised rest to those who were weary of working to achieve salvation if they would come to Him in faith (Matt. 11: 28).

The Creation of Man (vv. 4-7)

Verse 4 marks the beginning of the first *toledoth* section (see the Introduction). The text reads, "This is the history of the heavens and the earth when they were created." The word translated "history" is *toledoth* in Hebrew, and it means "to give birth" as in childbearing. It is properly rendered "generations" in the older English translations. In ten of its eleven uses, it introduces the descendants (or generations) of the person named. As an example, note the next *toledoth* section, which begins in Genesis 5:1 with the phrase "These are the generations of Adam." The phrase introduces the subject of the history of Adam's descendants which continues until the next *toledoth* section begins in Genesis 6:9.

In this passage, the subject of the *toledoth* is not a specific person but "the heavens and the earth." Thus the generations of the heavens and the earth speak of something which came from them—namely, man who was formed from the dust of the ground. From the created earth, God formed man. The next three chapters explain how God made the first two human beings, how they rebelled against Him, and how the results of their rebellion played out in their family.

Before we are introduced to Adam and Eve in the garden, the author reminds us of creation week, which he calls "the day that the LORD God made the earth and the heavens." The word "day" probably refers to the whole week of creation in contrast to its use in chapter 1, where the context clearly indicates a regular solar day. In verse 5 the author narrows his focus down to a specific time period when the dry land appeared but before plant and animal life appeared (2:5, cf.1:10). The earth was watered by a "mist from the ground" rather than by rain as we now know it (vv. 5-6). The main point in explaining what the world was like part way through the creation week is to let the reader see what the world was like without people. Note the words "And there was no man to till the ground" (v. 5). The bare earth was incomplete without man who would be given the job of cultivating it. During the six days of creation, it was man who was uppermost in the mind of God. In this way, we are introduced to the subject of the creation of man.

God Forms Man from Dust

Without even mentioning the creation of plant life on the third day and animal life on the sixth day, God draws our attention to how He made man when the text says that God "formed" man. A sculptor has in his mind both the design of the statue he will form and the intent to sculpt it from his material exactly to that design. So God had in His mind what man was to be like, and He formed him from the dust of the ground exactly as He intended. Man was not, as some evolutionists say, just a chance mutation from apes. And it was not only Adam that God was interested in forming; He "forms" people for His service today. When God called the prophet Jeremiah, He told him that He had "formed" him in the womb, using the same word as in Genesis 2:7. Jeremiah took comfort from this knowledge. In the same sense, we, too, were formed by God before we were born. God had a hand in our physical make-up. Thus we can rest assured that we are exactly what He wants us to be. God does not make mistakes.

Another valuable lesson from this passage comes from the fact that the first man was formed from "the dust of the ground." Man was made from the earth and is earthy (1 Cor. 15:47). All human beings are inseparably bound to the earth from which they are made. The idea that man in his origin is in any way part of God is wrong. God is the Creator; man is a created being. It is quite remarkable that chemical elements such as hydrogen, oxygen, sodium, and calcium, which make up the basic particles of earth, are the same elements from which our bodies are constituted. It should humble us to remember that we are "dust."

Dust is used in Scripture to illustrate what is of little worth. For example, when Abraham interceded for the wicked city of Sodom, he confessed to God, "Indeed now, I who am but dust and ashes have taken it upon myself to speak to the LORD" (18:27). It should humble us even more to know that our mighty God understands us. He "knows our frame and remembers that we are dust" (Ps. 103:14).

The main lesson about man in Genesis 2 is that he was made from the dust of the ground. The word "man" in Hebrew is *adam* from which we get the name of the first man. It is also related to the word for "ground," *adama*. Thus "Adam" and "ground" are closely linked. Adam was never meant to forget the connection. It is emphasized here in contrast to the next chapter when he did forget his dust-like quality and fell into temptation, wanting to be like God. All of us are mere dust, but we should remember that we do have dignity, because we are "God-formed" dust. God formed us to fulfill His purpose.

The Breath of Life

After forming the man's body, God supplied it with another element— life: "The LORD God ... breathed into his nostrils the breath of life." Suddenly, every physical function from Adam's toes to his brain sprang into being. Beyond that, he gained spiritual understanding (Job 32:8). Man had both physical life and spiritual life. Elihu, one of Job's comforters, testified to the truth that man has a body of dust and in-breathed life from God. He said, "I also have been formed out of clay" (Job. 33:6), and "the breath of the Almighty gives me life" (Job 33:4).

Thus "man became a living being," or soul. The phrase does not mean, as the Greeks taught, that God added something called a soul to the body, but that man was now a whole person, a soul with consciousness, mind, and emotions. The same expression is also used of animals (2:19). However, man is distinct from animals because he is made in the image of God and has the God-given breath of life. It is in God that we "live and move and have our being" (Acts 17:28). Genesis 2:7 should have assured the Israelites for whom Moses was writing—as it assures us—that God created them with care and attention, giving them both the physical and spiritual capacity to serve Him as He would desire.

The Garden in Eden (vv. 8-14)

The Planting of the Garden

The Bible says, "The LORD God planted a garden." God prepared the garden as an ideal work place and living space for man. The location was eastward in Eden, that is, somewhere east of where Adam had been created outside the garden. The region was called Eden, meaning "delight," describing its loveliness. It was a real garden, filled with shrubs and trees of every kind bearing delicious fruits. Aesthetically, it was a beautiful garden; every tree was pleasing to the eye. And it was a fruitful garden; the fruits were not only delicious but also good for food to nourish and sustain Adam.

God prepared Eden as a perfect environment for the man to carry out the functions He had purposed for him. Adam's first knowledge of God was of a powerful, wise Creator who paid special attention to him by placing him in the garden of delight and providing everything he needed. The garden is mentioned in other parts of Scripture: It is called the "garden of the LORD" in Genesis 13:10, the "garden of God" in Ezekiel 28:13, and the "Paradise of God" in Revelation 2:7.

The Tree of Life

Verse 8 is a summary of the planting of the garden, while verse 9 provides some important details about it. Among all the trees of the garden were two especially important trees which are to become a major focus in the next chapter. One was "the tree of life," which was in the center of the garden. This tree had the capacity to sustain life and was readily available to Adam. We understand by its name that the regular eating of its fruit would enable mortal man to live forever (3:22). In a coming age, it will be growing in the New Jerusalem, and its leaves will promote the health of the nations (Rev. 22:2). We have no idea how nourishment from it could halt the aging process in man, but the preservation of life is clearly implied from the description of the tree and the fact that the man was prohibited from approaching it after he sinned. God's purpose for the tree is not limited to our human understanding, and it may well include other features.

The Tree of the Knowledge of Good and Evil

The other important tree in the garden was called the "the tree of the knowledge of good and evil." We are not told exactly where it was located. Eating the fruit of this tree would result in the experience of "good and evil." We do not know whether there was any harmful or toxic substance in the fruit itself, but certainly the eating of it in disobedience to God would bring the knowledge of evil experientially. The importance of the tree is not so much the nature of the fruit, but the responsibility it gave to Adam. He already knew "good" because everything that God had made was good, but he had nothing with which to compare the good. When he ate the forbidden fruit, "evil" immediately became apparent to him in contrast to the good.

The Four Rivers

In addition to information about the two special trees, we learn of the remarkable water supply system. Evidently the luxuriance of the garden required an abundance of water supplied by a river that went "out of Eden" (v. 10). We may assume that because there was no rain in those days, the river had its source in an artesian spring. From the garden "it parted and became four riverheads."

The names of the rivers were the Pishon, the Gihon, the Heddekel, and the Euphrates. The first two cannot be positively identified with any known rivers. The third is linked on Assyrian monuments with the River Tigris. The Euphrates is the best-known river in the ancient world. The Pishon is described as encompassing the whole land of Havilah where there is gold, bdellium (an aromatic gum), and onyx (vv. 11-12), all of which suggest wealth and beauty. The location of Havilah is unknown, however, so we are left with a mystery. The Gihon was said to encompass the whole land of Cush (v. 13). Cush is referred to in other parts of Scripture related to both a section of current-day Arabia and to the land of Ethiopia. But as neither of these areas has a river encircling it, the mystery deepens. The Hiddekel was "one which goes toward the east of Assyria" (v. 14). If that river is associated with the Tigris of today then we have another problem, for the modern Tigris is on the western side of Assyria. The river we know as the Euphrates cannot be definitively identified with the river in Genesis 2.

The Location of Eden

The curiosity of many people regarding the location of the Garden of Eden has led them to try to identify these rivers. The mature Christian will disregard any speculation. In all likelihood, none of these ancient rivers still exists. The topography of the whole world was dramatically changed during the time of the great Flood. Therefore, the geographical features described in verses 11 to 14 do not exist in the modern world. "The world that then existed perished, being flooded with water" (2 Pet. 3:6).

The question then arises as to why all this information is included in Scripture. In answer we can suggest that perhaps Adam or his son Seth wrote the original records of this part of Genesis, and obviously they would have done that before the Flood. When they wrote, the people living then knew the names of rivers. As Moses collected and sorted materials available to him, he would want to include all the information he had so that the true story of the beginnings of the world and mankind would be preserved separate from the corrupted myths popular among the Babylonians and Egyptians of his day.

The similarity of names like Euphrates, Hiddekel, and Cush would have been names that were remembered by the survivors of the Flood and reused in their new world. An illustration of this is how the early English settlers in America reused existing English geographical names. Today, literally hundreds of towns in the United States bear the same names as older ones in England. In summary, we can say with certainty that the Garden of Eden was a wonderful place, that it was destroyed in the Flood, and that it cannot be located today.

Adam and His Responsibility (vv. 15-17)

God Assigns Adam Work in Eden

The Garden of Eden became Adam's home. "Then the LORD God took the man and put him in the garden of Eden to tend and to keep it." The word *tend* means "cultivate" or "till," and the word *keep* means "care for attentively." Even though the garden was God's horticultural masterpiece, it was designed to require Adam's constant care. We also learn that Adam needed work to give him life fulfillment.

The Garden of Eden was designed as a place where Adam was to actively serve God. Work is honorable. Even in the world-to-come there will be work for people to do in heaven. When sin and the curse have been removed, the Bible says that "His servants shall serve Him" (Rev. 22:3). The principle of work is no less true for all of us. God intends for us to be fulfilled as people and to glorify Him through work and service.

The Commandment of the Lord

Both Adam and the garden were direct creations from the hand of God. Both were perfect and had been pronounced "very good." Adam was without excuse. Being there, he had every reason to please a good God who had placed him in such ideal surroundings. God then gave Adam one small restraint in his life to test his love for Him.

"The LORD God commanded the man." In this way the subject of man's responsibility for obedience is introduced (vv. 16-17). But notice that even before God explained what the command was, He reminded Adam that he could eat freely of "every tree of the garden." God's provision included not only the trees as we know them but also "every herb that yields seed" (1:29). The variety of texture and flavor was almost limitless in the grains, seeds, fruits, roots, and foliage that were available to him. Adam was not even restricted from the Tree of Life in the center of the garden.

"You Shall Not Eat"

One responsibility was placed on Adam. It concerned the Tree of the Knowledge of Good and Evil, and of that tree God said, "You shall not eat." The privilege of obedience would actually place Adam in a new, higher relationship with God, because he could choose to obey God in order to please Him. It became an avenue through which he could express his love to God. Adam had every reason to obey God and no reason to disobey.

The consequence of disobedience was clearly spelled out by God: "You shall surely die." Spiritually, in his relationship to God, Adam would die immediately. He would be alienated from God. Physically, his body would begin a degenerative process that would end in physical death. Adam understood the consequences if he disobeyed. It is important for us, as students of Genesis, to see that death, as a result of disobedience to God, is a major theme in the book, as indeed it is all through the Scriptures. Spiritual death can be defined as "separation from God." It is the fact from which will spring man's need of a Savior.

The Creation of the Woman (vv. 18-23)

After God gave Adam his special responsibility and a clear warning if he failed to meet it, He made a remarkable announcement—that the man was incomplete. Everything else that had been created had been declared "good," but of Adam, God said, "It is not good that man should be alone; I will make him a helper comparable to him" (v. 18). "Not good" meant that Adam without a partner was, as yet, unfinished. Alone, he could not yet do everything that God had planned for him.

The Woman's Role as Helper and Counterpart

God declared that He would make for Adam a "helper comparable to him" (v. 18). The word helper is not a term that gives woman second-class status. The term is used of God Himself a number of times. Let's look at several examples:

- Moses called one of his sons Eliezer, which means "God is helper" (Ex. 18:4).
- In Deuteronomy 33:7, Moses prayed that the Lord would be a Helper for Judah.
- In 1 Samuel 7:12, Samuel named a stone Ebenezer ("stone of help") saying, "Thus far the LORD has helped us."
- Psalm 46:1 says, "God is our refuge and strength, a very present help in trouble."

So when God spoke of the woman as Adam's helper, He meant that she would provide what was lacking in Adam. Man has been made in such a way that he needs the help of a partner. Man and woman can only completely fulfill their God-given purpose when they are mutually assisting each other.

Observe carefully that woman was not only to be a helper to Adam but that she was to be "comparable to him." The same phrase is also translated "corresponding to him" and "complementing him." She would share the man's nature and have man's essential quality, but she would be his counterpart in several ways:

- Physically, she was his counterpart in intimacy.
- Emotionally, she was his counterpart in bringing balance to his masculinity.
- Socially, she was his counterpart in his relationships with men and women in the world.
- Spiritually, she was his counterpart in her response to his leadership in the home.

How beautifully God created man and woman for each other!

Adam Names the Animals

Before actually creating the woman, God arranged for Adam to familiarize himself with the animals whose creation was explained in chapter 1. God proceeded to bring them to Adam to see what he would call them (vv. 19-20). How God caused them to come to Adam, we are not told. As Adam studied each one, he gave it an appropriate name according to its nature and characteristics. Some critics have reasoned that the task was beyond the ability of a single person. We should remember, however, that Adam had come from the creative hand of God and was of superior intelligence; the task was well within his enormous capability. He did not need to revise any of the names he gave. "Whatever Adam called each living creature, that was its name."

Adam could not have helped but be impressed at the complexity, variety, and adaptability of the thousands of creatures. He would also have observed how vastly different he was from them. His intelligence and spirituality were not found in any of them. He knew most certainly that he had not recently evolved from them. None of the animals, from the antelope to the zebra, could provide the level of companionship he desired. Then, too, he saw that every animal had its mate to which it was exactly suited. But for Adam there was no suitable partner or helper. Of all the creatures God had made, Adam alone was really alone. God allowed him to see that it was "not good" for man to be alone, so that when Eve was created, Adam was thoroughly prepared to appreciate her.

God Forms Woman from Adam's Rib

The beautiful story of the creation of Eve from Adam's rib is specially revealed at this point (vv. 21-23). Her creation subsequent to man's does not mean she was an afterthought. Rather, it is deliberately separated from the story of Adam's creation to teach us some foundational truths of what God desires in male and female relationships.

Just as man's creation from dust teaches us that man belongs to the earth from which he came, so woman's creation from Adam's rib teaches us that she belongs to the man from whom she came. We are not told if God told Adam in advance of what He was about to do. The biblical text simple says: "And the LORD God caused a deep sleep to fall on Adam, and he slept; and He took one of his ribs, and closed up the flesh in its place. Then the rib which the LORD God had taken from man He made into a woman, and He brought her to the man" (vv. 21-22). Adam saw his companion and declared concerning her, "This is now bone of my bones and flesh of my flesh. She shall be called woman [Hebrew, *ish-shah*] because she was taken out of man [*ish*]" (v. 23). At this point, it would seem that Adam knew that God had used one of his ribs with some flesh attached to make her. He concluded rightly that she was his counterpart, made of his own bone and flesh, and made especially for him. Martin Luther fully understood this passage. When the great reformer and scholar came to appreciate his freedom in Christ to marry, he did so, and would affectionately call his wife, Catherine, "Kitty, my rib."

It is often said that Eve was not taken from the head of Adam so that he might intellectually dominate her; nor was she taken from his foot that he might tread her down. Rather, she was taken from his side that he might love her and protect her. The woman was formed from Adam's side to be his companion. Together they were to carry out the commission that God had given them. They were to "fill the earth and subdue it" and to "dress and keep" the garden.

And so, the first wedding took place in the Garden of Eden. Imagine, God Himself joining the couple in the holy union of marriage! God created the first marriage as a trilateral relationship. The man and the woman were to love each other, but always within the context of their relationship to God. The divine plan of marriage is one man and one woman becoming one flesh and living together in submission to God their Creator.

Christ Loved the Church and Gave Himself for It

This first marriage is an illustration of Christ and His Bride, the Church. God "caused" a far deeper "sleep" than Adam experienced to fall on the Lord Jesus Christ—the "sleep" of death by crucifixion. Christ came to earth seeking a Bride. As He hung on the cross at Calvary, His side was pierced, out of which flowed His life's blood (John 19:34). From that wound came the price that He paid to purchase the Church (Acts 20:28). Having bought her, He claimed her as His own. Paul calls it a "great mystery .... Christ and the church" (Eph. 5:32). As Adam was delighted with his bride, so the Lord Jesus will be delighted with His (Eph. 5:25-27). As believers, we are part of Christ's Bride and should respond to His love and affection by seeking to please Him in every way.

The Institution of Marriage (v. 24)

God established marriage as the first human institution, and the most basic. It preceded the other building blocks of society: human government, education, and religion. From the authority of the father in the family came forms of government, beginning with the patriarchal. From parental responsibility in marriage to teach both the knowledge of the world and of God came education and religion. Thus, marriage underlies the major building blocks of society.

Principles of Marriage

This foundational passage on marriage is quoted in four places in the New Testament. In each of them there is an important principle that emerges from Genesis 2.

Permanence

First is the principle of permanence in marriage (Matt. 19:3-9). Answering the Pharisees on the question of divorce, Jesus said,

Have you not read that He who made them at the beginning made them male and female, and said, 'For this reason a man shall leave his father and mother and be joined to his wife, and the two shall become one flesh'? So then, they are no longer two but one flesh. Therefore what God has joined together, let no man separate (Matt. 19:4-6).

No one should try and separate what God has declared as being "one." Marriage between one man and one woman was to be permanent. Mark Jesus' words carefully.

Faithfulness

The second principle is that of faithfulness in marriage. In writing to the Corinthian believers, Paul made it clear that the physical union of a man and his wife makes them "one flesh" and that their physical bodies are the Lord's (1 Cor. 6:16-7:2). Therefore, it is wrong for either one of them to commit adultery.

> Or do you not know that he who is joined to a harlot is one body with her? For "The two," He says, "shall become one flesh." But he who is joined to the Lord is one spirit with Him. Flee sexual immorality (1 Cor. 6:16-18a).

What the Corinthian believers did with their bodies was important because their bodies were included in their relationship with Christ that is described as membership in the body of Christ. "Do you not know that your bodies are members of Christ?" (1 Cor. 6:15). Any extramarital sexual intimacy is seen by God as a union with the other person and is a most serious matter. The apostle Paul went on to say that our bodies are sacred. They are temples of the Holy Spirit. They should never be defiled by illicit intimacy with anyone other than our spouses. He concludes by restating the necessity of faithfulness in marriage because it is a "one flesh union." "Let each man have his own wife and let each wife have her own husband" (1 Cor. 7:2).

Male Headship

The third principle that is based on Genesis 2 is that the man is the head of the home. In Eden, God gave the man headship in the marriage. God had made the woman from Adam's rib. She came from him. God also made her for Adam, and He demonstrated this by bringing her to him (v. 22). In 1 Corinthians 11, the apostle Paul explained the headship of man and the symbols associated with it in the church. Though male headship in marriage is not in line with popular thinking today, it is clearly taught in Scripture. God designed the male and female roles even before sin entered the world.

> For man is not from woman, but woman from man. Nor was man created for the woman, but woman for the man. For this reason the woman ought to have a symbol of authority on her head, because of the angels. Nevertheless neither is man independent of woman, nor woman independent of man, in the Lord. For as woman came from the man, even so man also comes through woman; but all things are from God (1 Cor. 11:8-12).

God was active in the entire process. After creating woman from man, He reminded the man that he was not independent of women. God points out that it is the woman who gives birth to the man, thus establishing his dependence on her. Consequently, there is to be a mutual dependence, since both are created in the image of God. Both are to please God by obeying the commands of God.

Male Responsibility

In addition to woman being made for the man, she was also flesh of his flesh and bone of his bone. Just as the New Testament expands on the priority of the man's role in marriage, it also expands on the responsibility of the husband to love and to care for his wife, based on the truth of their being one flesh. Paul instructed husbands at the church in Ephesus:

> So husbands ought to love their own wives as their own bodies; he who loves his wife loves himself. For no one ever hated his own flesh, but nourishes and cherishes it, just as the Lord does the church. For we are members of His body, of His flesh and of His bones. "For this reason a man shall leave his father and mother and be joined to his wife, and the two shall become one flesh" (Eph. 5:28-31).

Although he is the head of the home, he must never forget that it is his responsibility to demonstrate his love for his wife. "Christ loved the church and gave Himself for it" (Eph. 5:25). Not even the most dedicated Christian husband has carried out that responsibility to the extent that Christ did in relation to the Church. All husbands ought to continually strive to excel in loving their wives.

Innocence (v. 25)

The last verse of our chapter says, "And they were both naked, the man and his wife, and they were not ashamed." Adam and Eve were perfectly at ease with each other and did not have any fear that they could be exploited for evil. They had no consciousness of sin or moral guilt, but lived together in their own integrity. They were living in God's sight without a trace of shame, nor should they have had any. The significance of their nakedness will emerge in the next chapter, where its shame is unmistakably linked to their sin. It was only after their rebellion against God that consciousness of sin arose in them and they were uncomfortable with being naked. This verse is a bridge between the institution of pure and innocent marriage in chapter 2 and the shame and realization of sin that occurs in chapter 3.

In Conclusion

This chapter has described how Adam and Eve were formed by God and became the crown of everything He created. They were brought together in marriage by God in order to fulfill His purpose for them to enjoy Him, to fill the earth and subdue it, and to serve God together in caring for the garden. God set before them life and death by the presence of the two special trees, the Tree of Life and the Tree of the Knowledge of Good and Evil, and the command associated with the latter.

We, too, have important choices to make with far-reaching consequences. Like Adam and Eve, we have been placed in a God-chosen set of circumstances. Like them, we have life partners with whom we are to live in harmony, according to God's order. Like them, we have the command of God to guide us and the presence of God to surround us. Like them, we have a task to do as God's servants. May God give us grace to live up to the challenge God has set before us.

The Tragedy of Sin and the Triumph of Grace

Genesis 3 is one of the key chapters in the entire Bible. It is *doctrinally* important because it contains the reason why God's plan of redemption through Christ was necessary. That reason was *sin* that entered into the world, cutting off man's relationship with God. It tells us how humanity came into its fallen state through disobedience to God. It explains the origin of the problem of evil that has puzzled philosophers for centuries. That problem is easily demonstrated in the worldwide need for things like locks and lie detectors, armies and weapons, courts and jails, police and judges, orphanages and shelters.

The need for all these began in the Garden of Eden. But other consequences of sin which have touched almost everything that God created are explained here too. In bringing to light the problems caused by sin, the chapter provides a basis for solutions that are progressively revealed in the rest of the Bible. This chapter points to the central feature in those solutions, which is that God would provide a way to re-establish man's broken relationship with Himself. The first moves by God in this direction are revealed here in Genesis 3. Ultimately, God will restore the conditions of His original creation.

This chapter is *historically* important because the events recorded changed the course of human history. Genesis 3 is not, as some claim, a fable or a legend that was written just to teach a moral lesson. Rather, it is history—a record of the reality of sin and the resulting dilemma for man. It is the historical truth of Genesis 3 that gives meaning to the death of Christ.

Some students of ancient history have called this account a "creation myth" like those of Babylon and Sumer, concocted to satisfy people's curiosity. However, Genesis 3 is an *historical* account. All the myths from other sources about creation and the beginning of evil are either distortions of this account or inventions from the minds of ancient man. Adam and Eve were real people in a real garden talking to a real serpent. The New Testament confirms the literal truth of the serpent's deception of Eve and builds upon it. In 2 Corinthians 11:3, for example, the apostle Paul says, "I fear, lest somehow, as the serpent deceived Eve by his craftiness, so your minds may be corrupted from the simplicity that is in Christ." See also 1 Timothy 2:14.

The chapter is important *practically* because it offers useful insight on how we can deal with temptation. It will alert us as to the process and methods of temptation that Satan may use in trying to wreck the purpose of God in us. The disobedience of Adam and Eve cannot be blamed on the environment or on their background; their surroundings were ideal and they had no history. It was the process of temptation that caught them off guard. This chapter will help us understand the difference between the testing by which God *proves* His people and the tempting by which Satan seeks to *harm* them. There is also a warning to us of the enormous consequences of personal sin that may flow from a single disobedient act of rebellion against God.

Biblical Images of Satan

Adam and his helpmeet were fresh from the creative hand of God. They were physically perfect in every detail. Intellectually, God created them with a capacity far above that of the most brilliant minds in the world today. They were emotionally and psychologically healthy and balanced. God placed them in a perfect environment designed especially for them. In it, they were to develop their capacities and happiness to the fullest extent. Most wonderful of all, they were able to enjoy personal fellowship with God every day (v. 8).

Chapter 3 begins on an ominous note: "Now the serpent was more cunning...." The serpent was one of the created animals, maybe the most beautiful. The fact that snakes today are biologically incapable of talking is irrelevant. Clearly, in the temptation, Satan caused the serpent to talk and used it for his evil purposes. Though the name "Satan" is not used in these verses, there is no doubt that he is present. The book of Revelation clearly links him with the serpent: "That serpent of old, called the devil and Satan" (Rev. 12:9). His character as "the father of lies" (John 8:44) is evident in his conversation with Eve, and his cunning, stated in verse 1, prepares us for his tempting her. Satan spoke through the serpent in order to deceive the woman. But the emphasis in this story is not on Satan, probably to avoid the very human tendency of blaming the sin on Satan rather than accepting the truth of man's culpability and responsibility.

Satan is portrayed in the Bible in several different ways. As a *dragon*, he slaughters the saints (Rev. 12:9). As a *roaring lion*, he terrifies and attacks God's people to nullify their testimony (1 Pet. 5:8). And here as a *subtle serpent*, he tempts the man and the woman and uses the beauty and craftiness of the serpent to his own advantage. In addition to these characteristics, the Lord Jesus attributes wisdom to serpents (Matt. 10:16). No doubt Satan had listened carefully when Adam named each of the animals according to their characteristics. The serpent's attractiveness and wisdom must have stood out to him. As we consider the temptation of Adam and Eve in the garden, we ought to note that the fall of Satan, as a result of his pride, had already taken place. Satan was an angelic being of a very high order who rebelled against

God. He fell from being an exalted angel to being the enemy of God (see Isa.14: 4-21; Ezek. 28:11-19; 2 Pet. 2:4; Jude 6). Although the Bible does not tell us when this took place, it may have occurred during the first day of creation week.

It is clear from this account that Satan, through the serpent, intruded into Eve's life with evil intent. What God had created was "good" (1:31), but Satan determined to spoil that good. Adam and his wife were God's special delight, and because of this they became the focus of Satan's enmity against Him. Satan remains an intruder into the lives of God's people today by trying to wreck everything that God does.

One of Satan's favorite tactics is the one he used with the woman: he undermined her trust in God by creating doubt in her mind about God's good intentions. Satan tempted her in three specific ways:

- He questioned the truth of God's word.
- He contradicted what God had said.
- He maligned God's character.

Satan Questions God's Word and Man Falls (vv. 1-6)

Satan's Approach to Eve

The serpent approached Eve using all his cunning. He did not admit how he hated God and how he wanted to destroy God's world. He waited until she was alone, without Adam to counsel her. It was to Adam that God had given the command not to eat of the Tree of the Knowledge of Good and Evil (2:16-17). Eve learned God's command from Adam, who had heard it from God. The serpent by-passed Adam, the head of the home, and spoke directly to the woman. He started the discussion by talking about God, asking what appeared to be an innocent question: "Has God indeed said, 'You shall not eat of every tree of the garden'?" She was probably taken aback when he said, in effect, "Is it really true that you are not allowed to eat of every tree?" He did not explicitly deny what God had said, but subtly questioned God's integrity. Could it be that God was withholding something that might be to her advantage?

Eve probably did not realize that his enquiry assumed man's right to question not only God's word, but God Himself. She seems to have been caught off guard. And although she should have consulted with Adam, she did not. Satan's tactic of causing doubt about what God said was beginning to take root in her. It has been a favorite strategy of his ever since.

Eve's Reply (vv. 2-3)

Eve's response to the serpent was to try to explain that he was incorrect in his assumption. Certainly, she was not careful herself when she quoted what God had said. Three glaring dangers emerge from her reply to Satan:

- She added something to God's word.
- She left something out from God's word.
- She weakened the penalty for disobedience.

What she added was that they were not to *touch* the Tree of the Knowledge of Good and Evil, an addition that made God seem more demanding than He really was (cf. 2:17). This exaggeration indicates that she was beginning to think that God's test might be harder than was necessary—maybe even unfair. We, too, may be inclined to exaggerate God's demands, especially when we have rising doubts about the wisdom of them. It is always dangerous to add anything to God's directives, especially when it involves questioning God's intent.

The woman succumbed to the second danger when, in her reply, she omitted that they might *freely* eat of the fruit of all the trees in the garden. In saying that the fruit of the trees was simply *available*, she made light of the fact that it was freely given by a generous God (cf. 2:16). So the second danger was in making God appear less generous that He was.

The third danger in her reply was to weaken the effect of God's word, which was the force of the punishment for their disobedience. She misquoted God's warning to Adam about the penalty for eating the fruit of the forbidden tree. She quoted Him as saying "lest you die," when what God had actually said was "you shall surely die." In other words, there was no room for the possibility that they would not die (2:17; 3:3).

In summary, the woman exaggerated the intent of God, minimized the generosity of God, and weakened the penalty of God. She had already fallen into Satan's trap.

Satan Contradicts God's Word

Satan's reply in verse 4 was an emphatic denial of God's clear word to Adam that he would "surely die" (2:17). He now asserted, "You will not surely die." This was the first lie ever told, and it came from "the father of lies." It was a direct attack on the woman's faith in God because it insinuated that God lied to Adam when He told him that eating of the tree would result in death. She could reason that if what God had said about the penalty for disobedience was not true, how could she believe in Him at all? Satan claimed that disobedience to God does not have eternal consequences. This is a lie that Satan has used down through history, and it is widespread in our world today in several forms. There are those who deny hell or eternal punishment. Others believe in reincarnation and a chance at another life. Still others believe that humans are products of chance and there is no God to whom they are accountable. All these false ideas reinforce Satan's first lie that there is no consequence for man's disobedience.

Satan Accuses God of Evil Intent

Satan explained to Eve the reason why she would not die by suggesting that God was jealous and was intentionally keeping her back from her destiny—that of being like Him (v. 5). He said, "For God knows that in the day you eat of it your eyes will be opened, and you will be like God, knowing good and evil." Gaining knowledge of good and evil was intriguing, and the idea of becoming like God almost irresistible. Part of what Satan said was true—in one sense, she would know both good and evil—but not from the perspective of a sinless God. Rather, she would know it from the perspective of one caught in its clutches and condemned to death. In knowing both good and evil, she would find herself unable to do the good she might want to do and unable to stop doing evil she might not want to do. Satan deliberately deceived her into thinking that she would be better off by eating the fruit of the forbidden tree.

The Fall (v. 6)

The woman's eyes were, by this time, off her Creator and off her husband. Instead, she was focusing on herself. Her goal was no longer to glorify God, but to be self-fulfilled. At this point, she had already sinned—even before she ate the fruit. Her sin, like all sin, occurred internally first and then manifested itself externally. Sin touched her whole person: body, soul, and spirit. She saw that the tree was "good for food"; that was the bodily aspect. It was also "pleasant to the eyes"; its color and shape appealed to her aesthetic sense, which has to do with the soul. Finally, she believed the lie that it would give her wisdom. This was the intellectual or spiritual aspect. She was tempted to seek wisdom apart from God, which is both foolish and futile (Prov. 1:7; 1 Cor. 3:19). Thus Satan appealed to her body, her soul, and her spirit in tempting her to succumb—which she did.

The world system governed by Satan offers the same attractions to *our* bodies, souls, and spirits. The Holy Spirit said through the apostle John, "Do not love the world or the things in the world. If anyone loves the world, the love of the Father is not in him. For all that is in the world—the lust of the flesh, the lust of the eyes, and the pride of life—is not of the Father but is of the world" (1 John 2:15-16). John identified the three parts of the world system as the lust of the flesh, the lust of the eyes, and the pride of life. The lust of the flesh can be linked to the woman's desire for the fruit as food. The lust of the eyes relates to the fruit being "pleasant to the eyes." The pride of life equates to the wisdom she thought she would gain by eating the fruit. Satan's tactics in tempting people have not changed down through the centuries, and we would do well in our own lives to beware of their subtlety.

Adam and Eve's Temptation Contrasted with the Temptation of Jesus

A most profitable study in temptation is to contrast the defeat of Adam and Eve when they were tempted with the victory of the Lord Jesus when He was tempted, and then to compare both with the apostle John's teaching (cf. Genesis 2:1-6; Matt. 4:1-11; 1 John 2:15-16). In both situations, Satan the tempter sought to bring them down using similar tactics. He used physical food to arouse lust of the flesh: hunger for the fruit and the bread. He used the attractiveness of something visible to arouse lust of the eyes; for Eve it was the beautiful fruit and for Jesus it was spectacular angelic mid-air support. Finally, he used the desire for power and control to arouse pride of life: for the woman in the garden it was to be like God; for the Lord Jesus Christ it was to receive earthly kingdoms. The results were stark in contrast: the woman fell into the trap, but the Lord Jesus countered the temptation by quoting the written Word of God. He emerged victorious and became our great example.

The Act of Sin

The acts of Eve are described very simply: She "saw," she "took," and she "ate." When she ate the fruit of the Tree of the Knowledge of Good and Evil, she did not die immediately. She may have thought that the serpent was right after all. With her new discovery, she gave the forbidden fruit to Adam, "and he ate." Adam sinned by forsaking his God-given role of leader and allowing himself to be led by his wife. The Bible tells us that he was not deceived by the serpent as she had been (1 Tim. 2:14). He knew what the consequences would be, and then he willfully sinned. He consciously decided to follow his wife into sin rather than obey God and be separated from her. Ultimately his choice was between following her and following God. Adam's sin, like Eve's, was first in the mind and then in the act. Thus, the *Fall* occurred. By the term *Fall,* we mean that mankind fell from his state of innocence before God into a state of sinfulness and guilt before Him.

The Consequence of Guilt before God (v. 7)

The guilty pair's initial reaction was one of a strong sense of shame. The tempter had told them that their eyes would be opened and that they would know both good and evil. What he did not tell them was that they would see good and evil from the standpoint of sin, and that they would be deeply ashamed of it. Their shame was in their consciousness of guilt. They realized that the glory of their former innocence was now gone. They saw the lie Satan had perpetrated. They saw that instead of becoming like God in knowing evil, they had become like Satan, who was himself evil. They saw themselves degraded from their dignity as created beings and disgraced before God.

The fact that they both covered themselves and tried to hide from God confirms their shame. In sewing fig leaves for a covering, they were creating the first man-made religion. It was a pathetic attempt to cover their guilt and relieve their conscience. They tried to satisfy God by inventing something to meet a felt-need. It didn't work, and they hid themselves because they knew their clothing was unacceptable to God. They had disregarded God's law of innocence and happiness. Now they found they were under God's law of holiness which condemned them as sinners. They knew good but were incapable of doing it. They knew evil but were unable to resist it. This is the human dilemma that theologians call *depravity*.

Before they sinned, Adam and Eve had been naked but felt no shame (2:25); they were at ease with each other. Now they were aware of their nakedness. From that time to this, nudity has been associated with sin. Some sociologists believe that the shame of nudity is simply an inhibition introduced by Jews and Christians. The truth is that its source is in the awareness of sin that started in the Garden of Eden. Only where people are morally insensitive to sin is public nudity encouraged. In the Bible, both the saints in heaven and the glorified Son of Man are always pictured as being clothed (Rev. 1:13; 19:14).

The Consequence of Separation from God (v. 8)

Not only were the couple guilty before God—they immediately sensed a distance between themselves and their Maker. Having clothed themselves in garments of fig leaves, they heard God approaching them in the garden. An appearance by God in human form in the Old Testament is termed a *theophany*. We read of many such appearances made by the second Person of the Trinity. In their time of innocence, Adam and his wife had enjoyed close and personal fellowship with God as the highlight of their day. Now everything was different. When they heard the voice of the Lord, "they hid themselves from the presence of the LORD God among the trees of the garden." They did not want to see Him or be seen. They could not bear His presence, because they sensed the enormous gulf between His holiness and their sin. That gulf, which was introduced by their sin, still exists today between sinners and a holy God.

God Seeks Adam and Eve (vv. 9-13)

God Calls to Lost Man

God is faithful to His own holy character and must, therefore, confront sin and sinners. He did just this with Adam and Eve in the garden. First, He sought them and found them. Then, He confronted them with their sinful condition, which was evident by their own confession. God's approach to them sets the scene for the rest of the Bible, which records how God reached out to sinful man and carried out His plan to regain "paradise lost." God's plan was centered in the redemptive work of His Son by which He provided a way for man to be restored to fellowship with Himself. The prophet Habakkuk understood the distance between God and sinners when he said of God, "Your eyes are too pure to approve evil, and you cannot look on wickedness with favor" (Hab. 1:12). Yet it was God who sought man in order to restore what was lost, not man who sought God, trying to recover his own loss. God's first words to Adam after the Fall were, "Where are you?" He was already seeking.

Notice how God approached them. He came "walking," not with a big demonstration of His displeasure, but gently. It was in the "cool [breeze] of the day," the most pleasant time. Neither their garments of fig leaves nor their hiding place in the trees concealed them from God's sight. As sinners, they remained afraid among the trees until God came near.

God Questions Lost Man

God had two questions for Adam. First, "Where are you?" It was a rhetorical question; God knew where he was. He asked the question so Adam would have to acknowledge that he was trying to hide from God and was not able to enjoy His presence. No one can hide from God. David voiced this truth in Psalm 139: "Where can I go from Your Spirit? Or where can I flee from Your presence? If I ascend into heaven, You are there" (Ps. 139:7-8). The psalmist went on to say that no matter where he went, he could not escape the presence of God.

Adam then tried to defend himself, saying, "I heard Your voice in the garden, and I was afraid because I was naked; and I hid myself" (v. 10). Here he confessed his nakedness and also confessed that it made him ashamed, prompting him to hide.

The second question was in two parts. "Who told you that you were naked? Have you eaten from the tree of which I commanded you that you should not eat?" (v. 11). The question was posed in such a way as to emphasize that he had eaten from the tree specifically marked out as "off limits" to him. It made his eating a direct violation of God's clear commandment. He was also giving Adam an opportunity to acknowledge his sin. God directed His question toward the man. He deliberately by-passed the woman's part in the matter and focused only on Adam's responsibility and disobedience (see Rom. 5:12).

Adam's answer was to try and avoid responsibility by transferring the blame to his wife. How quickly the effects of sin were evident in him! Adam only offered excuses. In fact, more than simply blaming the woman, he implied that God Himself had a part in it by saying it was "the woman whom *You gave* to be with me…." (emphasis added). Instead to praising God for His goodness in giving him a partner, he blamed God for providing the woman who offered him the fruit! But the truth of his guilt comes out at the end of the verse: "I ate" (v. 12). God now turned His attention to the woman.

Eve's confession emerges from the Lord's question: "What is this you have done?" (v. 13). It has the force of "what in the world have you done?" Her answer, like Adam's, was to "play the blame game." She tried to transfer the responsibility to the serpent who had deceived her. But, like Adam, she had to confess, "I ate" (v. 13). How different it might have been, if they had not tried to shift the blame, we can only guess. In the end, both of them had to admit that they were guilty, and that was the correct verdict.

The New World Order as the Consequence of Sin (vv. 14-22)

This section is sometimes called the *curse*, but it is much more than that, for it includes provision for relief and hope for the future. In these verses, God the Judge pronounces His sentence. God's words are not commandments; rather, they are statements about the new world order about how things will be in the light of the presence of sin. A whole new order was to be imposed on the animal kingdom, on the serpent, on the woman, on Adam, upon his descendants, and on the ground itself. He spoke to the serpent first, then to the woman, and then to Adam. This was the same sequence as their involvement in the Fall (vv. 1-7).

The Oracle of Judgment to the Serpent

In the previous verses, the Lord gave the humans opportunity to defend themselves; He did not grant the same for the serpent. He treated the serpent as already condemned for He immediately pronounced a sentence on it (vv.14-15). The serpent may have been the head (the representative) of all the animals; certainly it had yielded itself to the devil as the instrument of evil. "Because you have done this" (deliberately deceived the woman) and because of his deliberate opposition to the order of God on earth, he was "cursed … *more* than all cattle" (emphasis added). This implies a general curse on the whole animal kingdom and a specific curse on the serpent. The general curse is borne out in the New Testament, which confirms that the whole of creation groans until now under the "bondage of corruption" (Rom. 8:20-22).

The serpent's anatomy must have been altered. It is now told, "On your belly you shall go, and you shall eat dust." Perhaps it was originally created with arms and legs. Its new form represents retrogression in the scale of beings. Being now without limbs, it was compelled to eat everything from the ground and so to swallow dust with its food. In the words of a Jewish commentary, "All its food had the flavor of dust." This will be true even in the Millennium, when serpents will eat dust (Isa. 65:25). Up to this point in God's pronouncement, only the creature had been in view. From verse 15 onwards, the focus moves from the serpent to Satan, whose presence was concealed within it.

The Germ of all Biblical Prophecies (v. 15)

God declared a prophecy about Satan's future in relation to the seed of the woman. This verse has been called "the germ of all subsequent prophecy." It is one of only two prophecies that are known to have survived the pre-flood period, the other one being Enoch's prophecy (see Jude 14-15). He spoke about the consequences of the Fall. The tranquility that the man and woman had enjoyed in their garden paradise, experiencing unhindered fellowship with God, would be lost. Their peace would be replaced by hostility on three levels.

Level 1: Enmity between the Woman and the Serpent

God said, "I will put enmity between you and the woman." Satan may have believed that he had won Eve over to following him and that she would be his ally in his plans to control humanity through her—she was, after all, to be the mother of the human race. God broke up that projected alliance. She would not be Satan's ally. Instead, there would be enmity between them. She would always know that Satan was a doomed being and the cause of all her misery.

Because of this, she would not be willing to serve Satan. Eve now saw him as the enemy of God. She was, therefore, better prepared to engage him in any future battle. Satan had won in his first objective, which was to seduce Adam and Eve away from the worship of God, but he failed in his second objective to win their allegiance and worship for himself.

Level 2: Enmity between Satan's Seed and the Woman's Seed

There was to be hostility between her "seed" and Satan's "seed." The term *seed*, as used in Genesis 3:15 and other passages, has caused a great deal of discussion among commentators. It is best to understand it in the same way it is used of Abraham and his seed, also recorded in Genesis: as both a *collective* term, referring to all his descendants (12:3; 13:16; 15:13), and as an *individual* term, referring to one particular descendant (4:25; 22:17-18; Gal. 3:17, 19). Thus, there are three ways to understand the word "seed": it relates (1) to Eve's descendants, that is, mankind in general; (2) to the chosen people through whom Messiah would come; and (3) ultimately, to the Lord Jesus Christ (Gal. 3:16, 19).

Satan's seed probably refers to evil people who ally themselves with his purposes in opposition to God, setting themselves against the Seed of the woman. Ultimately it may refer to Antichrist, the great world leader of the end times who will oppose Christ (1 John 2:18).

Jesus used this kind of terminology when He said to His enemies, "You are of your father the devil" (John 8:44). These people opposed the redemptive purposes of God. They would not acknowledge their hopeless condition but believed, instead, the lie of the devil. Cain, Adam's first-born, was evidently the first of these, as we shall see from Genesis 4. He was "of the wicked one and murdered his brother.... because his own works were evil and his brother's righteous" (1 John 3:12).

On this level, the prediction is that there will always be antagonism between those who are for and those who are against the purposes of God. Good and evil will continually be in conflict. In keeping with this hostility, Christ called His enemies a "generation of vipers" (serpents), and went on to say "how can you, being evil, speak good things?" (Matt. 12:34). See also Matthew 23:33 and Revelation 12:9.

Level 3: Enmity between the Christ and Satan

There will be a future battle between Satan (the serpent) and Christ (the Seed of the woman). The Lord God spoke to the serpent about the coming Seed and said, "He shall bruise your head and you shall bruise His heel." The imagery here is of a man in a standing position being bitten on the heel by a poisonous snake. He then kills the snake by crushing its head with his foot. Note the use of the personal pronouns—both are actual persons. There would be personal combat and a personal victory. Bible students will be aware that the ultimate Seed of the woman was the Lord Jesus Christ who came into direct combat with Satan at the cross.

Satan's hatred for Christ was evident during every part of Jesus' life on earth:

- When Herod attempted to kill Him along with the other babies in Bethlehem (Matt. 2:16)
- When, as a boy of twelve, Jesus was left in the Temple among the Pharisees, who were enemies (Luke 2:41-50)
- In the satanic temptations right after John the Baptist publicly introduced Him to ministry (Luke 4:1-13)
- In Nazareth, when the men of the synagogue would have thrown him over the cliff, had He not spirited Himself away (Luke 4:28-30)
- In the storm on the Sea of Galilee (Mark 4:35-39)
- In Jerusalem, when the Jews picked up stones to stone Him (John 8:59)
- In the trial and crucifixion, when the "bruising" occurred, and Satan must have thought he had finally won the conflict (Mark 15:22-26)

Suffering and Glory for the Seed of the Woman

But there is much more to this than the fact that there would be mortal combat between the Seed of the woman and Satan. The conflict would end with Christ triumphant. Note what God said to Satan. "He [the Seed of the woman] shall bruise your [Satan's] head and you shall bruise His [the Seed's] heel." Satan's power would be destroyed and his "captives" set free. This prophecy was fulfilled at Calvary where the Lord Jesus Christ "destroyed him who had the power of death, that is, the devil" (Heb. 2:14). The defeat of Satan at the cross, though final and irrevocable, will not be fully manifested until a coming day when he and his angels will be cast into eternal fire (Matt. 25:41). Paul referenced the truth of Satan's defeat when he assured the Roman believers, "The God of peace will soon crush Satan under your heel" (Rom. 16:20).

The other side of the prophecy is that, in the process of bruising the serpent's head, the Seed of the woman would be bruised on the heel. This means that the Seed would Himself be "wounded," but only on the "heel." In his redemptive work, Christ was "wounded for our transgressions, He was bruised for our iniquities" (Isa. 53:5). But His wounds and death were not the end. He rose from the grave in victory. His suffering and death climaxed in resurrection and glory. What a triumph! This is the first prophecy concerning both the suffering and glory of the coming Savior.

Hope for the Guilty Pair

The effect of this prophecy created high hopes in Adam and Eve. Although both they and the natural world around them were under the curse, their subjection was "in hope" (Rom. 8:20). Although their struggles with childbirth, marital roles, growing food, broken fellowship with God, and death itself were all part of the judgment, there was hope of a coming Victor who would turn it all around and restore them and their world to their pre-fall condition.

In the ancient names of the constellations of stars, there are at least four pairs of star signs that clearly indicate a victor treading down the head of a serpent while he himself is being wounded:

- Hercules has his foot on the head of Draco.
- Ophiuchus has his foot on the head of Scorpio.
- Orion is treading down the head of Lepus.
- Leo, the final constellation in the Zodiac, has his foot on the head of Hydra the dragon.

These signs were probably designated long before the Flood to keep alive the great primeval promise of Genesis 3:15.

The Oracle to the Woman (v. 16)

Turning to the woman, God announced two consequences of her sin: pain in procreation and subjection to her husband. The physical pain would be associated with childbirth. Added to this was the grief associated with the rearing of children, because they would be born possessing sinful natures. She would produce new life through suffering. What was originally designed to be the joyful function of reproduction would now be marred by pain and sorrow.

The second part of the prophecy has to do with her "desire" toward her husband. This is generally understood to mean that the woman would be drawn to her husband. However, the use of the same word in Genesis 4:7 clearly indicates that the word "desire" has to do with the prompting to commit evil or exercise control. If this meaning is taken, then the verse should be paraphrased, "you wanted to control your husband, but *he* shall rule over *you.*" Because Eve's desire had been to influence her husband to follow her in eating the forbidden fruit, her judgment was that her husband would rule over her. This reading is supported by the next verse, which finds Adam guilty because he "heeded the voice of [his] wife."

The woman had taken the lead; she had stepped outside of the boundary of the role God had ordained for her in their partnership, that of being a helper to

Adam. She had acted independently. She had led her husband to sin and would now be mastered by him. The word *rule* is a strong one that describes dominion and lordship. Male domination was part of the woman's punishment. Throughout human history, the male domination of the family and society has been a perpetual reminder of the Fall. The Christian application is that husbands are not to take advantage of their authority but to rule their wives by loving them as Christ loved the church (Eph. 5:22-25).

The Oracle to the Man (vv. 17-19)

The effect of Adam sinning willfully, obeying his wife rather than God, was that he would be forced to work hard in order to grow food from the cursed ground. The earth that had previously been so fruitful when Adam tilled and dressed it would now produce a much smaller yield from much greater work. Not only that—it would also produce thorns and thistles that would further diminish its harvest. Working hard by the sweat of his brow to grow food from resistant ground, Adam would constantly be reminded that he had sinned. The weeds would choke the grain. The thorns would scratch his body. His food would be bread made from grain, which had to be planted, harvested, ground, and baked: "In the sweat of your face you shall eat bread." In the end, death would triumph, and his body would return to the dust. The ground was cursed "for his sake": hard work was God's plan to help keep Adam from further rebellion.

Adam and Eve were fully aware of the four primary consequences of their sin. For her it was "sorrow" and "pain" (v. 16). For him, it was "sweat" and "death"—his return to the "dust" (vv. 17-19).

Note that these very consequences were among the sufferings of Christ for our sins. It is most instructive to read that Christ was a "man of sorrows" (Isa. 53:3). He also suffered the pain of physical torture, part of which came from the crown of thorns that was pressed on His head (Mark 15:17). Thorns were part of Adam's curse, too. In the Garden of Gethsemane, Jesus' "sweat became like great drops of blood falling down to the ground" (Luke 22:44). And as He gave up His spirit after six hours on the cross, He was brought to "the dust of death" (Ps. 22:15).

Adam's judgment was the consequence of his obeying his wife and disobeying God. He was not deceived by her, but sinned willfully, choosing to join her even if it meant separation from God. Adam sinned by eating, so he would suffer in order to eat. They brought pain into the world, so they would experience pain in their respective lives. Thus there are three aspects to the judgment on Adam:

- The ground was cursed.
- Adam was condemned to live by sweat and toil.
- The end would be physical death.

Adam's Faith in Naming Eve (v. 20)

In naming his wife *Eve,* which means "life" or "living," Adam demonstrated that he believed she would be the mother of children in general and of the coming Seed in particular. He also believed that the Seed would crush the head of the serpent. He anticipated the coming One who would take the sting out of death. In believing this, he overcame the power of death. The point is this: Adam accepted his sinfulness before God and became a believer in a coming Savior.

No doubt, Eve became a believer at this time, too. The editor of these ancient documents then added a note about Eve: "she was the mother of all living." Life would go on through her and her children. This statement precludes the possibility of any humans existing before Adam and Eve.

God Prepares Coats of Skin (v. 21)

God provided clothing for the sinners. "For Adam and his wife the LORD God made tunics of skin, and clothed them." This is one of the most wonderful object lessons of God's grace in the Bible. It is true that making clothes for them was an act of kindness, but the truth goes much deeper than that. Adam and Eve realized they were naked before God (3:10). Their fig leaf aprons were inadequate. God then demonstrated the truth of sacrifice for sin. He took animals (probably sheep) and shed their blood in order to make garments from their skins. God was teaching them that sin could be "covered" by the death of another, a *substitutionary sacrifice.* In all likelihood, Adam and Eve probably recognized that it was the coming Seed who would become that sacrifice. He would have to shed His blood for the atonement (covering) of sin.

It is remarkable that God should offer the first sacrifice. He covered the guilty couple with coats of skin in pure grace. In sacrificing the animal, He illustrated some of the great truths of the gospel. He demonstrated that "it is the blood that makes atonement for the soul" (Lev. 17:11) and that "without shedding of blood there is no remission" (Heb. 9:22). The clothing of skins clearly shows three great truths of salvation:

- Shedding of blood was stipulated. It was a *blood sacrifice.*
- Sacrifice of an innocent victim was necessary to pay the penalty of sin. It was a *penal sacrifice.*
- It was necessary for the substitute to fulfill the requirements in the place of the sinner. It was a *substitutionary sacrifice.*

All this was illustrated in the Garden of Eden and ultimately fulfilled by Jesus, the Son of Man, who gave His life "a ransom for many" (Mark 10:45). It was God who proposed the solution: *He* sacrificed the victims; *He* prepared the clothing; *He* actually dressed them in the skins; and *He* finally accepted them in their new "garments of salvation" (Isa. 61:10).

The Consequence of Eviction from the Garden (vv. 23-24)

Adam and Eve, even though they were repentant, were expelled from their paradise home. They were reluctant to go, so they had to be driven out. Perhaps, from their perspective, they feared losing the presence of God but, from God's gracious point of view, they must not be allowed to partake of the Tree of Life and live forever in their sinful condition (v. 22). It was a sad admission for God to say that man, because he had fallen into a depraved state, now knew evil. Adam was helpless to prevent sin's control and growth. It would certainly have been intolerable if he had lived physically forever. What would life on earth be like if some of the truly evil leaders of the past had lived even five hundred years, let alone forever? The Tree of Life was still in the center of the garden, so God prevented unlimited extension of physical life by driving Adam and Eve out. Their expulsion was a punishment designed for their good. Although they would be exposed to physical death, they would have the opportunity to gain eternal *spiritual* life.

Man had been made from the dust of the earth. He had chosen earthly principles; now he had to live by them. He had to cultivate the dust outside the garden and make bread from the grain it produced. He needed to experience the misery caused by sin to prompt him to seek deliverance. God's *love* imposed the difficult conditions on his life that would help him realize his lost condition. God's *grace* made provision for his eternal salvation based on the sacrifice of the coming Seed. God's *mercy* prevented him from taking the fruit of the Tree of Life so that he would not have to live forever tainted by sin.

Cherubim, and a flaming sword which turned in every direction, now guarded access to the Tree of Life. Cherubim, the keepers of the holiness of God, are associated in Scripture with God's throne (Ps. 18:10; Ezek. 1:4-28; 10:1-22). Replicas of the cherubim were placed above the mercy seat in the Most Holy Place in the Tabernacle (Ex. 25:17-22). God prevented Adam and Eve from returning to show that the Tree of Life would be preserved until the time of the end when sin would be rooted out and death would be abolished by the victory of the Seed of the woman (1 Cor. 15:26). Note that the Tree of Life appears again in the very last chapter of Scripture as part of the eternal day in the heavenly Jerusalem (Rev. 22:2, 14).

In Conclusion

Genesis 3 has presented us with some vital basic truths. We have seen how sin entered into the world through Satan's temptation of Adam and Eve. We have seen that when they yielded to temptation they immediately lost their innocence, and their relationship with God was broken. Eventually their physical bodies would die. God announced a new order for the world that was now tainted by sin. The serpent was cursed. God placed hostility between the serpent and the woman and between her children and those called the children of Satan.

Ultimately, there would be hostility between the messianic Seed, who would be born of a woman, and Satan. However, the Seed of the woman would, in the end, triumph over the serpent. In the process, He would be wounded Himself. He would both suffer and be glorified.

As for Adam and Eve's future on earth, they were expelled from the Garden of Eden. Outside the garden, toil, suffering, and pain would be part of their daily life. The woman would suffer pain in childbirth and be subject to her husband. Adam and Eve accepted God's judgment, and Adam named his wife Eve, meaning "life." They accepted the clothing of skins God made for them that demonstrated the need for blood sacrifice for sin. God mercifully blocked the way to the Tree of Life lest they live forever in their sinful state. This is the scene out of which comes the unfolding story of salvation in Scripture.

The Rebellion of Ancient Civilization

The events of Genesis 4 grow out of the events of the previous chapter, where the first two people were tempted to sin by the subtlety of Satan. They yielded to the temptation to disobey the clear command God had given them. Thus they became guilty sinners before a holy God. The result of this was that God judged both the guilty couple and the fruitful earth in which they lived. However, God gave them a promise that the cursed creation would be restored when the Seed of the woman defeated Satan. He also made them clothes of skins and demonstrated how fellowship with Himself could be restored through the blood sacrifice of a victim in their place.

The Effects of Sin

We now learn that the sin that began in Adam and Eve quickly spread within their family to corrupt their children and then society in general. It reveals the origin of social sin in the world and man's responsibility to deal with it. We also learn how peoples' relationship with God changed because they were now fallen beings. To demonstrate their faith, they worshipped Him by offering blood sacrifices that pointed to the coming Savior—the One who would be the ultimate sacrifice for sin.

The children of Israel (for whom Moses was compiling this historical record) would need to keep alive the hope of a Redeemer through the rite of sacrificial offerings when they entered Canaan. Moses knew that Canaan's culture was morally and spiritually corrupt, and it would be necessary for the Israelites to understand the roots of paganism in the land so that they could avoid the dangers. The stark lines drawn in this chapter between the character and behavior of the righteous and the ungodly would have served as a strong warning to Moses' audience of the conflict they could expect with the pagan inhabitants of Canaan.

The story line focuses primarily on Cain, the firstborn son of Adam and Eve. It explains the murder of his brother Abel and the consequences of that act on his life and family. Cain and Abel were not fictional or mythological characters—they were real people. Just as in the case of Adam and Eve, they are referred to as historical people by several New Testament writers as well as by the Lord Jesus (see Matt. 23:35; Luke 11:51; Heb. 11:4; 12:24; 1 John 3:12; Jude 11).

The Births of Cain and Abel (vv. 1-2)

The story begins with the conception and birth of Cain. The text says that Adam "knew" his wife, a common Hebrew term for marital sexual union (cf. 1 Sam. 1:19). The resulting child was the first human baby ever born on planet Earth. At his birth, Eve exclaimed, "I have gotten a man from the LORD." Cain's name means "gotten." Note that she defined him as "a *man* from the LORD" (emphasis added). She was anticipating his development and manhood. She might have thought that he was the promised Seed who would undo the damage caused by sin (3:15). Later it would become evident that he was not the promised Seed, but whatever she thought, it is evident that Eve acknowledged God's part in the birth of the child ("from the LORD"). She believed God would fulfill His promise to provide a deliverer from the power and penalty of sin. Eve then bore another son, whom they named Abel. His name may mean "breath" or "vanity." Some commentators think Abel may have been Cain's twin because of the statement "then she bore again" without the mention of conception, as in the case of Cain.

The Occupations of Cain and Abel

As they grew to manhood, Cain and Abel took up different occupations. Abel's occupation is mentioned first as a "keeper of sheep." He was exercising dominion over animals, a task that God had given man (1:28). God did not authorize eating meat until after the Flood, so we assume that people used these animals for sacrifices in their worship of God and the hides and wool for clothing (1:29; 9:3).

Cain was a "tiller of the ground," another honorable occupation. His father Adam had been sent out of the Garden of Eden to "till the ground" (3:23). Cain simply followed in his father's footsteps as a farmer. Cain's harvests would have provided food for the family. There is no reason to doubt that Adam and Eve had many other children as time progressed. As the first generation, they possessed near perfect human bodies and even after the curse lived ten times longer than people do today. Adam himself lived 930 years. It is not unreasonable to think that they might have had at least two hundred childbearing years during which a great number of children would have been born.

We ought to mention the age-old question of skeptics as to who Adam and Eve's children married. The obvious answer is that they married their own siblings, who were genetically only one generation from Adam. Later, as the effects of sin and the curse further corrupted the genetic structure, it obviously became necessary to establish rules prohibiting sibling marriages. The Bible is very clear on the fact that Adam and Eve were the parents of all human beings. There was no other genetic source of people on earth.

The Offerings of Cain and Abel, and God's Response (vv. 3-5)

The narrative in Genesis 4 focuses on the offerings that the two brothers brought to God. Their offerings are associated with their occupations in life and may not have been the first offerings they made. As a farmer, Cain brought an "offering of the fruit of the ground to the LORD" (v. 3). It is quite possible that Cain had previously obtained lambs from Abel for his offerings. However, it seems that he began to think that the fruit of his own labor would be better than the clearly revealed plan of God. Abel the shepherd brought "of the firstlings of his flock and of their fat" (v. 4). One commentator has suggested that he brought "the fattest of the firstlings of the flock." The idea is that Abel brought the best that he had in order to please God, while Cain merely brought an offering to discharge a duty or, perhaps worse, to express his own rebellious heart.

The response of God to the offerings draws a clear line between them. "The LORD respected Abel and his offering, but He did not respect Cain and his offering." Some have asked how God demonstrated His acceptance of one and not the other. One suggestion is that the smoke may have ascended straight up when Abel offered his sacrifice, whereas it did not in the case of Cain's. Or perhaps God spoke audibly. We do not know.

The method by which God showed His pleasure or displeasure is not important to the theme. What is important is that one was acceptable to God, and the other was unacceptable. Why? The answer, while not directly stated in the text, is that Abel had obeyed the instructions God had given about bringing sacrifices, whereas Cain had not. It is significant that, in the record of God's response, the emphasis is on the *person* who brought the offering. It speaks of "Abel and his offering" and "Cain and his offering" (vv. 4-5). The heart attitude of the worshipper was more important than the nature of the offering he brought. It therefore seems evident that both Cain and Abel knew what God wanted, but when it came time for the offering, Abel obeyed, and Cain did not.

The explanation for God's rejection of Cain and his offering can best be seen in the light of the incident which immediately precedes it in the text (3:20-24). God made garments of skin as coverings for Adam and Eve after they sinned. Then He evicted them from the garden. Now He graciously made it possible for them to approach Him by the same way He had demonstrated when He made clothing for them, which was by the blood sacrifice of animals. Adam and Eve surely taught the necessity of blood sacrifice to their children and had, no doubt, offered them in their children's presence.

Cain chose to approach God on his own terms. The problem was his heart attitude before God; he brought the fruit of his labor, and thus did not express faith in God's appointed way. Light on this may come from the New Testament, where we read of the "way of Cain" in Jude 11. He came with the wrong offering in the wrong spirit. The "evil" of his offering was in his disobedience to God; he brought the products of the cursed ground in rebellion against God's instructions.

Abel's Faith and His Gifts

The reason for the acceptance of Abel's sacrifice is clearly stated in the New Testament. "By faith Abel offered a more excellent sacrifice than Cain" (Heb. 11:4). Abel knew that "without faith it is impossible to please [God]" (Heb. 11:6). Faith is not just an abstract idea; faith is "the substance of things hoped for, the evidence of things not seen" (Heb. 11:1). Faith comes by, or through, hearing (Rom. 10:17). And what had Abel heard? He had heard that people could only approach God through animal sacrifices that pointed forward to the Savior (who we know to be the Lord Jesus Christ) as the one true sacrifice for sin. Abel simply placed his faith in God's revealed word and acted on it. He believed what God said about the need for blood sacrifice to cover his sin. Hebrews 9:22 confirms this truth in a succinct way: "Without shedding of blood there is no remission [forgiveness]."

"By Faith . . . Abel Obtained Witness"

The Hebrews passage mentioned above goes on to say that, through his faith, Abel "obtained witness that he was righteous" (Heb. 11:4; cf. Matt. 23:35). This means that he was justified (declared righteous) by his faith (Rom. 5:1). Then, it says that God testified of "his gifts," that is, the firstlings of the flock. God called his gifts "better" or "more excellent" than Cain's. Abel's lambs were better than Cain's produce because God had appointed blood sacrifice as the only means of atonement for sin. The blood of Abel's lambs could not actually take away sin, but they did point to the true Lamb who died on Calvary (cf. 1 Pet. 1:18-19). In summary, Abel's offering was accepted because of *his faith in the word of God* and because he presented *his gifts* (sacrifices) *according to the word of God.* He was saved by his faith in a coming Savior, and he demonstrated his faith by his offering. He was a believer.

The writer of Hebrews says that Abel "still speaks" (Heb. 11:4). What is he saying?

- His *faith* speaks to all who need to put their trust in what God says.
- His *offering* testifies to those who understand the need of the sinner for the sacrificial death of Christ.
- His *death* speaks of the rejection that prophets usually faced in the fulfilling of their prophetic ministry (Luke 11:49-51).

Cain's Angry Response

When God did not respect Cain's offering, Cain became "very angry, and his countenance fell." These words paint a picture of a man so angry that his face became distorted. Cain was enraged because he was jealous that God accepted his brother's sacrifice and not his. Cain's attitude was not that of a humble believer trying to please God but of a rebel whose self-righteous ideas had been rejected. The outward show of godliness in his offering now revealed his inner rebellion and hatred. The Bible testifies of Cain that "his works were evil, and his brother's righteous" (1 John 3:12).

God Warns Cain (vv. 6-7)

God had shown concern for Adam and Eve when they sinned; He now did the same for Cain. God took the initiative to come to the sinner; the sinner did not approach Him. God appealed to Cain's reason and asked him to explain why he was angry and why his countenance had fallen. In this, God was gracious to him. He asked Cain to examine his anger in the light of the situation. Perhaps he would repent and believe. God went on to say that, if he did "well," he would be accepted. He undoubtedly meant that Cain would do well by simply obeying God and bringing the right sacrifice with the right attitude. God would graciously accept a blood offering if he brought it.

The alternative was that, if he did not do well, sin would control him and ultimately destroy him. Sin is pictured here as a wild beast, crouching, ready to pounce at the right opportunity. God said, "Sin lies at the door." It is worth noting that this is the first specific use of the word "sin" in the Bible, and it gives a striking picture of its character as a wild animal ready to spring on its prey.

The word picture of sin is followed by an interesting phrase: "And its desire is for you, but you should rule over it." This passage should be compared with Genesis 3:16 where we noted that the word *desire* meant "to prompt to evil." As Eve prompted Adam to partake of the fruit, so, in this passage, sin was prompting Cain to do evil. Because the events that led up to the Fall must have been known to Cain, he should have realized that God was warning him of the consequences if he gave in to temptation. God went on to tell Cain that there was a way out of the dilemma. He should respond to the attack of sin by resisting it: "You should rule over it." God wanted Cain to gain mastery over sin, not yield to its attacks. It was a matter of the will. In New Testament language, he was to "resist the devil" (James 4:7).

Cain Murders Abel (v. 8)

Cain did not want to master his inclination to sin. He rejected God's warning. Verse 8 records that Cain went out in the field to meet Abel. Prior to this, all Bible versions say that Cain spoke to his brother. Some versions of the biblical text state that Cain initiated the meeting with the words "Let us go out to the field." It appears that Cain was carrying out a previously-prepared plan. It then says, "Cain rose up against his brother Abel and killed him." This was the world's first premeditated murder, and it illustrates the terrible outcome of sin's entrance into the world.

The apostle John's comment gives us the reason: "Cain … was of that wicked one and murdered his brother. And why did he murder him? Because his works were evil and his brother's righteous" (1 John 3:12). From this verse we learn two things. First, Cain was "of the wicked one" and, therefore, one of the serpent's "seed" (3:15). Satan himself was probably orchestrating the temptation behind the scenes. He would know by Cain's character that he could not be the promised Seed of the woman, but he could also see that Abel might be or was, at least, the line from which the Seed might come.

Thus, Satan prompted Cain to prevent the coming of the Seed. Satan had continued these attempts throughout history, from man's fall in the Garden of Eden until the sealing of the borrowed tomb in which Christ was laid. However, God's plan prevailed, and Christ arose from the dead "in a mighty triumph o'er his foes."

Second, we learn from the apostle John is that "[Cain's] works were evil." They were so evil that, instead of heeding God's warning, he immediately rebelled against it and deliberately carried out his intentions to commit murder. Jude spoke of those who have gone in the "way of Cain" (Jude 11). It means that, like Cain,

- they practice a self-styled form of worship in opposition to God's revealed will. Cain brought fruit rather than a lamb.
- they place their faith in human works rather than in God's grace. They trust in their own self-effort.
- they deliberately disobey and rebel against God's clearly revealed instructions. Cain knew what God wanted and rejected it.

The "way of Cain" is a road that begins in unbelief and leads to rebellion against God. It results in all kinds of personal and social sins, the beginnings of which are given to us in this important chapter. These include murder, war, rebellion, sexual sin, false religion, persecution of the righteous, and any expression of human pride and arrogance.

Cain is Called to Account (vv. 9-10)

After the murder, God called Cain to account with the question, "Where is Abel your brother?" He immediately sought out Cain and confronted him with his sin. It was a rhetorical question designed to give Cain an opportunity to humble himself before God and confess what he had done. This is a lesson for us. God's question also suggests that He was concerned, not only with Cain's attitude and actions toward Him, but also with the care he gave to his brother Abel. God's question should cause us to consider how we are caring for our "brother."

The question is similar to the one God asked of Adam when he was hiding in the Garden of Eden (3:9). Just as with Adam, God wanted Cain to humbly admit his sin. However, Cain's response was even worse than Adam's. Adam made excuses (3:10-12), but he did confess his sin. Cain, on the other hand, was defiant in his answer: "I do not know. Am I my brother's keeper?" Consider Cain's response:

- It was a lie. He knew very well where the body of Abel was.
- It challenged God's right to question him or hold him accountable.
- It was a "put down" to Abel's calling to be a shepherd. Literally, he said, "Am I a keeper [shepherd] of shepherds?"

Cain had the audacity to calmly face it out with God. He denied any responsibility for his sin. Cain's answer shows him to be an example of the power that sin has to harden a man's heart and pervert his reasoning. We can all learn from this story that God is everywhere and knows all about our sin, that sin cannot be covered up by an impudent response, and that we are accountable to Him for our sins. We should also be sobered by the knowledge that sin tends to harden our hearts toward God, as it hardened Cain's.

The Witness of Abel's Blood

God spoke again to Cain—this time in judgment: "What have you done?" Without waiting for him to answer, God assumed his guilt by presenting the damning evidence. "The voice of your brother's blood cries out to Me from the ground." There may not have been any human witnesses to the murder, and Cain may have been able to silence his brother's prophetic ministry and to stop his acts of worship, but he could not still the voice of his blood. Cain is found guilty.

The voice of Abel's blood that cried out to God for vengeance can be widely applied in our day. Today's "Cains" are the providers of pornography and prostitution. They are the godless professors in colleges and universities. They are the false teachers and preachers in many liberal churches. They are the leaders of false cults where the truth of God is denied. They are the abusers of women and children. The "blood" of their "victims" cries out to God for vengeance. In one sense, Abel's blood crying from the ground foreshadowed all the suffering for righteousness of God's people down through history. The climax of unmerited suffering came when the enemies of the Lord Jesus Christ cried out for His crucifixion saying, "His blood be on us" (Matt. 27:25).

The author of Hebrews speaks of Abel's blood in contrast to the blood of Jesus (Heb. 12:24). Jesus' blood is called "the blood of sprinkling," because it atoned for sin once for all, having been foreshadowed by the blood of animals that was shed time and again. It is *better* than the blood of Abel because Abel's blood only condemned his killer, while Jesus' blood paid for the sins of those for whom He died. Every redeemed person can testify that the blood of Jesus "speaks better things" than the blood of Abel.

The Curse on Cain (vv. 11-15)

God spoke quickly and forcefully to pronounce judgment on Cain. It was clear that no repentance or confession would come from him. He spoke more sharply to Cain than He had to Adam. To Adam, the ground was cursed, so that hard labor was required to extract a living. But to Cain God said, "So now you are cursed from the earth, which has opened its mouth to receive your brother's blood from your hand." Unlike Adam, Cain would not be able to till the ground and reap its fruit. God banished him from the fertile land and condemned him to become a wandering fugitive. The curse on Cain was not to prevent him from repenting or from exercising saving faith, but there is no evidence that he ever did.

Cain immediately protested God's judgment, complaining that it was greater than he could bear. He spoke to God like an injured person, as if he were the victim. He seemed to think that God was being overly harsh. He objected about three things:

- That God was driving him out from the face of the ground
- That he would have to hide like a fugitive
- That other people would seek to kill him

Cain complained that the sentence would cut him off from relationships with home and family, and even from God Himself. His words to God, "I shall be hidden from Your face," seem to indicate that Cain saw God as his only protector and would, therefore, like to have Him nearby. It is interesting that though he was angry with God, he feared the possibility that God might be too distant from him.

God did spare Cain's life and provided protection for him to deter anyone from killing him. If they did, there would be a penalty of sevenfold vengeance on them (v. 15). Then the Lord appointed a sign or "mark" by which people would understand the protective decree of God. That mark would also remind them of God's view of the sanctity of human life. We do not know what that sign might have been, but it did demonstrate God's care for the sinner as well as the saint. God did not bring in the death penalty for murder at this time; that came later (9:6). As to the reason why God permitted the first murderer to live rather than be executed, we can only point to His sovereign grace.

The Family of Cain and Early Civilization (vv. 16-24)

The remainder of Genesis 4 gives us the only glimpse we have of the world before the time of the Flood, usually called the *antediluvian world*. A remarkable civilization came into being in a relatively short time. Long before either Adam or Cain died, the earth's population on the earth would have amounted to tens of thousands, and by the time of the Flood there could have been hundreds of millions. However, when the Flood did come, virtually all traces of early civilization were destroyed. Apart from the Genesis record, there are only legendary recollections of the original "golden age" or a "lost" continent called Atlantis. Because these verses provide the bulk of all the evidence on the subject, they are most important. They tell us of man and his relationship to God in those ancient times. They give us a most intriguing picture of life as it then was. But they also leave us with as many questions as answers. Modern scholars have paid scant attention to the once great civilization on earth and, for the most part, have left the field open to fiction writers.

This passage traces the development of Cain's family tree for seven generations, covering a period of more than sixteen hundred years. If, as seems very probable, they are parallel to the generations of Adam's son Seth, then the people of the seventh generation were those who died in the Flood. There is more in this passage, however, than Cain's genealogy. It outlines the development of various aspects of culture as it formed among the growing human population. It also traces the results of God's judgment on Cain for the murder of his brother. It explains how man without God was seeking to carry out the cultural mandate to "subdue the earth" that God gave before the Fall (1:28). It ends in a strange mix of good and evil. It soon became evident that the effects of sin cannot be neutralized or redeemed by human culture devoid of God.

Cain in the Land of Nod

The passage begins with Cain's departure from the presence of the Lord. It pictures a man in unbelief and rebellion against God. When he wanted God's protection, he complained about the possibility of being hidden from His face (v. 14). Now, however, he clearly reveals his unbelief by deliberately removing himself from God's presence, as Judas Iscariot did when he "went out" from the presence of Jesus (cf. John 13:30). God had asked Cain to "do well" by offering the acceptable sacrifice. God would have accepted him if he had done so (4:7). Instead, he chose to go out from God's presence. How sad. As a symbol of spiritual separation from the Lord, Cain and his rebellious actions are a warning to all who may be tempted to depart from Him. Cain "dwelt in the land of Nod." The word "Nod" means wanderings, so we understand that it was an area of land probably so-named by Cain because God had condemned him to be a wanderer and a vagabond on the earth (cf. v. 12). Nod was east of Eden. It was on that side of the garden that the cherubim were stationed to guard the Tree of Life (3:24). Cain seems to have gone further east.

Enoch and the First City

The first thing mentioned about Cain after God cursed him is that "Cain knew his wife [presumably one of his sisters], and she conceived and bore Enoch." Cain built a city and named it after his son, no doubt to preserve his son's name. In Psalm 49, we read of the ungodly who give their name to their works and their lands (v. 11). It seems that Cain was doing this, promoting himself and his son above God. Although he had been cursed to be a wanderer, Cain was attempting to evade the effects of the curse by building a city in defiance of God's directive. In that city, the Cainite civilization was going to take shape. Cain did everything possible to improve his human condition without

God. The world is still trying to do this, despite the failure of every civilization thus far. The city of Enoch was to be a lasting monument to this first endeavor. It is the first city mentioned in the Bible. Note that the first generation of people in the world, far from living in caves as evolutionists suggest, began to build cities. And if they built cities, they must have had advanced technology.

Four more generations of Cain's descendants are given to us in verse 18, two of whom have the Hebrew word for God, *El,* in their names, which may indicate some belief in the existence of God by their parents. We cannot tell from the meanings of their names whether they had saving faith in Him. What the list of names does do is support the truth of the historical account of the line of Cain. The list can be compared in its structure to the line of Seth in chapter 5. Both lines conclude with a man who had three important sons. Lamech, in Cain's line, had three sons, as listed in the following chart. Noah, in Seth's line, had three sons: Shem, Ham, and Japheth.

Descendants of Cain and Seth

The Line of Cain	The Line of Seth
(Genesis 4)	(Genesis 5)
Adam	Adam
Cain	Seth
Enoch	Enosh
Irad	Kenan
Mehujael	Mahalalel
Methushael	Jared
Lamech	Enoch
Jabal, Jubal, Tubal-Cain	Methusaleh
	Lamech
	Noah
	Shem, Ham, Japheth

The Rebellion of Lamech

Lamech was the seventh from Adam in the line of Cain. He, alone, is singled out as the person in Cain's line who led the way in open rebellion against God. He and his sons were also innovators of technology. The first thing mentioned about him is that he married two wives, Adah and Zillah. This was in direct violation of the principle of monogamy (one woman for one man) that God had clearly ordained for marriage and procreation (2:23-24). Jesus reiterated the same principle in the New Testament (Matt. 19:5). Lamech's action led the way for the practice of bigamy and polygamy, which have been a blight on the human family ever since.

Two reasons may have motivated Lamech to take a second wife. Physical lust is the obvious one. The other reason may have been to have more children in order to gain prestige and power in a world of family clans. Three of Lamech's sons come in for special mention in relation to the development of technology and culture. Jabal, whose name means "wanderer," invented the tent as a portable house, allowing him to travel as a nomadic trader more widely and for longer periods.

Jabal's brother Jubal was an inventive genius and originated stringed instruments like the harp, and wind instruments, like the flute (v. 21). The lyre, or harp, is often pictured on the oldest of existing records. Arts and crafts began to flourish and probably appealed to the sensual side of Cain's descendants. The longevity of life in those days no doubt contributed to rapid technological development.

Tubal-Cain was born to Zillah, Lamech's second wife. He became the founder of the science of metallurgy in both bronze and iron (v. 21). From the theme of Lamech's song that follows, it seems that he crafted the metals into weapons of aggression. Their civilization may have been much more advanced than historians have thought possible. Their technology was used for evil purposes even before it was used for good, just as in our own times.

Lamech's Song

This is the first poetry in Genesis and is sometimes called a taunt or a sword song because of its content. The reason for the mention of Lamech's two wives in the previous verses becomes clear as he sings this song to them. The song's lyrics indicate the progress of sin in the lives of people before the Flood. Adam repented of his sin and taught his sons to offer sacrifices to the Lord (3:20-24; 4:3-4). Later, in Cain's case, he understood what he had done, but he did not repent. Rather, he "went out from the presence of the LORD" (vv. 8-11; 16). Now, when Lamech, Cain's descendant, sins, he goes a step further— he exults in his sin. He is an example of arrogance and rebellion.

In his song, Lamech told his two wives that he had killed a man who had apparently attempted to wound him. When Cain sinned, he sought protection against the world. God assured him that if anyone killed him, vengeance would be taken sevenfold (v. 15). Lamech went much further than that. First, when he was wounded, he overreacted by killing his assailant. Second, he took the place of God when he challenged the world that "if Cain shall be avenged sevenfold, then Lamech seventy-sevenfold." Jesus may well have had this in mind when he spoke of *forgiving* a brother who sins against you "unto seventy times seven" (Matt. 18:21-22). In his song, Lamech was threatening to take vengeance into his own hands.

This is self-centered arrogance that knows no bounds. Even Cain was willing to wait for God to do the avenging. But here, Lamech was himself taking responsibility for all retribution. It shows how much the ancient civilization was engrossed in evil. Lamech, as the seventh generation from Adam and representative of the descendants of Cain, illustrates the spirit of his age in rebellion against God and going in the "way of Cain." One commentator suggests that the purpose of the poem was to warn his wives, Adah and Zillah, against encouraging any men who may have been trying to seduce them. The world was probably becoming more and more sexually liberal, and he was warning them about the consequences if they complied.

The Birth of Seth (vv. 25-26)

Although Genesis chapter 4 commences with rebellion and murder, it concludes on a happier note with the good news of another son born to Adam named Seth. His line will present us with a new and different focus. Instead of rebelling against God, "men began to call on the name of the LORD" (4:26). If the Cainites manifested the seed of the serpent, then the Sethites evidenced the hope of the coming Seed of the woman (3:15). In naming their son Seth (which means "appointed" or "substituted"), Adam and Eve were expressing faith that this son would be the means through whom God's promise would be fulfilled. He would be the appointed "substitute" for Abel.

In the course of time, Seth's son Enosh was born. His name means "frailty," and he was probably so named because Seth realized the spiritual need of man compared with the gracious provision of God. It was then that men began to call on the name of the Lord. This phrase means that instead of individually bringing sacrifices to God in order to express faith, people gathered together to worship God. This is the earliest reference to the public worship of Yahweh. The word "call" frequently means public worship in the Scriptures, as in nations or families that "call" on His name (Ps. 79:6; Jer. 10:25). We can safely assume that Adam and Eve attended the gatherings of believers.

The name of "Yahweh" or "Jehovah," usually indicated in English Bibles as "LORD," is the name known and used by the people with whom He was in a covenant relationship. Over the period of time covered by Genesis, God's people knew Him by this name in a limited sense, that is, as the One who *made* the covenant promises. When God delivered the Israelites from Egypt and brought them into the Promised Land, they experienced the full significance of the name "LORD"—the One who *fulfilled* those promises (cf. Ex. 6:3).

In Conclusion

This chapter has been overshadowed by the influence of Cain in the affairs of man. He brought an offering to God in unbelief and defiance of God's instructions. When God rejected his offering, he became angry and rejected God's offer of pardon. He turned around and deliberately killed his brother. When confronted by God, he challenged His right to hold him accountable. Cain was cursed by God, prevented from tilling the ground, and condemned to be a vagabond on the earth. Cain protested, and God showed him mercy. Then

Cain's descendants are listed, but they, too, went "in the way of Cain" and their civilization and culture became corrupt and evil. We should remember that the culture of Cain is also our culture. In politics, in the military, in religion, and in family life, the spirit of Cain is everywhere. But then there are those who call on the name of the Lord—the community of worshippers of the true God within a corrupt society.

We have seen the blood of Abel, the victim of sin, crying out to God for vengeance. One day. that cry and the cries of the blood of millions of such victims will be answered. Now, however, we can find refuge in the blood of Christ that is pictured so clearly by the lamb that Abel offered as a sacrifice. John the Baptist introduced Christ as "the Lamb of God who takes away the sin of the world!" (John 1:29).

The Patriarchs, from Adam to Noah

As the world's population grew rapidly, the first civilization developed. Genesis 4 speaks of established cities, of advanced technology in agriculture, manufacturing, and metallurgy, of trade, and of musical entertainment, all of which evolved during this period. These advances are traced through the descendants of Cain. It was Cain who rebelled against God, who murdered his brother, and who challenged God's authority. Moses records that "Cain went out from the presence of the LORD" (4:16), a literal and deliberate act that was the basis of the downward path followed by his descendants.

The Lineage of Seth

Chapter 5 contains genealogical details about the ten generations from Adam to Noah, and then switches the focus to Seth, another son born to Adam and Eve. Seth is particularly important because it was through his lineage that the future Messiah would come to crush the head of the serpent (3:15). The names of the ten men chosen from the line of Seth for inclusion in this chapter were men who were faithful to God in an increasingly godless age.
Martin Luther noted that their long lives overlapped for hundreds of years. Most of them were alive together at any one time in their history. He said:

> This is the greatest glory of the primitive world, that it had so many good, wise, and holy men at the same time. We must not think that these are ordinary names of plain people; but next to Christ and John the Baptist, they were the most outstanding heroes this world has ever produced. And on the Last Day we shall behold and admire their grandeur.... what they endured from the old serpent, how they comforted and maintained themselves by means of the hope of the Seed against the outrages of the world... how much envy, hatred, and contempt they endured on account of the glory of the blessed Seed (Luther's Works, vol. 1, Concordia Publishing House, St. Louis, 1958).

We can be encouraged from their example because, like them, we live in a morally corrupt world. Certainly, every generation needs outstanding people such as these. In ancient times, decadence invaded both the line of Cain and the line of Seth. Neither line, as a whole, was necessarily righteous or godly.

Cain's line particularly, though, gives evidence of the malignant growth of sin as it infected humanity and civilization, while Seth's line included great heroes of faith. By the time of the Flood, wickedness had increased to such a degree that God judged it fit for destruction.

The Generations of Adam

The purpose of chapter 5 is to verify the direct historical human link between Adam and Noah. This portion reinforces the truth that the history of the human race between creation and the Flood is not some vague mythological tale but the true story of actual people in ancient times. These are successive generations of people who lived a specific number of years. They fathered sons. These sons were names that were known and remembered. The people described here were not, as some would say, evolving humanoids that were slowly changing into fully-developed humans. Rather, because they were genetically nearer to the first created man and woman, they were physically and mentally the most perfect human beings that ever lived. These men named are not, by any means, *all* the ancients who lived before the Flood; the world population no doubt grew very rapidly during this time. These men are remembered, in particular, because they are the key figures in the lineage leading from Adam to Noah.

The first verse begins with the usual formula for each new section in Genesis: "The genealogy of" (Hebrew, *toledoth,* translated "generations," "genealogy," "history," or "account." See the Introduction and comments on Genesis 2:4). This second *toledoth* section is called "the genealogy of Adam" (5:1 - 6:8). It traces the descendants of Adam through the line of Seth and ends with the declaration from God that He would destroy everything living on the face of the earth because, by the time of Noah, human civilization had become so wicked.

In the beginning, Satan lied to Eve, saying that if she ate the fruit of the Tree of the Knowledge of Good and Evil she would not die (3:4). Genesis 5 is God's answer to Satan's lie, for it records the death of every person listed with one exception—Enoch (whom we shall study in detail later in this chapter). The phrase "and he died" becomes a dark refrain, occurring eight times. The lives of all men end in death because of sin. In the New Testament, the apostle Paul reiterated the truth of this when he said, "through one man sin entered the world, and death through sin, and thus death spread to all men, because all sinned" (Rom. 5:12). The reality of death due to sin is a central point of this chapter.

God Names Them Mankind (vv. 1-2)

A sometimes-overlooked fact at the beginning of this section is the statement that it is a "book." This means it was a written document, not merely oral tradition. Perhaps Adam himself wrote some of it, for it is likely that writing was invented long before Adam died. It is possible that Moses possessed the clay tablets he had written.

The genealogy is introduced by repeating some information from the earlier creation account. "In the day that God created man, He made him in the likeness of God" (5:1; cf. 1:26-28). This brief review reminds us of Adam's original wonderful state with the prospect of a wonderful future. God made Adam in His image; that is, Adam was made to reflect God's spiritual nature, possessing some of His attributes such as truth, wisdom, love, holiness, etc. With these attributes, he was to represent God on the earth and exercise dominion over the animal creation, while enjoying constant fellowship with God Himself.

Verse 2 says that God "called them Mankind in the day they were created." The reader should know that the Hebrew word for "Adam" and "man" or "mankind" is the same. It is the context that guides the translator to decide which one to use. In this verse, where the subject includes both man and woman, the New King James Version (NKJV) text is probably correct, calling them "Mankind" rather than "Adam," as in many older versions.

Seth in the Image and Likeness of Adam (v. 3)

There is one thing mentioned about the birth of Seth that is unique in all these generations. "Adam ... begot a son in his own likeness, after his image." No other son in Scripture is said to be in the likeness of his father. Why, we may ask. It is significant that it occurs at the beginning of the chapter that introduces the godly line of Seth in contrast to the ungodly line of Cain in chapter 4. While Seth is described as being in the likeness and image of Adam, Cain is not. This is an obvious reference to verse 1, where we are told that Adam was created in the image and likeness of God. Even after the Fall, Adam still possessed some elements of the image of God. Seth, unlike Cain, seems to have had a likeness to Adam insofar as Adam retained part of the image and likeness of God. He inherited that same quality from his father and sought to model it in his life. Unlike Cain, Seth demonstrated this likeness when he followed Adam in worshipping the true God.

The image of God is mentioned again in Genesis 9:6 in connection with Noah. After the Flood, God reasserted the value of human life on the basis of man being made in His image. God said to Noah, "Whoever sheds man's blood, by man his blood shall be shed; *for in the image of God He made man*" (emphasis added). Thus, after the Flood, man still bore a continuing element of the image and likeness of God.

In the New Testament, we are told that the believer has "put on the new man who is renewed in knowledge according to the image of Him who created him" (Col. 3:10; see also James 3:9). In 2 Corinthians 3:18 Paul says that believers "are being transformed into the same image from glory to glory, just as by the Spirit of the Lord." Thus, we learn that it is the ministry of the Holy Spirit to change us into the image of the Lord Jesus Christ from one degree of glory to another so that we become increasingly like Him. As we allow the Spirit to control our lives, we become more and more like Jesus. As we are changed into His image, we will influence other believers to follow us in the same way we follow Him (1 Cor. 11:1). In so doing, they will be blessed, as we have been.

The Genealogical Pattern (vv. 3-32)

The actual genealogy begins in verse 3 and follows a pattern that is consistent throughout the chapter, with the exception of Enoch. The record of each generation includes:

- The name of the patriarch
- How long he lived before a particular son—not necessarily his first child—was born
- The name of that son
- How long he lived after the birth of that son
- His age when he died

For example, when Adam was 130 years old, he produced a son whom he named Seth (v. 3). Adam then lived eight hundred more years and had other sons and daughters (v. 4). Finally, the total number of years Adam lived was 930 years (v. 5). We are told one final thing: "and he died."

The unfolding of the story of man contains the message that every life ends in death. The funeral bell tolls its doleful note: "and he died." Reflect on this repeated refrain. It signifies the consequences of sin. If there was ever any doubt that God's warning to Adam and Eve—"You shall surely die"—would actually be fulfilled, Adam's death dispelled it, and every subsequent death confirmed it. Assuming Adam was the first human being to die of natural causes, his death signaled to everyone living at that time that life would end in physical death. Paul rightly states, "Sin entered the world, and death through sin" (Rom. 5:12). If man's rebellion against God is the theme in chapter 4, then man's death is the theme of this chapter.

Ages and Death of the Ancients

Adam lived 930 years ... and he died
Seth lived 912 years ... and he died
Enosh lived 905 years ... and he died
Cainan lived 910 years ... and he died
Mahaleleel lived 895 years ... and he died
Jared lived 962 years ... and he died
Methuselah lived 969 years ... and he died
Lamech lived 777 years ... and he died

No doubt, Adam and Eve had many sons and daughters, but only Cain, Abel, and Seth are mentioned by name in the biblical record. This chapter follows the line of the coming Messiah, hardly mentioning others who were born, while the line of Cain in chapter 4 was recorded separately as it was not connected to the history of salvation through the coming Seed.

The Longevity of the Ancients

Compared to today's life expectancy, the lengthy life spans of these people were remarkable. The average life span of the men listed above was 907 years. How can we explain their longevity as compared to that of, say, Moses, who lived for 120 years? There are no conclusive answers, but we can consider several theories. One is that the environmental conditions were different. There was no rain as we know it; the ground was watered by "a mist [that] went up from the earth" (2:6). It has been suggested that there was a canopy of vapor above the earth that created something like a tropical greenhouse. The canopy would have filtered out more of the ultraviolet rays of the sun. When the Flood came, so the theory goes, the canopy collapsed, and the present cycle of direct sunshine, evaporation, and rain began. Did this affect man's longevity? That is open to question. The author remembers hearing this theory as a college student and relating it to his well-versed grandfather. The old man, then in his nineties, retorted, "Then how is it that Noah lived 350 years after the Flood?"!

Another suggestion is that longevity is connected to sin and the Fall. The physical condition of man deteriorated due to the increasing effects of sin, so life spans became shorter. However, this theory fails in light of the fact that Noah lived for 950 years, longer than any other recorded life (including Adam), except for Jared and Methuselah. Others have said that the word "years" should read "months." If that were so, it would mean that Seth became a father at nine years of age, and Enoch at five and a half! What we can be sure of is that what is written in the Word of God about the life spans of these men is true. The names listed in our chapter are repeated in 1 Chronicles 1:1-4 and Luke 3:36-38. They were believed to be literal, historical men by writers of both the Old and the New Testaments. We can be confident that they were.

What Genealogies Teach Us

What do genealogies like this one teach us?

- They teach that life has a terminal point toward which we are all moving.
- They teach that time is valuable and precious, and the believer, particularly, will use it wisely and well. Every one of us ought to live "the rest of his time … for the will of God" (1 Pet. 4:2).
- They teach that the time given to us may easily be lost or squandered. We ought to work while it is day, for the night is coming when no man can work (John 9:4). We are to redeem the time, because the days are evil (Eph. 5:16).

Thus, every one of us is reminded of the brevity of time, the value of time, and the ease with which time may be lost.

This genealogy teaches us that God, especially, remembers those who are faithful to Him. Calvin comments on this in his volume on Genesis. He said that the designer of this catalog of names wanted to inform us that, among the great number of people in the ancient world, there were always some who worshipped God and who were wonderfully preserved by "celestial guardianship." Believers have always been in the minority, but that should not discourage us. God is on the throne, and if history teaches us anything, it is that God keeps His people in mind. The entire history of God's people is the story of a remnant—a minority—that has been preserved by God's grace.

Enoch (vv. 18-27)

One man in this genealogy stands out from the others. That man is Enoch, the seventh from Adam, the son of Jared, about whom we know almost nothing except the information given in this passage. Enoch was the one man for whom the funeral bell did not toll. His spiritual character was such that he walked with God straight into eternity, without passing through death. In the case of Enoch, instead of the usual death announcement, we read the mysterious phrase "and he was not."

Enoch may be contrasted with his contemporary in the line of Cain, that is, Lamech (4:18-24). Both were the seventh generation from Adam. The author of Genesis selects both of them for some expanded comment. Lamech rebelled against God and boasted about his own godless accomplishments (4:19-24). In sharp contrast, we read the comment about Enoch who "walked with God" and bore the testimony that he "pleased God" (5:22, 24; Heb. 11:5). Every generation has its "Lamechs" and its "Enochs" living side by side. The "Lamechs" are known for their disobedience to God and rebellion against Him. The "Enochs" are known for their obedience and faithfulness to the Lord.

There were two ways in which Enoch is considered a prophet. The first had to do with the birth of his son. At the age of sixty-five, Enoch became the father of Methuselah. The time of Methuselah's birth marked a milestone in Enoch's life. It was "then" that he began to walk with God (v. 22). The name Enoch gave his son is most significant. Though it is not absolutely certain, many commentators believe that Methuselah means "when he is dead, it shall come." If this is correct, it is a veiled prophecy of the coming of the great Flood. In other words, Enoch's son Methuselah was a living reminder about the coming judgment on the wicked world of which Enoch himself was a prophet (Jude 14-15). It is possible that when Methuselah was born, Enoch received a special revelation from God concerning the Flood. At the same time, God promised him that the Flood would not come as long as Methuselah was alive, so Enoch gave him a name to reflect the prophetic warning: "when he is dead, it [the Flood] shall come."

Note how this prophecy was remarkably fulfilled: Methuselah lived for 969 years, the oldest human being on record. When his son Lamech was born, he was 187 (v. 25). Lamech was 182 when Noah was born (v. 28). Adding these together (187+182), Methuselah was 369 years old when Noah, his grandson, was born. Noah was six hundred years old when the Flood came (6:7). That very year, his 969th (600+369), was the year of Methuselah's death. Thus, the prophecy at his birth was fulfilled, just as God had said.

The fact that Methuselah lived longer than any other person reminds us of the patience of God and His reluctance to pour out His judgment. Peter, too, speaks of God's patience during those days. He says that God "waited in the days of Noah while the ark was being prepared" (1 Pet. 3:20). We read that God is "not willing that any should perish, but that all come to repentance" (2 Pet. 3:9). Even now, God is "slow" to bring about the judgment on this world of which the Bible speaks so much.

It is in the New Testament that we are told the second way in which Enoch was a prophet. Jude was writing to 1st century believers about living in times of apostasy (Jude 5-13). He used the illustration of Enoch living in similar times among apostates:

> Now Enoch, the seventh from Adam, prophesied … saying, "Behold, the Lord comes with ten thousands of His saints, to execute judgment on all, to convict all who are ungodly among them of all their ungodly deeds which they have committed in an ungodly way, and of all the harsh things which ungodly sinners have spoken against Him" (Jude 14-15).

Enoch, therefore, was the first human prophet to prophesy directly about the coming of the Lord in judgment. He was born in the creation year 622. Adam lived to be 930 years old. We conclude, therefore, that Adam and Enoch's lives overlapped by 308 years and that they may well have known each other. God revealed to Adam the victory of the Seed of the woman. If they did know each other, they may have talked together regarding the further revelation to Enoch of the Lord's coming in judgment with ten thousands of His saints.

"Enoch walked with God"

The phrase "Enoch walked with God" describes his life for the next three hundred years. He began to walk with God when his son was born. We should notice that the phrase occurs twice in this chapter, in verses 22 and 24 respectively. Both times, "walked with God" replaces the usual information cited in the genealogy. It is a deliberate change in the pattern referred to earlier in this chapter.

Notice the changes in the second and the fourth parts of the pattern regarding Enoch. Regarding Jared, it says, "After he begot Enoch *Jared lived* 800 years" (v. 19, emphasis added). Now notice the parallel phrase in regard to Enoch:

"After he begot Methuselah, *Enoch walked with God*" (v. 22, emphasis added). Instead of "Enoch lived," it says, "Enoch walked with God." Thus, it makes the point that Enoch did not just live an ordinary life; he "walked with God."

At the end of Enoch's life on earth, there is another break in the pattern in the genealogy. Concerning Jared, it says, "So all the days of Jared were 962 years; *and he died*" (v. 20, emphasis added). But of Enoch it says, "So all the days of Enoch were 365 years. *And Enoch walked with God*" (vv. 23-24, emphasis added).

Here the point is that Enoch did not just die; he "walked with God." And, while he was walking with God, "he was not, for God took him" (v. 24). Thus, both Enoch's life and his departure from life were marked by the fact that he walked with God. This was what made the difference. Enoch, therefore, provides a clear model for those who seek to walk with the Lord.

Another interesting fact about Enoch is the two features that he shared in common with two other notable saints later in the biblical record. First, the only other person of whom it is said that he "walked with God" was Noah (6:9). Second, the only other person that went to heaven without dying was Elijah, who lived nearly twenty-five hundred years later (2 Kings 2:11).

Enoch's "Translation" to Heaven

As Enoch walked with God, suddenly "he was not, for God took him." From the human perspective, he simply disappeared (v.24). People could only see that "he was not." There were no remains, no evidence, and no grave. From God's perspective, Enoch simply went to heaven from earth without dying. In Psalm 73:24, which says, "You will guide me with Your counsel, and afterward receive me to glory," the word "receive" is the same as the word "took" in our passage. The blessed hope for believers living today is that, at any moment, the Lord Jesus Christ could come and take us to be with Him in heaven. We will have the same experience that Enoch had (John 14:3; 1 Thess. 4:17-18). Then we shall "all be changed ... in the twinkling of an eye, at the last trumpet" (1 Cor. 15:51-52).

Walking With God

For Enoch, walking with God probably did not mean that he literally walked side by side with Him as Adam and Eve had evidently done in the Garden of Eden before the Fall (3:8). Enoch shared the fallen nature of man and, like other men, could not look upon God and live. The metaphor of walking with another person describes the *relationship* between them. The idea includes fellowship, nearness, a sense of oneness, personal conversation, and intimacy. It assumes that both are going in the same direction and that they are constantly moving forward. For three hundred years, Enoch's life moved in step with God. When we walk with God, it does not mean that we spend all day studying theology or reading the Bible. Consider different facets of walking with God:

- Walking with God involves, first, *believing Him*. We learn from Hebrews 11:5 that faith was an outstanding feature in Enoch's life. Enoch trusted God, and God trusted Enoch. When God spoke, Enoch believed Him and sought to respond.

- Walking with God is *agreeing with Him*. There was no disharmony between Enoch and God. Enoch's will was subject to God's will. The two walked together, and they agreed (Amos 3:3).

- Walking with God involves *progressing in the faith*. It is growing in the ways of God and increasing in the knowledge of God. It is constantly reaching forward to those things that are before (Phil. 3:14).

- Walking with God is *fellowship*. It means keeping in step with Him, not allowing oneself to get either ahead of Him or lag behind Him. God becomes part of every decision and action in life because He is constantly near.

- Walking with God is *enjoyment*. For three hundred years Enoch learned that in God's presence there is "fullness of joy" (Ps. 16:11). Those years were like heaven-on-earth to him.

- Walking with God requires *separation from the world*. The contemporary of Enoch in the line of Cain was Lamech; both men were the seventh from Adam. We have seen how Lamech walked away from God; murder, rebellion, and bigamy marked his life and his generation (4:19-24). In contrast, Enoch was walking with God. He did not succumb to the rebellious attitude of his generation. Jude describes Enoch's time as one of "ungodly deeds ... committed in an ungodly way" (Jude 15). Enoch observed the vanity of living for earthly things alone and rejected that mindset. Instead, he prized godly values and heavenly things. He lived to "please God" (Heb. 11:5). In applying these truths to our own lives, it is clear that we have but two choices: we either live in rebellion against God, valuing earthly things, or we live to please God, valuing heavenly things.

- Walking with God is *focusing on the future*. Just as walking home physically has a destination in view, so walking with God looks to being at home with Him. Enoch's reward was to be at home with God. By faith "Enoch was translated so that he did not see death" (Heb. 11:5). We, too, need to keep the focus on the future rather than the present.

The Scriptures reveal that the future apostasy will reach its full height during the time of the Great Tribulation after the church has been taken away. At the end of the Tribulation, the Lord Jesus will come with His saints to judge the wicked. The wicked are called "ungodly" four times in Jude 14-15, and the focus of their ungodliness is "against Him." Their sin of apostasy will be of the same nature as Enoch's contemporaries. But there is comfort here for persecuted saints on earth during the Tribulation: in the end, judgment will fall on those who rebel against the truth. May God give us grace to walk with God the way Enoch did.

The Birth of Noah and Lamech's Prophecy (vv. 25-32)

Enoch's son was Methuselah, who lived until the year of the Flood. Methuselah's son was Lamech, who died five years before his father at age 777. Lamech's son was Noah, the only one of the ten ancient patriarchs who was still alive at the time of the Flood (vv. 25-27).

The last five verses of chapter 5 complete the genealogy of the generations from Adam to Noah. Noah's father Lamech was, like Enoch, a prophet. When Lamech named Noah, he prophesied, "This one will comfort us concerning our work and the toil of our hands, because of the ground which the LORD has cursed" (v. 29). This is not the easiest prophecy in Genesis to understand, but let us notice some of the elements in it.

Speaking of his newborn son Noah, he said, "This one will comfort us." First, Noah was to bring comfort, or rest, to humanity. Second, that comfort or rest would afford some kind of relief from the "toil of [their] hands." This acknowledges that the "toil" was difficult and miserable because of "the ground that the Lord had cursed." The need for the prophecy was due to the curse on the ground. After the Fall, God had said to Adam, "Cursed is the ground for your sake; in toil you shall eat of it all the days of your life. Both thorns and thistles it shall bring forth" (3:17-18). The curse was the result of sin. The resulting toil, the endless work required to extract a living from the ground, was a continual burden on the people. They well knew that the curse was the reason for their struggles. The prophecy says that Noah would, somehow, bring relief to the people.

Comfort Concerning Their Toil

Lamech's prophecy said that Noah was going to "comfort them concerning their work." How would this be? One possibility is that, looking at the big picture, Noah brought spiritual comfort by building the ark in which the line of the promised Savior would be preserved during the judgment of the Flood. The prophecy, then, is a statement that God destined Noah to be the channel of comfort and rest to the human race, because he was in the direct line of the coming Messiah.

Another way to look at the prophecy is to link it to the blessing of God on Noah and his family after the Flood. In that blessing, God modified the effects of the curse on the ground. Up until then, people had been vegetarians and were only eating what they could grow by tilling the ground or gathering from plants and trees. After the Flood had "cleansed" the wickedness of the world, God promised them that "every moving thing that lives shall be food for you" (9:2-3). Now they could add "flesh" to their diet. With this post-flood blessing of God, their diet could now include meat, fish, and poultry, and thus they would be "comforted." In other words, they were no longer so dependent on food cultivated from the ground for daily sustenance.

The last two verses in chapter 5 tell us that Lamech was 777 years old when he died and that Noah was five hundred years old when he "begot Shem, Ham, and Japheth." The fact that his three sons are all mentioned at the same time does not necessarily mean that they were triplets, or that they were all born in that year. It simply means that that the eldest of them was born then. They are not even named in chronological order. Ham was the youngest (9:24); Japheth was the oldest (10:21). Shem is mentioned first here, probably because it was through his line that the Messiah would come.

In Conclusion

Genesis 5 lists the ten outstanding ancients in the ten generations from Adam to Noah. Through them, the line of Messiah was preserved, and through them the truth of God was held high in the time before the Flood. As spiritual leaders, they remained faithful to God while the moral and spiritual values of the culture around them were disintegrating. Man retained something of the image and likeness of Adam, who was created in the image of God. Among them were outstanding examples of those who walked with God, like Enoch, whom God took to be with Himself. In the unfolding plan of God, as predicted by his father Lamech, Noah would bring comfort concerning the toil forced upon man because of the cursed ground.

Noah and the Ark

Chapter 6 concludes the section entitled "the genealogy of Adam" that begins in 5:1 (cf. notes on 5:1) and traces the record of ten generations from Adam to Noah, particularly the ten ancients. These were the great and godly men of their times who formed the ancestral line of the coming Messiah. Their history began with Adam, who was made in "the likeness of God" (5:1), and ended with Noah, who "found grace in the eyes of the Lord" (6:8). Humanity in general, however, was sinking into evil. The section comes to a climax with the statement that the "wickedness of man was great in the earth, and ... every intent of the thoughts of his heart was only evil continually" (v. 5). The section also shows that the curse of death that God announced to Adam was carried out on all ten generations, with one notable exception, that of Enoch. The commentary on Enoch clearly contrasts his walking with God with the living and dying cycle of the other men listed.

Wickedness in the Days of Noah

Chapter 5 ends with the births of Noah's three sons. The first eight verses of chapter 6 describe the wickedness of the world in the days of Noah. There is good reason for us to pay close attention to these verses, for the Lord Jesus Himself invited us to compare the world of Noah's day with the world at the time of the coming of the Son of Man. In His sermon on the Mount of Olives, He predicted, "As the days of Noah were, so also will the coming of the Son of Man be" (Matt. 24:37). The generation of the last days will not expect judgment and will continue the regular routine of life, until it is too late. If the civilization of Noah's day is like the civilization at the end of this age, it is important that we examine it carefully.

The Characteristics of a Dying World

In Genesis chapters 4 and 5 Moses has been clearly showing that the civilization of the pre-flood world had a growing propensity for evil. Note again some of the marks or characteristics of that civilization:

- Urban development (4:17)
- Popular entertainment (4:21)
- Expanding industry and technology (4:22)

- Polygamy and sensuality in marriage relationships (4:23)
- Murder (4:23)
- Violent revenge and internal discord (4:24)
- Rebellion against God and His revelation (Job 22:17)
- Denial of God's power (Job. 22:17)

To these, add two more characteristics: population explosion (v. 1) and satanic activity (v. 2). Together, these resulted in the growth of iniquity exponentially, which in turn brought about God's intervention and judgment.

The Sons of God and the Daughters of Men (vv. 1-2)

One significant aspect of the days of Noah was that the "sons of God saw the daughters of men ... and they took wives for themselves of all whom they chose." This strange union is placed in the context of the multiplication of people on the earth. There is no doubt that these unions were a further development in the progress of evil.

The respective identities of the "sons of God" and the "daughters of men" have been interpreted in several different ways. Some take it that the former refers to the line of Seth (Genesis 4) and the latter to the line of Cain (Genesis 5). This view ignores the fact that the descendants of both Seth and Cain were part of the wicked world that God judged. All of them, with the exception of the family of Noah, were destroyed in the Flood. It also fails to explain how one group were all "sons" and the other all "daughters." Were all the good Sethites male (sons of God), and all the bad Cainites female (daughters of men)? Obviously not. Nor was there any command from God that forbade such marriages. This explanation proves unsatisfactory.

A second interpretation of the term "sons of God" is that they were nobility (kings) who married women commoners in a kind of royal polygamy. However, this does not explain why their children would be "giants."

A third interpretation, which was held by the early church fathers and supported by several factors, is the oldest. It says that the sons of God were angelic beings who had sexual unions with human women to whom they were attracted. The first grounds for this interpretation is that the precise term used here refers to fallen angels in its other three biblical uses, all in the ancient book of Job (1:6; 2:1; 38:7). In other passages, similar language is used that also refers to angels (Ps. 29:1; 89:6; Dan. 3:25). The second support for this view is that the Septuagint, a Greek version of the Old Testament from the pre-Christian era, uses the term "angels of God."

The third reason is that the New Testament confirms in two passages (2 Peter 2:4-6; Jude 6-7) that the sons of God referenced in Genesis 6 were, indeed, angels. In Jude we learn that "angels ... did not keep their proper domain, but left their own habitation." In the next verse, the sin of the angels is compared to the unnatural sexual relations of the people of Sodom. To make this even clearer, Peter links the fall of angels with the days of Noah: "God did not spare the angels who sinned, but cast them down to hell ... but [He] saved Noah ... bringing in the flood on the world of the ungodly."

Do Angels Marry?

How do we reconcile the marriages of angels to humans with the words of the Lord Jesus in Matthew 22:30? On that occasion, the Lord made a clear statement that those who will participate in the resurrection "neither marry nor are given in marriage, but are as the angels of God in heaven." The logical conclusion is that angels do not marry in heaven. It does, however, leave room for angelic beings to be married on earth. It also does not say that they are sexless. We do know that some angels have bodies and are able to eat (cf. 18:8).

What we can say then, with reasonable certainty, is that there was some form of sexual relationship and marriage between the sons of God (presumably fallen angels) and human women. These rebellious angels were able to invade the bodies of the daughters of men. As to how, we do not know, but that it did indeed happen is evident from Scripture. This sexual activity was beyond the bounds of God's limits for them. The purpose of these unions is not stated, but the context indicates that it was a satanic attempt to thwart the plan of God in providing a Redeemer. Satan wanted to completely corrupt the human race to prevent the birth of the Seed of the woman predicted to crush him. He nearly succeeded.

This is a strange incident that gives rise to difficult questions. But when considering this section we must not lose sight of the main point, which is that the growing wickedness of people was aided by demonic activity as they overstepped the bounds that God has set. Man's evil was beyond self-help and was leading him quickly toward judgment. The great apostasy of the people who lived before the Flood is clearly seen in these verses.

The Response of God (v. 3)

Evil continued to abound but was not to go unchecked. God took notice of it. He said, "My Spirit shall not strive with man forever." God put a time limit on how long man would continue in his debauchery. There has been some debate over the word "spirit." The more natural meaning is that it refers to God's Holy Spirit who strives (or contends) with people in convicting them of their sin (John 16:8). With the accelerating wickedness and the certainty of the coming Flood in view, God said that His Spirit would soon cease from His usual activity of convicting the world of sin. At that time, He would impose the threatened judgment.

Another interpretation is that "spirit" refers to the "breath of life" that God breathed into man at creation (2:7). Proponents of this view say that the word "strive" is better translated "abide," as in the margin of some Bibles. Thus it would mean that the breath, or life, of man would be taken away in the coming Flood. The interpretation of God's Holy Spirit no longer convicting people of sin is to be preferred.

The period of 120 years is probably the length of time that God gave to mankind after His warning and before the judgment came, "when the longsuffering of God waited in the days of Noah, while the ark was being prepared" (1 Pet. 3:20). In the same way, He is "longsuffering toward us, not willing that any should perish but that all should come to repentance" (2 Pet. 3:9). God extended His grace to man. Note, also, the reminder that man is "indeed flesh" (that is, subject to physical death). This was true, no matter what involvement the sons of God may have had. The passage does not tell us whom the Spirit of God used to announce this prophecy, but we do know that Lamech had prophesied at Methuselah's birth and that Methuselah was still alive until the year of the Flood. We also know that Noah was a "preacher of righteousness" (2 Pet. 2:5). It is quite possible that he was God's prophet.

The Giants in Those Days (v. 4)

During the 120 years prior to the Flood we are told that "there were giants on the earth … and also afterward." These were the children born to the sons of God and the daughters of men. The word *giant* comes from a root word meaning "to fall" and seems to carry the idea of "fallen." It is linked to the fallen state of the mongrel children. In Hebrew, the word *nephilim* is only used twice in the Bible, here and in Numbers 13. In our passage, the nephilim were called "mighty men" and "men of renown." Their notoriety probably came about because of their military ability and wicked pursuits. Like many powerful and exceedingly wicked leaders throughout history, they were honored by the world but condemned by God. Therefore, God literally poured out His judgment on them in the Flood.

Verse 4 also indicates that these were not the only nephilim that ever existed. In Numbers 13:32-33, the spies had just returned to Moses from their excursion into Canaan. Two of them, Caleb and Joshua, urged the Israelites to immediately invade the land, but the other ten spies gave a bad report. They had seen the descendants of Anak—giants (translated "men of great stature" here)—and persuaded the Israelites not to advance. Since Moses probably wrote Genesis while on the wilderness journey, he knew full well that giants existed. When their wickedness was ripe for judgment, God used Joshua and the Israelites to destroy them. It is significant that nephilim appear in two societies that had reached their pinnacle of wickedness just before God destroyed them both in judgment.

God's Reaction to Man's Wickedness (vv. 5-7)

This passage sums up the wickedness of man and reveals God's decision with respect to it. In calculating the enormity of their iniquity, the Lord noted their motivation and their deeds (v. 5). Man's every intent was evil. The word *intent* implies purpose or design and comes from the imagery of a potter molding his pots according to the pattern, or intent, in his mind. The use of the word in this context ("every intent of the thoughts of his heart was only evil continually") reveals a deliberate mindset to commit evil. The people were forming wicked philosophies and practicing obscene and filthy acts; they were trying to shape society according to their evil designs. It gives credence to the idea in verse 4 of demonic immorality between the sons of God and the daughters of men.

The statement in verse 6 that "the LORD was sorry that He had made man on the earth, and He was grieved in His heart" has puzzled some Bible students. God's reaction seems to compromise His immutability that the prophet Malachi spoke of: "I am the LORD, I do not change" (Mal. 3:6). The truth is that God is always the same. In His grace, He offered those wicked people a chance to repent and find safety in the ark through the preaching of Noah. In His love, He grieved that they did not repent. God acted in keeping with His absolute attributes. When God seems to "change his mind," it is because man has changed. God always responds consistently in accordance with His multi-faceted character.

The terrible effect of sin on the world and on people had been growing for sixteen hundred years and had reached the point where their holy Creator announced His intention to destroy the whole earth. The Spirit of God, in guiding the writers of Scripture, used language that we humans could readily understand. He conveyed God's feelings with stark simplicity in stating that He was sorry that He had made man. The depravity of man had negatively affected the whole earth. Thus, the judgment of God in the Flood would end the life of "man and beast, creeping thing and birds of the air" (v. 7). All people, animals, and birds dependent on the land would perish.

Grace for Noah (v. 8)

This is the last verse in this *toledoth* covering the ten generations from Adam to Noah (5:1-6:8). Noah, as a recipient of God's grace, provides a fitting end to it. In this verse, we have the third mention of Noah's name. First, it was prophesied that he would bring comfort (5:29). Second, we were told his age at the birth of his sons (5:32). Now he is described as a man who "found grace in the eyes of the LORD," and there is encouragement for us here.

In this verse we have the first mention of *grace* in Scripture. As with many key biblical terms, the first mention often brings important insight into their later use. Note the background of this passage. Noah, in the years before the Flood, was living in perhaps the worst sinful conditions this world has ever seen. He is set in sharp contrast with those who would soon be subject to God's condemning judgment. "But Noah," the Bible says. Even though he towered above his generation, yet he is portrayed here as one on whom God bestowed divine favor. That's grace. Even Noah did not *deserve* to be saved.

His salvation was a gracious gift from God. Just at this moment, God's grace shines like a light through the life of Noah. It provides hope for the future. There is a lesson for all that may live in corrupt social conditions, that God's grace has reached us, and we, too, are to shine like lights in the world.

The Genealogy of Noah (v. 9)

Genesis 6:9 through chapter 9 comprises the third major section of Genesis. This one concerns "the genealogy of Noah" and deals with what became of Noah. It follows the themes of the previous two sections ("the history of the heavens and the earth" [2:4-4:26] and "the genealogy of Adam" [5:1-6:8]).

The genealogy of Noah begins with the judgment of the Flood and Noah's salvation by means of the ark. After the Flood, God gave Noah and his family a new beginning in a cleansed world. Noah built an altar and worshipped God, who made a new covenant with him. The section ends with Noah's drunkenness and the activities of his sons during the incident that brought on another curse. Our present study will confine itself to the first part of this section in Genesis 6:9–22.

Noah, a Righteous Man in an Unrighteous World

In the face of impending, catastrophic judgment, one man among the millions on earth stood out as a man of character, morality, and godliness. Noah was that man. The movements of the narrative surround him and God's estimation of him as compared to the surrounding rebellious world, because Noah was God's standard of righteousness. His story is the lengthiest of any man in Genesis thus far.

Noah's Spiritual Stature

The character of Noah is contrasted with the corruption of the world. His spiritual stature is described in three ways: he was a "just" (righteous) man; he was "perfect" (blameless) in his generation; and he "walked with God." As a just man, he had found grace in the eyes of the Lord (v. 8). Noah's righteousness is confirmed again in Genesis 7:1 where God said, "I have seen that you are righteous before Me."

Noah is the first person in the Bible called righteous. The word itself carries with it the concepts of honesty, virtue, and holiness, but it is also a common biblical word for the spiritual standing of a believer. Therefore, it does not mean that God saved him *because* he was righteous, but that he was *declared* righteous on the basis of his faith in God. In the words of Hebrews 11:7, he "became heir of the righteousness which is according to faith." Noah, no doubt, believed the promises of Genesis 3:15 concerning the coming Seed of the woman who would suffer in the process of defeating Satan.

It is most instructive for us to note that the spiritual elements of Noah's life all occurred in the proper order:

- God's grace (v. 8)
- Noah's faith (Heb. 11:7)
- Noah's righteous standing before God (Heb. 11:7)
- Noah's righteous living before men (v. 9)

For us, too, God takes the initiative by acting in grace towards us. Then, we express our faith in Him by trusting in the Lord Jesus Christ as Savior (Eph. 2:8). Thus, "by faith" we are "justified," or declared righteous, before God (Rom. 5:1). Finally, we are to live righteously in the world. The word *righteous* summarizes Noah's life. He was righteous before God, he lived righteously, and he preached righteousness to the world by reminding people of their unrighteousness in God's sight (2 Pet. 2:5).

The second phrase used to describe Noah's character is "perfect" or blameless. That is, he was a man of integrity and wholeness. He refused to join in the moral wickedness of his generation. No one could accuse him of being contaminated by the sin around him. Rather, he was seen in stark contrast to his culture. He was perfect in that he was completely God's man.

Third, Noah was described not only as righteous and perfect, but also as a man who "walked with God." Before he was born, his grandfather, Enoch, had also walked with God (5:22). In connection with Enoch, we have noted that this involves agreeing with God, trusting in Him, growing in faith, fellowship with God, and separation from the world. This also describes how Noah walked with God. The spiritual stature of Noah encourages us to strive after righteousness, blamelessness, and a closer walk with our God.

The question may be asked as to how Noah's sons escaped the moral pollution of the world. All of them were born within one hundred years of the Flood and lived in an extremely corrupt society. There are, perhaps, two clues in the godly example of their parents and grandparents. Methuselah, their grandfather, would no doubt have reminded them of the prophetic meaning of his name: "when he dies, it will come." That they put their faith in God is evident from the fact that God preserved them in the ark. When Methuselah died, their expectancy must have reached a very high point as they waited for God to act. The second clue may have been that their father kept them working with him as he directed the building of the ark. He would actively encourage them and keep them busy, like godly parents raising children in a corrupt world. Noah set a good example for Christian parents today: keep your children deeply grounded in the Scripture and occupy their time constructively.

Noah's Faith   (Hebrews 11:7)

The New Testament commentary about Noah in Hebrews 11 is instructive. His faith was in what God had told him. "By faith, Noah, being divinely warned of things not yet seen ... prepared an ark." When warned by God, he believed what he heard. Even though Noah had never seen a flood—probably not even rain—yet he believed God. During the many years he was building the ark, he kept his faith in God, in spite of those who scoffed. May we, like Noah, believe God even though "scoffers will come ... saying, 'Where is the promise of His coming?'" (2 Pet. 3:3-4).

According to Hebrews 11:7, Noah's faith is also remarkable because he was motivated to act on it by building the ark. In faith, Noah took God seriously. He worked on the ark for one hundred years, convinced that the Flood would come. One more thing about Noah's faith mentioned in the Hebrews passage is that it moved him to have godly fear. He believed that a holy God would surely punish those who rebelled against Him. Few Christians today share Noah's fear of God. He believed that he should live in the light of God's holy wrath against sin. We all can profit by remembering these three things about Noah's faith: it was based on God's Word; it motivated him to obedience; and it moved him to have godly fear.

In preparing the ark for the saving of his household, Noah "condemned the world." He was not only constructing a means of escaping the coming judgment; he was demonstrating to the watching world that all who did not enter the ark would be lost. More than that, he believed that the entire world system (religious, political, technological, etc) was so corrupt that God would destroy it all. Noah is an example to God's people today who also live in a corrupt world and whose lives and actions condemn it.

The Earth's Corruption and Violence (vv. 11-13)

In contrast to the character of Noah, the man of faith who walked with God, we are shown the corruption of the people around him (v. 11). Job's commentary on what happened is helpful here. "Will you keep to the old way which wicked men have trod, who were cut down before their time, whose foundations were swept away by a flood? They said to God, 'Depart from us! What can the Almighty do to them?'" (Job 22:15-17). It was their desire to push God out of their lives that caused them to be swept away in the Flood. They questioned God's ability to do anything to them, and they told Him to go away while they pursued their immorality, rebellion, and violence. It is a sobering truth for us to consider in our times when the world's attitude toward God is becoming more and more like that of the pre-flood peoples.

God's Inspection and Conclusion

In verse 11, the corruption of the earth is simply stated. In verse 12, we are told that God *saw* that it was corrupt. When it says that God "looked," we are not to conclude that God saw with physical eyes, as a human would. Nor, when it says that God found the earth to be corrupt, are we to conclude that He did not know what was going on until that moment. Biblical authors often used human language to describe divine activities to help their readers better understand God and His actions. This is called *anthropomorphic* language, which is language that attributes human characteristics to God. In this verse we are told that God saw the corrupt and violent world with a view to what He was going to do about it.

Many civilizations have come and gone, and these same characteristics have marked the end of all of them. The tendency in every civilization is to abandon their dependence on God and become independent of His moral standards. The result has inevitably been catastrophe. The corruption in Noah's day was universal because it says, "all flesh had corrupted their way on the earth." Some commentators think that animal life was corrupted, too. The same phrase "all flesh" is used in the next chapter and includes animals that also perished in the Flood (7:21). But though they may have been corrupted physically they were not, like people, moral creatures and were not, therefore, subject to moral judgment.

Having made His divine inspection and assessed everything to be corrupt and violent, God told Noah, "The end of all flesh has come before Me" (v. 13). God revealed to Noah that He would destroy both the people and the earth itself. Language like this can only mean that the Flood must have been worldwide and not just confined to a local area. Many critics have declared that a worldwide flood was impossible. They regard it as just a theme for children's toys and coloring books. But the critics are wrong. This is the sober language of historical fact. Other writers of Scripture speak plainly of a universal flood. The apostle Peter declared that, "the world that then existed perished, being flooded with water" (2 Pet. 3:6). Isaiah spoke of a universal flood when he said, "the waters of Noah would no longer cover the earth" (Isa. 54:9), and the Lord Jesus Himself said that "the flood came and took them all away" (Matt. 24:39).

There is wordplay here that should not be missed. The Hebrew for *corrupt* and *corrupted* in verse 12 is the same word used for *destroy* in verse 13. The people had "corrupted their way," so God would destroy (literally "corrupt") them. In both places, the meaning of the word is that of ruining or devastating. The same word is used of the destruction of Sodom in Genesis 13:10. In Romans 1, the apostle Paul, in describing how "the wrath of God is revealed ... against all ungodliness and unrighteousness of men," said that God "gave them up to uncleanness .... to vile passions .... [and] to a debased mind" (Rom. 1:18, 24, 26, 28). God would complete the destruction that the corrupt people had already begun. Consider well that it was God who took the initiative in the judgment. He said, "I will destroy them." It was God's retribution for their sin—another sobering truth for us all.

The Construction of the Ark (vv. 14-16)

In light of the announcement of worldwide destruction, God told Noah, "Make yourself an ark of gopherwood" (v. 14). The word *ark* used here occurs in the Bible in only two places. One is in reference to the boat that Noah built, and the other to the vessel of reeds in which the baby Moses was hidden by his mother along the Nile River (Ex. 3:2). It is not the same word as the one used for the ark of the covenant in the book of Exodus. The word in our passage may be a borrowed Egyptian word describing a large, barge-like vessel that Egyptians used to transport obelisks. It is not unlikely that Moses, the probable author of Genesis, would use Egyptian terms, because he was educated in Egypt. Gopherwood, which was no doubt very suitable for the purpose, is not identifiable with any particular species of wood known today. The "barge" was to contain rooms, or compartments. The word for "rooms" can mean "nests." They were to be used to accommodate the different sizes and characteristics of the animals, birds, and creeping things that would occupy the ark.

The Covering of Pitch

God told Noah that the ark was to be covered both inside and out with pitch to make it thoroughly waterproof. The words for "cover" and "pitch" come from the same root that is also the word for *atonement* in the Old Testament. Because of its typical use here, Bible scholars have seen Genesis 6:14 as the specific first reference to atonement (meaning "covering") in the Bible. The aspect of atonement emphasized in Genesis 3 is that blood had to be shed to provide the covering; the emphasis here in chapter 6 is on the adequacy of the covering. The idea in the Old Testament that man could be reconciled with God was based on the *covering* of a blood sacrifice. As Leviticus 17:11 says, "It is the blood that makes atonement [covering] for the soul." Pitch was the ideal covering for the ark, therefore it is a good illustration of atonement. The covering of pitch kept out the waters of judgment and provided safety for Noah's family inside. For the believer, the blood of Christ is our covering in that it protects us from the judgment we deserve, and it satisfies God's requirements for justice.

The ark was to be three hundred cubits long, fifty cubits wide, and thirty cubits high (v. 15). In today's measurements, a cubit would be about eighteen inches long, possibly a little longer. Thus, the ark would be 450 feet long, seventy-five feet wide, and forty-five feet high. This was enormous by ancient standards. It was the largest boat ever built of wood and the largest ship ever built until steel ships were invented in the 1800s. Marine engineers today say the proportions are excellent for maximum seaworthiness. Scientists have determined that there would be ample room in a vessel that size to accommodate a pair of each of the thousands of animal species and still have room for food provisions.

The occupants of the ark would be housed on three floors, or decks (v. 16). The ark was to have a window the size of a cubit. The language is not precise, but it was probably an open space around the circumference near the roof that would provide both light and ventilation inside. Other than the window, there was to be one large door through which the people and the animals would enter and eventually leave. Building a very large ship like the ark would require considerable technology. These requirements should not surprise Bible students, considering the technology that Cain's descendants achieved (4:16-24).

The Lesson of the Door

We should learn a lesson from the door in the side of the ark. Anyone who wished to be saved from the Flood needed to go through it. There was no other way into the safety of the ark. There was a time coming when it would no longer be open, so there was some urgency about taking advantage of it. Nowhere in the Bible is it stated that the door in the ark was a type of Christ, but surely it does picture Him as the one and only "door" to everlasting life. He said, "I am the door, if anyone enters by Me, he will be saved" (John 10:9). The door of the ark is an illustration of Christ, the "Door" of deliverance from the penalty of sin. It is available to all as the only refuge from the judgment of God on a condemned world of which they are a part.

Noah, our Example

There are several important lessons to be learned from the building of the ark. First, there is the *obedience* of Noah in following God's direction without any other confirmation. Second, there is the *perseverance* of Noah in building faithfully over a very long period of time. We are not specifically told when God told Noah to start building, but it was likely soon after He announced that judgment would come after 120 years (6:3). Building a large ship on dry ground before a jeering crowd for that long a time required a great deal of courage and perseverance, but Noah continued until the task was complete. Finally, there is the *faithfulness* of Noah in his service to God under difficult circumstances. He had no converts, yet he remained as a faithful "preacher of righteousness" in an evil world. Obedience, tenacity, and faithfulness are qualities that all true believers should possess in the service of God.

Judgment and Grace (vv. 17-18)

After describing the means of deliverance from judgment, God now specified what kind of judgment would come. God told Noah clearly, "I Myself am bringing the flood of waters on the earth to destroy from under heaven all flesh" (v. 17). The particular word for *flood* is only used here and in Psalm 29:10 in reference to the Flood of Noah's day. After making the announcement, however, grace appears in the form of a promise. God said to him, "But I will establish My covenant with you." This is the first mention of *covenant* or promise in the Bible. God was speaking of the covenant that He would make with Noah after the Flood (9:9-17). God also specifically enumerated the eight people who would be saved. God knew that no one else would respond in faith to Noah's preaching and that all who were outside the ark would be lost.

The Inhabitants of the Ark (vv. 19-21)

God gave Noah instructions about the animals and birds that would occupy the ark. He was responsible to bring in two of every kind of animal, bird, and reptile that came to him, so that each species could be preserved. Noah was also to gather food necessary for his family as well as what was needed for the creatures. We can only speculate as to the details. It has been suggested that some of the larger animals may have gone into a state of hibernation, much as bears do during the northern winters. That way, there would be little need for food or cleanup. Were the reptiles and larger animals on the ark young so that they would not need to occupy such a large space? Did the animals get there by some migratory instinct? How did Noah and his family get them to their right places or "rooms" in the ark? Did God subdue the natures of the wilder animals, like lions? We must assume much of the supernatural hand of God in it all and accept by faith what we are not told and cannot work out. Certainly, to try to imagine the thousands of insects, birds, and animals as they flew or walked into the ark and then settled in peacefully with one another without harm, is mind-boggling. The salvation of Noah and the animals in the ark was an act of God, and we should not be surprised if some elements of it required supernatural power.

In Conclusion

The conclusion of chapter 6 focuses most fittingly on Noah's obedience. "Thus Noah did; according to all that God commanded him, so he did." Twice in that sentence it tells us that Noah "did" build the ark, even though it took more than one hundred years. Obedience to God is the outstanding characteristic of Noah in the whole narrative. He began as the recipient of the grace of God (v. 8). He lived his life in obedience to the word of God.

The Worldwide Flood

The ark was finished. The last nail had been driven and the final pail of pitch applied. Noah, the "preacher of righteousness," had given his final prophetic warning to the people of his generation. Though he preached for more than one hundred years, not a single person outside his own family responded in faith. Now Noah simply waited for a word from God to enter the ark, just as God had directed him to do many years before when He promised to make a covenant with him (6:18).

Instructions for Loading the Ark (vv. 1-4)

At the right time, God gave Noah instructions to "come into the ark" along with his household, and He gave two reasons for doing so. First, God said, "I have seen that you are righteous before Me in this generation" (v. 1). Noah (and only Noah) was righteous in his standing before God on the basis of his faith in Him. He is described in Hebrews 11:7 as an "heir of the righteousness which is according to faith." God preserved him in the ark because, using New Testament language, he was justified, that is, "declared righteous" (Rom. 3:21-26).

Second, his entrance was imperative, because in seven days God would send rain that would continue without let-up for forty days (v. 4). The long-predicted Flood was about to happen. The important thing in this passage is that, in giving details about what would happen, when it would happen and how long the deluge would last, God was reassuring Noah that He was in control. Even after all the animals were inside, there would be seven days of final preparations before the rain would begin to fall (v. 4).

When that seven day waiting period was over, God said he would "destroy" or blot out from the face of the earth all living things that He had made (v. 4). The word *destroy* is the same word used in Genesis 6:7 when God first announced, "I will destroy man whom I have created from the face of the earth."

Seven of Each Clean Animal

God had previously told Noah to bring a pair of every kind of creature into the ark. In this final command to enter, God added one additional requirement.

One pair of every creature, a male and a female, would preserve the species. Now God said to take seven of each kind of "clean" animal into the ark. There has been no mention of clean animals before this, and we must assume that these would have been defined in the same way as the clean animals of Moses' day described in Leviticus 11.

As explained there, clean animals were to be used primarily as food and secondarily as sacrifices. Sheep, goats, and cattle would fall into both categories, but other ritually clean animals, like deer, were only for food, not sacrifice. The reason for the extra pairs of clean animals on the ark was in anticipation of a God-given concession after the Flood that would permit people to eat meat (9:3). Up until the time of the Flood it appears that humans were vegetarians. After the Flood, they raised domestic animals of their own for food. The additional animals would also allow Noah to offer a sacrifice upon leaving the ark, which he did (8:20).

The coming rainstorm was to last "forty days and forty nights" (v. 4). This oddly-worded time period is used in two other passages of Scripture, and all three are associated with significant events in redemption history that marked a new order of things. In the first, Noah was in the ark during the cataclysm of the Flood and emerged to make a new start on earth with his family with a covenant of promise from God (9:9). In the second, Moses was on Mount Sinai receiving the tables of the Law and the covenant regarding the worship and administration of Israel (Ex. 24:12 - 31:18). The third time, the term is used of the period that the Lord Jesus was alone in the wilderness, fasting and being tempted by Satan. He was preparing for His public ministry that would bring in a new covenant ratified by His own blood (Luke 4:13-29). Note that all three forty day periods were preparation for covenants from God.

Noah and the Animals Enter the Ark (vv. 5-9)

God's instructions had been clear; Noah's obedience was immediate. He had been obedient in building the ark: "Make for yourself an ark of gopherwood" (6:14). He had been obedient when God told him to stock the ark with provisions (6:21-22). Now he was obedient in moving into the ark with his wife, three sons and their wives, and all creatures great and small (v. 7). They went in "to Noah," that is, Noah arranged for their accommodation in the ark (v. 9). Their orderly entrance "two by two" must have been a spectacular sight.

The Date of the Flood

The date for the Flood is specifically stated as occurring when Noah was six hundred years old. It was a significant year because it was the same year that Methuselah died according to the prophecy of his name (see comments on Genesis 5:22-25). The date of the Flood can be ascertained quite easily from the dates and times recorded in Scripture. It happened in the year 1656 after the creation of Adam (See the chart on the next page and Genesis 5).

Seth was born when Adam was	130
Enos was born when Seth was	105
Cainan was born when Enos was	90
Mahalalel was born when Cainan was	70
Jared was born when Mahalalel was	65
Enoch was born when Jared was	162
Methuselah was born when Enoch was	65
Lamech was born when Methuselah was	182
Noah was born when Lamech was	187
Noah in the year of the Flood was	600
The Flood occurred in the year of Adam	1656

From a time perspective, Adam and Methuselah's lives overlapped for 243 years. Adam and Lamech's life spans crossed for fifty-six years. It is, therefore, quite likely that Noah had the direct testimony of at least two men who had actually conversed with Adam. If this is so, we need not worry that truth became distorted through re-telling.

The Coming of the Flood (vv. 10-16)

After the final period of seven days, "The waters of the flood were on the earth" (v. 10). This is a summary statement that the rains began—and right on schedule. "On the very same day, Noah [and his family] entered the ark" (v. 13). It was the six hundredth year of Noah, the second month and the seventh day, the first specific chronological date in the Bible. This precise dating lends credibility to the Flood story. Hardly any other event in the Bible is as comprehensively dated as is the Flood. No less than eighteen time notations are recorded. It is as if Noah made daily journal entries as the various things happened, from the Flood's prophecy to its completed purpose.

On that particular day, "the fountains of the great deep were broken up, and the windows of heaven were opened" (v. 11). There seem to have been two great reservoirs of water, one of which is called "the fountains of the great deep." These were probably subterranean waters that God caused to rupture, releasing an enormous volume of water upward to cover the world. The other reservoir, called the "windows of heaven," may have been a vapor canopy suspended over the entire earth that collapsed and came down in the form of rain. Exactly how God did this has been a matter of much speculation. Some have suggested causes such as the tilting of the earth's axis, a collision of the earth with asteroids or meteorites, slipping of the earth's crust or tectonic plates, or a near miss from a passing comet, among others. The important thing for us is not *how* God did it, which we are not told, but *that* He did it, which is exactly what we are told.

The deluge continued for forty days and forty nights, starting on the same day that Noah and his family entered the ark (vv. 12-13). The next two verses describe the four categories of creatures that were preserved: beasts, cattle, creeping things, and birds. These are the same as the ones mentioned at the time of creation with the exception of the sea creatures, which obviously did not need to be preserved in the ark. In verse 15 we are told that all flesh in which is the "breath of life" went into the ark. This describes all creatures that breathe air, which excludes fish.

In verse 16 there is a flashback to the moment when all the animals and family of Noah were safely inside the ark. Without any help from Noah, the great door in the side of the ark swung shut. There was a finality about this act of God that preserved the safety of those inside and sealed the fate of those outside. When God shut the door, it was shut. The Lord Jesus commented, "As in the days of Noah ... they were eating and drinking, marrying and giving in marriage, until the day that Noah entered the ark, and did not know until the flood came and took them all away" (Matt. 24:38-39).

We should not fail to see that the one who shut the door was the LORD (v. 16). Note that the word "LORD" spelled with capitals indicates the Hebrew name *Yahweh* or *Jehovah*. It is to be distinguished from "God" (in Hebrew, *Elohim*) and "Lord" spelled with lower-case letters, which is the translation of *Adonai,* meaning "master." All three are names for God, but they emphasize His different characteristics. Bible students should carefully consider the particular names and titles of God in their contexts. Note how two of these names are used in this chapter, and indeed they are both used in verse 16. The divine Person who commanded Noah to obey is called God - *Elohim* – the powerful Creator (vv. 9, 16). The divine Person who invited Noah into the ark and who shut the door to protect them for the future was the LORD, the covenant-keeping God. Keeping these distinctions in mind will enhance your study of the Scriptures.

The Extent of the Flood (vv. 17-24)

Note the language in these next verses that indicate a progressive rise in the water level, culminating in the total inundation of the whole earth by water:

- In verse 17, the waters "increased and lifted up the ark."
- In verse 18, the waters "prevailed and greatly increased on the earth."
- In verse 19, they "prevailed exceedingly, and all the high hills were covered."
- In verse 20, "the waters prevailed fifteen cubits upward, and the mountains were covered."

The phrase "fifteen cubits upward" relates to the depth that the ark would have had to float to avoid being grounded on a mountain peak. We may also take into account the fact that mountains then were not necessarily as high as they are today. The Flood itself may have had an enormous effect on the shape of the earth's crust, including the mountains.

Judgment and Grace

The very solemn language in verses 21 and 22 describes the destruction of every human being, every animal, and every bird in the whole world, except those that were in the ark. "Everything that had breath died." There is not a word about the horror of those who were overtaken by the catastrophe. Neither is there a word of sympathy for them from God or from those in the ark. God was acting as a holy God must act. It was the most complete devastation the world has ever seen. God as the Creator exercised His power and freedom over creation to judge it in deadly anger. The Flood is a warning to every succeeding generation, including our own, that man cannot trifle with a holy God.

Principles of God's Judgment

The events concerning the Flood in Genesis 6 and 7 illustrate some of the principles by which God judges people. It may be helpful to consider these:

- *God's judgments are based on His perfect justice* (7:23). God is in no way capricious or arbitrary. He is fair and just in His retribution for sin, as the Flood narrative vividly illustrates.

- *God's judgments have purpose* (6:11-13). The world and its people were corrupt, and the whole earth needed cleansing.

- *God's judgments are forewarned* (6:13). He warns those who deserve judgment so that it is perfectly clear what is happening. Thus He warned Noah, and Noah warned the people (2 Pet. 2:5).

- *God's judgments allow for repentance* (6:3). The Spirit of God had striven with a wicked generation to give them opportunity to change. Even after His announcement to destroy the earth, another hundred years went by before it occurred. And even after giving the command to enter the ark, it was another seven days before the door was shut (7:4).

- *God's judgments are certain* (7:21-22). Unless man repents, judgment must come, as did the Flood. God will fulfill every promise He makes.

- *God's judgments end in death* (7:21-22). Because the wages of sin is death, the ultimate end of judgment is death, which the Flood accomplished.

Ponder a poignant quote from Sir Thomas Browne: "That there was a deluge once seems not to me to be so great a miracle as that there is not always one."

In Conclusion

Chapter 7 concludes by telling us that the waters prevailed on the earth covering the mountains for five months (150 days). The purpose of the Flood was to destroy the whole population of the world because of the enormity of their sin. Nothing less than a universal flood could accomplish this purpose. But inside the ark were the only remnants of humanity and the animal world. They were perfectly safe, waiting for a new beginning to come. In that ark lay the hope for a new world, the people through whom the plans of a gracious God would be carried out.

Leaving the Ark

The important elements in Noah's life are well summarized in Hebrews 11. "By faith Noah, being divinely warned of things not yet seen, moved with godly fear, prepared an ark for the saving of his household, by which he condemned the world and became heir of the righteousness which is according to faith" (Heb. 11:7). By the time the ark came to rest on the mountains of Ararat, these things had been accomplished. These events remain to this day one of the most outstanding examples of God's grace and justice ever revealed to man.

The subsiding floodwaters revealed a world that had been utterly devastated. The terrible offenses against God's holiness had all been vindicated. But not only had God displayed His wrath, He had also expressed His grace, evidenced by the lovely sight of the ark at rest. The ark had come through the storm, and its precious contents—Noah, his family, and the whole range of living creatures—were safe. We see here a powerful illustration of the salvation of the believer in Christ today. Though the ark had borne the fury of God's judgment, the ones who had sought protection inside were safe. The ark pictures Christ, who bore the wrath of God for our sake. We are safe in Him. By faith in Christ, believers have passed from death into life and will never be subject to God's condemnation (John 5:24; Rom.8:1).

God Remembered Noah (vv. 1-3)

Chapter 7 ended in the middle of the Flood year. The floodwaters had covered the earth for one hundred and fifty days since "the fountains of the great deep were broken up and the windows of heaven were opened" (7:11, 24). When the ark landed after five months afloat, Noah still had seven more months to wait until they could disembark. Chapter 8 begins, "Then God remembered Noah and every living thing, and all the animals that were with him in the ark." When the Scripture says "God remembered Noah," it is not implying that He had forgotten him. It means that after carrying out His righteous judgment on the earth, God once again turned His attention to Noah to act in love and care on Noah's behalf. We will read the phrase again in Genesis 30:22, where it says that "God remembered Rachel," meaning that He had heard her petition and allowed her to finally conceive and bear a son (Joseph).

Sometimes we, too, are tempted to feel that God has abandoned us; we need to learn the lesson of waiting for God to act on our behalf. As surely as God remembered Noah, so He will remember us at exactly the right time.

Note that the inspired writer used "God" in this verse, not "LORD." The reason for the particular use of "God" here relates to His sustaining care of animals (as well as people) in His role as Creator. Animals have no personal relationship with God, but God *is* concerned for their welfare.

In remembering Noah, God began to remove the water. "God made a wind to pass over the earth, and the waters subsided" (v. 1). Some have suggested that the wind is a reference to the Spirit of God, but it is better to view it as natural wind. The second way in which God remembered Noah was that the "fountains of the deep" wer e closed and the "windows of heaven" were stopped (v. 2). The stores of water in both places had probably dried up by this point in time. We are not told where all the water went, but there must have been vast geological changes in the earth's surface during the Flood and shortly thereafter. These would have included the movement of the earth's crust, the up-thrust of mountain ranges, and the depression of the sea bottoms. The third way God remembered Noah was by providing a sign through the sending out of the dove, on which we shall comment below. Finally, God remembered Noah by breaking His silence and speaking to him again, directing him to leave the ark (v. 16).

The dating of the various aspects of the Flood is given accurately to the very day. Noah completed the ark when he was six hundred years old. The Flood started on the seventeenth day of the second month and the ark floated for one hundred and fifty days (v. 3). No doubt Noah kept careful records of these events. The chart below clarifies the timing of the events. The accurate dates indicate real events, not legendary myths, as some writers suggest.

Chronology of the Flood

(Dating from the 600th year of Noah, the year of
the ark's completion, which is 1656 years from Adam)

1656, 2nd month, 10th day	Noah begins to board the ark (7:1, 11).
1656, 2nd month, 17th day	The flood begins (7:11).
1656, 3rd month, 26th day	The rains end (7:12).
1656, 7th month, 17th day	The ark lands (8:4).
1656, 10th month, 1st day	The mountain tops are seen (8:5).
1656, 11th month, 11th day	The raven and the dove sent out (8:6-9).
1656, 11th month, 18th day	The dove brings an olive leaf (8:11).
1656, 11th month, 25th day	The dove does not return (8:12).
1657, 1st month, 1st day	Noah removes the covering (8:13).
1657, 2nd month, 27th day	All the ark's occupants disembark (8:14-19).

The Landing on Ararat (vv. 4-5)

As the water level began to decrease, the ark came to rest "on the mountains of Ararat." There is a high mountain known as Mount Ararat on the border between the countries of Turkey and Azerbaijan that is 16,254 feet high. Several sightings of parts of a barge-like structure have been reported on the upper reaches of this glacier-covered mountain. So far, though, hard evidence is not available. Search parties continue to look for it. It should be noted, however, that the text does not say "Mount Ararat" but *mountains* (plural) of Ararat, a country (cf. 2 Kings 19:37; Isa. 37:38; Jer. 51:27). In biblical times the whole area was known as Ararat. Another reason for rejecting Mount Ararat as the site where the ark rested is that it stands alone, not among surrounding mountains, whereas our text says that when Noah looked out of the ark he saw "the tops of [other] mountains." We cannot be certain, therefore, that the present peak named Ararat is the place, although it may be.

When the ark came to rest on solid ground after five months "at sea," there must have been praise and rejoicing among Noah's family members, realizing that the waters were receding and God's promises were being fulfilled. It was gracious of God, indeed, to bring the ark to rest in an elevated spot; its passengers did not have to endure the turbulent sea for any longer than necessary while the water continued to recede. How typical of our God to be so thoughtful!

Note the date of this event. It may be more than mere coincidence that the ark came to rest on the seventeenth day of the seventh month, for it was on that very same day in the Jewish calendar year that the Lord Jesus Christ rose from the dead, having passed through divine judgment. It is in Him that we find our spiritual salvation and "rest."

The Raven and the Dove (vv. 6-12)

After forty more days, Noah released a raven. He must have known of the habits of these birds and used one to his advantage to determine the level of the water as it decreased. The raven, a carrion-eating bird, kept going to and fro and evidently found floating carcasses on which to feed (v. 7). Noah also sent out a dove (v. 8), a bird that lives in the lower lands. When the dove came back to the ark and lit on Noah's outstretched hand, he knew that it had not found place to land; the waters had not receded from the valleys. Seven days later, he released the dove again, and this time the bird returned with an olive leaf in its beak. The leaf would indicate that olive trees were already sending out new shoots. Since the olive tree is a lowland tree and usually domestic, Noah knew that the floodwaters were still going down. When the dove failed to return after another seven days, Noah knew that the earth was habitable again.

The raven and the dove have been used as illustrations of biblical truth. Some see a connection between Noah's dove and the Holy Spirit who descended *like* a dove on the Lord Jesus at His baptism (Mark 1:10). Noah's dove was the harbinger of a new creation; the Holy Spirit's descent on Christ was the harbinger of the new covenant. We sometimes speak of the dove as a symbol of peace, but the dove with the olive leaf in its beak pointed to new life more than it did to peace (v. 11). Others have seen the initial sending out of the raven and the dove as typical of the two natures in the believer. The raven, an unclean bird, was satisfied with carrion (flesh), which pictures the old nature; the dove came back and found rest in the ark (Christ), picturing the new nature.

The End of the Flood (vv. 13-14)

Although the earth was once again habitable, Noah waited another twenty-nine days before he removed the covering (presumably part of the roof) of the ark. But they still did not disembark. The God who shut the door had not opened it. Though he could easily have fretted, Noah seemed content to wait until it was the right time. The earth had not yet sprouted enough new life to support humans, animals, and birds in sufficient numbers. They waited nearly two more months until Noah could see that the vegetation was rejuvenated enough to provide sustenance for all the living creatures. But even then he did not make a move until God spoke.

The New Commission to Noah (vv. 15-19)

At last, one year and seventeen days after Noah had heard God say "Come into the ark, you and all your household" (7:1), he heard God's voice again, saying, "Go out of the ark, you and your wife, and your sons, and your sons' wives" (v. 16). It is interesting that God was still dealing with Noah directly. The other seven members of Noah's family seem to simply have been beneficiaries of God's dealings with him. The whole menagerie of animals and birds were included in God's command, and Noah was told to bring them out with him. God made their going out just as orderly as their going in had been. There was no mad rush for the door. They had waited for the signal from God, and when it came, they went out to the new conditions on the earth. There would never be another ark of that type, nor any need for one.

The command for both man and beast included the same words that God had given in the beginning when they were first created: "Be fruitful and multiply on the earth" (v. 17; cf. 1:22, 28). It was always God's desire to fill His earth with life that would be in submission to Him. It must have been a wonderful moment for Noah to step out of the ark, confident that the God who had commanded him to build it more than one hundred years before was still directing him personally as he began life in a new world. The promise of deliverance from the terrible judgment of the Flood had been fulfilled. The promise of a new life was just beginning.

Noah and his company were immediately obedient to the command of God to leave the ark. Obedience had marked every recorded step of Noah's life thus far (cf. 6:9, 14, 21-22; 7:1-5, 9; 8:16). Obedience is also the mark of a person who loves the Lord Jesus, who said, "He who has my commandments and keeps them, it is he who loves Me" (John 14:21).

Noah Worships God (vv. 20-22)

The first thing Noah did when he disembarked from the ark was to build an altar "to the LORD." This is the first mention in the Bible of an altar, which means "place of sacrifice or slaughter." Although sacrifices had previously been offered to God (such as Cain and Abel's), no mention of using an altar exists. That Noah "built" the altar probably indicates it was made of stones. Noah sacrificed burnt offerings of every clean animal and bird that he had taken with him on the ark. Literally, he gave to God one seventh of all his domestic animals—an act of significant faith on his part, seeing he gave up a considerable portion of a potential food source for his family. Note that he built the altar "to the *LORD*." Noah was responding in appreciation and worship to the One who had kept His promise to preserve him through the Flood.

The term *burnt offering* means that the animals were not only killed, but that they were burned up completely. Smoke ascended into the sky, picturing God's reception and acceptance of the offering. The burnt offering, as later described and commanded in the book of Leviticus, served a different purpose than the sin offering. The burnt offering was all for God; it was the expression of a heart that overflowed with praise and worship. It was also a beautiful expression of the delight God took in the worship of His people, because it looked forward to the willing sacrifice of the Lord Jesus, the One who gave Himself up completely out of obedience to the Father to purchase salvation for mankind. Noah's offering was a pleasing aroma to God that prefigured the Father's delight with the sacrifice of His Son. The phrase "sweet smelling aroma" in reference to acceptable sacrifices is used forty-two times in the Old Testament. In Ephesians 5:2 we read, "Christ also has loved us and given Himself for us, an offering and a sacrifice to God for a sweet smelling aroma."

The whole scene is most instructive. Noah's act of worship pictures three things:

- The wrath of God being appeased through an acceptable sacrifice
- The gratitude of the worshipper to God, who has saved him
- The worshipper's dedication to God, who will care for him in the future

These same three elements are part of the believer's worship as we acknowledge God's grace, offer Him praise and thanksgiving, and commit to live for Him.

God Responds

God was pleased with Noah's act of worship because it was genuine. When it says that "He smelled a soothing aroma," it means that He was satisfied with both the quality of the sacrifice and the dedication of the worshipper. Then

God said in His heart, "I will never again curse the ground for man's sake, although the imagination of man's heart is evil from his youth." The curse mentioned here is not the judgment of the Flood, but the curse of Genesis 3:17, which will prevail until the time of the new earth. The similarity of the language in both cases is convincing. The curse on the ground would not be removed at the time of Noah, but mankind could take comfort that there would never again be universal destruction by flood ("nor will I again destroy every living thing *as I have done,*" emphasis added). The Flood was an unforgettable lesson for all men in every age that sin inevitably brings about God's judgment, but as a means of judgment it would not be repeated. The conditions of the post-flood earth are more fully explained in the next chapter.

The phrase "although the imagination of man's heart is evil from his youth" has puzzled many. It appears at first to be a reason for *judging* the earth rather than a reason for not judging it. But the opposite is so. Man's inclination towards evil is really an occasion for God to display His grace, for it is the grace of God which reaches out to those whose heart is bent to "only evil continually." Grace is grace because it operates against the background of sin; as man is completely unable to save himself (owing to his depraved state), God's grace abounds toward him and enables him to be brought into fellowship with Himself. Even righteous Noah needed, and found, grace in the eyes of the Lord (6:8). Believers today are saved by grace: "By grace you have been saved through faith, and that not of yourselves, it is the gift of God, not of works, lest any man should boast" (Eph. 2:8-9).

The Promise of God

God's wonderful and gracious promise to Noah in verse 22 (that He would never again destroy every living thing by a flood) will last "while the earth remains." However, one day in the future, the "earth and the works that are in it will be burned up" (2 Pet. 3:10). Then, the ground that was cursed will be consumed, and the curse with it. Until that time, however, people will have to deal with the regular cycles of nature and the physical processes associated with them. These include "seedtime and harvest, and cold and heat, and winter and summer, and day and night." The effects of the Flood may well have given rise to new weather patterns such as winds, storms, rain, drought, etc. If the earth had a canopy of water vapor over it before the Flood, the "greenhouse effect" would have provided a worldwide, tropical-type climate. After the Flood, seasonal patterns in the weather came into being that affected the tilling of the ground for food. There would be "seedtime and harvest," a time to plant and a time to reap.

In Conclusion

Chapter 8 has recorded God's dealings with Noah as the floodwater subsided. The ark rested on firm ground, the mountaintops were observed, and the raven and the dove revealed the approaching time suitable for disembarking. Finally the cover was removed, and God commanded them to leave. They found a cleansed world in which to make a new beginning. The key point of the chapter is that God preserved Noah in the ark and "remembered" him in the preparations for a new life. In thanksgiving and dedication, he built an altar to the Lord and offered burnt sacrifices of every clean animal and bird. In his offering, he responded to God's grace and dedicated himself to Jehovah, the covenant-keeping God. God accepted his offering and promised Noah that He would never again destroy the earth by means of a flood.

Noah realized the enormity of man's sin before the Flood. He experienced the wonderful grace of God to cover sin in the present, and believed the promise of God for the future.

God's Covenant with Noah

Noah and his family had just emerged from the ark to start life all over again on the cleansed earth. In chapter 9, God repeats the commandment that He first gave to Adam to be fruitful and to multiply (v. 1; cf. 1:28). In fact, there are a number of common factors in God's dealing with Adam after creation and His dealings with Noah in the post-flood earth. The parallels are easy to see because both Adam and Noah were present at the beginning of a new order in the world; from each of them came everything that followed. No doubt, Moses had these similarities in mind when he wrote the book of Genesis. The chart below lists some of them. Note particularly the last four in relation to our chapter:

Parallels Between Genesis 1 & 2 and Genesis 8 & 9

God sent a wind	1:2	8:1
Waters were separated from land	1:9	8:5
Birds sent out to fly	1:20	8:6
Living creatures of every kind	1:25	8:17
"Be fruitful and multiply"	1:28	8:17; 9:1
Dominion given over animals	1:26, 28	9:2
Food prescribed to eat	1:29-30	9:3
One prohibition on food	2:17	9:5-6

A New Start (vv. 1-7)

This section of God's word to Noah both opens and closes with the repetition of the command to propagate and fill the earth (vv. 1 and 7). God seems to be emphasizing the importance of multiplying and dispersing people over the earth as quickly as possible.

The reason for prioritizing this was probably to provide man with the power to rule over the animal world (v. 2). God was going to instill into every wild beast, bird, and fish, the fear and dread of man to provide protection for man. Wild animals would instinctively shun man's company. It may be that, prior to the Flood, animals had no fear of humans and got out of control. Consequently, they were destroyed along with the people (cf. 6:7). Notice, however, that "cattle" (domestic animals) were excluded from the God-given fear of man, although they were included in other contexts (cf. 1:28; 8:17). These animals would, therefore, be easy to raise and use for food and clothing. God said to Noah, "they are given into your hand" (v. 2). People were free to handle them as they pleased, but always as responsible stewards of God's creation. There is no license given here to abuse animals.

Animals in general would also become food for man (v. 3). Evidently people had been vegetarian up until this time. It is not clear why this change was made. Possibly, God wanted to show man that his life-giving sustenance derived from the death of other living creatures. This would have been a picture of the biblical truth that, ultimately, eternal life would only come through the death of the Seed of the woman. Whatever the reason, God told Noah, "Every moving thing that lives shall be food for you." There were no restrictions. Much later, the nation of Israel's diet was limited to include only those animals considered "clean." However, other people groups were free to eat whatever animals they desired, just as they had been free to eat of the "green herbs" (v. 3; 1:29). Centuries later, the dietary restrictions given under the Old Testament economy were lifted for Jewish believers, and Gentile Christians were assured that they were free from them too (Acts 10:9-16).

The Restriction on Eating Blood

God stipulated one restriction regarding the consumption of meat: "You shall not eat flesh with its life, that is, its blood" (v. 4). In other words, people could eat meat as long as it no longer had blood in it. Blood represents the life, and therefore it is sacred. God, who is the Giver of life, and to whom life belongs, says, "The life of the flesh is in the blood" (Lev. 17:11). Thus, blood—even the blood of animals—was to be treated with great sanctity to show reverence for the life God has created.

Consider the implication of this truth in connection with the modern practice of abortion, in which both the blood and the life of the unborn infant are treated as mere tissue. Consider, too, the value of blood that was shed on the sacrificial altars during the Old Testament period. That blood—animal blood—was accepted by God as a substitute for the life of the guilty sinner until the Lamb of God, the Lord Jesus Christ, "put away sin by the sacrifice of Himself" (Heb. 9:26).

The Blood and Human Government

Because life is precious in the sight of God, there will be a reckoning with Him over the wrongful shedding of blood. In the Mosaic Law, if a beast killed a man, the beast was to be put to death (Ex. 21:28). If a man killed another man willfully, then he too was to be put to death. The word "require" used twice in verse 5 is a judicial term, which carries the idea (in this context) that God is the Judge who exacts a severe penalty for an infraction of His sacred law. The responsibility to enforce this law was given to "every man's brother," although it was God who said, "I will require the life of man" (v. 5). This is, therefore, a command to establish some form of government, a legally constituted authority, to ensure that murderers are apprehended and executed (v. 6). God was delegating the authority for justice over to man. Killing, as an act of justice by civil authority, is not at all the same as murdering a fellow man. It would be understood that the God-given authority to carry out capital punishment, the most severe of penalties, implied the added authority to establish laws and penalties to govern human activity in general.

Before the Flood, when there was no human government, there was no constituted authority to either punish or prevent crime. Thus, the moral condition of people degenerated to the point that God had to judge them all. After the Flood, the principle of human government was established, and it still continues. The Bible does not specify a particular *type* of government, but it does emphasize the *fact* of government. The present dispensation still requires government. Although all governments are imperfect, they are better than no government at all (see Matt. 26:52; Acts 25:11; Rom. 13:4).

The reason why man's blood is even more sacred than that of animals is that he is made in God's image (v. 6; cf. 1:26). Therefore, neither beast nor man was permitted to take man's life. The rightness of capital punishment is not based on the deterrent factor but on the truth of the image of God in man. The section closes with the command to be fruitful and to multiply, repeated for the third time (v. 7; 8:17; 9:1).

God's Covenant with Noah (vv. 8-17)

The Promises of the Covenant

In response to Noah's offering, God made an unconditional promise to him regarding the preservation of people, birds, cattle, and beasts in the post-flood world as representatives of all living creatures born after the Flood (vv. 8-11). It is the first time in Scripture that the word "covenant" is mentioned (the word in Genesis 6:18 being simply a reference to the covenant given here). The word is used seven times in this passage, emphasizing its importance. A biblical *covenant* is a promise made by God and fulfilled by God alone. There are several covenants in Scripture. They climax in the new covenant, which was ratified by the death of the Lord Jesus Christ. In this commentary, we cannot deal with the subject of covenants generally, but a study of them will richly reward the student of the Bible. This covenant is often called the Noahic covenant because it was given to Noah. Its provisions and promises are still in force while "earth remains" with "seed time and harvest" (8:22).

The provisions of the Noahic covenant are mainly described in the previous verses (8:20-9:7). They are given in light of God's judgment in the Flood and Noah's sacrifices of worship and dedication that God accepted (8:20-21). They are also given on the basis of the sanctity of life, the truth of which underlies everything else in the covenant. It can be summarized as follows:

- Life will never again be universally destroyed by a flood (8:21; 9:11).
- Life will be preserved by regular and continuing climatic conditions (8:22).
- Life should be propagated to fill the earth (9:1, 7).
- Animals will live in fear of people and are given to man (9:2).
- Animals are given to humans for food (9:3).
- The life (blood) of animals is not to be eaten (9:4).
- God protects human life by requiring the life of the killer, be it man or animal (9:5).
- Human life is to be protected by human government (9:5).
- Human life is highly valuable because man is made in the image of God (9:6).
- God Himself established the covenant with Noah, his descendants, and the animal world (9:9-10).

The covenant is unconditional: the fulfillment of the promises God made are not dependent in any way on man. God established this covenant without any agreement from man and in spite of the fact that "man's heart is evil from his youth" (8:21). It is, therefore, a covenant of grace. When men and women comply with the provisions of the covenant, they will enjoy the benefits of those provisions. And the beneficiaries are not only people, but also non-rational animals, which shows that the covenant does not have to be understood to be experienced and enjoyed.

The Sign of the Covenant

God gave the rainbow as a visible sign to Noah and his family of His pledge to keep His word (vv. 12-17). A rainbow is an appropriate sign for this covenant in that, like the covenant, God initiated it, and man can do nothing to either create it or destroy it.

Was the rainbow a new phenomenon after the Flood? Most commentators think not. They say that it was just given a new significance at that time. Others contend that it is only the post-flood atmospheric conditions that allow rainbows to be formed. If the second view is correct, this would have been the first rainbow that Noah had ever seen. How much more striking a sight it must have been, if this was indeed its first occurrence! But we cannot be dogmatic.

God also said, "When I bring a cloud over the earth ... I will remember My covenant which is between Me and you and every living creature of all flesh" (vv. 14-15). The phrase "I will remember" echoes the first verse in chapter 8 ("And God remembered Noah," when he was still in the ark). Now God promises to remember His covenant. The great truth here is that God's covenant turns judgment into grace. The storm of the Flood was passed, and the beauty of God's marvelous grace now shone as a confirmation of His promise. The rainbow seen against the cloud is a sign of God's grace breaking in on the darkness of man's sin and being displayed in all its varied beauty. It shows the triumph of grace over sin and judgment. The apostle John observed this symbol of grace surrounding the throne of God in heaven (Rev. 4:3).

In the context of the whole Flood story, the rainbow pictures God's gracious promise to preserve and protect His creation. We, today, should remember this every time we see a rainbow. We should also remember that if we are going to enjoy the beneficial results of the covenant, we, too, should propagate, protect, and preserve life that is so precious to God.

The Last Days of Noah (vv. 18-29)

Chapter 9 ends with the occasion of Noah's drunkenness and nakedness followed by the dishonorable behavior of his son Ham. This relatively minor incident is the setting for Noah's prophetic oracle that was profoundly significant and had far-reaching implications, in that Canaan was cursed, while Shem and Japheth received a blessing. There are some puzzling elements to ponder, but they will be less puzzling if we see them in the larger context of the whole book of Genesis and Moses' purpose in writing it. This passage will emphasize the themes of blessing and cursing, which are recurrent themes in Genesis.

The Sons of Noah

It is fitting that Noah's three adult sons are introduced to the reader at the beginning of this section because the focus now shifts to them. Their names are given in what we may term the usual order: Shem, Ham, and Japheth (cf. 5:32; 6:10; 7:13; 9:18; 10:1). This is probably not their birth order. Ham seems to have been the youngest (9:24), and Japheth, the oldest (10:21). Thus, their birth order was probably Japheth, Shem, and Ham. Concerning Ham, it says, "And Ham was the father of Canaan," a fact that is key to understanding the curse upon Canaan. The three sons are very important because all of humanity has descended from them, as verse 19 indicates. It appears from this statement that, although Noah lived 350 years after the Flood, he had no more sons.

The Drunkenness of Noah

Noah, the man who walked with God so consistently for six hundred years before the Flood, was caught off guard. At least a couple of years must have elapsed since they left the ark, for he had become a farmer, planted a vineyard, harvested the grapes, and made wine. In this incident, Noah, who had been the hero of the Flood, drank too much wine, became drunk, "uncovered himself," and passed out on his bed (vv. 20-21).

The narrative neither specifically condemns nor exonerates Noah. His act was most likely one of self-indulgence. Drunkenness *is* condemned throughout Scripture. It would seem that, after Noah's great personal victories both before and during the Flood, Satan found a weak spot and exploited it. Satan is a like a "roaring lion, seeking whom he may devour" (1 Pet. 5:8). We do well to remember that the believer who thinks he is spiritually strong should "take heed lest he fall" (1 Cor. 10:12).

The Sin of Ham

While Noah was in his drunken sleep, Ham entered the tent and "saw" him there. The word "saw" in this context implies that he gazed at his father with some satisfaction (vv. 22-23). One explanation for Ham's act is that he lusted in a homosexual way after his father, and he may have assaulted him. However, there is no biblical evidence to support this view. It is much more likely that Ham held some kind of resentment against his father and, when he saw his father naked, he rejoiced and tried to get his brothers to join him in dishonoring their father with scorn and merriment. When it says he "told" his brothers it means he took delight in telling them. In Old Testament times, nakedness was a shameful condition. In the Garden of Eden, both Adam and Eve reacted strongly and negatively about their nakedness when they sinned (3:10). Thus it was a terrible dishonor to Noah for Ham to make fun of his nakedness.

Shem and Japheth would not join Ham in reveling in their father's shame. They understood that seeing their father naked would not only be disgusting, but had the potential to feed their sinful nature (cf. Gal. 5:16). So they took a garment and walked backwards into their father's tent so that they could cover him while avoiding seeing him. In doing this, they did the opposite of their brother Ham: they honored their father. Their act is an illustration of the apostle Peter's admonition: "Have fervent love for one another, for 'love will cover a multitude of sins'" (1 Pet. 4:8). They must have sensed that Ham was expressing rebellion against Noah's spiritual leadership and, ultimately, against God. Ham enjoyed his father's failure. It was a flagrant violation of filial honor that God would later stipulate in the fifth commandment, "Honor your father and your mother" (Ex. 20:12). Ham's sin was a serious violation of the authority that God had delegated to the head of the family. Even through Noah's drunkenness was a sin, Ham's sin was far greater, for it revealed a serious character flaw.

The Curse Concerning Canaan

Noah awoke from his sleep to discover from the position of the robe that he had acted shamefully and that someone had intervened. He soon found out what had happened and realized the seriousness of the disgrace that Ham had brought upon him. He then, inspired by the Spirit of God, uttered one of the great messianic prophecies of the Old Testament (vv. 25-27).

There are some remarkable similarities between this prophecy and the ones that God Himself spoke in the Garden of Eden to Adam, Eve, and the serpent

(3:14-19). The first prophecy was given after Adam sinned; this one was given after Noah and Ham sinned. Both Adam and Noah were commanded by God to fill the earth. Each of them was the ancestor of all living people. Both sinned by partaking of a fruit. Each was in a naked state and was provided with a covering by someone else. In both cases, the prophecy that was given included both a curse and a blessing.

Canaan, not Ham

Noah's prophecy concerned his grandson Canaan, the fourth son of Ham (cf. 10:6). We may immediately ask the question: why is Canaan cursed when it was Ham who acted sinfully against Noah? First, observe that the prophecy is looking down through history to future nations, the descendants of the people mentioned; the names of Canaan, Shem and Japheth are all used *representatively* of their descendants. So the reason why Noah cursed Canaan's name may well be because Noah anticipated in Canaan the evil traits that marked his father, Ham. These traits would not be characteristic of all Hamitic people; only of Canaanites, who formed just one of the four branches of Ham's line. When Israel subjugated the Canaanites in the days of Joshua, the prophecy was fulfilled.

We should remember that Moses was writing the Genesis story to encourage the Israelites on their journey through the wilderness to the land of Canaan. God had already told them they would conquer Canaan and destroy its people. The purpose of this prophecy, then, was to give the Israelites confidence to move into Canaan, knowing that God had long ago pronounced judgment on the Canaanites for their moral delinquency. Moses' readers were reminded from Genesis of how God destroyed some of the Canaanites in Sodom with fire and brimstone (Genesis 19). When the Israelites drew nearer to Canaan, Moses warned them of the dangers of the land that were linked with the sin of Ham. He said, "None of you shall approach anyone who is near of kin to him to uncover his nakedness.... Do not defile yourselves with any of these things; for by all these the nations are defiled, which I am casting out before you. For the land is defiled; therefore I visit the punishment of its iniquity upon it" (Lev. 18:6; 24-25). Although the Canaanites, as a nation, were cursed, God did show grace to individuals like the prostitute Rahab and her family in Jericho (Josh. 2:11). Not only that, but Rahab was in the Messiah's ancestral line (Matt. 1:5).

One Race of Men

It should be noted that this curse has often been used to justify the idea that all Hamitic people were destined to become the servants of Japhetic and Semitic people. Nothing could be further from the truth. The issue of distinction between races is actually contradicted by the clear implication in this passage that there is only one race of men—we all come from the family of Noah. Consider

Paul's remarkable statement in Acts 17:26-27: "And He has made from one blood every nation of men to dwell on all the face of the earth, and has determined their pre-appointed times and the boundaries of their habitation, so that they should seek the Lord, in the hope that they might grope for Him and find Him." God's great purpose in creating nations was that they should seek the Lord. It is still true.

The Curse on Canaan

The phrase "a servant of servants" in verse 25 appears only here in the Bible. Its meaning has been much debated. Although both verses 26 and 27 say "and may Canaan be his servant," referencing both Shem and Japheth, there is no historical or biblical record of Canaanites being placed in the most abject form of slavery by their fellow descendants. In point of fact, both the Phoenician and Hittite peoples were descended from Canaan and yet were among the greatest nations in the ancient world. Others have thought that the reference to Canaan applies to all Ham's descendants, especially the black peoples of Africa. However, history has recorded that the Hamitic peoples have been no more in bondage to other people groups than those who came from the lines of Shem and Japheth.

The main intent of the prophecy seems to refer to the time when the Canaanites were enslaved during and after the Israelites' invasion of Canaan under Joshua (cf. 1 Kings 9:20-21). If this interpretation is correct, the prophecy had a specific, rather than a general, fulfillment. Certainly, this prophecy does not deal with the future of the other Hamitic peoples who descended from Canaan's three older brothers. We do know that Ham's descendants became great inventors and technicians. And we also know that millions of them have come into the blessing of salvation in Christ.

The Blessings on Shem and Japheth

Noah turns from Canaan to his son Shem who, along with Japheth, had shown respect for him in his humiliation. Shem's life and character must have demonstrated his faith in God for Noah exclaimed, "Blessed be the LORD, the God of Shem" (v. 26). The use of God's personal, covenant-keeping name indicates that Shem followed God and believed His promises, particularly the promise of the coming Redeemer (3:15). It was through Shem (that is, the Semitic people) that God gave the Scriptures. It was through Shem that God provided the Redeemer, the Lord Jesus Christ. Just as God determined that Messiah would come through Adam's son Seth, so He chose to continue the line through Noah's son, Shem.

Turning now to Japheth, Noah said, "May God enlarge Japheth, and may he dwell in the tents of Shem" (v. 27). Japheth's name actually derives from a word that means "enlarge." It indicates both size and numbers. The Indo-European peoples, as well as the majority of the Oriental people, have come from Japheth's line. Their widespread habitation and huge numbers attest to their enlargement. However, more important is the second phrase, which says that Japheth was to "dwell in the tents of Shem." This expression means to "have fellowship with Shem." In other words, the Japhetic people would enter into the spiritual blessings of the Semitic people, the ones who would bring them the Scriptures and the Redeemer. The prophecy concludes in the same way as the one concerning Shem: "And may Canaan be his servant."

The important thing about the threefold prophecy of curses and blessings is the dominant idea of Canaan's curse and slavery as the background for the invasion of the Israelites under Joshua. When Moses explained it to the Israelites in the wilderness, they would have been encouraged. God brought their forefather Abraham to the land of Canaan. God made them a nation during their many years in Egypt. Now God was going to give them the land of Canaan and, in so doing, take it away from the cursed and sinful Canaanites. In order for the Israelites to receive their blessing, the curse on the Canaanites—whose cup of iniquity was now full—had to be put in force. This is what the Israelites in the wilderness were to clearly understand from these words of Moses.

The Death of Noah

Noah lived 350 years after the Flood, a total of 950 years (vv. 28-29). His age is the third oldest recorded age after Methuselah (969 years) and Jared (962 years). Assuming there are no gaps in the genealogies of Genesis 11, Noah must have lived fifty-eight years into the life of Abraham. We will consider the possibility of gaps in the discussion on that chapter. Noah's death marks the end of one of the greatest human lives ever lived. Consider again the New Testament summary: "By faith Noah, being divinely warned of things not yet seen, moved with godly fear, prepared an ark for the saving of his household, by which he condemned the world and became heir of the righteousness which is according to faith" (Heb. 11:7).

In Conclusion

The conclusion of the Noah story in chapter 9 deals with God's covenant with him concerning post-flood life on earth in light of the fact that human life was sacred and man was made in His image. People were commanded to propagate and fill the earth. Government was to be established to protect life, and the rainbow was given as a sign of God's promise. The chapter records the prophecy of Noah concerning the descendants of his grandson Canaan, whose judgment would be carried out by the Israelites when they invaded Canaan.

Ancient Nations and Their Dispersion

One of the themes of Genesis is that God is going to bless all people on earth through the great promises that He gave to Abraham. The early chapters provide background information to help understand the place of Abraham. Genesis begins with creation, the Fall, the Flood, and how peoples surrounding Abraham came to be what they were *spiritually* and where they were *geographically*. Genesis 10 and 11 explain their geographical dispersion and spiritual decline during the period between the Flood and the call of Abraham. The focus is always toward Abraham, whom God called out from a pagan world and through whom God planned to accomplish His worldwide purpose. Given the context provided by these chapters, the reader will understand the background out of which Abram (his original name) came.

A New Section

Chapter 10 marks the fourth *toledoth* section after creation, and it maintains the orderly progress of the book. It is a description of the peoples and nations that descended from each of Noah's sons (Shem, Ham, and Japheth) and how they were dispersed around the earth until the birth of Abraham (10:1-11:26).

The Importance of the History of Noah's Sons

Many Bible students neglect chapters 10 and 11 because they contain many unfamiliar names and places. However, we shall see that these chapters are significant and strategic to Moses' purpose for writing the whole chronicle. Moses wrote this history for the Israelites in the wilderness to show them how their roots had developed from pagan sources. They would also see the filial connections they had with other people groups and would understand the basic unity of all the peoples of the world. They would perceive that God had chosen them *out* from among the world to be a special people for a special purpose. These chapters of Genesis show that the cradle of civilization was in the Near East and demonstrate the remarkable universal outlook of the Old Testament. It is important that we, too, understand how God moves in history so that we can be assured that the God who has *been* at work is *still* at work. He is, indeed, the God who is sovereign over all.

It should be noted that most of the events listed in chapter 10 actually occurred *after* the events surrounding the tower of Babel in chapter 11. The two chapters are in thematic rather than chronological order (cf. Genesis 1 and 2). Chapter 10 deals with *who* the scattered people were and *where* they went; chapter 11 deals with *why* they were scattered. Chapter 10 speaks of many languages that resulted from God's initiative at Babel (vv. 5, 20, 31). Genesis 11:1 specifically states that the whole earth spoke only one language, a fact that was only true before Babel. The chapter then proceeds to recount how these many languages came into being.

The Genealogy of the Sons of Noah (vv. 1-32)

The Table of Nations

Chapter 10 is often called the Table of Nations. It is based on Noah's prophecy regarding the future of his three sons, and it shows how the prophecies began to be fulfilled. A close look will reveal that it is very carefully arranged. The chapter falls into three parts, each having to do with one of Noah's sons:

- The sons of Japheth (vv. 2-5)
- The sons of Ham (vv. 6-20)
- The sons of Shem (vv. 21-32)

The order (Japheth, Ham, Shem) has to do with how closely their fortunes would be linked to that of the Israelites. Japheth's descendants would have little to do with Israel's history and are described first. Ham's descendants would have much more to do with Israel's future, and are covered next. Shem's descendants were the ancestors of the Israelites, so they were of great importance to Israel. They are dealt with last, this being the most prominent place, and through them the reader is led directly to Abraham.

One more feature of chapter 10 is the parallel construction of each of the three segments concerning Japheth, Ham, and Shem that will be evident if the reader refers to the passages noted. Each segment contains:

- The names of their sons (vv. 2, 6, 21)
- The names of their son's sons (vv. 3-4, 7-19, 23-30)
- A similar inscription about their lands, their languages, their families, and their nations (vv. 5, 20, 31)

Moses used four features—geography, language, genealogy, and politics—as building blocks to describe the early advances of the post-flood world. All of this demonstrates the care with which he arranged the details about the history of real peoples who lived in a real world. It stands in stark contrast to the mythology of many other peoples that is often vague and far removed from reality. Abraham, himself, is a mythological hero figure of other cultures, but the accounts of him in the Bible are the true ones.

Many of the names and places cited in this chapter can still be identified; enough to assure us that names and places we can no longer identify really did exist.

The Descendants of Japheth (vv. 1-5)

The chapter is framed by an introduction in the first verse and a summary conclusion in the final one (v. 32). From verse 2, we learn that Japheth had seven sons: Gomer, Magog, Madai, Javan, Tubal, Meshech, and Tiras. These men became the heads of tribes and nations that then derived their names from them. Frequently, the area where they would settle also assumed that same name.

Thus, Gomer is the name of one of Japheth's sons as well as the name of the tribe that he started and the name of the area where the tribe settled. The name of Gomer was still in use more than one thousand years later (Ezekiel 38:6). Indeed, five of the seven names associated with Japheth's sons are country or place names mentioned in Ezekiel 38. All seven appear to have settled at first in the area of modern-day Turkey and eastward to the Caucasus, that is, between the Aegean and the Caspian Seas.

Of the seven sons of Japheth, two are selected for further attention: Gomer and Javan. Ethnologists believe that Gomer was the progenitor of the Indo-European people, who migrated both northwest into Europe and east into North India. Gomer's three sons are cited (v. 3). His brother Javan was the forefather of the Ionians, or Greeks. Another brother, Madai, is thought to be the ancestor of the Medes, who settled near the Caspian Sea.

The Sons of Ham (vv. 6-20)

Ham had four sons: Cush, Mizraim, Put, and Canaan (v. 6). They became the founders of well-known post-flood civilizations such as Egyptian, Babylonian, Mayan, Aztec and Sumerian. They settled first to the east and south of the Mediterranean Sea, including Arabia, and then moved farther away. It is incorrect to think that the Hamitic peoples can all be classified physically as Negroid. A study of peoples such as the Canaanites mentioned here will confirm this.

Five sons of Cush and two of his grandsons are listed in verse 7. In verse 8, Cush's sixth son, Nimrod, is listed separately. Some interesting and enlightening facts about him are added in verses 9, 10, and 11. Nimrod was a very well known figure in the mythologies of the Middle East. Cush named him Nimrod, which means "let us rebel," probably to indicate Cush's own attitude toward God at the time. Nimrod seems to have been trained to plan an organized rebellion against God and His purposes. Unlike the rest of Cush's sons, Nimrod's descendants settled in the Tigris-Euphrates valley and stayed there even after the confusion of tongues.

Nimrod, the Mighty One

Nimrod is described as "a mighty one on the earth" (v. 8). As a tyrant, he would have influenced many others to follow him in his rebellious ways. He is also described as a "mighty hunter before the LORD" (v. 9). This phrase could mean that he was a hunter of wild animals, but more likely it means that he was skillful in coercing people to acknowledge him as their imperial leader in rebellion, or "in the face of," the Lord. Note the word used—LORD—is the covenant name for God. The negative context of its use here may indicate his hatred for the covenant promises of God.

Extra-biblical sources indicate that Nimrod was also known as Marduk, and that his wife's name was Semeramis. When he died, she claimed to bear a child without a father, whom she named Tammuz. It was the beginning of the "Mother and Child" cult as the central point of the religion of Babylon, which became the mother of all false religions. It may have been an attempt by Satan to preempt the virgin birth of the Seed of the woman with a false substitute. The theme of Babylonian false religion runs all through Scripture from Genesis to Revelation. It culminates in Revelation 17 and 18, in which Babylon and its false worship are described as the "mother of harlots." Just as Babylon reaches its pinnacle of power, it will be destroyed by Christ coming in power and glory against the backdrop of the triumphant singing of the "Hallelujah Chorus" (Revelation 19).

The Beginning of Babylon

Nimrod lived in Babel, the original capital of the land of Shinar (also known as Sumeria), the area that included the surrounding cities of Erech, Accad, and Calneh (v. 10; cf. Dan. 1:2). Nimrod extended his influence northwards up the Tigris River to the land of Assyria and built Nineveh, Rehoboth, Ir, and Calah. Nineveh later became the capital of the great Assyrian Empire. Nimrod was actively involved in false religion and political exploitation. The Holy Spirit inspired Moses to include this information here because both Babylon and Assyria would become the political enemies of Israel from the time of Solomon to the Exile (vv. 10-12).

Egypt and Philistia

The second son of Ham who is brought to our attention is Mizraim (vv. 6, 13-14), the founder of Egypt. The original word commonly translated "Egypt" in the Bible is Mizraim. Egypt, to the southwest of Israel, became another powerful nation and was also one of Israel's long-term enemies. The Philistines, another inveterate enemy of Israel, are mentioned in verse 14.

The Sons of Canaan (vv. 15-20)

The youngest son of Ham was Canaan, whose descendants would occupy the land of Canaan that Israel invaded in about 1405 BC. His son Sidon was the father of the Phoenicians, who lived to the north of Canaan. Heth was the father of the Hittites, who settled farther to the north (v. 15). His other sons gave names to the Canaanite tribes that were occupying the land of Canaan when the Israelites arrived. These names were associated with the curse on Canaan, and the Israelites would gain from this insight a better understanding of the mission and destiny that God had given them. Then, it says, "the families of the Canaanites were dispersed" (v. 18). We do know that the Hittites went north to establish a powerful kingdom in what we call Turkey today. The general borders of the Canaanites lands were also listed, from Sidon in the north to Gaza in the south (v. 19).

The Sons of Shem (vv. 21-32)

The genealogy of Shem's sons begins with a description of Shem as "the father of all the children of Eber." Many commentators believe that Shem provided this section of Genesis. He lists himself last because he knew from Noah's prophecy that the knowledge of God was to be transmitted through his line. He lists his descendants to the fifth generation, probably because he had more knowledge of them. By contrast, Ham's genealogy extends only to the third generation, and Japheth's, to the second. Five sons of Shem are listed, plus seven grandsons, one of whom was Eber. His name comes from a root word meaning "to cross over" and was probably so-named because he came from beyond the Euphrates. The term *Hebrew* was derived from his name. From his line, several generations later, came the patriarch "Abram the Hebrew."

The Dividing of the Earth in the Days of Peleg

One of Eber's sons of special interest was Peleg, because "in his days the earth was divided." The phrase must refer to a significant happening, for his is the only one of more than eighty names in this chapter whose meaning is given in the text. Peleg's name means "division," and of course the question arises as to what kind of division is meant when "the earth was divided." Some commentators contend that it has to do with the division of the peoples of the earth that resulted from the confusion of languages as given in chapter 11. They point to another reference to division in verse 5 where the "peoples of the Gentiles were separated [divided], everyone according to his own language" and to verse 32 where "the nations were divided on the earth after the flood." In both verses, however, a different word is used from the one in verse 25.

Other commentators think that the reference is to the land being divided by what we now call the continental drift. From the time of creation, there was one great landmass (1:19). After the Flood, the earth's crust may have adjusted itself by the drift of the continents. Look at any world map and notice how the continents seem to "fit" together. The drift was probably rapid at first, then it gradually slowed to its present almost insignificant pace. Neither theory can be proved at this point.

Settling of Arabia

Peleg's brother Joktan had thirteen sons, who are listed (vv. 26-30). Every one of them appears to have settled in Arabia, mostly in the south in modern-day Yemen. Shem's family is summarized in verse 31 just as Japheth's was in verse 5 and Ham's was in verse 20. Note, again, that all three of these verses refer to distinct languages and therefore to a time after the occasion of the building of the tower of Babel.

In Conclusion

The last verse in this chapter summarizes the families of the sons of Noah from which emerged the ancient nations. Twenty-six of them came from Shem, thirty from Ham, and fourteen from Japheth—seventy in all. This chapter has provided some important insights. First, it has shown the unity of the human race. Second, it has demonstrated how reliable the Bible is; its historical data is increasingly confirmed to be true by recent findings in linguistics, anthropology and archeology. Third, it sheds light on a period of history between the time of the Flood and the time of Abraham. Fourth, it provides a good illustration of the hand of God at work among the nations, even though they have since been scattered and fragmented.

The Tower of Babel

Anarchy and rebellion against God marked the world before the Flood. After the Flood, Noah's family made a fresh start. His three sons and their wives produced sons who became the heads of family clans, and these clans grew into nations. In this chapter, we learn *why* the dispersion of the people took place much earlier than would have happened naturally. The spirit of rebellion against God soon reared its ugly head, and within one hundred years evil leaders organized a united rebellion against God. In response, God stopped their rebellion by confusing their language. Groups speaking one language were unable to communicate to groups speaking another language. The result was their separation from one another and the frustration of their rebellion.

The chapter can be divided into three parts. The first nine verses conclude the *toledoth* section called "the genealogy of the sons of Noah" (10:1–11:9). They show clearly that the fresh start after the Flood soon ended in rebellion and judgment at Babel. The second part of the chapter is a short section called "the genealogy of Shem" (vv. 10-26). It enlarges on the descendants of Noah's son Shem and leads to the birth of Abram, whom God chose to be the patriarch of the Hebrew people. The last few verses of the chapter introduce a much longer *toledoth* called "the genealogy of Terah" (11:27–25:11). It prepares the reader for the story of Abraham by explaining the circumstances of his birth, the removal of the family to Haran on the way to Canaan, and the death of Terah.

Genesis 11 is clearly transitional, bridging the gap between God's worldwide judgment at Babel and His grace to His chosen servant, Abraham. It narrows the Genesis story from dealing with the people of the whole earth to dealing with the one man through whom the Redeemer would come.

Themes in Genesis 11

This chapter demonstrates once again that fallen man tends to dethrone God and exalt himself. It illustrates the spirit of worldliness that results from leaving God out of the equation of life. When this happens, man strives to be his own master, allowing the lust of the flesh, the lust of the eyes, and the pride of life to guide his way (1 John 2:15-16). Worldliness is opposed to godliness, and we should pay close attention to this illustration of Babel.

We learn here of the origin of the city of Babylon that is symbolic of man's opposition to God throughout the Bible. It was at Babylon that man turned away from the eternal God to form his own religions that have continued throughout history (Isa. 47:8-13). Babylon is the *city of man* in contrast to Jerusalem, the *city of God*. And so it will continue until the last days. It was Babylon that destroyed Jerusalem and took the Jews into exile in 586 BC. During that time, Babylon continued to persecute God's people (Dan. 3:1-30). And Babylon will be the capital of Antichrist in the last days (Rev. 17:1–18:24). But at that time, both the city and all that it stands for will be destroyed when the mighty angel cries, "Babylon the Great is fallen," and the answering chorus of a multitude in heaven sings, "Alleluia! For the Lord God Omnipotent reigns!" (Rev. 18:2; 19:6).

The chapter also teaches that God is sovereign in the affairs of the world. He did not then—and never will—hand over His control to the designs of unruly and ungodly men. At exactly the right moment, He intervened to accomplish His own purpose. Just as His sovereignty was demonstrated in His dealings concerning the judgment of the Flood, so it is demonstrated in His dealings with the wicked people of Babel.

The Decision to Build the Tower (vv. 1-4)

The date of Babel and related events is not absolutely certain, but many scholars place it about 2240 BC. It may be that there are gaps in the genealogical record, in which case the period between the Flood and Babel would have been considerably longer than we can assume if we add up the dates given in the biblical text. If no allowance is made for gaps, then it occurred about one hundred years after the Flood. This means that Noah would have been alive during the building of Babel and its tower (because he lived for 350 years after the Flood). Assuming he was still alive, we can only wonder why the Scripture is silent as to any part he might have played in resisting the rebellion.

Noah's sons and their descendants spoke the only language there was (v. 1). The word "speech" is literally "lip" and means that they had one vocabulary, one set of words. That original language may have been Semitic (like Hebrew and Arabic), because the names and places mentioned before Babel have meanings in Hebrew and related Semitic languages. Some have thought that perhaps Shem did not participate in the rebellion of Babel, and for that reason his language was not "confused."

As the population grew, the people moved "eastward." Our text says "from the east," but most commentators believe that "eastward" is to be preferred. The main point is that they came to the land of Shinar and settled there (v. 2). Shinar is the fertile plain in the lower Tigris-Euphrates valley. With productive farming, it was not long before the abundant food supplies gave them time and opportunity to develop urban communities with permanent public buildings— even walls—to protect themselves from large wild animals.

Such public building projects would have necessitated the unified cooperation of the people with the emerging leadership. The Bible indicates that Nimrod had become an outstanding figure—a "mighty one in the earth" as well as a "mighty hunter before [or in the face of] the LORD" (10:9). In all probability, it was he who rose to prominence in Shinar and chose to centralize power under his leadership, rather than "multiply and fill the earth" as God had commanded. With Babylon under his control, he added to his empire the cities of Erech, Akkad, and Calneh, south of Babylon (10:10). He then moved northward to control three other cities (10:11). We conclude that Satan motivated Nimrod to build his capitol at Babel, from which he hoped to rule the world. Inspired by Nimrod's leadership, the people said, "Come let us make bricks ... come let us build ourselves a city and a tower" (vv. 3-4). It was man's first attempt at world government. Nimrod lived until 2230 BC, ten years after the probable year of the confusion of tongues in 2240 BC.

The tower was to be the central point of their city. It was very likely in the form of a stepped pyramid called a *ziggurat,* several of which have been unearthed in the area. A temple and an astrological observation platform were usually built at the top. (Some of the ziggurats unearthed in recent times have the signs of the Zodiac engraved on them.) Nimrod's tower was probably like this. The phrase "whose top is in the heavens" (v. 4) does not mean that the tower was so high it would reach heaven, but that the zodiacal signs of the heavens were inscribed in the temple at its top. It was here that the leaders practiced occult astrology. The building of the tower signified the peoples' anti-God purposes.

The Purposes of the Tower of Babel

Romans 1:18-32 is a commentary on the downward path taken by humankind at the time of Babel. The rebels wanted to build a city, which may sound innocent enough, but it was a city not centered on the Lord. Rather, it was modeled after the city of Cain (4:17). It symbolized man organizing himself independently of God. They said, "Let us make a name for ourselves." Thus the first purpose was for *human independence* of God.

The second purpose was *false religion*. To have its "top is in the heavens" sounds spiritual, but their astrology was a man-made religion that replaced the worship of the one true God. Instead of looking to Him for guidance and bringing sacrifices to Him, they consulted their priests who were experts in pagan astrology. They were trusting in whatever occult (that is, hidden) knowledge the astrologers might gain from their observations of the stars. It was false religion, because although they might claim that the wisdom came from God, its true source was the evil one. God originally created those constellations to be "for signs" (1:14), which may well have been symbolic representations of the coming Seed of the woman, the Redeemer. The symbolism spoke of His suffering and future glory. But these false priests were purporting to use the constellations to tell the future. They twisted the original meanings concerning Messiah and maintained that the movements of the stars taught the future of nations and kings. Of course, in order to gain control of the people, the occult priests claimed that only they were able to interpret the meanings.

The third purpose for the tower was for *human honor* in the place of God's honor. They said, "Let us make a name for ourselves," a motto echoed by much of humanity throughout history. They were not interested in honoring the living God, but rather of gaining recognition for themselves and attention from others. The incongruity between the stated religious purpose for the tower and the intention of the builders to make a name for themselves is obvious.

People had departed a long way from great Noah, who built an altar, brought sacrifices, and worshiped God. Like Eve in the Garden of Eden, they were listening to the subtle voice of the serpent. Once again, Satan was tempting people to be like God, and once again they fell into his trap. The people did not want to "be scattered abroad over the face of the whole earth." They disdained God's commandment to "fill the earth," believing it to be neither wise nor right.

In doing so, they rejected God. In rebellion, they turned to *human unity*, the fourth purpose, as a way to fill the void. They were not afraid of inculcating wrong doctrine or of disobeying God. Their primary fear was disunity. Their sin was not in building the city or the tower, but in attempting to unite and live together in rebellion against God. They saw power in unity and were determined to achieve it on their terms—even at the cost of God's favor, truth, and righteousness. They seemed to discount the possibility that God might judge them. Human power structures like theirs are still common in our world, and the pressure is on many of God's people to join them at the expense of truth. That, we dare not do.

God's Response to Their Arrogance (vv. 5-9)

During Nimrod's rebellion in Babel, the "Lord came down to see the city and the tower." This does not mean that the Lord did not know what was going on until He "came down" from heaven to inspect the activities of man. Anthropomorphic language is being used here to speak of God in humanly-understandable terms. God is omniscient and always aware of everything that is going on. The point here, is that God took judicial notice of the pursuit of man in building the tower and the city with a view to doing something about it. Perhaps the builders thought God would take no notice—if so, they were wrong.

The Lord made three observations. First, He observed their unity and their common language. These factors would allow their false religion to flourish. Second, He saw the building of the city and the tower. These were just the initial results of their rebellious ideas; similar projects would surely follow. Third, if they continued, "nothing that they propose to do will be withheld from them." The religious leaders may have been on the verge of discovering satanic secrets through astrology, or of using their unity, language, and satanic involvement to accomplish other things that God would not tolerate. They had arrogantly boasted in their ability, and God took their arrogance seriously.

The people had made an evil resolution: "Come, let us build ourselves a city, and a tower" (v. 4). Using the same terminology, God declared "Come, let Us go down and there confuse their language." God was not the slightest bit threatened by them or their plans, but He jealously guards His deity and will not allow anyone else to infringe on it. So God directly opposed their scheme. It is ironic that, no matter how high they built their tower, God still had to "come down" to see it. Notice, also, that God referred to Himself as "Us," as if He called a council among the persons of the Godhead. God's *let Us* is in contrast to the *let us* voiced three times by the people: "Let us make bricks.... let us build ourselves a city .... let us make a name for ourselves" (vv. 3-4).

We cannot be sure as to exactly when God intervened. It would appear that, even if the tower was finished, the building of the city was not, as verse 8 states that they "ceased building the city." It makes sense that God intruded when they began their pagan worship in the temple at the top of the tower. God saw the potential of spiritual calamity for the whole human population, so He took steps to prevent it.

The Confusion of Languages

It is not hard to imagine all the chaos in and around Babel when God confused their language. People suddenly found it impossible to understand one another and were, themselves, unable to be understood. Presumably, individual families and clans still had uniform languages and were able to communicate among themselves. But life would never be the same again. The omnipotent God changed everything. The building of the city obviously could not continue. Business could no longer be conducted. Government was brought to a standstill. And—most important of all—the practice of their pagan and occult religion was stopped.

The People were Scattered

The people could not continue to live in a cooperative, urban community. There was no alternative but for each language group to move out to a rural setting where they could farm and raise animals to provide for the basic necessities of life. In one masterstroke, God put an end to their evil plans, rebellious activities, and urban community and gave them no choice but to do what He had previously commanded. The scattering that they had feared most (v. 4) became their only option.

God observed their common language and their unity, and His response embraced both (v. 6). In response to their language, He confused their speech. In response to their unity, He scattered them "over the face of all the earth." By doing this, God removed what they intended to be the capstone of primeval history. With the scattering the unified history of people on earth came to an end. From this point forward, the narrative of Scripture focuses on only one people group—the descendants of Abraham—and the blessing that comes through them to the whole world.

The Name of the City

"Therefore it is called Babel." *Babel* means "gate of God," which seems to be the name by which it was known when Nimrod was leading the rebellion. By using that name, people were led to believe in its spirituality. There is, however, a play-on-words in verse 9. Babel is similar in sound to the Hebrew word "balel," which means "confused." So the thought is that, following the confusion of the language, it was appropriately called Babel, because God created a "babble" of the languages of all the earth. The *gate of God* was turned into the *confusion of men*. It was "from there," from the place of unity, that they were forced to scatter. They left the city with their dream unfulfilled. Later, it was inhabited by descendants of Shem and called Babylon.

The Multiplication of Languages

Ever since Babel, the language barrier has continued to be a dividing factor in the world. We do not know how many resulted from God's initiative at Babel, but there are roughly three thousand languages in the world today. There is a coming future day, however, when the confusion caused by multiple languages will be done away. The prophet says, "Then I will restore to the peoples a pure language, that they all may call on the name of the LORD" (Zeph. 3:9). Although distinct nations will still exist, the language barrier will be eliminated. On the day of Pentecost, visitors to Jerusalem experienced a foretaste of this when a number of language groups all heard the message of the gospel in their own tongue (Acts 2:6-11).

The Genealogy of Shem (vv. 10-26)

Although this passage contains some of the same information as the Table of Nations in chapter 10, it serves a much different purpose. The Table of Nations explains the general development of civilization in the ancient world. The genealogy of Shem prepares us for the call of Abram, one of Shem's descendants, and is the fifth *toledoth* section.

This small section is simply a genealogy that traces the ancestry of Abram through ten generations back to Shem. That connection becomes most important in the fulfillment of the promise of the coming Seed of the woman. The initial promise was given to Adam and Eve (3:15). It was enlarged upon through the revelation given to Noah concerning Shem (9:26). It will be further expanded in the promise given to Abram (12:1-3). It is a remarkable fact, that the book of Genesis records the names of virtually every person in Messiah's line covering more than two thousand years from Adam to Abram.

It may also be of interest to compare this genealogy with the genealogy of Genesis 5, which traces the line through ten generations from Adam to Noah. Every generation mentioned there, with the exception of Enoch, ends with the phrase "and he died." The emphasis in that chapter is that death ruled the human race. The generations listed in Genesis 11 also died, but their deaths are not stated. The emphasis is different here. It begins with Shem, who was blessed after the Flood (9:26), and ends with Abram, who was both the object and the means of blessing. These ten generations comprise the line through which the blessing came and which was prospered by God's grace.

Three Common Questions

Concerning the genealogy of Shem, there are several commonly asked questions. The first is the issue of why the longevity of the ancients declined after the Flood. Noah died at age 950, whereas Shem lived for only six hundred years, Arphaxad for 438 years, and Terah, the father of Abram, for only 205 years (cf. v. 32). Some have speculated that shortened life spans resulted from increased solar radiation after the Flood, which was, in turn, brought about by the loss of the supposed vapor canopy over the earth. Whatever the reason, we can be sure that the information given in Scripture is accurate.

The second question is a textual one relating to why the genealogy in Luke 3:36 includes the name of Cainan between Arphaxad and Shelah (or Salah). If this name belongs there, then it must have been left out of the Genesis 11 lists. The name is found in some (but not the oldest) manuscripts of the Septuagint (the Greek translation of the Old Testament) that Luke may have referred to when writing his gospel. Nevertheless, the name Cainan does not appear in Genesis 10:24, nor in Genesis 11 or 1 Chronicles 1:18. The most likely explanation is that it was a copyist error in Luke 3. The name properly occurs in verse 37 between Enos and Mahalalel and may have been inserted by a careless copyist in Luke 3:36.

The third question concerns the time between the Flood and Babel. Was there enough time for the population to grow to satisfy the requirements of the Babel story? It is best to take the biblical record from Shem to Terah as literal and complete. To the knowledge of this writer, there is no biblical support for the view that there are gaps in the genealogies. Archeologists who tend to base their theories on dating methods and not on Scripture insist that man is much older than the Bible indicates. But any alleged gaps need to be shown to be consistent with the biblical revelation, not vice versa.

This short section ends with the births of Terah's three sons: Abram, Nahor, and Haran (v. 26).

The Genealogy of Terah (vv. 27-32)

The next section is called the "genealogy of Terah" and continues through Genesis 25:11. It would seem that, at some point, Shem passed on to Abram the data he had written on cuneiform tablets together with the records that he had obtained from the pre-flood ancients through Noah. Shem may have sensed that the promise of the Seed would come through Terah, or he may have even heard that God had called Abram. From the biblical text we can deduce that Abram lived 150 years concurrently with Shem.

The section begins, "This is the genealogy of [or, what became of] Terah," which the reader will now recognize as the beginning of a new section, according to the pattern of the book. This long section will embrace the whole life of Abraham. It contains the promise of the blessing to Abraham and to his seed. It is the pivotal section of the whole book of Genesis. It will emphasize the development of the purposes of God concerning the land and the seed. It begins with the last five verses of Genesis 11, where the relationships within the family of Terah are explained. The importance of this will become clear when we consider the marriages of Abraham's son Isaac and his grandson Jacob.

We are introduced to Terah's three sons: Abram, Nahor, and Haran (v. 27). From this family will come the three patriarchs and their wives. Verse 26 indicates that Abram was born when Terah was seventy years old. The names of Haran and Nahor are associated with cities in the Euphrates valley (24:10; 28:10). Haran died in the city of Ur in the lower Euphrates area. Haran's son Lot stayed with Terah's family and, presumably, Abram became his guardian. Lot will become a significant figure in later events in the life of Abraham. Haran's daughter Milcah married her uncle Nahor. Their son Bethuel was the father of Rebekah and Laban, both of whom we shall meet in connection with Isaac and Jacob. Nothing further is said of Haran's other daughter, Iscah. Abram married Sarai, who we later find out was his sister (20:12). Close marriages such as Abram and Nahor's were not uncommon in those early days, nor frowned upon. The inherent genetic dangers of such marriages that we fear today did not exist then. The one thing we learn about Sarai is that she was barren; she bore no children in either Ur or the city of Haran. Terah, Nahor, and Abram were all idol worshippers, as Joshua makes clear (Josh. 24:2).

The Lineage of Terah

Terah		
Haran + (?)	Nahor + (?)	Abram + (Sarai)
Iscah, Lot, Milcah	Bethuel	
	Laban, Rebekah	Isaac + (Rebekah)
	Leah, Rachel	Jacob + (Leah & Rachel), Esau

The Journey to Haran

After Haran died in Ur, Terah left the city accompanied by Abram, Sarai, and Lot. Ur was a well-known and highly civilized city. It had a famous library and was so large that archeologists are still investigating the ruins of its walls and public buildings. Terah may have received some kind of direction from the Lord, for he seems to have taken the lead. The record says that he "took his son Abram and his grandson Lot ... and his daughter-in-law Sarai, his son Abram's wife, they went out with them from Ur of the Chaldeans to go to the land of Canaan" (v. 31). We also know, however, that Abram himself received a definite call from God while still in Ur. Stephen (the first Christian martyr), under the inspiration of the Holy Spirit, spoke of it in his great speech to the Sanhedrin council in Jerusalem. He said, "The God of glory appeared to our father Abraham when he was in Mesopotamia, before he dwelt in Haran, and said to him, 'Depart from your country and from your relatives, and come to a land that I will show you'" (Acts 7:2-3). Abram "went out, not knowing where he was going" (Heb. 11:8). Abram's response to God's call is a great example of a person who clearly senses God's direction in his life and takes a giant step of faith in obedience to it.

The party traveled north along the Euphrates River past Babylon until they reached the city of Haran, about halfway from Ur to Canaan. There they stopped and "dwelt" for about twenty-five years. Haran is identified with a site north of the Euphrates River that was not on the usual route to Canaan. The site today is in southeastern Turkey. Terah and Abram knew from the beginning that Canaan was their destination. As to why they stopped in Haran for an extended period is not as clear. Possibly, Haran was their ancestral home. Terah was now well up in years and may not have wished to travel farther. Whatever the reason, Terah and his family stayed in Haran until he died at the age of 205 (v. 32).

In Conclusion

Genesis 11 is a pivotal chapter. It records how the people in the land of Shinar built their city and tower in rebellion against God's command to multiply and fill the earth. The Lord stopped them by confusing their language and thus ensured their scattering. It follows the line of Shem through the generations to Abram, establishing Abram's Semitic roots. Finally, it tells of Abram and Sarai's marriage, their childlessness, and their move from Ur to Haran on their way to Canaan. It sets the stage for the Lord to bring Abram into the land of promise and give him a son who would be in the line of the promised Seed of the woman.

The Call of Abram

The first eleven chapters of Genesis have described the history of the world, from creation to the formation of the nations. Up to this point, Genesis has, in narrative form, explained why God's intervention on behalf of man was so desperately needed (chapters 3-11). Men rebelled against God and proved utterly incapable of living peaceably with Him or with one another. Events surrounding the Fall, the Flood, and Babel clearly demonstrated man's sinful nature. God now unfolds His plan to bring a Savior into the world through whom man could be reconciled to Himself.

Beginning with chapter 12, the historical perspective narrows to just one man—Abraham—whose biography occupies the next fourteen chapters. This fact alone should impress us with the importance God places on him. In fact, in the scheme of Genesis, the whole scope of history from Adam to this point is really an introduction to Abraham and his very significant place in biblical history. It is through Abraham that two key ideas of Genesis are developed. The first is *the promised seed,* that is, the ancestral line from Adam to the chosen people and from them on to the Messiah. The second is *the promised land,* the region God selected for His chosen people that would ultimately be the location on earth of the kingdom over which Messiah would rule.

The Significance of Abraham to the Israelites

Abraham was described by Isaiah as a "rock" from which the nation of Israel was hewn (Isa. 51:1). He was the original ancestor of the family clan from which they as a nation had developed while in Egypt, so his story was especially important to that generation. Just as Abraham (originally an idol-worshiper according to Joshua 24:2) had been called by God to "get out" of his homeland and go to Canaan, so the Israelites had to "get out" of the land they had called "home" for many years and go to Canaan. God revealed to Abraham that the nation he would father would be God's very own people. They would inherit the land of Canaan and be the recipients of special blessings in the future. They were now on the doorstep of entering into the promises God had made to Abraham. Moses knew that if God had been faithful to their father Abraham, then He would be faithful to them, too. Thus Moses presents this account of Abraham's life to encourage them to claim God's promises.

The Israelites were not the only ones destined to learn from Abraham's story. Just as Abraham was also Israel's *spiritual* father—their example of how to live by faith—so every believer is a spiritual child of Abraham and has the opportunity to exemplify his faith. Every true believer needs to get out of the grip of the world and into the sphere of God's blessing and promise.

Abraham the Patriarch

Abraham was the first of three *patriarchs* whose biographies form the rest of the Genesis narrative. The patriarchs were Abraham, Isaac, and Jacob. Abraham's original name was Abram (17:5). He could trace his lineage for two thousand years, directly back to Adam. Several hundred years before, Noah had prophesied that God's original promise to Adam and Eve would be fulfilled through his son Shem (9:25-27; cf. 3:15). Abram was the tenth generation in Shem's line, and it was to him that God revealed the next great block of truth in redemption history. To properly understand salvation history, it is important for us to get a good grasp on these promises and their fulfillment.

Abraham's importance to us is reflected in four significant areas:

- He is the great example of *the life of faith.* In the record of the heroes of faith in Hebrews 11, more space is devoted to Abraham's faith than to that of any other person.

- Abraham's right standing before God became the New Testament example of *the truth of justification* (see Romans 4).

- The covenant promises God made with Abraham are of crucial importance in understanding *the doctrine of future things* in the Bible, especially concerning the nation of Israel.

- Abraham is an example of the fact that individual people can have *a personal relationship with God.* Abraham was known as the "friend of God." King Jehoshaphat reminded God in prayer that Abraham was "Your friend forever" (2 Chron. 20:7). Isaiah assured the people that they were special because they were descended from "Abraham My friend" (Isa. 41:8). James tells us that the reason Abraham was called the "friend of God" is because he believed God. (James 2:23).

Abraham's Seed

In the study of Abraham we notice that his descendants are called his "seed." It is well to keep in mind the three ways by which the seed of Abraham is described in the Bible:

- His natural descendants through his son Isaac are called seed, and they still claim that identity four thousand years later. Almost no other people group can claim with any certainty an ancestor who lived that long ago. The Jews are the natural seed of Abraham.

- His spiritual descendants—those who are justified (in right standing) with God by faith in the same way that Abraham was justified by faith— are called his seed (Gal. 3:29).

- One particular descendant, the Lord Jesus Christ, is also called Abraham's seed (Gal. 3:16). The very first prophecy in the Bible proclaimed that the "Seed of the woman" would triumph over Satan (3:15).

We will see in Genesis that some of the promises made about Abraham's seed concern his natural seed and have to do with those who are ethnic Jews descended from him (12:7). Other promises are concerned with Abraham's spiritual seed, that is, those believing Gentiles and Jews who follow his example of being justified by faith.

God Calls Abram (v. 1)

The first few verses of this chapter are key in Genesis. They explain the purposes that God was going to accomplish through Abram. They explain the beginning of the nation of Israel as a worshiping community and as the channel through which the Savior would come.

We learned from chapter 11 that Terah took Abram, Sarai, and Lot from their home in Ur (in the lower Euphrates Valley) to Haran (in what is today southeastern Turkey). Haran lay about half way between Ur and the land of Canaan, not by the shortest route, across desert, but along the trade route of the time, known as the Fertile Crescent. The first four verses of Genesis 12 seem to explain what God had previously said. "Now the Lord had said to Abram: Get out of your country … to a land that I will show you." The original text does not, however, include the word *had* and simply says, "Now the Lord said to Abram…." We understand that this was his second call; it came after Terah died (Acts 7:4). The Bible does not say why Abram did not go all the way to Canaan when he was first called. Perhaps he stayed in Haran to settle family affairs, or perhaps Terah became ill and Abram did not want to leave him. It says that he "dwelt" or settled there, which indicates that he broke or delayed his journey for a time (11:31).

If Abram's stay in Haran was a delay in his obedience to God's previous command, it was really disobedience, or at the least incomplete obedience. Many believers are also guilty of going part way in following the Lord or fully carrying out his commands. Some are delayed by business, some by pet sins, some by material things, some by family pressure, some by fear of the unknown. Perhaps the Lord Jesus was thinking of Abram when He challenged one of His followers with the cost of discipleship. When the man said, "Lord, let me first go and bury my father," Jesus answered him, "Follow Me, and let the dead bury their own dead" (Matt. 8:21-22). Jesus was making the point that a true disciple will follow Him at any cost, no matter what. Someone has well said, "Obedience is only obedience when it is immediate and complete." Abram was to put his faith in God and then act on it. We, too, should be careful not to come to the end of our lives and regret our partial obedience.

The Command to Get Out (vv. 1-3)

The call to Abram involved two commands, each of which was linked to three wonderful promises from God. Note that God's covenant keeping name of LORD is used, implying that God could be trusted to fulfill these promises. The first command was "Get out of your country." God's commands are not always easy to follow, and this one was no exception. The faith required was staggering. Faith, from this point on, became the great principle of Abram's life. But an even greater challenge to his faith was in the fact that God did not reveal where he was to go. He simply said, "to a land that I will show you."

Thus, Abram had to leave three things, each of which was increasingly dear to him: his country, his relatives, and his father's house. It was to be separation from every aspect of the old life as a necessary condition of blessing. He had to totally abandon all that had been significant to him, and he had to do it not knowing what was coming next, trusting in God alone for an unknown future. Because the environment in both Ur and Haran was not conducive to spiritual growth, he had to get out. His obedience by faith is an example for us who are called upon to believe God and obey Him, even when we do not understand all the implications.

The Promise of Nationhood

God now announced three promises that were dependent on Abram obeying God's call (v. 2). The first was that God would make of him a great nation. That is, his descendants would multiply to become a nation and would take their place among the nations of the world. We know that nation as Israel today, and although small in size, it is one of the top ten military powers in the world. This early promise of becoming a great nation was especially important to the Israelites in the wilderness. It would remind them that God had been true to His promise made to Abram hundreds of years earlier. Under Moses' leadership, they were on their way to Canaan to possess the very land God had promised to Abram. What an encouragement for the Israelites! But to Abram's faith, the promise that his descendants would reach the status of nationhood was a stretch—he was seventy-five years old, he had no children, and his wife was barren (11:30).

The Promises of Blessing and a Great Name

The second promise was that God would bless him; He would shower him with favor. The word "blessing" is key and occurs five times in these three verses. God would bless him in the sense that Abram was to be specially favored by God, both physically and spiritually. Within the scope of Abram's life this blessing certainly included fertility, through which he and Sarai would have a son. The third promise was that God would make Abram's name great (v. 2). The builders of the tower of Babel had wanted to make "a name" for themselves by their act of rebellion (11:4). Their names are not remembered, but God's plan to make Abram's name great *has* been accomplished—his name is well known by at least half of all the earth's people, even today. Thus, there were three promises made to Abram connected with his willingness to obey God's command to leave his country, his relatives, and his father's house.

The Command to Be a Blessing

The second commandment to Abram was that he should be a blessing. Although the wording at the end of verse 2 makes it appear to be part of the previous promises, it is actually the second imperative given to Abram. It was the promises of God in verse 2 that enabled him to obey the command to be a blessing to others. He was to be a blessing in the future when he, in his descendants, became God's missionary nation to the world. They would transmit the good news of God's saving purpose to all the families of earth (v. 3). Those who believed the good news would come into God's favor and be blessed. So Abram was instructed to be a blessing by making it possible for them to receive God's salvation by faith. The New Testament twice links gospel outreach to the command to Abram to "be a blessing" (Acts 3:25; Gal. 3:8).

Three More Promises

This second command, like the first one, was followed by three promises and had to do with God's protection of Abram (v. 3). Anyone who treated him badly or showed him disrespect would fall under God's curse. They would be removed from the place of blessing and be given over to judgment. The remainder of the book of Genesis will bear testimony to this promise. World history, in addition, has shown that those who mistreated Abraham's descendants were penalized by God. Prime examples are Assyria, Babylon, Egypt, and in more recent times, Germany.

The third promise to Abram was the most significant. It states, "And in you all the families of the earth shall be blessed." He was to be a channel of blessing for the whole world. No one would experience God's blessing apart from the blessing that was given through Abram and his seed. God's goal was to make the blessing available to all people, and Abram was to be the key to it in three ways:

- By *proclamation*: The good news of God's salvation as revealed to him was to be spread by speaking it.
- By *generation* (having children), that is, Abram's descendants would be specially cared for by God to accomplish His purpose in preserving His truth and by providing the Savior at the foreordained time.
- Ultimately, his seed was *Christ,* who was to be the Savior through whom man could be justified by faith (Gal. 3:8, 16).

The Abrahamic Covenant (vv. 1-7)

When considered together, these promises form the original covenant that God made with Abram. It was a most important revelation as it provided for the future of Israel as a literal nation, for the future of the other peoples who would be blessed through Abram, and for the specific land (granted in perpetuity) to be given to Abram's descendants (vv. 2, 3, 7). There are three other passages in Genesis that will add to the provisions of the covenant (13:14-17; 15:1-7; 17:1-18). We will consider these as we proceed through the book.

Get a good grasp of this covenant and all its provisions because there are many Christians who believe that the covenant is fulfilled spiritually in the Church, and not literally with Israel. The interpretation of many prophetic Scriptures hangs on whether these verses are taken literally or spiritually. It is important for the reader to take them literally. Dozens of prophecies regarding Israel have already been literally fulfilled. There is no reason why those that remain will not also be literally fulfilled.

Abram's Pilgrim Journey to Canaan (vv. 4-6)

When God called Abram the second time, he obeyed without delay (v. 4). "So Abram departed as the Lord had spoken to him." Obedience is the focus of the story here and is emphasized by the use of the word "departed" three times in verses 4 and 5. God told him to "Get out" (v. 1). In response to God's word, Abram "departed" (v. 4). At this point in his life, Abram began to live the life of a *pilgrim*. A pilgrim is a person on a journey to a better place. As a pilgrim, Abram looked for a city whose Builder and Maker was God (Heb. 11:10). He had left his permanent home in the east and from then on lived the life of a bedouin in Canaan, moving from place to place. We do not read that he settled down anywhere permanently in Canaan.

A genuine Christian is a pilgrim as well. The apostle Peter called the believers to whom he wrote his epistles "pilgrims." He said that believers are aliens and strangers in a hostile world (1 Pet. 1:1; 2:11). We should recognize that this world is not our home. Since this is true, our values and goals should not be based on earthly things that are passing away. Rather, they should be based on eternity's values. Pilgrims are easily recognized because they look, speak, and act differently than the people that belong to the world.

Abram's Traveling Companions (v. 5)

Abram took with him his wife, Sarai, and his nephew, Lot, the son of his deceased brother, Haran. He was wealthy and "gathered" all his possessions, which no doubt included flocks and herds of animals. Beside these, he took the "people" whom he had "acquired in Haran." This expression seems not to refer to the acquisition of servants, for different Hebrew words would have been used. It may well mean that Abram had already been sharing his faith in the Lord and that these were people who believed God and joined themselves to Abram as fellow pilgrims. They believed his testimony and observed his good example. Thus, they wanted to follow his faith and make a new start in life.

The journey from Haran to Canaan was long—about four hundred miles. Haran was on a major east/west trade route through Syria. In Syria they would probably have turned south on another well-traveled route called The King's Highway, through Damascus and then on toward Canaan. Along these routes, Abram and his caravan would have moved slowly, taking several weeks, bearing in mind the difficulty in driving many flocks and herds.

A problem of chronology arises concerning Abram's age, recorded in Genesis 12:4 as being seventy-five when he left Haran. Terah was seventy when he fathered Abram, presumably his first-born son (11:26). Therefore, Terah would have been at least 145 when Abram left Haran, as Acts 7:4 tells us that he died before Abram left. The problem is that Genesis 11:32 says that Terah was 205 when he died in Haran. Three solutions are offered, none of which are without difficulty. One solution is that Abram may not have been Terah's firstborn child. If he was born when Terah was 130, Terah would have been 205 when he died and Abram left Haran. The difficulty with this is: why should Abram have been surprised (17:17) at being able to father a child (Isaac) at one hundred years of age if his father had been 130 when he himself was born? A second solution offered is that Terah did not, in fact, die before Abram left Haran. This calls into question the clear statement in Acts. A third suggestion is to accept the Samaritan text (generally viewed as inferior) of Genesis 11:32 that cites Terah's age at death as 145 in preference to the Hebrew text. It is wise not to be dogmatic about any of these views.

Shechem, the Place of Promise (v. 6)

When they reached Canaan, the first place they stopped at was Shechem, near a well-known landmark of the time called the Terebinth tree of Moreh. The landmark may have been a grove of trees that belonged to a Canaanite named Moreh. Some expositors think it might have been a place where Canaanite priests declared oracles; thus, a rather ominous note is struck. Even if that is not the case, the next phrase is significant: "And the Canaanites were then in the land." This was alien territory for the patriarch. He pitched his tent in a land not his own, one that was occupied by a pagan people. We sense tension here; the Canaanites were to be enemies of Abram's seed for hundreds of years. In fact, they were still in control of the land several hundred years later when the Israelites, under Moses, approached.

It was in Shechem, surrounded by Canaanites, that God appeared to Abram (v. 7). This is the first mention in Genesis of an actual appearance of God (cf. 17:1; 18:1; 26:2, 24; 35:9). God had certainly "walked" and spoken with Adam, Enoch, and Noah, and perhaps there was some visible presence, but the Scripture does not say so. In this instance, however, there certainly was an actual visible manifestation. We conclude that the second Person of the Trinity appeared, because God is Spirit and has never been seen by man (John 4:24; cf. 1:18). To Abram, God's appearance was a divine welcome to the land. It would have assured him that he was in the right place. Shechem was right in the middle of the land; therefore, there could be no mistake about which land God meant when He said, "To your descendants I will give *this* land" (v. 7, emphasis added). God's promise to Abram and his descendants amounted to a divine title deed, given on the first day the patriarch camped there. It has remained in effect for four thousand years. Because God promised the land to Abram and his descendants, it has been commonly called the *Promised Land,* although the phrase does not appear in Genesis.

The Altar at Shechem (v. 7)

When God announced to Abram that this was the land He had promised to him and his descendants, Abram built an altar to Jehovah. It was the first altar built in the land of Canaan to the true God, and it was devoted to the worship of the LORD, the covenant-keeping God. The word *altar* means "place of sacrifice," and undoubtedly Abram offered a sacrifice to God in thanksgiving, just as Noah had done after the Flood (8:20-21). Both men had cause to give thanks, because God had fulfilled His promises to each of them. In addition, Abram, like Noah, offered his sacrifice as an expression of worship to God. The imagery of the smoke rising would convey that his worship was a sweet aroma to God. It is remarkable that the first thing Abram did in the land was to worship God.

The Altar at Bethel (v. 8)

Abram then moved about thirty-five miles south to a place between Bethel and Ai. There he built another altar to the Lord and "called on the name of the LORD." This phrase may mean that he preached or proclaimed to the pagan Canaanites concerning the name and nature of the Lord while he was worshipping Him by sacrifice on the altar. What a witness it would have been to them! They would learn from Abram's lips that his God was the one true God who wanted to bless them. Maybe he explained the significance of the animal being sacrificed, that it pictured the coming Redeemer. By "calling on the name of the LORD," Abram followed his worship with a verbal testimony. God's plan for His people to declare Him to the world by their worship and their witness has never changed; all believers should be witnesses as well as worshippers.

From there, he "journeyed, going on still toward the South," or the Negev (v. 9), the name by which it is still known today. Abram had traversed the land from north to south. In the Negev he found a drier climate with enough pasture for his flocks and herds. It was in that general area between Hebron and

Beersheba that he spent the rest of his days. Three particular aspects marked Abram's life:

- *His tent* (v. 8). Abram was a pilgrim, an alien in a strange land, and always separate from the surrounding pagan communities. He tried to keep his people from becoming identified with Canaanite culture. He did not settle with them in their cities.

- *His altars,* which symbolized his worship of the true God. With God as his primary focus, it was important that he maintain his worship, because the Canaanite's religion was corrupt and false.

- *His witness.* Not only did he probably influence some people from Haran to join him, but he kept on being a witness of the true God before the idol-worshipping Canaanites.

Abram Tested by the Famine (vv. 10-20)

Immediately after God gave the great covenant promises to Abram regarding the future of his descendants in the land, something happened to threaten their fulfillment, placing the possibility of Sarai ever being the mother of Abram's child in jeopardy.

When Abram and his company were in the Negev, a drought caused a severe famine in the area. It may have seemed an incongruous situation to Abram because he had just been assured of the blessing of God (v. 2). He might wonder, how there could be a famine in the land of promise? Without rain there could be no crops, nor pasture for the herds. It was a critical situation, and it required immediate action. He might even have thought that God had deceived him. But the truth is that God was teaching Abram some important lessons about trusting Him. The right response for Abram would have been to depend on the Lord and hold Him to His promises, even though the circumstances looked negative.

Abram's Bad Choice

Abram did not consult the Lord or consider His interests. There is no mention of prayer for help or guidance. The text simply says, "Abram went down to Egypt to sojourn there" (v. 10). Egypt was not usually affected by droughts, because the River Nile supplied sufficient life-giving water and because the source of the Nile lay far enough to the south to be subject to a different weather pattern. To Abram, Egypt seemed like the natural place to go. The word *sojourn* refers to a temporary stay, which is what Abram intended. But it is surprising how quickly the man of faith abandoned his disposition to trust God and sought out his own ways to face difficult circumstances.

The Plot

As Abram crossed into Egypt, he encountered a situation that caused his faith to falter (vv. 11-13). It concerned his beautiful wife. Abram realized when he left his "father's house" that her beauty might be a threat to his own safety (20:13). Pagan princes might want her for themselves and would possibly kill Abram to get her. Perhaps he had already seen admiration in their eyes as he approached Egypt.

Abram was in a difficult situation. If he and Sarai returned to Canaan they faced starvation, but if they went forward he might be killed, and Sarai might be taken by another man. He found himself giving way to the compromise he seems to have previously planned. If the Egyptians inquired, Sarai was to say that she was his sister (v. 13), and hopefully he would be spared. Actually, the story about Sarai being his sister was partly true because she *was* his half sister (20:12). The intent of the ruse, however, was to deceive the Egyptians.

Abram was advising Sarai to tell a lie, and the indications are that she was a willing party to the scheme for Abram's sake. There are two phrases that indicate Abram's motivation: "that it may be well with me for your sake" and "that I may live because of you." It may be that he was thinking of the promise of God that would be fulfilled through him, but it seems more likely that it was a purely selfish plot to save himself. Abram caused the whole sorry mess. He based his decision on self, carried it out by deceit, and ended up a hypocrite.

The Compromise of Faith

As they entered Egypt, the Egyptians did indeed notice Sarai's beauty (vv. 14-16). In fact, the princes of Pharaoh noticed her and "commended her to Pharaoh." The word *commended* means "praised" in this context. It is the first time the Hebrew word *halal* is used, the common expression for "praise" still used by believers around the world in the word *hallelujah*. By this time, there was nothing Abram could have done to prevent Sarai being taken. Even Sarai herself seems completely passive in the incident. She was taken away to the house of Pharaoh. A surprising turn in the story is that Pharaoh treated Abram well for her sake and gave him large numbers of sheep, oxen, donkeys, camels, and servants (v. 16; cf. v. 13).

The whole situation was one of compromise. Abram and Sarai both compromised the truth when they agreed to deceive. They seemed willing to compromise the covenant promises of God that they had just received at Shechem. Abram fell at his strongest point—his faith—and Sarai along with him. They compromised their faith in God by replacing it with fear. They missed out on experiencing how God would have provided for their needs in what seemed like impossible circumstances, something that many missionaries and others have since been able to testify to. Abram and Sarai were even willing to compromise their own marriage relationship. If God had left them to their own devices, the consequences would have spelled disaster. But God preserved Abram's marriage for the later birth of Isaac; before Pharaoh married Sarai, God mercifully intervened.

Pharaoh Rebukes Abram

It is not hard to imagine Abram visiting Sarai while she was being prepared for marriage and the two of them trying to console each other (vv. 17-20). They could not change anything—but God could and did. He afflicted Pharaoh and his house with some unexplained plague. Whatever its nature, Pharaoh perceived it was due to Sarai already being married. Pharaoh called Abram and confronted him with his lying: "What is this you have done to me?" He rebuked Abram harshly for not telling the truth. He asked him two more rhetorical questions: "Why did you not tell me that she was your wife?" and "Why did you say, 'she is my sister'?" (vv. 18-19). Obviously Pharaoh was utterly disgusted by Abram's behavior, and he let him know in no uncertain terms. It is always sad when a believer loses his testimony and the people of the world rebuke him. Pharaoh sent Abram and Sarai away and had them summarily escorted out of the country.

In Conclusion

At the point where his story in Genesis begins, Abram was seventy-five years old and destined to live another one hundred years, during which time he would father two major people groups. But more importantly in terms of faith, Abraham became the spiritual father of a great host of believers; we, his spiritual children, have observed some lessons about faith in this chapter.

Chapter 12 began with one of the greatest revelations any human has ever been privileged to receive and ended with that same person failing to trust in the One who gave the revelation. It began with Abram being called to the land by the covenant-keeping God with the promise of wealth, greatness, honor, posterity, and protection. It ended with Abram being sent back to the land by a pagan king in disgrace.

However, the incident, in its context, also shows that God exercises mercy towards His people when they do fail. The truth exemplified here is that the failures of God's people do not nullify God's promises. Although Abram jeopardized Sarai's purity and the future of the covenant, God intervened. And although Abram suffered the consequences of his sin, God's purpose was not thwarted: God had promised the land, so Abram was sent back to it. He promised protection, so Sarai was protected to allow her to become the mother of the covenant people and, ultimately, of the Messiah.

In this chapter, Abram made two choices: one by faith and one by sight. What happened as a result of each one illustrates the huge implications that can result from the choices we make. Abram certainly prospered materially from deceiving Pharaoh, but it was not long before the needs of those same animals became a source of tension between him and Lot. And in all probability, Abram acquired Hagar as part of Pharaoh's gift; the handmaid would be a factor in another set of problems a few years later.

Abram's choice "by sight" demonstrates how vulnerable believers can be to failure, how easily we can become entangled in a web of sin, and how quickly we can lose our testimony before the world. Yes, most of us are as vulnerable to temptation as Abram was. Like him, we are adept at rationalizing our plans when we get into compromising situations. This chapter is a powerful reminder that the danger of personal sin and disgrace is never far away from believers who, like Abram, have been called to blessing. We need to pay attention to what the Lord Jesus said to His disciples: "Watch and pray, lest you enter into temptation" (Matt. 26:41). May God help us to be careful and prayerful.

The Choices of Abram and Lot

Abram returned to Canaan a wiser man. In this chapter, we will see how his renewed faith is contrasted with his failure in Egypt. He looked beyond the material and the transitory to that which is invisible and eternal. He made serious choices based solely on God's promise that the land would belong to his descendants. That promise is the dominant theme in the story of Abram. After returning to Canaan, tension developed between his and Lot's herdsmen with respect to sufficient grazing ground for their animals. The tension resulted in Abram and Lot making certain choices. Abram based his choice on his faith in God; Lot based his choice on what he saw. Because he believed God, Abram put aside selfish and material interests and worked for a peaceful settlement of the issue. God honored his faith by reiterating and expanding the promise.

Abram Returns to Bethel (vv. 1-5)

Verses 1 through 5 provide the background for the significant choices that Abram and Lot would make. Abram was wealthy when he went to Egypt, and the gifts Pharaoh gave him in regard to Sarai had enriched him further. The text emphasizes Abram's wealth: "Abram was very rich in livestock, in silver, and in gold." He returned to the land with "all that he had": Sarai, Lot and his family, servants, his own herds, Lot's herds, and the herdsmen who managed them. They traveled northeast from Egypt and came to the South, or the Negev, where it appears that he stopped and camped for a time, perhaps around Beersheba, the area where he would later live. In due time, they proceeded further north until they came to "the mountain east of Bethel" (12:8) where he had previously erected his tent, built an altar, and called on the name of the Lord. It was there that he had last sensed God's presence.

The Place

With his failure in Egypt behind him, the patriarch marked a new beginning as a pilgrim in the Promised Land and in his spiritual relationship with God (vv. 3-4). Abram's return to that place is emphasized. It is called *"the place* where his tent had been at the beginning" and *"the place* of the altar which he had made there at first" (emphases added). Returning to the land of Canaan was not enough; he had to get back to Bethel, the place where he had first established his new life in Canaan, where he had worshipped God with sacrifices at the altar (vv. 3-4, cf. 12:8). On his first visit to Bethel, he had "called on the name of the LORD"; that is, he publicly proclaimed the nature of God to those who watched him offering sacrifices and were willing to listen. When he came back to the land, he went straight to the same "place," that is, Bethel. It is instructive that he did not go to Shechem to try to recapture the vision God had given him there (12:7), but to Bethel to reestablish his worship at the altar and his testimony in the land. The *place* marked his restoration to the Lord. The keys to Abram's restoration were first, his worship at the altar—putting God in His rightful place—and second, his calling out to God in confession and prayer. When Abram got back on the pathway of faith, the Canaanites all around noticed the worshiping saint before the altar where the sacrifice was consumed and accepted.

Back to Bethel

Abram's return to Bethel and his calling on the name of the Lord is a good illustration for believers who retrace their own spiritual steps after failing God in some way. We, too, get ourselves into wrong places and end up in compromising situations. Then comes that longing to get back into fellowship with God and make a new start. In sorrow for our sin and penitent before God, we too find God waiting to receive us. We have to get back, in spirit, to the place where we went astray. When we do, we will once again find sweet fellowship walking with the Lord in the light of His Word. Back to the place where we once were obedient to all that we knew. Back to the practice of true worship and communion with God. Back to "simply trusting every day." Back to Bethel.

Lot's Flocks, Herds, and Tents

The paragraph ends with an observation that "Lot also ... had flocks and herds and tents" (v. 5). Like Abram, Lot had become very wealthy in livestock. An interesting sidelight is that the two men were "between Bethel [house of God] and Ai [heap of ruins]" (v. 3). Abram and Lot were on the verge of making choices, with one looking one way toward the house of God and the other looking the other way toward Sodom, which would become a heap of ruins. Lot's tents are mentioned, which become significant later in the story.

Wealth Leads to Strife and Choices (vv. 6-13)

Abram and Lot were not back in the land very long before strife developed. The flash point came when there was not enough pastureland around Bethel for all of their combined herds of animals. The reason is not hard to find, for "the Canaanites and the Perizzites then dwelt in the land," and no doubt they inhabited the best parts of it. Strife erupted between Abram and Lot's herdsmen. The word for *strife* indicates that there were claims and counter claims. Their inability to dwell together is twice mentioned in verse 6. The spiritual lesson for us is important. Second Timothy 2:24 says "a servant of the Lord must not quarrel." It was not enough for Abram, the spiritual man, to leave Ur, Haran, and Egypt and make his home in the land of promise. He must also separate from the members of his own family who were hindering his spiritual desires and goals. Lot represents the worldly Christian who is not living to please God. Lot and Abram had to separate.

Abram's Offer

Abram offered a solution to the strife that was in keeping with his faith in God. He said to Lot, "Is not the whole land before you? Please separate from me. If you take the left, then I will go to the right." He allowed Lot to make the choice without any strings attached or any pressure from him. Abram was utterly selfless, although, as the head of the clan, he had the right to dictate whatever would be to his own advantage. He based his offer to Lot on several things:

- *The promise of God* (12:7). He knew that God had given him the whole land, and he did not need to take any action to reserve any of it for himself.
- *His desire for peace.* "Let there be no strife between you and me." Peace was more desirable than his own personal advantage.
- *He and Lot were related.* "We are brethren."
- *His previous experience with God.* He had already renounced all that he could see with his eyes for that which was invisible. So another step toward the invisible "city which has foundations" was an advance in walking by faith (Heb. 11:10).

There are some important lessons for us here:

- There is the lesson of *humility,* as Abram did not grasp for what was his right.
- There is the lesson of *faith,* for he believed that whatever Lot chose would not affect what God was going to give him.
- There is the lesson of *generosity,* for Abram deferred to Lot, giving him the first choice.
- Finally, there is the lesson of *wisdom,* for Abram realized that the incompatibility between himself and Lot would be best served by separation. His spiritual goals were going to be hindered if he continued in close association Lot and his worldly goals.

Lot's Choice

Lot took advantage of the opportunity Abram gave him (vv. 10-13). He was not an evil man, but he was a believer out of fellowship with God. From the high country around Bethel and Ai he could see the lower Jordan Valley. He "lifted his eyes" and liked what he saw. He described it in generous terms. He saw a "plain" that was "well watered everywhere," like the "garden of the LORD" and like the "land of Egypt." The "garden of the LORD" probably refers to the Garden of Eden, where God had placed Adam and Eve. Lot compared what he saw with what he had been told of the Garden of Eden. He also compared it to the land of Egypt, and he liked the prospect of living in a similar place.

Little did Lot know that what he thought would be paradise would turn out to be more like perdition. As he looked with his eyes, a move to the plain of Jordan seemed very advantageous to him. How wrong he was. He looked for what we call the "American dream"—status, business success, pleasure, comfort. When Lot chose to take his family and flocks to the plain of Jordan, he started down a long slippery slope that ended in disaster. Lot became the father of those who are possessed by their possessions. Notice the progression of Lot's choice:

*   Lot "saw" (v. 10)
*   He "chose" (v. 11)
*   He "journeyed east" (v. 11)
*   He "pitched his tent" (settled) in the cities of the valley (v. 12)
*   He moved "as far as Sodom" (v. 12)

His choice was a bad one from several angles. He certainly did not seek wisdom from his uncle Abram. Nor does it appear that he took the matter to God in prayer. He seems not to have taken into account the possible bad effects that a move so near to a desperately corrupt civilization would have on his own family and herdsmen. Perhaps he thought that a city would be a good place for his daughters to find wealthy husbands. His choice was made on the basis of the lust of the flesh, the lust of the eyes, and the pride of life (1 John 2:15-16). There are a couple of ominous notes struck in the description here that give reason for pause. The first is that destruction was coming: the choice was made "before" the Lord destroyed Sodom and Gomorrah (v. 10). The second is that the men of Sodom were "exceedingly wicked and sinful," that is, even by Canaanite standards they were evil. And the third is that their sin was "against the LORD," indicating that God was especially offended by their wickedness.

Lot's Choice is a Warning

Lot's choice is a clear warning to us. Many believers make choices about where to live on the basis of their business interests, pleasant surroundings, economic class of the people from the world's viewpoint, or the reputation of the local school for their children. They see themselves as a Daniel in Babylon and being a good testimony for God there. But not every Christian is a Daniel. It you are not sure that God has sent you to "Sodom," you make a mistake if you go there. If you put your job ahead of your family's spiritual life; if you put social advance ahead of the fellowship of God's people; if you let your choice of a nice place to live keep you from church, then you have moved from the highlands to the lowlands, and you are just like Lot. The result may well harm you and your family. What happened to Lot may happen to you. As a result of his choice, Lot lost his testimony, his friends, his family, and his fortune. Without the witness of Scripture in 2 Peter 2:7-8, we would hardly know that Lot was a believer at all.

God's Further Promise to Abram (vv. 14-18)

Note carefully that "after Lot had separated from him," God spoke to Abram again. Because Abram chose to walk by faith and not by sight, God reaffirmed the promises He had previously made and added to them. Abram could afford to be generous in offering the land to Lot because he already knew that God was going to give it all to his own descendants, so it didn't matter how much or how little of it Lot claimed. Abram knew that God meant what he said, and he could rest in that. His faith is all the more remarkable in that the only thing he ever owned in Canaan was a burial site. Abram's faith was the "substance of things hoped for" (Heb. 11:1).

"Lift your eyes"

There are strong links in this section to the previous one. Lot had "lifted his eyes and saw all the plain of Jordan" (v. 10). God now said to Abram, "Lift your eyes now and look"—not just in one direction, but in all directions. God told Abram to look north, south, east, and west, and said, "all the land which you see I give to you and your descendants forever." Lot chose selfishly and obtained a little—and only temporarily at that. Abram waited for God to give it and got it all. How much better to receive it from God's hand than to take it one's self. What God had promised *geographically* in verse 14, He promised *numerically* in verse 16. "I will make your descendants as the dust of the earth." In other words, the number of his descendants would be too many to count.

God also promised the land to Abram *experientially* when He instructed him to "walk in the land through its length and its width, for I give it to you" (v. 17). In that way Abram would see all the beauties, all the possibilities, and all the wealth of the land which would one day be the center of the world. There the Davidic kingdom would be established. There the Savior would spend His earthly days, give His life, rise from the dead, and ascend to heaven. There Christ will return in power and great glory and set up His earthly kingdom for a thousand years.

Many believers today have had the privilege of surveying the land of Israel from the same vantage points that Abram did. But what must Abram have thought when he claimed it all by faith, then actually saw much of it as well! How different was Lot, who temporarily held a little piece of the lowest point then lost it. Whatever remains of that area today is somewhere below what we call the Dead Sea. It has been well said, "God always gives the very best to those who leave the choice with Him." Back in Ur, God had said of the land, "I will show you" (Acts 7:3). When Abram arrived in Shechem, God said, "This is the land I will give you." Now God says, "All the land which you see I give to you … forever" (v. 15).

In doing as God directed (traversing the whole land), Abram experienced an ever growing appreciation for the inheritance God had given him. For the next one hundred years, Abram no doubt found the land that Lot rejected to be a place of peace, joy, and contentment as he walked with God. Who among us would trade Abram's life for that of Lot? In applying this passage to ourselves, have we claimed the spiritual inheritance that is ours in Christ? Have we claimed the great promises in the Word?

The Promise Awaits Fulfillment

Though Abram surveyed the land, he never actually owned it himself, nor have his descendants during most of the intervening four thousand years. This means that the promise has not yet been literally fulfilled. The question, therefore, arises as to whether the promise may have been fulfilled spiritually, meaning that Abram's seed are really believers in every age. Many commentators tell us that we should not interpret the promises literally and physically. They think that the promises do not refer to the Middle East or the Jewish people, but to believing people. However, the places mentioned in these chapters such as Shechem, Haran, Sodom, Bethel, and Ur are all literal places with ruins left to this day. Abram took these promises literally; indeed, they would not have made sense to him without a literal interpretation. It is the deeply-held view of the writer that these promises must be interpreted literally by Bible readers today.

None of the patriarchs (Abram, Isaac, and Jacob) lived to see God's promises fulfilled. They saw them from afar, but faith made them real. We await their complete fulfillment at a future time. The fact that the Jews have remained an identifiable people for four thousand years and have recently established themselves as a sovereign nation is a striking testimony to the truth that God is still working out His purposes in them.

In the last verse, we read that Abram moved his tent and dwelt by the Terebinth trees of Mamre (v. 18). Mamre was near the place where the town of Hebron was later built. It was named after an Amorite chief (14:13) and was evidently marked by a large and well known grove of trees. The first thing he did in his new location was to build another altar where he and Sarai could worship the Lord and offer sacrifices. There were now three altars in Canaan built by Abram to stand as a witness to the one true God: at Shechem, at Bethel, and at Mamre.

In Conclusion

This section has followed Abram from his faithless venture into Egypt back into the land, and especially to Bethel, where he restored his walk with God. In turn, he was prepared for the next test, concerning pastureland for the animals. He gave Lot the choice, then God came to him with an even greater promise than the previous ones. God gave Abram the best when he left the choice with God.

The Blessings of Victory

After returning to the land of Canaan from Egypt, Abram renewed his fellowship with God at the altar he had previously built at Bethel. It was while he was still in that area that strife erupted between Lot's herdsmen and his own over the shortage of grazing land. In an act of great faith, Abram gave the choice of the land to Lot, believing that no matter which part Lot chose, the whole land had been given to him (Abram) and his descendants (12:7). At the same time that his grasp on the temporary things of earth was loosening, his grasp on the eternal was strengthening. When Lot left, God confirmed the two great promises He had made to Abram about the land and his seed, the latter of which guaranteed a huge posterity to Abram, as numerous as the dust of the earth (13:16).

Abram then "moved his tent" to the Oaks of Mamre, later called Hebron, apparently making an agreement with the local Amorite king for protection in case of attack (14:13). The altar he had built there (13:18) would have served as a center of worship for his family and a witness to the surrounding pagans. After living there for several years, the events of chapter 14 began to unfold.

Lot's Dilemma in Sodom

All was not well with Lot. Having chosen to live in the fertile valley of the Jordan river, he eventually gave up living the nomadic life and settled in the city of Sodom (14:12). The Bible says that Lot was "oppressed with the filthy conduct of the wicked" (2 Pet. 3:7) in Sodom, but not oppressed enough, it seems, to leave or to remove his family from the inherent spiritual danger of that environment. There was the potential threat of physical danger, too. The city was planning to rebel against Chedorlaomer, King of Elam, to whom Sodom had been paying tribute for many years. Lot would have known that trouble was on the horizon. When war erupted, he found himself caught up in its effects.

We should be aware of the strong connection between chapter 13, in which Lot chose the valley of the Jordan for selfish reasons, and chapter 14, where that choice led him into long-term trouble and heartache. Abram continued to demonstrate his faith by the choices *he* made and sets an example for us of how to participate in world affairs without becoming drawn into the dangers they present.

The Battle of the Kings (vv. 1-12)

This chapter gives the first detailed description of the execution of a battle in recorded history, although there is a great deal of evidence of warring from very early times. This was a battle between two confederacies of city-states. The aggressor was a coalition of four cities from the Lower Euphrates Valley and the defender a coalition of five cities from the Jordan Valley in Canaan. As such, it was typical of wars in the ancient world. City states, each governed by a fortified city, would band together and attack other such cities in order to dominate them and enforce tribute as a means of enriching themselves and extending their influence.

The Warring Parties

The first three states of the eastern confederacy named Shinar, Ellasar, and Elam were well known ancient peoples of the Euphrates Valley. Goiim, which translated means "nations," was likely a tribe of northeast Babylonia. Their kings are all named in our text, and while there are, as yet, no known references to them outside the Bible, their names are linguistically authentic. Chedorlaomer was the acknowledged leader of the group (vv. 1-4).

A possible reason for their initial attack some thirteen years earlier was to obtain metals that were mined in the area. The five targeted cities were Sodom, Gomorrah, Admah, Zeboiim, and Zoar, all in the plain of Jordan near the Salt Sea, now known as the Dead Sea. For twelve years they all "served" the kings of the East (that is, paid tribute money), but the next year they "rebelled." The subsequent attack in the year following their rebellion that is described in this chapter was a punitive action. Lot had been separated from Abram for some time by now and, living as he was in Sodom itself, would have been well aware of the threatening situation. In spite of this, he chose to stay. Like many believers down through history who gain material prosperity in the world system, he hoped that the danger of his compromise with it would not materialize.

The Battle of Siddim Valley

The invasion of the eastern kings was preceded by a military campaign against several other cities in Canaan. Having traveled from the Euphrates Valley via the arc of the Fertile Crescent, the combined forces traveled south, past the Sea of Galilee, through the Jordan Valley, and on to the Gulf of Aqaba. Along the northern part of this route, they attacked several peoples including the Rephaim, the Zuzim, and the Emim. They bypassed the Sodom area initially and attacked the Horites as far as El-Paran on the Gulf of Aqaba. Then they turned northwest to Kadesh and finally east, to assail the Amorites. At that point, the armies of the five Sodom cities met the campaigning armies of the East in the Valley of Siddim. The details of the military operation and the use of known place names lend authenticity to the fact of this battle (vv. 5-12).

The eastern confederacy, led by the King of Elam, quickly defeated the Sodomites, who fled in disarray. Some hid in the asphalt pits nearby, while others escaped into the mountains. It is likely that their debauched lifestyle made them poor soldiers, with the result that they were easy prey for the enemy. The invading army sacked Sodom and Gomorrah and took captives, including Lot and material goods. Moses described Lot as "Abram's brother's son" to emphasize the relationship between them and the part that Abram would play in the story. The confederacy then began the long trek back to the Euphrates Valley with all of its captives and booty.

Abram's Pursuit and Defeat of the Kings (vv. 13-16)

A breathless runner who had escaped from the battle scene arrived at Abram's tent near Mamre with the news that the Sodomites had been badly defeated and that Lot had been captured. Abram immediately armed 318 of his trained men and, joined by his three Amorite allies, pursued the five kings now traveling north. It was no doubt a sizeable expeditionary force, but small in comparison to the thousands they were going after. Abram led the force. They could travel much faster with their camels and infantry than the army they were chasing, who were slowed down by the spoils of war, chained captives, and herds of animals. Notice that for the first time Abram is called "the Hebrew." This is the name by which the descendants of Eber in Abram's line were known (10:4; 39:14) and by which they identified themselves to foreigners (cf. 40:15; 43:32). The term continued to be one of their designations throughout the Old Testament era, and their language is still called "Hebrew." By calling him a Hebrew, Moses (the author of Genesis) was signifying that Abram was clearly distinguished from the other inhabitants of Canaan.

Abram took steps quickly and decisively for the benefit of his nephew. He could have done nothing, reasoning that Lot deserved what he was getting. Instead, his initiative demonstrates his great compassion for Lot, though he must have been well aware of Lot's worldliness. Abram obviously put himself at risk, considering the size and nature of his impromptu army compared with the organized forces of the five kings. With that risk in mind, he trusted that God was going to give him victory. We can compare this incident to Gideon's victory with his three hundred men over the 135,000 Midianites many years later (Judges 7).

Abram proved to be a competent military leader; his battle strategy shows all the marks of an excellent military operation (vv. 14-15). From his starting point in Mamre, he would move directly north through the hill country, passing the Sea of Galilee, until he came to Dan. (Dan was originally named Laish; a later copyist probably edited the text to read "Dan" after the conquest of Canaan.) There Abram divided his army into two columns for a double-pronged attack. Not only did he outflank the retreating army on two sides; he also attacked by night, surprising them. Perhaps he caught them in the midst of revelry. However that may have been, they fled with Abram in pursuit as far as Hobah north of Damascus, abandoning their spoils and captives along the way. They were completely routed by Abram's modest troops and hurried home in humiliation and defeat. It is not surprising that no mention of this battle has been found in Babylonian chronicles as they usually only recorded their victories. Abram did not gloat over the victory for he knew that it was God who had brought it about.

Abram and the Two Kings (vv. 17-24)

Abram's victory was the first fulfillment of the prophecy that God would make his name great (12:2). He had now become respected as a powerful prince and a hero who, along with his Amorite allies, had defeated King Chedorlaomer and rescued Sodom and Gomorrah's inhabitants. News of the victory traveled ahead of him. As Abram was nearing home, two kings met him in the Valley of Shaveh. This valley cannot be identified but was probably somewhere between Salem and Mamre. The contrast between these two kings is most striking, and Abram would have understood that their respective reasons for meeting him were going to require him to make some significant choices.

The King of Sodom

Bera, King of Sodom, had escaped capture in the Battle of Sodom (v. 10) and arrived now with his entourage to greet the homecoming troops. It says King Bera "went out" to meet Abram. He had good reason for doing so: Abram, as the expedition leader, had in his possession many people and a great amount of goods that had previously belonged to him—and which he hoped to retrieve. In his reasoning, the better he treated Abram, the greater were his chances of getting them back. He had come at least thirty miles from Sodom to meet Abram.

The King of Salem

While the King of Sodom was still giving homage to Abram for the victory, another king appeared—Melchizedek, King of Salem. He had not been involved in the battle but appeared now with gifts for the victor. He brought out bread and wine because he was a priest of "God Most High." There seems to be a deliberate contrast here between Bera, who "went out" to Abram, and Melchizedek, who "brought out" bread and wine to him. One had his own self-centered agenda; the other came to honor Abram and his God. The encounter of Abram with these two kings is indeed an intriguing story.

The Blessing of Melchizedek

The bread and wine that Melchizedek brought to Abram was not intended to alleviate hunger and thirst—after all, Abram had all the spoils of war—but to be a token of refreshment in honor of a great triumph. It may be that the bread and wine were symbolic of the completed victory or a kind of thank offering to Abram's God. What we should not miss is the importance of Melchizedek's blessing. It is mentioned twice, in verses 18 and 19. First, he blessed Abram; thanking God that Abram belonged to God Most High. Then he blessed God Himself, acknowledging that it was His power which had given Abram success and that the Most High God was greater than the false gods of the Canaanites.

Who was Melchizedek?

Melchizedek was most certainly a literal king. Salem is usually linked with Jerusalem ("city of peace"), the eventual site of Israel's glorious capital city from which King David and his successors ruled. In a future day, the "greater David" will rule the world in righteousness and peace from His throne in Jerusalem. In addition to being a king, Melchizedek was also a priest. Priests speak to God on behalf of others. They offer up prayers and sacrifices to God. This is the first occurrence of the word "priest" in the Bible, and it belongs to this interesting person.

Melchizedek is called "the priest of God Most High" (v. 18). The term *God Most High* (Hebrew *El Elyon)* is one of the many names of God, and it stresses His absolute superiority over other so-called gods. He is the one sovereign God to whom both Melchizedek and Abram belonged as believing brothers. Both men used the name "Most High God" in their worship (vv. 20, 22). The name "Most High" is a designation of God used in the New Testament, too: in connection with Christ (Luke 1:32, 35, 76); by the legion of spirits (Luke 8:28); by Stephen (Acts 7:48); and by the demon-possessed girl in Philippi (Acts 6:17).

Melchizedek, a Type of Christ the Priest and King

Most conservative commentators believe that Melchizedek was a more significant figure than simply a regional king, based on two passages that refer to him. One is Psalm 110 verses 1 and 4, and the other is Hebrews 5–7. In these passages, Melchizedek is portrayed as a type of Christ, who is a "priest forever according to the order of Melchizedek" (Ps. 110:4; Heb. 5:6).

Melchizedek prefigures the priesthood of the Lord Jesus Christ in a number of ways:

- Both are marked by righteousness and peace (Rom. 5:1; Heb. 7:1-3).
- Both are kings as well as priests and outside the Law of Moses (Ps. 110:1-4; Zech. 6:12-13).
- They are both dependent on personal qualifications, not their family line (Heb. 7:16).
- Both are presented in Scripture as timeless (Heb. 7:3).

- The priesthood of both is superior to the Levitical priesthood (Heb. 7:11).
- Both provide bread and wine, symbols of suffering and victory (14:18; John 6:51-53).

Thus, Christ as a priest in the order (or nature) of Melchizedek is pictured in the New Testament as both Priest and King.

As to Melchizedek's identity, several ideas have been suggested. Some think he may have been Shem, who outlived Abram by thirty-five years (assuming there are no gaps in the chronology of Genesis 11). Others see Melchizedek as a theophany, an appearance of the pre-incarnate Christ, citing the words "without father or mother" from Hebrews 7 to justify that conclusion. Still others think he was merely a Canaanite priest who knew nothing of Abram's God. It is best to take the text at its face value and see Melchizedek simply as a faithful and godly priest of the one true God. Certainly, in his position as both king and priest, he foreshadowed Christ.

Abram Gives Melchizedek a Tithe of all the Spoils

Abram would have perceived Melchizedek's blessing as a confirmation of the blessing he had received when he first entered the land (12:2, 7). It assured him that God's blessing was more enduring than the spoils of war. His faith was now stimulated to rest on the Lord rather than on the material goods he had retrieved from the battle. In recognition of the majesty of God, he selected one tenth (a "tithe") of all the rescued goods and presented them to Melchizedek (v. 20). Abram was much more concerned about acknowledging the "Possessor of heaven and earth" than he was about obtaining possessions. Melchizedek, the priest, represented the true God to Abram, and he gave him priority above everything else.

Abram Gives Back the Spoils to the King of Sodom

Abram's clear spiritual sight and strong faith stand out at this point in his life (vv. 21-24). He was able to discern what was from God and what was from the world. He was astute enough to recognize the twisted motives of the King of Sodom in his "generosity" in bargaining for all the people in exchange for the spoils. He well knew that everything about Sodom ran counter to the purposes of God. For this reason, Abram did not want to give the King of Sodom any reason to claim that he had contributed anything to his prosperity or to God's blessing of him. What was important to Abram was that the promises concerning his seed would be fulfilled by God's power alone and without any help from this pagan king. When God's blessing came and was evident to others, Abram would be sure that the only explanation for it was God's supernatural intervention. This test of Abram is also a good test for God's people today who would discern between the natural and the supernatural. The king of Sodom offered a deal. Abram responded, in effect, "No deal; you take it all" (v. 23). His pre-determined response was "I have lifted up my hand to the LORD, God Most High, Possessor of heaven and earth."

Abram's action is a good example for today's Christian ministries that are often all too quick to seek money from pagan foundations and institutions. How many of us receive pleas for financial support from Christian organizations that will happily accept help from almost any source without question. And how many of us assume that because some potential benefit is legal it is right to pursue. How much better for us to decide before God what is morally right for us to do and not just govern our giving by what is allowed by the law of the land.

In Conclusion

In the narrative of chapter 14, Abram had his faith tested, and he passed with flying colors. He fought two battles. The first was the military defeat of four kings which achieved Lot's rescue against great odds. The second was more subtle, difficult, and far-reaching, as he faced the friendly—but worldly— temptations of Sodom and its king. By faith, Abram trusted God and did not let the worldly king get even a small "foot in the door" of his life. Notice something else that is instructive. Abram did not force his faith and convictions on his Amorite allies who had helped him in the rescue operation. They no doubt took their fair share of the spoils, and of course the king of Sodom received back the rest (v. 24).

As for Lot—during his brief time as a prisoner of war, he must have had time to mourn the prospect of living out his days as a wretched slave in a foreign land. If it had not been for Abram's courage and compassion, slavery would have been the bitter consequence of his selfish choice to obtain what he considered to be the best of everything the world had to offer. It is interesting that, even though Lot was the reason for Abram's involvement in this situation, he does not figure personally in the narrative following his rescue. We do know that he returned to Sodom and ended up in much more trouble than what is recorded here. Lot is an example of so many worldly-minded believers who have lived after him, and his foolishness still stands as a warning to us all.

The Covenant with Abram Ratified

Ever since God first called Abram out of Ur of the Chaldees, his faith in God's promises, demonstrated by his obedience, had been tested many times; sometimes he "passed," sometimes he "failed." In this chapter, God confirms His promises about the land and about Abram's seed, first by a pronouncement and then by a solemn ceremony. Up to this point, the focus has been primarily on the land; it now shifts initially to his seed, and then back to the land. God had promised Abram descendants as numerous as the dust of the earth, but as yet he still did not even have one son. The birth of his promised heir was actually to be deferred for another twenty years or so, and the record of it in Genesis would not appear for another six chapters. During the intervening period, Abram's faith would need to endure while waiting for that hope to be fulfilled.

The Importance of Chapter 15

This is a key chapter in the understanding of the whole book of Genesis for several reasons:

- It substantiates the truth of salvation by faith. It answers the question as to how a person can be made right with God.
- It records how God ratified His covenant with Abram by a special sacrifice. Even the great covenant of Moses given hundreds of years later did not replace this covenant of grace (Gal. 3:15-22).
- It gives us another example of how Abram dealt in faith with delays in the fulfillment of God's promises. Once again his faith shines.

God's Promise and Abram's Question (vv. 1-6)

The chapter begins "after these things," linking its context with chapter 14. Abram's faith had been strengthened when God gave him the victory over the four kings of the eastern confederacy. He had grown in faith when he was blessed by King Melchizedek, the priest of the Most High God, and when he then refused to keep any of the spoils of victory for himself. He chose instead to trust the Lord, the Possessor of heaven and earth. Abram would have seen from the events of chapter 14 how he could one day possess the *land,* but he could not see how the promise of *innumerable descendants* could be fulfilled. Naturally, he was anxious and fearful about that. The entire chapter concerns how God ratified the covenant that he would indeed have all those descendants. Both visibly and audibly, Jehovah appeared to him, saying "Do not be afraid, Abram" to allay his great concern over not having a son according to the promise given him years before. It is the first of hundreds of times the phrase "do not be afraid" is used in the Bible. It is possible that Abram may have also feared a possible reprisal by the four kings from the East. Many commentators have linked this possibility with the fact that Abram gave away the booty (probably including shields) with God's assurance that *He* would be his shield, that is, his protection.

God said to Abram, "I am your shield." The word *shield* comes from the same root word as *delivered* as used in Melchizedek's blessing on God Most High—the one who "delivered" Abram's enemies into his hand (14:20). As God protected him in that context, so God would shield or protect his life so that he could live to father the son God had promised him. God also said to Abram, "I am your ... exceedingly great reward." Most commentators prefer the alternate reading in the margin—"Your reward shall be very great"—in view of Abram's response in verse 2—"What will you give me?" The great reward in Abram's eyes was that he would have a son. A paraphrase of God's word to him might be "Don't be afraid that you might never have a son. I will protect you as a Shield, and your future son will be your great reward."

Obviously, Abram did not understand God to mean that He, personally, was Abram's reward. Abram was concerned that he still had no seed, and he seemed to hold God responsible for that. In calling God "Lord" (*Adonai* means "master") both here and in verse 8 he was submitting to God's ways, but he was getting impatient. His nephew Lot, who might have been an heir, had returned to Sodom. The legal heir to an inheritance in childless families, according to the custom of that day, was the household steward, who was, in this case, Eliezer of Damascus. In speaking with God, Abram pressed this point with a strong word play between the word for "Damascus" (*dammeseq*) and the word for "heir" *(ben-meseq)*. Abram was trying to force God into revealing what He was going to do. He complained, "Look, You have given me no offspring," which was to say, "God, it is really Your fault." Abram is like many believers who are often unwilling to trust God for the future unless they know exactly how He is going to work it out. God's practice is often to deliberately veil the future to give us further opportunities to trust Him.

God's Pledge Concerning Abram's Heir

God made it perfectly clear to Abram that Eliezer would not be his heir, promising instead that his heir would come from his own body (vv. 4-5). God then invited Abram outside at night to give him an "object lesson" about his descendants whom He had previously likened numerically to the dust of the earth (13:16). Now He made the same point again. "Look now toward heaven, and count the stars if you are able to number them.... So shall your descendants be." God was implying that Abram's descendants would be innumerable. From our perspective four thousand years later, we know that Abram's descendants are, indeed, without number. They include the Jews who issued from Isaac, Ishmael's seed, and the descendants of others Ketura bore to him (25:1-2). To these we can add Abram's spiritual seed, the true believers down through history (Rom. 4:11-12; 9:7-8). Some commentators have suggested that the illustration of the "dust of the earth" means the physical seed of Abram (the Jews) and that the "stars of the sky" represent his spiritual seed (Jewish and Gentile believers). That distinction can hardly be drawn from our passage.

Abram's Faith and Righteousness

Verse 6 states, "And he believed in the LORD, and He accounted it to him for righteousness." With these words, the author makes a most important statement about Abram's faith. He is not saying that Abram's eternal salvation was secured just at this moment or with particular reference to what God had just told him. Rather, verse 6 is a general observation about Abram's faith as a conclusion to this dialogue (vv. 1-5). Abram had exercised faith back in Ur and had demonstrated it many times up to this point in his life. The statement is followed by God's ratification of the covenant promise (vv. 7-21); thus, Abram's faith is the central point of the chapter.

The word *believe* occurs here for the first time in Scripture, and as is often the case, its first use is a key to its future usage. Here it relates to saving faith, a vital doctrine throughout the Bible. Note several important aspects of Abram's faith:

- It was *personal.* It had as its object the Lord Himself.
- It was *responsive.* Abram was responding to the word of the Lord.
- It resulted in his gaining *righteousness,* which he did not and could not achieve himself.
- He demonstrated his faith by *sacrifices,* which acknowledged atonement for his sin.
- His faith was *reckoned* as righteousness; a righteous standing was credited to him, as he was not inherently righteous. This concept is associated with the New Testament truth of *justification*, which means to be "declared righteous." When Abram's faith was "credited to his account" as righteousness, God was making him fit to stand before Himself, the holy God.

Genesis 15:6 is quoted three times in the New Testament (Rom. 4:3; Gal. 3:6; James 2:23). In Romans, Abraham's faith is the model for all who would be justified with God. In Galatians, Paul contrasts the "works of the law" with the "hearing of faith." He quotes Genesis 15:6 regarding Jews who claimed that both works and faith were necessary to salvation and concludes that "only those who are of faith are sons of Abraham" (Gal. 3:7). In the James passage, the author shows that true faith will always evidence itself in appropriate works because "faith without works is dead" (James 2:26).

Confirmation of the Covenant with Abram (vv. 7-17)

What follows is a most interesting passage in which God confirms the promise and the declaration He made to the patriarch. Moses, recording this for the Israelites in the wilderness, wanted them to understand that the promises about the seed and the land were rock solid. They learned of the unique way by which God assured Abram that the certainty of the covenant was as sure as God Himself.

The Expansion of the Promises to Abram

Keep clearly in mind the expanding terms of the promises as God revealed them to Abram. *First*, when he was still in his native country, God told him to go to a land He would direct him to, and He promised him so many descendants there that they would be called a "nation" (12:1-2). God reiterated the promise a *second* time when Abram first arrived in Canaan and added "to your descendants I will give this land" (12:7). Once again the promise concerned both the land and the seed. God appeared a *third* time to Abram after he returned from Egypt. On that occasion, God expanded the promise more widely when He said, "All the land I will I give to you and your descendants forever, and I will make your descendants as the dust of the earth" (13:15-16). Then God appeared to him a *fourth* time, as we have seen in the first part of chapter 15. After Abram reminded God that, as yet, he had no offspring, God assured him that one born from his own body would be his heir. He also said, "I give you this land to inherit it" (15:1-7). Thus, both the seed and the land were promised four times, and each time the terms of the promise were expanded. Ultimately, the seed of Abram would be as the stars of the sky, and the land would stretch from Egypt to the Euphrates (vv. 5, 18).

Abram's Request for a Confirmation of the Promise

Abram believed God, but he wanted assurance, so he asked, "Lord GOD, how shall I know that I will inherit it?" (v. 8). He was not doubting God's promise, but he wanted some confirmation, some indication, some sign that he would indeed inherit the land. Like Gideon, Abram wanted visible assurance regarding the promise God made to him (Judges 6:17-21).

God's Reply—The Ritual of a Formal Covenant

God confirmed the promises by means of a formal ceremony (vv. 9-10). A covenant is a formal binding agreement between the parties involved. Abram would have fully understood ratifying a covenant by such a ceremony; covenants of this type were the normal practice in his day and were common in the selling of property. When the two parties had verbally agreed on the terms of the covenant, they would carry out a ceremony in which both parties bound themselves to the agreed terms. In the ceremony, both parties walked between the two halves of an animal sacrifice, indicating their agreement. The slain halves of the animal indicated the penalty of death should either party break their side of it.

Although Abram participated in the preparations for this ceremony, it was God who actively enacted it, demonstrating that He was the only responsible party in this particular agreement. There is another reference to such a covenant in Jeremiah 34:18. The covenant ceremony would conclude with the meat of the sacrifice being roasted and eaten in celebration of the agreement.

Abram made preparations for this covenant ceremony just as God asked him to (vv. 9-10). Instead of a single animal, God told him to prepare five: a cow, a female goat, a male sheep (ram), a turtledove, and a young pigeon. These were the five sacrificial animals that were acceptable to God under the Mosaic Law that came later. Abram proceeded to kill them and to divide the three animals in two. Without any further instructions from God, he placed the halves of the three animals opposite each other and the two undivided birds opposite each other. Thus, there were two rows of animals with a space in between. Whether they were positioned on an altar or on the ground, we are not told.

The Symbolism of the Ceremony

Two unusual things occurred next. The first was a long delay. After he prepared the animals and the birds, nothing happened for the rest of the day. Abram was waiting for God to make the next move. While he waited, vultures appeared and would have feasted on the carcasses, but Abram took it upon himself to drive them away (v. 11). The second unusual feature was that, when the sun had set, a nightmarish sleep fell on Abram (v. 12) in which he was enveloped by "horror and great darkness." God was teaching Abram some things regarding the future (his own being that he would die in peace at a good old age [v. 15]).

Although the promise was secure, there was to be a long delay until Abram's descendants inherited their promised possessions. This delay was symbolized by Abram's long wait during the day. During that time, Satan (symbolized by the vultures) would try to thwart God's purpose. Satan did indeed attempt to stop the Savior coming many times down through history. These attempts included events like the corruption of the human gene pool by the sons of God before the Flood, King Saul's attempts to kill David (God's appointed king), and Herod's attack on the baby boys in Bethlehem.

The meaning of the "horror and great darkness" was a prophetic message for the Hebrew nation. Their history would include many periods of suffering, and one of the darkest times was predicted here. God told Abram, "Know certainly that your descendants will be strangers in a land that is not theirs, and will serve them, and they will afflict them four hundred years" (v. 13). This was a reference to the Israelites being enslaved and mistreated in Egypt before their deliverance under Moses. Only after that time of suffering would they "come out with great possessions" (v. 14). Abram's descendants would receive that bounty at their point of departure from Egypt, when the Egyptians gladly bestowed their valuables on them.

The prophecy of the coming "horror and great darkness" in this passage may also refer to the sufferings of Abram's greatest descendant, the Lord Jesus Christ, that He endured during three hours of darkness on Calvary's cross at the hand of God. The inauguration of the covenant with Abram is reminiscent of the inauguration of the new covenant in Christ's blood (Matt. 27:45).

Four Hundred Years

The Lord told Abram that his descendants would be strangers in a foreign land for four hundred years (v. 13). It is worth noting that the word "afflict" in verse 13 is the same word used in Exodus 1:11 where the Egyptian taskmasters were said to "afflict" the Israelites with burdens. The actual period has often been brought into question because of the number "430 years" mentioned in Exodus 12:40 and similar references in Acts 7:6 and Galatians 3:17.*

The 430 years in Exodus 12:40 probably speaks of the period between God making this covenant with Abram and the Israelites leaving Egypt under Moses. It was significant in two ways. First, it was a time of learning and waiting for the people of God which would last for four generations (v. 16). God was preparing them for their future in the land. The hostility around them taught them to believe God, to love God, and to serve God. Second, the four hundred years was significant to demonstrate God's patience in waiting for the proper time to enforce His judgment on the Amorites, whose iniquity was not yet "complete" (v. 16).

The name *Amorites* as used in this passage is a collective name for all ten tribes of the Canaanites as listed in verses 19-21. The "incompleteness" of

---

* Editor's Note

Among scholars there is much disagreement as to the period to which the 430 years applies. The debate is linked to views on when the Israelites entered Canaan. The discussions are quite involved and lengthy and are not suitable for discussion in this volume. For further information the reader is directed to *A Survey of the Old Testament* by Andrew E. Hill and John H. Walton (Grand Rapids, Michigan: Zondervan, 1996, p107-10) and an article entitled "Duration of the Egyptian Bondage" in Bibliotheca Sacre (October 1969).

their iniquity has to do with one of the principles of God's judgment whereby He waits to inflict judgment until iniquity reaches a predetermined level. In the case of the people before the Flood, God "waited in the days of Noah" before He judged them. Here, in regard to the wickedness of the Amorites, He did not send in the Israelites to cast them out until their wickedness fully justified the action (cf. 6:5; 1 Pet. 3:20). The Lord Jesus also referred to this principle in Matthew 23:32.

The Smoking Oven and a Burning Torch

After God's verbal explanations to Abram in verses 13 to 16, He appeared visibly as smoke and fire to ratify the covenant (v. 17). In the darkness, Abram saw a smoking oven and a burning torch pass between the pieces of the sacrifice. This was a *theophany*, a manifestation of God. The smoking oven was a cylindrical firepot commonly used in homes of that day. The symbol of fire to depict God is not unusual in Scripture. God appeared at Mt. Horeb in a burning bush when He called Moses (Ex. 3:2-6). God led His people through the wilderness with a pillar of fire by night (Ex. 13:21), and He appeared on Mt. Sinai in a consuming fire to give the Law (Ex. 19:18).

Abram was not invited to follow the firepot, which would have been the normal practice in a covenant ceremony. Only the smoking oven and the flaming torch, representing the Lord, passed through. The fact that God alone passed between the pieces means that it was God alone who bound Himself to fulfill the obligations of the covenant. This was an unconditional covenant; the fulfillment of which was not dependent on Abram doing anything at all. God's solemn oath to Abram guaranteed that the promises would be fulfilled.

The Covenant Explained (vv. 18-19)

The covenant with Abram concerned both his descendants and the land. God explained to him the extent of the land with specific and literal borders in which his descendants were to live as a literal people. It would stretch from the "river of Egypt" in the southwest (Wadi Arish in the Sinai Peninsula) to the Euphrates River in the northeast. Ten Canaanite tribes that occupied the land in the days of Abram are listed by name. Thus, Canaan was delineated geographically and ethnically. Except for a very brief time during the reign of Solomon, Israel has not yet occupied all this land. It will be fully theirs in the millennial period when Messiah rules the world.

The covenant began to be fulfilled in the time of the Exodus from Egypt to Canaan (Ex. 2:24). It was further fulfilled when Jesus, the Son of God, came into the world (Luke 1:72-73). The fulfillment will be fully realized when the nation of Israel comes into possession of all the promises of God in the future (Acts 3:13, 25). Even Israel's repeated disobedience has not nullified it (cf. Luke 1:46-55; Acts 3:17-26; Heb. 6:13-18).

In Conclusion

When we consider the unconditional love of God for Abram, we can rejoice in God's unconditional love showered on us through His Son, the Lord Jesus Christ. He went through the "fire" of Calvary to deliver us from our sin and give us eternal life according to the new covenant. This new covenant, like the covenant with Abram, assures us of its complete fulfillment because it is not based upon what we do, but on what He has done. Like Abram, we have been justified (declared righteous) before God. "If God is for us, who can be against us?" (Rom. 8:31). And, like Abram, we too have to wait for God's timing to see our salvation's complete fulfillment.

The Birth of Ishmael

The faith of Abram, God's friend, has so far proved to be one of mountains and valleys. In the previous two chapters his faith was in the highlands. It was by faith that Abram allowed Lot to have first choice of the land, believing God would make ample provision for his own needs. In the battle with the kings of the Euphrates Valley (a much superior force) he trusted God and found Him faithful in that He gave him the victory. After giving Melchizedek (in his role as a priest of the Most High God) a tenth of the victory spoils, he gave the king of Sodom the remainder because he did not want it said that anyone but God had enriched him. In these incidents Abram demonstrated a vital trust in God.

In chapter 16, we observe Abram in the valley of unbelief because he loses sight of God's promises. Many years earlier, he had failed to trust God to provide for him when Canaan suffered a famine, and he fled to Egypt. On that occasion, his faith failed in relation to the first subject of God's promises—that of the land. In this chapter, Abram's faith stumbles again, this time in regard to his descendants, the second sphere of God's promises to him.

Abram's Faltering Faith

Ten years had passed without a fulfillment of God's promise to give Abram a son. Even though God had reassured him that his own son, not his household steward, would be his heir (15:4), Sarai was still barren. Abram was keenly aware that their "biological clocks" were ticking; he was eighty-five years old, and Sarai was seventy-five. But what they did not know was that the very thing they feared—the physical impossibility of conceiving a child—was the very thing for which God was waiting. In the long delay, there is no doubt that God was not only testing Abram's faith, but arranging circumstances so that when he and Sarai did have a child, it would be obvious that it was entirely God's doing. God was not going to step into the situation until they had to depend on Him alone, knowing that nature had passed them by. However, Abram's faith failed. He and Sarai took matters into their own hands.

Abram and Hagar (vv. 1-6)

The pathos of the situation is evident in the first verse, which states that "Sarai … had borne [Abram] no children." The focus is on Sarai. She must have been thinking about just how God's promise could be fulfilled. She had given up hope of having children, because it now seemed physically impossible. But she did have an Egyptian maidservant named Hagar. Hagar belonged to Sarai; therefore, everything Hagar had was Sarai's. If Hagar had a child, therefore, it would belong to her, Sarai. She concluded that if the child were fathered by Abram, she (Sarai) and Abram would have a child, and the promise of God would be fulfilled. She stated correctly that it was God who had restrained her from bearing children (v. 2) but implied that God was to blame for making the situation more difficult than necessary for her. To get around what she perceived as God's reluctance, she reasoned that her husband should marry Hagar. She suggested to Abram, "Please, go in to my maid. Perhaps I shall obtain children by her" (v. 2).

Her plan looked really brave and selfless. Consider the following aspects in its favor:

- Having children by proxy was an accepted custom of the times (cf. 30:3).
- It was generous of her to voluntarily share her husband.
- God had not specifically stated that Sarai would be the mother of Abram's heir (see 15:4). She might have reasoned that the promise could still be fulfilled if a different woman bore Abram a child.

The truth is, however, that her plan was wrong from the outset because (1) it violated the marriage principle of "one man and one woman" that had been clearly set out by God in the Garden of Eden (2:18-25) and (2) it violated the principle of faith, in that it took the choice out of God's hands as to how He was going to carry out His promise to give Abram a son. Sarai thought she had a better idea than God.

Abram's Error

The fateful words are "Abram heeded the voice of Sarai." He should have known better. By listening to her and doing what she suggested, Abram became responsible for the outcome. He gave in to pressure from Sarai when she was obviously frustrated and embarrassed by her childlessness. Even worse, Abram left God out of the equation; he acted out of human reasoning alone.

We are reminded of a similar incident that took place in the Garden of Eden (3:6, 17): just as Eve took the forbidden fruit and gave it to Adam, so "Sarai ... took Hagar, and gave her to her husband to be his wife" (v. 3). Both Adam and Abram were wrong to neglect the word from God in order to please their wives.

Hagar is termed Abram's wife, not concubine, though it is obvious that, being a maid, she would not have been elevated to the same status that Sarai held in the household. Note that God refers to Hagar as "Sarai's maid" in verse 8 and as "the bondwoman" in Genesis 21:12-13. Sarai is the only one that God terms "your [Abram's] wife" (see 17:15 and 19; 18: 9–10).

Hagar Conceives Ishmael

When Hagar's pregnancy was confirmed, all three characters in the story responded in a sinful way to the problems it created (vv. 4-6). If no other passage existed in the Bible about the evil of polygamy, this one alone would be sufficient warning against it. Polygamy results in envy, jealousy, and strife in the home. Although people commonly practiced polygamy in Old Testament times, there is no biblical record of a happy polygamous marriage. God instituted marriage between one man and one woman (2:22-25). Any other arrangement is a violation of God's law.

Hagar Despises Sarai

When Hagar realized that she was pregnant, she despised Sarai (v. 4). Perhaps she looked down on her for being unable to bear children. Maybe she thought that Sarai's barrenness indicated God's displeasure with her due to some sin. Her feelings of superiority must have been evident to everyone in Abram's encampment. Though her attitude is easy to understand from a human point of view, it did not reflect a humble thankfulness to God or quiet submissiveness to her mistress. Instead, she gloated over her good fortune and compared it to Sarai's misfortune.

Sarai Retaliates Against Hagar

Sarai realized that her authority was being undermined. Bitterness toward Hagar soon overwhelmed her such that she acted irrationally by blaming Abram for Hagar's pride (v. 5). She poured out her complaints to him and demanded action, even though the whole idea had been hers. Sarai had sinned when she tried to achieve God's purpose by her own efforts. She sinned when she allowed bitterness to dictate her behavior. She sinned again when she blamed Abram for her own scheme. She is an example of many believers who leave the pathway of faith and then blame others when life become unpleasant. How easily situations deteriorate and our perspective becomes distorted when we act in unbelief!

Abram Sides with Sarai

Abram's response to Sarai's outburst was hardly better than that of either of the two women (v. 6). He knew Sarai, and it was inadequate for him to simply say to her, "Indeed your maid is in your hand; do to her as you please." He did not act responsibly as the head of the home. Abram knew that Sarai would treat Hagar badly. It was with Abram's permission that she "dealt harshly" with her. Note how he distanced himself by calling her "your maid" instead of "my wife." As a result, Hagar had little recourse but to try and run back toward Egypt, her homeland. The three sinful responses by Sarai, Hagar, and Abram form the dark side of the story. It was wrong to allow their situation to be dictated by social customs. It gives us cause to think how often we, too, allow the world and culture to govern what the faithful should do, rather than trust and obey our sovereign God.

The Angel and Hagar (vv. 7-14)

Hagar escaped from the encampment and began her journey back to Egypt. She reached a place described as "a spring of water in the wilderness, by the spring on the way to Shur" in a physically exhausted state. The Angel of the Lord found her in this condition.

Who was "the Angel of the LORD" mentioned four times in this passage (vv. 7-11)? He was a manifestation of the Lord Himself, none other than the second Person of the Trinity. This Old Testament term is used to refer to pre-incarnate appearances of the Lord Jesus Christ. He appeared as such to Abraham when he offered Isaac on the altar (22:11), to Jacob when He wrestled with him (32:24-30), to Moses at the burning bush (Ex. 3:2), and to Gideon before the battle with the Midianites (Judges 6:11). In each of these instances, He instructed people in crisis, just as He did when He appeared to Hagar. What He had to say was always more important than the fact of His appearance. Note that He is called *the* Angel or "messenger," not just *an* angel. More significantly, in verse 13, He is called "the LORD," and Hagar recognized Him and called Him "the God who sees."

The Angel Questions Hagar

The journey was proving too much for Hagar—she was, after all, pregnant—and she sensed that she could go no further. However, turning back also seemed impossible; she did not want to endure any more of Sarai's harsh treatment. Right there, in her misery by the spring, the Angel appeared to her. It is often the way of God to allow believers to come to the end of their own resources and to reach a point where all hope seems lost. It is then that He reveals Himself to them and provides a solution to the crisis. That is what Hagar experienced.

The Angel addressed Hagar by her name and her station in life, showing that He knew her personally. He gently probed her with questions intended to get her to admit her own dilemma. He asked, "Where have you come from, and where are you going?" She confessed that she was running away from her mistress. It was tantamount to saying that she couldn't take the abuse and humiliation any more.

The Prophecy about Hagar's Son

The Angel was direct with His answer: "Return and submit yourself under Sarai's hand," that is, Sarai's authority (v. 9). These would not have been easy words to hear, but they were certainly clearly understood. The Angel continued by giving her a remarkable prophecy (vv. 10-12). The message was really a set of promises and prophecies from God to Hagar.

The first promise was that her descendants would be so numerous that they could not be counted (v. 10). The second promise was that the child she was carrying was a boy. She was told to name him *Ishmael,* which means "God hears." The Angel explained that the name was appropriate because "the LORD has heard your affliction." In this way the name Ishmael would remind people for all time how the promise-keeping God responded to Hagar's cry in the wilderness. All of this has come to pass. Hagar's descendants by Abram are numbered in the hundreds of millions. The Arab peoples claim Abraham and Hagar as their first parents and Ishmael as their father. The meaning of the name Ishmael has also comforted countless Christian people who find that when they pray in the hour of their distress, *God hears.* The theme of "hearing" will appear again in the next chapter, as well as in chapter 21 (cf. 17:20; 21:17).

After assuring Hagar that God had heard her affliction He added a prophecy to the promise. Hagar's son would be a "wild man," or a wild donkey of a man (v. 12). This figure is not used of Ishmael in a contemptuous sense, as we might suppose. The onager, or wild donkey, was a beautiful and swift animal of the desert that, when fully grown, could be neither caught nor tamed (cf. Job. 39:5-8). A mustang would be a more familiar illustration of Ishmael's character for us today. The wild donkey was intended to illustrate Hagar's own tendency to sudden impulse, and these strong feelings would be magnified in her son. He would love the freedom of the wilderness and resist the confinement of city life. He would be known for the less disciplined life of a desert nomad: noisy, frugal, constantly on the move with his camels and horses. His descendants, the bedouins who inhabit the desert and who excel in animal husbandry, are known by these characteristics.

The prophecy went on to say that "his hand will be against every man, and every man's hand will be against him" (v. 12). It speaks of the aggressive and defiant spirit with which he would face other people. There would be constant feuds with neighbors over the rights to pastures or wells. "He shall dwell in the presence of all his brethren," meaning that, although he would not inherit the blessing of the land, as would Abram's heir, he would live in their presence independently as a free man looking on. History has confirmed this in what happened, not only to Ishmael and his immediate family, but also to the descendants of Ishmael who now occupy the huge peninsula of Arabia and large territories to the west and north.

El Roi: The God Who Sees

Hagar had an extraordinary and rare experience in receiving a direct revelation from God. She was told to go back to the point where she went wrong and start over. How would she respond? Initially, Hagar responded to the Angel with surprise. She understood that God has seen her in her predicament and cared for her, so she called Him "the God-who-sees." The original construction of this phrase can be understood to include a second aspect that not only had God *seen* her in her need, but in manifesting Himself to her as an Angel, *He* could *be* seen. Then Hagar expressed her surprise that she was still alive after having seen God, for she asked, "Have I also here seen Him who sees me?" More simply stated, she said, "Am I still alive after seeing God?" She knew that the God who had seen her had discerned that she was a rebel and that she was running away. She acknowledged that He who had appeared to her was personally interested in her.

How instructive this is for us, even when we are running away from God. He is the "God who sees." He sees where we are going and sees what we need. He waits for us to realize that He is the all-seeing God. From that time on, the well where Hagar rested was called "Beer Lahai Roi," meaning the "well of the One who lives and sees me." The well was a reminder that God is alive and provides for the needs of His people.

The Birth of Ishmael (vv. 15-16)

Hagar obeyed the Angel of the Lord and returned to Abram and Sarai. She must have come back a changed woman, having placed her trust in God. The Lord sent her back to the same tense situation with Sarai, but she now had faith, hope, and a message from God. Undoubtedly, she related her experience at the well to Abram. In due time, she gave birth to a son, at which point Abram was eighty-six years old. Abram named him Ishmael, just as the Angel had instructed Hagar.

In Conclusion

Although Abram is often called "the father of the faithful," his faith is certainly not evident in this chapter. Abram stumbled in agreeing to Sarai's suggestion that he take Hagar so he could produce a son, and he stumbled again over his responsibility toward them both. God, however, did not fail Hagar in her need. The whole incident reminds us that no matter how faint the cry, God hears. Hagar herself named the Angel El Roi, which reminds us that God "sees." The chapter ends with the same tensions with which it began. Sarai was still barren, and the relationship between her and Hagar was still strained. But it teaches us that God had great plans for Abram's son Ishmael, plans that have become apparent during subsequent history.

The Pledge and Sign of the Covenant

In view of the events in the previous chapter, it is not surprising that no details are given of the next thirteen years of Abram's life. There are no recorded visits from the Lord, no progress in his faith to account for, and nothing extraordinary happened to him. Nor do we read of any significant failure on his part. It was neither a time of great loss or great victory, but the Lord kept His hand on His chosen man during this period of silence in the biblical record.

The Covenant of Grace

In this chapter, God reveals more about the covenant promises to Abram that He gave in Genesis 12 and 13 and later ratified in chapter 15. It may be that God allowed the thirteen-year delay between the events of chapters 16 and 17 to teach Abram to trust Him more implicitly regarding the promises, especially after his undue haste in agreeing to Sarai's proposition to father a child by Hagar. In Genesis 17, God again pledged His covenant and gave a sign. The actual word "covenant" is used only once in all the earlier chapters (15:18), whereas in this chapter it is used thirteen times, and on every occasion God is speaking. Nine times He calls it "My covenant," three times an "everlasting covenant," and once a "covenant between Me and you." It was entirely God's covenant. God designed it, ratified it, and carried it out. The covenant was a demonstration of God's grace, meaning that it was God alone who acted; He imposed no conditions on Abram. God asked nothing from Abram except to believe that the promises would be fulfilled. God illustrated His grace to Abram by being the sole party to pass between the pieces of the sacrifice in the covenant ceremony. Now God pledges to keep His promise by changing Abram's name to Abraham, "because I have made you a father of many nations" (v. 4). Note the use of the past tense, underlining the certainty of fulfillment.

God Appears to Abram (v. 1)

Chapter 17 is almost entirely composed of God's direct revelation to Abram. In verse 1 "the LORD appeared to Abram," and in verse 22 "God went up from Abraham." The occasion was so special that God revealed Himself by a new name: "God Almighty" (Hebrew El Shaddai). By this name, God was pledging to Abram that He was both able and willing to give him the long promised seed even though, at ninety-nine, Abram's body "was as good as dead" and Sarai's the same (Rom. 4:19).

El Shaddai was the third name by which Abram knew God. In the beginning, God revealed Himself to Abram as *Elohim*, the God of creation (Acts 7:2). Later it was through the name LORD (Yahweh) that Abram was given the ever-widening promise of God's saving purpose through the coming Seed (12:1). Now God revealed himself as the Almighty God who would overcome the impossible to fulfill His promise (17:1). The title of God Almighty occurs forty-eight times in the Old Testament. Because the root meaning of the word *shaddai* can be viewed in different ways, commentators have not always agreed about its significance. A majority of scholars believe it to mean "strong and powerful." A quick comparison of the six times it is used in Genesis will bear this out (17:21; 28:3; 35:11; 43:14; 48:3; 49:25). In this passage, God assures Abram of His power to bless him by giving him and Sarai the long promised son and heir. Like Abram, we too have El Shaddai as our God. What an encouragement it is to know that our God is strong and powerful! He fulfills His promises, even when the circumstances seem impossible.

Having revealed His name to Abram, God commanded him to walk before Him and be blameless, or perfect. To walk before God is to live openly and consciously under God's watchful eye. He had failed to do this when he schemed with Sarai to have a son by Hagar. He had failed to believe then that God was all-powerful. For us, to walk before God emphasizes our responsibility to please Him. The second command to Abram was to be perfect, mature in respect to godliness. The meaning here emphasizes his need to be a complete man of faith. It does not mean that Abram was to make himself worthy to obtain God's promises. Rather, he would do those things that were consistent with God's covenant purposes. It is important to keep this distinction in mind, because this command is in the context of God's covenant of grace. Abraham, like us, would never become worthy of God's kindness, but he was to live his life in response to God's grace, so as to please Him.

The Promise to Establish the Covenant (vv. 2-3)

After pledging again to fulfill His covenant promises, God established it visually and gave Abram a sign (vv. 9-14). God did it all. The word *make* is literally "to give," meaning that it was a gift from God rather than a two party contract. In response, "Abram fell on his face, and God talked with him." Abram bowed down low in an act of worship. He showed his unworthiness before God Almighty. At the feet of the exalted Lord, he was at the place where consecration begins. He took the posture of a servant before his master and demonstrated that he was appropriating the promise of the covenant to himself by an act of worship. Abram is a model for any believer in believing God's covenant, accepting God's conditions, and humbling himself to worship.

The Covenant is Given (vv. 4-14)

Initially, God spoke of the divine side of the covenant saying, "As for Me" (v. 4). Later, in verse 9, He would talk of Abram's side of it: "As for you." From God's perspective, the covenant promise was specifically with Abram. He said, "You shall be a father of many nations." But the promise reached far beyond Abram being the patriarch of just one nation; some of the nations he would father are mentioned in Genesis, such as the Israelites through his wife Sarah, the Midianites through Ketura (25:2), the Ishmaelites through Hagar (25:12), and the Edomites via his grandson Esau (36:43). For Abram, it was a great and rare honor to be the father of not one, but many nations.

Abram Becomes Abraham

God then gave Abram a new name. He said, "Your name shall be Abraham, for I have made you a father of many nations" (v. 5). For ninety-nine years he had been called Abram ("exalted father"). That name most likely referred to the rank and stature of his father, Terah. In calling his son Abram, Terah signified that he was of a distinguished lineage and high birth. Now Abram was to be known as *Abraham,* which means "father of a multitude." It was to be a perpetual reminder to him of God's promise that he would be the father of many nations.

The new name might well have surprised Abraham's family and others in the household. As the father of only one son at that time—Ishmael—to announce that he was to be called the father of many nations would have taken great faith, both to speak and to accept. However, by now he had come to believe that his wife, Sarai, was to bear a son who would bring him many descendants. When God gave him his new name, He was pledging that He would fulfill His promise. Whenever God changes someone's name, it is because something has changed in their lives. It was Nehemiah who explained what happened in the life of Abraham: God changed his name because He "found his heart faithful" (Neh. 9:7-8). The name Abram is only used in the Bible twice after this chapter in Genesis, both references in the context of the change in his name (1 Chron. 1:27; Neh. 9:7).

The Covenant Promises Expanded

In verse 6 God continued by saying that He would make him exceedingly fruitful, to the extent that not only nations would come from him, but also kings (i.e. the line of David). God then revealed two additional features of the promises. First, that in a special way He would be their God and second, that the covenant would be everlasting. The word *everlasting* sometimes means "for all time." It also means "all during the time when certain conditions exist." Whichever meaning is intended here, the covenant would most certainly be fulfilled without any conditions attached.

In a sense, the words "I will ... be God to you and your descendants" (v. 7) are the core of the covenant. This promise alone far outweighed any of the particular benefits. It was not Abraham deciding that the Lord would be his God, but God who was promising to forever be Abraham's God. None of us can possibly need a promise greater than that. God then amplified the promise to include the time when Abraham's descendants would actually obtain possession of the land, and even then, God said, "I will be their God" (v. 8).

Abraham, the Friend of God

The relationship between Abraham and God was remarkable for its closeness and intimacy. Three times the Bible calls him "the friend of God": in 2 Chronicles 20:6-7, in Isaiah 41:8, and in James 2:23. Perhaps the most significant of these is the Isaiah passage, where the Lord Himself says: "But you Israel, are My Servant, Jacob, whom I have chosen, the descendants of Abraham My friend." It was in the making of the covenant that Abraham became the friend of God. As the covenant promises were unfolded, Abraham drew ever closer to God in his faith and worship. Friendship with God is an open possibility for every believer. When the Lord Jesus was talking to His disciples, He said, "No longer do I call you servants, for a servant does not know what his master is doing; but I have called you friends, for all things that I heard from My Father I have made known to you" (John 15:15). The closer we draw to Him, the greater the bond of friendship develops. Who would have thought that divine/human friendship was possible?

The Sign of the Abrahamic Covenant (vv. 9-14)

A sign is a tangible indication of an object or an action other than itself. The rite of circumcision was a sign instituted by God that was designed to affirm, every time it was performed, that God would honor His covenant. Just as the sign of the rainbow is a reminder that God will never again destroy the world with a flood, so circumcision was a sign that God would faithfully fulfill His promise to His chosen people.

Abraham's Responsibility

God carefully explained His side of the covenant in verses 4 to 8, beginning with the words "As for Me." Here we read of Abraham's side of the covenant, "As for you" (v. 9). Abraham would demonstrate his belief in the covenant by carrying out the rite of circumcision. The moral obligations of the covenant were not clearly spelled out at this time; they were told to Moses on Mt. Sinai (Exodus 20).

At this point, Abraham was just instructed to practice the rite, which was like a brand mark demonstrating that his household and his descendants belonged to God. The rite was to be a permanent practice "throughout their generations" and was to be performed on all males, including servants and foreigners acquired by purchase. Newborn sons were to be circumcised on the eighth day after birth. Circumcision was not unknown among the peoples of ancient times, but the practice on infant boys was not known and seems to have begun with Abraham.

Circumcision and its Meaning

Circumcision was (and is) a simple surgical procedure on the male sex organ through which the "seed" of the father is transmitted and the race perpetuated. Thus, circumcision was associated with the purity of the ongoing line of Abraham's descendants. However, more importantly, it was identified with the moral and spiritual purity of God's people. The procedure suggests the "removal" of heathen ways, just as it did in the days of Joshua, when all the male Israelites born in the wilderness were circumcised immediately after they entered Canaan. At that time, Joshua said, "This day I have rolled away the reproach of Egypt from you" (Josh. 5:9). Not long before, Moses had reminded them that physical circumcision was a sign of the purity of heart that was to characterize them (Deut.10:16). In the New Testament, Paul spoke of the meaning of circumcision as the "putting off the body of the sins of the flesh, by the circumcision [death] of Christ" (Col. 2:11). In both Old and New Testaments, therefore, the meaning symbolized separation from evil practices.

A second aspect of circumcision was its being a sign of the unity of God's people. Any uncircumcised person among them would be "cut off from his people; he has broken My covenant" (v. 14). Gentiles could be circumcised if they believed in God and became part of the community of Israel (vv. 12-13; cf. Ex. 12:45). A third aspect of the biblical teaching of circumcision was that it was a sign of Abraham's right standing before God. Paul argues that Abraham was justified (declared righteous) by faith before he was circumcised and later received circumcision as the sign and seal of his justification (v. 11; Rom. 4:11). It pointed to the reality of righteousness by faith without works.

The external rites and ceremonies of Israel that became part of the Mosaic Law, including circumcision, were never transferred to the Church. However, circumcision is commonly practiced by doctors today as a physically healthy procedure. Some Christians regard infant baptism as a rite that replaces circumcision. They believe that it "brings the infant into the covenant community," that is, the church. However, nowhere does the Bible teach this. Baptism is a public ceremony confirming the new believer's faith in Christ (Acts 8:36-37).

The Covenant and Abraham's Family (vv. 15-22)

Sarai becomes Sarah

After God informed Abraham of the covenant sign of circumcision, God specifically brought Sarai into the covenant (vv. 15-17). Up to this point, it had been implied, but never specifically stated, that Sarai would bear the promised seed. Now God made that clear, and in connection with that confirmation He changed her name to Sarah. The meanings of Sarai and Sarah are similar, that is, "princess." Nevertheless, the change in her name reflected a change in her life, as it did in Abraham's. As a "princess," she would be connected with royalty, for her line would include kings who would rule over their peoples (v.16). David and Solomon are examples.

Abraham Laughs

When God finished speaking, "Abraham fell on his face and laughed." Was this the laughter of unbelief or of joy? Some think that Abraham's reaction reflected doubt because he wondered in his heart "Shall a child be born to a man who is one hundred years old? And shall Sarah, who is ninety years old, bear a child?" However, it is more likely that he was simply incredulous that such a wonderful thing could happen. We might put it this way: "That's unbelievable! Who would have thought that such a thing could happen!" Abraham believed what God said while speaking of what seemed to be the impossible barrier—their advanced ages. This interpretation is supported by the fact that Abraham fell on his face before God, an act of worship not unbelief. Notice also that God did not rebuke him as He did Sarah when *she* laughed in unbelief (cf. 18:12-13). Abraham's laughter and response showed how amazed and happy he was.

Abraham's Prayer for Ishmael

Despite this wonderful revelation, Abraham could not forget that he already had a son—Ishmael (vv. 18-20). The boy was thirteen-years old by this time, and Abraham loved him dearly. So the question that troubled Abraham was: If there was to be another son, would Ishmael receive any blessing? Abraham prayed, "Oh, that Ishmael might live before You!" It was a prayer for God's blessing on Ishmael. Abraham wanted to ensure that Ishmael would not be left out.

God Names Isaac

Before answering Abraham's concern for Ishmael, God wanted Abraham to be absolutely clear about who the promised seed was (v. 19). He repeated that Sarah would bear him a son and that he was to name him Isaac (meaning "laughter" because Abraham laughed with joy when God promised he would be born). The covenant promises would be fulfilled through Isaac and his descendants after him forever.

God Blesses Ishmael

With obvious reference to the meaning of Ishmael's name ("God hears"), God said to Abraham, "I have heard you." He promised that Ishmael would have a fourfold blessing:

- He would be fruitful (i.e. have children).

- God would "multiply him exceedingly," meaning that his descendants would be numerous.

- He would father twelve princes, indicating that his sons would be the heads of twelve clans. These twelve princes are listed in Genesis 25:12-16.

- God promised that Ishmael would become a great nation.

It should be noted that, as great as these blessings were, there is no element in them that links Ishmael or his descendants to God's covenant with Abraham. Thus, there is a clear distinction between the descendants of the two half-brothers. God ended His message to Abraham with the information that Sarah's son would be born about the same season next year (v. 21). Then God departed from Abraham (v. 22).

Abraham Circumcises His Household (vv. 23-27)

In the final section of the chapter Abraham obeyed God's command and immediately circumcised every male in his household, including Ishmael and himself. The matter was one of urgency because it was linked with the blessings of the covenant, and it was one of obedience because he had been commanded to do it.

In Conclusion

Chapter 17 reveals a name of God that showed He was powerful enough to fulfill His covenant with Abram—God Almighty. By faith, Abram bowed in worship, and God changed his name to Abraham. God then expanded the terms of the covenant and commanded circumcision as the visible sign of it, marking out Abraham's descendants for special favor from God and obligating them to keep themselves pure among the nations. Sarai's name was changed to Sarah. When Abraham prayed on behalf of Ishmael, God gave him a separate blessing, but the covenant blessing was to come through Isaac, who was yet to be born to Sarah. Abraham obeyed God and circumcised all the males in his household. Abraham leaves us an example of a dedicated believer; like him, we are to become a useful "vessel ready for the Master's use" (2 Tim. 2:21).

God's Promise and Abraham's Prayer

Chapter 18 records another visit from the Lord to Abraham. It is remarkably different to the encounter in chapter 17 in which the Lord appeared as God Almighty and very likely in some glorious form that prompted Abraham to fall on his face before Him (17:3). That appearance was probably reminiscent of the first time the "God of glory" appeared to him (Acts 7:2). In contrast to those visits, God now appears to Abraham as a human visitor to his home.

This visit was the prelude to several significant events in this chapter: first, the giving of further assurance of the birth of Abraham and Sarah's long-promised son; second, Sarah's laughter of unbelief; then, as Abraham was bidding his visitors farewell, advance news of the judgment that was about to fall on Sodom and Abraham's remarkable intercessory prayer on behalf of any righteous inhabitants of Sodom.

The Visit of the Heavenly Trio (vv. 1–8)

On a hot afternoon in the shade of the great trees of Mamre, the patriarch was sitting in the entrance to his tent. He looked up to see three men standing before him. He had not seen them approach, and in all probability they did not walk up to the tent but simply appeared. He ran to meet them and bowed low, indicating his deep respect for them as visitors and his intention to make every effort to entertain them generously.

Because of their human appearance, Abraham did not at first realize that one of the men was none other than the Angel of the Lord, the second Person of the Trinity, and that the other two were angels. Occasionally human kings have mingled incognito among their subjects, but how wonderful that the God of the universe came as an unknown guest to the home of one of His servants to receive hospitality! As the "friend of God," Abraham received Him into his own home, where they had fellowship and a meal. The Lord Jesus did a similar thing on the day He walked with the Emmaus disciples and entered their home for a meal. Only later did they, like Abraham, realize who their visitor was (Luke 24:13-32). The other two visitors were angels, as is clear from the next chapter (19:1).

Abraham spoke to the leader of the three saying, "My Lord, if I have now found favor in Your sight do not pass on by Your servant" (v. 3). Perhaps

Abraham wondered if the strangers had anything to do with the Lord's promises to him about Sarah finally bearing him a son. He certainly went to great trouble to serve them.

Abraham offered to wash their feet, to give them rest in the shade of a tree, and to bring them a "morsel of bread" so that they could be refreshed. It was a classic understatement to speak of the feast he was arranging as a "morsel," or as we might say, "just a bite." The writer of Hebrews alluded to this incident when he exhorted believers to show hospitality to strangers by saying that "some have unwittingly entertained angels" (Heb. 13:2). These passages are strong encouragements for believers to use their homes to show hospitality to people outside their usual circles. We may not always appreciate the biblical importance of entertaining guests in God's name. Abraham gave his guests a lavish meal with the best that he could provide.

The three visitors accepted Abraham's offer of hospitality by saying, "Do as you have said" (v. 5). Abraham hurried to have the meal prepared. He asked Sarah to make cakes from fine meal. He selected a choice calf for slaughter and roasting. He had butter and milk brought and the whole meal served to them. All of these preparations must have taken considerable time, but the guests showed no sign of impatience. Abraham stood respectfully nearby, ready to meet their every desire (v. 8).

The Challenge to Sarah's Faith (vv. 9-15)

When the three visitors had eaten, they asked Abraham where Sarah was. The fact that they knew her name would have confirmed his growing awareness that they were no mere humans. Abraham told them that she was inside the tent. Note that all three were included in the "they said" of verse 9, whereas only one of them responded to Abraham in verse 10. The speaker was the Lord Himself, who was the spokesman from then on. He said, "I will certainly return to you according to the time of life, and behold, Sarah your wife shall have a son." These words were evidently intended for Sarah's ears, who was listening behind the tent walls. The Angel confirmed what God had previously told Abraham, adding the word "certainly" (18:10; cf. 17:19). The tension of the story increases when the narrator reminds the reader again that Sarah was beyond the age of childbearing (v. 11).

Sarah Laughs in Unbelief

No doubt Sarah was aware of the promise, but maybe she clung to her unbelief, so sure that her lifelong barrenness and change of life were insuperable barriers (v. 12). What she heard prompted her to laugh "within herself." It was not a laugh of joy like Abraham's when he heard the same promise (17:15-17). It was a cynical laugh. As far as she was concerned, it was impossible for her and Abraham to have a child. When she referred to her husband as "lord" in this verse, she was simply using a common term of respect for him.

"Is Anything Too Hard for the Lord?"

The Lord perceived Sarah's derisive yet silent laugh behind the tent flap and said to Abraham, "Why did Sarah laugh, saying 'Shall I surely bear a child, since I am old?'" Though she had not spoken audibly, He let her know that He knew the thoughts and intents of her heart (vv. 13-15). This knowledge proved that He was God. He was prodding her to examine her unbelief. He went on to challenge her faith saying, "Is anything too hard for the Lord?" Then He repeated the promise, "At the appointed time … Sarah shall have a son." The truth began to dawn on her that God was not only able to give her a son, but faithful and willing to do so. Her realization of God's presence stimulated the growth of her faith (Heb.11:11).

The rhetorical question "Is anything too hard for the Lord?" has become one of the great sayings of the Bible. Our God is the God of the impossible. To cite one of several examples: In the account of the birth of the Savior, the angel spoke to the virgin Mary, telling her that she would bear a son. After stating that the child would be conceived by the Holy Spirit, he concluded by saying, "For with God nothing will be impossible" (Luke 1:31-37). See other examples in Jeremiah 32:17-27 and Luke 18:27. We can take great encouragement from such a statement when our own circumstances seem impossible.

Wonderful!

The word *hard* in the question "Is anything too hard for the Lord?" is used in other places in the Bible and translated "wonderful." Its significance lies in its meaning, which is "surpassing," "extraordinary," or "full of wonder." David spoke of God's extraordinary knowledge of all his ways and used this word in saying, "Such knowledge is too *wonderful* for me " (Ps. 139:6). In Isaiah 9:6, it describes one of the titles of the coming King whose "name shall be called Wonderful Counselor." Thus we have, as Abraham did, a God who Himself is Wonderful and for whom nothing is too *difficult* or *wonderful*.

God Tells Abraham of the Judgment on Sodom (vv. 16-21)

The reminder of "the God of the impossible" in verse 14 is followed by one of the best examples of intercessory prayer in the entire Bible, from which we may learn much. The theme of the prayer in this passage is the underlying biblical theme of the justice of God. We learn that even Abraham's intercession was not going to alter God's decision to judge the evil cities of the plains. The people of these cities deserved God's judgment and would receive it notwithstanding Abraham's prayer. It is his prayer, however, that teaches us that the destruction was just. Sodom and Gomorrah were ripe for judgment, especially in view of the fact that they had witnessed God's power in Abraham's brilliant military operation that resulted in their deliverance from the power of the kings of the East. They had heard Abraham say, "I have lifted up my hand to God Most High, the Possessor of heaven and earth" (14:22). In spite of this, they continued in their evil ways in flagrant disrespect of the one, true, holy God.

Abraham's Guests Leave

After the encounter with Abraham and Sarah, the three "men" rose up and headed toward Sodom (vv. 16-17). Abraham walked some distance with them to send them on their way. As they walked, the Lord spoke in a reflective way that Abraham could hear: "Shall I hide from Abraham what I am doing?" (v. 17). We should notice that it was God who directed the whole interlude. It was He who raised the subject of Sodom's judgment. He then waited for Abraham's intercession. Finally, it was He who brought the whole matter to a close by simply leaving after promising not to destroy Sodom if there were ten righteous people dwelling there (vv. 32-33). When we see God's sovereign direction over the whole scene, we will not get sidetracked into wondering if Sodom might have been saved had Abraham prayed for longer.

The Confidence of Friends

As we have noted before, the Bible calls Abraham God's "friend." One proof of their friendship in this passage is how God confided in Abraham by revealing His intentions to destroy Sodom, "for," He said, "I have known him" (v. 19). God's knowledge of Abraham carries the thought that He knew him as an intimate friend and could trust him with His secrets and plans. In New Testament times, the Lord Jesus treated His disciples in the same way. He said in John 15:15, "I have called you friends, for all things that I heard from My Father I have made known to you." Friendship with God is available to all who "walk with the Lord in the light of His Word." The Bible says, "The secret of the Lord is with those who fear Him" (Ps. 25:14).

As His friend, God not only revealed to Abraham what He was planning to do, He also explained why He was telling him. The first reason was because "all the nations of the earth shall be blessed in him" (v. 18). When his descendants became a nation, they would be entrusted with the Scriptures and prophetic revelation from God. This would be the first of many occasions of sharing His plans and purposes for the world, the nations of which would ultimately be blessed by the provision of a Redeemer. The second reason was to enable Abraham to explain to his descendants that God's judgment on Sodom was just (v. 19). The judgment was to be understood as an illustration of God's justice and righteous standards. Sodom's deserved destruction would motivate both his immediate and future "household" to "keep the way of the LORD to do righteousness and justice." By living righteously, they would enjoy the blessings that God had promised Abraham. That God is just or righteous in what He does is the most prominent theme of the chapter. The Israelites in the wilderness, for whom Moses was writing, would also need to understand this because they were going to be His instruments to utterly destroy pagan nations in Canaan.

They needed to know that their destruction would not be arbitrary, but just. God's people needed to be reminded of His standards for them, too. He was going to expect them to represent Him well. Therefore, the knowledge of this event would instill in them godly fear, and God could fulfill "what He [had] spoken to [Abraham]."

The Outcry Against Sodom

God spoke of the great "outcry against Sodom" (v. 20). The word "outcry" can be understood either as an outcry against Sodom caused by its wickedness (19:13) or the cry of its own rebellion against the Lord. Whichever it was, God purposed to "go down" and investigate (v. 21) it. This expression is similar to what we read in regard to Babel when the "Lord came down to see the city" before judging it (11:5). In both cases, if their condition matched the outcry, they would be judged. God's investigation does not imply that He did not already fully know the situation. He is omniscient and knows everything. He "came down" so that the people might know that God had actually seen and considered the full situation before acting in a just and terrible judgment. Sodom's judgment was no doubt made more severe because they had heard the witness of Abraham and Melchizedek (14:18-24).

The destruction of these sinful cities should speak powerfully to the nations of today's world. Many of them have had a strong witness of God's righteousness and yet have both ignored and rejected it. Despite warnings, they continue their downward path into corruption and evil, without giving God one thought.

While the Lord was talking to Abraham, His two companions "turned away and went toward Sodom" (v. 22). Abraham seems to have realized that they had started their mission. Instead of returning home, he remained with the Lord and began his great prayer of intercession.

Abraham's Prayer (vv. 21-33)

The Basis of Abraham's Prayer

It is well to note the progression in this chapter of Abraham's relationship with God that led up to his great prayer. It is an example to us. It began with God's initiative to reveal Himself to Abraham (v. 1). For us too, it is God who takes the initiative and gives us His Word. As Abraham came closer to God, he gladly welcomed God's company (vv. 2-3). We, also, are to welcome God's Word by reading it with a view to knowing God and obeying Him. The result for Abraham was fellowship with God around a common meal (vv. 4-8). We will experience greater closeness to God when we "dine" with Him in the common sphere of His Word and prayer (Rev. 3:20). Abraham's fellowship with God led to further revelation and a greater understanding of God's will, especially about the coming judgment on Sodom (vv. 9-22). We will learn more of His revealed purposes if we stay close to Him (Col. 1:9). With his growing understanding of God's purpose in judgment, Abraham's response was to approach God (v. 23) and intercede for the people who would be affected. And we who discern that our world is under judgment should respond by being people of prayer and intercession.

"Would You also destroy the righteous with the wicked?"

Abraham began by showing his concern for those around him: "Would You also destroy the righteous with the wicked?" (v. 23). The Sodomites were described as "exceedingly wicked and sinful against the LORD" in Genesis 13:13. By using the word *righteous,* Abraham referred to people who, like him, believed in the true God. Lot, for instance, was called "righteous" in the New Testament (2 Pet. 2:7). Naturally, Abraham was anxious about Lot and his family. Although he had undoubtedly compromised his testimony by his life in Sodom, Lot was a true believer in God. Abraham may well have hoped that Lot had influenced as many as forty-nine others to believe in God, including his own family. Abraham may also have been concerned for other residents of Sodom whom he had come to know after rescuing them from the eastern confederacy (Genesis 14). He would hope that they might still turn to God. He may also have been prompted to pray out of fear that surrounding nations might blaspheme the name of God when the cities of the plain were destroyed. Thus, Abraham began to pray that God would spare judgment on "the city" (v. 24; he probably had Sodom in mind) if sufficient righteous people could be found. His prayers were exploratory and most perceptive. He knew that God would be just, but he obviously did not know the situation in those cities as well as God did.

Abraham's prayer took the form of a series of questions and responses relating to the number of righteous people for whose sake the Lord would spare the whole city of Sodom. All six of his petitions reveal genuine humility and reverence for God. He did not demand God to act, or try to overcome His reluctance, or haggle with Him. Abraham made his pleas on the basis that God would act justly and not destroy the righteous along with the wicked. Note that the One to whom Abraham was speaking was the LORD" (vv. 22 and 26), but when he began to intercede he addressed God by "Lord," that is, *Adonai,* master (vv. 27, 30, 31, 32).

Abraham was acknowledging God's absolute authority in the situation. He never denied that God was completely justified in destroying the wicked. But, being convinced that there were righteous people living there, he wanted to know if God would spare the city for their sake. The answer was a resounding "yes." God takes no pleasure in the death of the wicked; rather, he longs for them to turn from their wicked way and live (Ezek. 33:11).

What should true believers, the "righteous," do when surrounded by evil? This passage teaches us that they should remain steadfastly true to the Lord. It also teaches that the righteous can make a difference for the good of the larger society in a pagan world. What an encouragement that even a tiny minority may have a remarkable restraining influence on the judgment of a whole city! Christians who sense the burden of growing wickedness should continue to bear a testimony as lights against the dark backdrop of evil. Finally, this passage teaches us that the righteous must teach their children to be righteous and pray that they might not be swept away with the wicked. The God of justice is also a God of mercy.

Abraham Perseveres in Prayer

Beginning with the supposition that there might be fifty righteous people in Sodom, Abraham asked God, "Would you destroy the place and not spare it for the fifty righteous that were in it?" (v. 23), reasoning "Far be it from You ... to slay the righteous with the wicked" (v. 25). Note that Abraham appealed to God's mercy and His righteous character. He said, "Shall not the Judge of all the earth do right?" Abraham's God was not a local tribal god, but the "Judge of all the earth." In answer to his prayer, God said, "If I find in Sodom fifty righteous within the city, then I will spare all the place for their sakes" (v. 26).

The second appeal reduced the critical number to forty-five, with the same merciful answer from God (vv. 27-28). Abraham humbly admitted he was only "dust and ashes," a most appropriate attitude for a praying believer (cf. Ps. 103:14). The number was lowered to forty and then to thirty (vv. 29-30). Abraham was concerned that the Lord not be angry with him for his persistence. Twice more the number was reduced, first to twenty and then to ten. Again God assured him, "I will not destroy it for the sake of ten" (vv. 31-32). Ten may possibly have been the number of Lot's family. It can be inferred from the text that Lot had, in addition to his wife, two married daughters and their husbands, two sons and two unmarried daughters (19:8, 12, 14). It would seem that the Lord stopped the dialogue at this point by leaving Abraham. But even if Abraham had petitioned for only five righteous in Sodom, it would not have saved the city, for only three ultimately escaped the holocaust.

The Results of Abraham's Prayer

Chapter 19 verse 24 says that God did indeed destroy Sodom and Gomorrah, having confirmed that their sin *was* "very grievous" (v. 20). Was Abraham's prayer, therefore, fruitless? Not at all. In regard to Sodom, it was never Abraham's intention to thwart the righteous judgment of God. He wanted the Judge to "do right." What he prayed for was that the righteous be saved. God answered that prayer, for He did preserve Lot (and those in his care).

In Conclusion

Abraham's six petitions can be compared to Elijah's seven petitions on Mt. Carmel (1 Kings 18:41-46) in terms of persistence. The Lord Jesus commends persistence in prayer (Luke 18:1-8). Abraham's prayer is a wonderful model for every believer in several ways:

- It reveals the mercy and care of God towards the righteous, however few.
- It exemplifies the humble attitude of the intercessor, who confesses "I who am but dust and ashes" as he prays to the Judge of all the earth.
- It shows how God answers His people's prayers in most specific ways.

Thus, we have an instructive model of the prayer of the righteous to God, the righteous Judge.

The Deliverance of Lot from Sodom

In chapter 19 the scene shifts from the quietness of the tents of Abraham among the Hebron hills to rioting mobs of evildoers in Sodom, the chief city of the plains of the Jordan. The two chapters also reveal the marked contrast between their leading characters, Abraham and Lot. They each received visits from angelic beings, but for very different reasons.

Lot, a Resident of Sodom

The chapter vividly illustrates the severity of God's judgment in the destruction of Sodom and the tragedy of Lot's worldliness in the destruction of his family. It concludes the story that began when Lot chose the well-watered plains of the Jordan and settled there (chapter 14). When he made that choice, he had no thought for the glory of God or the welfare of his family. Lot was drawn to Sodom, little by little, by his worldly aspirations. At first, he "pitched his tent toward Sodom" (13:12). Then he "dwelt in Sodom"(14:12). He even deliberately returned there after being rescued by Abraham. Now we find him "sitting in the gate of Sodom" (19:1). He gradually rose in his worldly pursuits from being a herder of domestic animals to becoming an officer in the gate of the city, this being the place of commercial, judicial, and political activities in all ancient cities.

Sodom was undoubtedly one of the most morally bankrupt cities this world has ever seen. The influence of its wicked and worldly environment had left its mark on Lot. He seems to have forgotten that he had participated with Abraham in one of the highest callings ever given to men, when the God of glory first appeared to Abraham back in Ur. He had been there when the great revelations from God came to Abraham in Haran, Shechem, and Bethel. When he was captured by the eastern confederacy, he knew that it was God who had given Abraham's tiny army the power to rescue him and the other captives. Yet there he was, enmeshed in Sodom's business and political affairs, probably because of his desire for power and influence. However, the greatest lesson from this chapter is that the destruction of Sodom and Gomorrah is an example of God's righteous judgment that hangs over all wicked societies today. God says that they were "an example to those who afterward would live ungodly" (2 Pet. 2:6).

"Righteous Lot"

It may surprise us that the Bible calls Lot a believer. Peter calls him "righteous Lot" and describes his abhorrence of the lifestyle of the Sodomites by saying "that he was oppressed with the filthy conduct of the wicked." He spoke of him as "that righteous man, dwelling among them, [who] tormented his righteous soul from day to day by seeing and hearing their lawless deeds" (2 Pet. 2:7-8). Lot seemed to rationalize his concern over the wickedness of Sodom by his intention to merely "sojourn" there, that is, live there temporarily. Both his concern and his good intentions were, unfortunately, dimmed by the worldly attraction Sodom had for him. He may have prided himself in his ability to get along in such an environment. Like many believers today, he was trying to get the best of both worlds. He ended up losing virtually everything he valued except his eternal salvation.

The Angels See the Sin of Sodom (vv. 1-11)

While Lot was sitting in the gate of Sodom, he saw two men approach (vv. 1-3). The passage identifies them as the angels who had just left Abraham's company by describing them as *the* angels (with the definite article). He thought they were influential visitors from out of town and hurried to offer them hospitality. After bowing with his face to the ground, he invited them in. When they said "No," preferring to stay outside, Lot insisted that they come in because he knew the moral depravity of the Sodomites. Their initial refusal was probably intended to test Lot's willingness to do his best for their welfare. When they came inside, Lot made them a feast and baked unleavened bread for them, which they ate (v. 3). Why his wife did not participate in the hospitality we are only left to surmise.

What happened next seems almost unthinkable (vv. 4-5). The men of the city had seen the two visitors, and they gathered outside Lot's door demanding that they be allowed to homosexually rape them. It was not just a wicked minority but "both young and old, all the people from every quarter" who surrounded the house. It was a shocking display of depraved people who wanted to violate both a host and his guests. No wonder the Lord had said to Abraham, "The outcry against Sodom and against Gomorrah is great, and ... their sin is very grievous" (18:20).

Homosexual activity is clearly condemned here in this, the first book of the Bible. The sin is called *sodomy* after the name of this very city. Later, in the Law of Moses, it was made a capital offense, along with bestiality and incest (Lev. 18:22; 20:13). In Romans, Paul calls homosexuality a sin. Because men rejected God, they worshipped the creature more than the Creator, resulting in God giving them up to "vile passions" in which both women and men departed from the natural desires and "burned in their lust for one another" (Rom. 1:18-32). Homosexuality is *not* an acceptable alternative lifestyle, but a gross departure from the law of God and His purpose for mankind. God designed sexual intimacy to be confined to a man and a woman within the bonds of marriage. All other forms of sexual activity pervert God's design and are pronounced in the Bible as sinful.

Lot's Futile Attempt to Stop the Outrage

Lot showed courage in seeking to halt the Sodomites' depraved plans. It was his duty, according to custom, to protect his guests, even at the risk of his own life. He went outside, shut the door behind him, and pled with the men, "Do not do so wickedly!" (vv. 6-7). He displayed even more courage when he offered his two virgin daughters to satisfy the lusts of the unholy mob (v. 8). Though this offer is almost unthinkable to us, Lot did it to protect the visitors, whom he may have guessed by this time were really angels. It was a tragic compromise situation into which Lot was pressed to offer to pay a terrible price. It was an attempt to avoid one sin by committing another. It should also be pointed out that although Lot's daughters were virgins in their bodies, they were already debauched in their minds. This is obvious by the dishonorable plan they carried out after they left Sodom (vv. 30-38).

The men outside did not agree to the "deal" Lot offered. Instead, they became angry with him and accused him of acting like a judge (v. 9). Like some antagonists of God today, they called good "evil" and evil "good." Perhaps, in the past, Lot had tried to act as a moral guide to them (cf. 2 Pet.2:7-8), especially after Abraham had rescued them all from enslavement to the kings of the East. Lot pled with them to do nothing to his visitors. They threatened him with even worse harm unless he stood out of the way, and they pressed hard against him, attempting to break down the door.

When Lot failed to save the visitors by the only strategy he knew, the angels intervened. They opened the door and forcefully pulled Lot inside, shutting out the mob. Then they struck them with blindness. The men were confused as well as blinded so that they could not even find the door (v. 11). Most certainly, it was God's supernatural intervention to save Lot's life and dignity.

The Destruction of Sodom (vv. 12-29)

While the mob milled around in the street outside, the angels specifically told Lot to warn any close family members in the city: "Take them out of this place!" They explained their mission: "the outcry against [Sodom] has grown great before the face of the LORD, and the LORD has sent us to destroy it." It was a message like that of John the Baptist, who talked about fleeing from the wrath to come (Matt. 3:7). Surely, if Lot's testimony could influence anybody it would be those within the circle of his immediate family.

Lot's family, however, was in the last stages of debauchery and disintegration, to the point that, when Lot warned his sons-in-law that they should leave the city, they thought he was joking (v. 14). His compromise with the worldliness of Sodom had been so great that his warning had no impact on them—nor, presumably, on his daughters who had married them. But what else could Lot expect? There is no record that he even *tried* to warn his sons. (We are assuming Lot actually had sons and the angels were not just listing off possible family members in verse 12.) Perhaps he knew it would be useless. What an indictment on Lot as a believing father! We who live in a world under God's judgment should not miss the deeply sobering lesson for ourselves and our families. The Bible says "Do not love the world or the things of the world" (1 John 2:15).

Lot's Hesitation

The next morning the angels urgently told Lot, "Arise, take your wife and your two daughters who are here, lest you be consumed in the punishment of the city" (v. 15). But they were not completely sure they wanted to go, and he "lingered" (v. 16). While they hesitated, the angels literally had to pull all four of them out of the city by the hand. Then one of the angels urgently commanded them to run for their lives saying, "Do not look behind you nor stay anywhere in the plain. Escape to the mountains, lest you be destroyed" (v. 17). The word for *destroyed* in the original text is the same as the word translated *consumed* in verse 15. It literally means "swept away." It is the word Abraham used in his intercessory prayer when he asked, "Would you also destroy the righteous with the wicked?", which shows that Lot's deliverance by the angels was in answer to Abraham's prayer (cf. 18:23).

Even outside the city, Lot hesitated again and asked for a concession, saying he was afraid to escape to the mountain "lest some evil overtake me and I die" (v. 18). He didn't think he could survive there and obviously did not trust God to keep him safe there. Lot's carnal bent of life is evident in every mention of him. He asked if he could go live in the city of Zoar, cited "insignificant" (v. 22, margin translation). If they granted his request, the city would have to be spared for his sake.

Lot seems to have little idea of what the angels were doing on his behalf or of the holocaust which was about to erupt. He still hoped to be comfortable in the world. He is like some of the people in the city of Pompei when it was destroyed by an eruption of Mt. Vesuvius. Peoples' remains can be seen in the streets to this day, still clutching their jewelry.

It is surprising that Lot's request was granted. The little city of Zoar was spared by the mercy and grace of God, and Lot was allowed to run to it (v. 21). Lot's prayer seems to have accomplished more than Abraham's. The answer to it may encourage us to continue in prayer for God's mercy and leave the results with Him. Lot's wife had no doubt been partially responsible for the delaying tactics up to this point, and she appears to have lagged behind. The angel's last words are striking, "Hurry, escape there. For I cannot do anything until you arrive there" (v. 22). The lesson for believers is clear. We must flee the world's attractions before we are overtaken by them and ruined, and we should treat each decision along life's path as significant in the light of the future.

The Destruction of Sodom and Gomorrah

The sun had risen by the time Lot reached Zoar, and at this point the Lord rained brimstone and fire on Sodom and Gomorrah (v. 24). Only two cities are mentioned in this verse, but we know from other passages that Admah and Zenoiim were also destroyed (cf. Deut. 29:23 and Hosea 11:8). What was the brimstone and fire that destroyed the four cities of the plain? There have been no lack of suggestions. A volcanic eruption might have rained down its fiery contents on the cities. Modern research has found little to corroborate this idea. Others have suggested that it might have come from explosions triggered by an earthquake or that there was a nuclear explosion, and still others think that material rained down on that part of the earth from outer space. The Bible simply says that God supernaturally and literally rained down some kind of fiery material from "out of the heavens," which selectively destroyed four of the five cities of the plain, everything that grew on the ground, and the plain (ground) itself (v. 25).

Lot's Wife

Lot's wife had been forcefully taken out of the city. Despite being told not to look back, she could not resist doing just that, longing for the life she had enjoyed in Sodom. Her heart was still in the city. She had not arrived in Zoar when the sun came up and fiery judgment came down. When she lingered and looked back, she was overcome by the fire and brimstone. She died on the spot and became a "pillar of salt." Brimstone is usually thought of as sulphur and is associated in Scripture with fire and God's judgment (Isa. 34:9; Rev. 14:10, 19:20, etc). Lot's wife was encrusted by salt and became a memorial pillar of disobedience. There are some standing salt formations remaining in the area of the Dead Sea to this day that are still termed "Lot's wife" by local people. Jesus warned His hearers to "remember Lot's wife" in the context of His message on His Second Coming, the times of which He likened to the days of Sodom (Luke 17:28-32). She is a warning to all who will not make a clean break with the world.

Abraham Views the Aftermath

The same morning that Sodom was destroyed (v. 28), Abraham went to the place where, only the day before, he had stood before the Angel of the Lord and interceded for Lot (18:23). It was probably on the hills to the east of Hebron from where the valley of the Jordan is visible. What must his thoughts have been as he remembered God's revelations the day before? As he looked toward Sodom and Gomorrah, he saw "the smoke of the land which went up like the smoke of a furnace." The destruction was all over in a very short time.

Verse 29 tells us that "God remembered Abraham," which indicates that Lot's escape "out of the midst of the overthrow" was in direct answer to Abraham's prayer to spare the righteous living in Sodom. It is interesting that only Lot is mentioned as being rescued, both here and in 2 Peter 2:6-9 (the New Testament commentary on this story). He was the only righteous one in God's sight. Peter tells us that God turned the cities of Sodom and Gomorrah into ashes, condemning them to destruction. Then he reminds us that the Lord knows how to deliver the godly out of temptation, that is, trial. If God delivered righteous Lot in response to Abraham's prayer, we have a strong encouragement both to pray earnestly and to trust God for special mercy ourselves.

Lot's Descendants (vv. 30-38)

There is a tragic sequel to Lot's deliverance. With his daughters he arrived in Zoar, which was at the south-eastern end of the valley in the plains of the Jordan. It was now surrounded by devastation. The people of Zoar (who were few in number, owing to it being a "little" city) probably resented the fact that Lot was the only survivor. Now that the fertile plains had been destroyed, the economy of the city was gone. If Lot still owned his vast herds, they were now all gone. He and his daughters did not stay in Zoar long, for verse 30 tells us that "Lot went up out of Zoar and dwelt in the mountains, and his two daughters were with him." The angel in Sodom had commanded them to "escape to the mountains" in the first place (v. 17). Why they did not return to Abraham's camp, we are not told. Perhaps pride stood in Lot's way. It must have been a miserable existence in the mountains. What a contrast to the wealth and luxury they had enjoyed in Sodom! We do not know how long they were there before the following recorded incident took place, but the implication from the word "dwelt" is that they made the mountains their home.

Lot's Disgrace

The daughters thought that, because of their current situation, they would never marry. Maybe they reasoned that no man would want to have anything to do with survivors of a cursed city. Looking ahead, they realized that, not only would their father never have descendants, but that they would have no one to care for them when they grew old. They do not seem to have even considered simply trusting God, as Abraham had demonstrated. In their twisted frame of mind, they decided that the answer to their dilemma was to have children by their father (vv. 30-38). To accomplish this, they would have to commit the sin of incest. They knew that Lot would never agree, so they figured out how they could make him inebriated and then carry out their plans. We should notice that although they must have had negligible possessions living as cave dwellers, they did have a stock of wine. There is often a connection between the consumption of alcohol and sexual impurity.

Starting with the eldest, they made Lot drunk on successive days, put him in bed, and followed through with their wicked acts. Lot was completely unaware of what happened. As a result, both of his daughters became pregnant. They both bore sons (vv. 37-38). The name of the firstborn's son was Moab, meaning "from the father," and the younger daughter's son was named Ben-Ammi, which means "son of my people."

The Moabites and the Ammonites

Moab became the progenitor of the Moabite people, who inhabited the area east of the Dead Sea. Ben-Ammi became the father of the Ammonite people, who occupied the area to the north of the Moabites and east of the Jordan. The capital city of the country of Jordan today takes its name, Amman, from the Ammonite people. At this point, Lot's biblical history ends in his terrible compromise and just fades away. He is one of a number of men in the Bible who started well but ended their lives in failure, men like Isaac, Saul, and Solomon.

The Moabites and Ammonites were Israel's constant enemies in subsequent history. Moab was the nation that would trouble the Israelites just before they entered the Promised Land. They committed the worst carnal seduction in Israel's history, and the cruelest religious perversion (Lev. 18:21; Num. 25:1-18). However, the biblical record shows that God did extend mercy to certain individuals among them: Ruth was a Moabitess who became the great-grandmother of King David and an ancestor of Jesus. Naanah, an Ammonite maiden, became wife to Solomon and the mother of Rehoboam, his successor. She, too, was an ancestor of Jesus. For the most part, the Moabites and Ammonites have become amalgamated with the Arab peoples, but two passages indicate that they may be revived in the last days (Jer. 48:7; 49:6).

In Conclusion

The account of Lot and his family teaches us a number of important lessons. It teaches the danger of choosing to live in wicked surroundings for the purpose of wealth and influence, without a thought for God or family. Lot lost all he held dear. He lost his wife, who could not tear herself away from the life she had come to love. He lost family and home, presumably ending his days in a cave on a mountainside. He was deceived into an incestuous relationship with two of his surviving daughters and, thereby, lost his honor. All this illustrates that it is foolish for a believer to become attached to the things of this world. They will corrupt him or her, just as surely as they corrupted poor Lot.

The example for the believer in this story is not Lot, but Abraham standing before the Lord interceding for others. Instead of grasping for what the world offers, he trusted and obeyed his God. God then confided in him concerning what He was going to do and allowed him the privilege of fellowship with Him. Abraham is known as the "friend of God," while Lot is known as a friend of the world.

Abraham and Abimelech

After the destruction of Sodom and Gomorrah, the narrative in Genesis again picks up the story of Abraham, which is central to the book. Only recently God had confirmed His promise that Abraham and Sarah would have a son and had instituted the sign of circumcision to mark out the special character of Abraham's descendants. God's power had been demonstrated by the destruction of Sodom and the deliverance of Lot, in answer to Abraham's prayer. Abraham was now poised for the birth of his son and further blessing from God.

A Detour in Abraham's Pilgrimage

Suddenly, the story of Abraham makes a detour. We read that he journeyed south from Hebron and came to stay in the vicinity of Gerar, a city of the Philistines about thirty miles southwest of Hebron. The events in Abraham's life are linked with this city in this chapter and the next. The Philistine people were beginning to establish themselves in what we now call the Gaza Strip, although the main body of them did not arrive from Crete until later. There is no explanation in the Bible for Abraham's move. Some commentators suggest that he needed more grazing and better pasture land for his flocks and herds. Others think that Abraham was attracted to Gerar because it was on a trade route to Egypt, where he could more easily take advantage of markets in Egypt and Philistia to trade his vast herds. Gerar was ruled by Abimelech, whose name is more likely a title meaning "king" rather than a personal name, much as the Egyptians used the title "pharaoh" for their rulers.

An Error Repeated (vv. 1-7)

What happened next is almost unbelievable. When Abraham moved to Gerar, he said of Sarah, "She is my sister." It was exactly what he had done in Egypt with disastrous results (cf. 12:13). We find it hard to understand how Abraham could tell the same lie for the same reason, knowing what happened before. Sarah may have still been attractive, even at age ninety. Her rank as the sister of a wealthy prince or chieftain also made her desirable as part of a king's harem. Abraham's deception would be easier to accept if there had been no communication from God for a long time, but this was not the case. God had just appeared to him and specifically stated that, at the proper time, Sarah would have a son (18:10). It is even possible that she was already pregnant with Isaac. The actions of Abraham and Sarah are most difficult chapters to understand—and especially hard to reconcile with Abraham's faith. What happened, according to the record, is stated simply: "And Abimelech the king sent and took Sarah." She then became part of Abimelech's harem.

What was Abraham Thinking?

The suspense is dramatic. On the very threshold of Isaac's birth story, this incident puts the fulfillment of God's promises to Abraham in jeopardy. What was Abraham thinking? Did he reason that because God had prevented Pharaoh from consummating the marriage in Egypt that He would do it again? Did he think that God would automatically rectify his mistakes without consequence? If so, he was presuming on God's grace and tempting God—both grave sins.

Nothing is Too Difficult for God!

When Abraham allowed Sarah to be taken into the harem of a Philistine king, he added one more impossibility factor which, with the others, demonstrates God's sovereignty in a remarkable way if he and Sarah were ever to have a son. Consider some of the impossibilities that God overcame:

- Sarah was physically unable to have children.
- Apart from her barrenness, she was of advanced age when not even a fertile woman could expect to have children.
- Abraham was past the age of fathering a child as well, at nearly one hundred-years old.
- Abraham had put Sarah in jeopardy of becoming an Egyptian princess in Egypt, from which she escaped only by the grace of God.
- Abraham did it again in Gerar, and it was only by God's grace that he received Sarah back without harm.

Together, these *impossibilities* assure us that nothing is too difficult for God (18:14).

Although fear of what might happen had evidently gripped Abraham, there was another contributing factor. This course of action was not a spur-of-the-moment decision. According to verse 13, Abraham and Sarah had agreed before they entered Canaan that she would call Abraham her brother wherever they went. They acted on their intention to deceive, which arose out of their mistrust of God's ability to protect the truth. Abraham and Sarah were clearly guilty, but God held Abimelech accountable for his own failure in this chapter. He may have considered Sarah to have political value: She was the "sister" of a powerful chieftain, and marriage is one of the tools kings have always used in the art of diplomacy.

God Intervenes

Before Abimelech consummated his marriage with Sarah, God came to him in a dream with a stern warning. Dreams were the usual mode of revelation God used in dealing with pagans. This dream amounted to a dialogue between God and Abimelech. God abruptly told him that he was a "dead man" because the woman he had taken was, He said, "a man's wife" (v. 3). God threatened him with a fatal illness. Abimelech certainly seems to have feared God and have a better understanding of Him than the mass of heathen around him. In his dream, Abimelech answered God with a surprising question: "Lord, will You slay a righteous nation also?" (v. 4). He was alluding to God's recent destruction of Sodom—an unrighteous and wicked nation. He questioned God's integrity in judging *his* nation, which he believed was comparatively "righteous."

Abimelech continued to defend himself, quoting Abraham's own claim that Sarah was his sister. In addition, Sarah herself had said of Abraham, "He is my brother." He went on to protest, "In the integrity of my heart and the innocence of my hands I have done this" (v. 5). He assumed that kings had the right to take unmarried women into their harems. But that was not his right before *God*, and God held him responsible. God acknowledged to him that he had not deliberately taken Sarah knowing that she was Abraham's wife, but that did not clear him of guilt before God if he had consummated the marriage, or as He put it, of "sinning against Me" (v. 6). Joseph used this same language when Potiphar's wife tempted him to commit immorality. He replied, "How then can I do this great wickedness, and sin against God?" (39:9).

Abimelech's guilt is implied when God commanded him, "Restore this man's wife; for he is a prophet, and he will pray for you and you shall live. But if you do not restore her, know that you shall surely die, you and all who are yours" (v. 7). He needed not only to give Sarah back to Abraham but to also seek Abraham's mediation. He was guilty before God, even though his conscience had not accused him. This is the first use of the word "prophet" in the Bible. It refers to Abraham's ability to speak on behalf of God, to represent Him. In this case, Abraham would intercede in prayer for Abimelech's life. In a similar way, the prophet Samuel prayed for the nation of Israel in the days of King Saul (1 Sam. 12:19).

Abimelech Confronts Abraham (vv. 8–13)

Abimelech responded to God's warning immediately, probably out of high respect for God and Abraham; however, he did not send Sarah back to Abraham straight away. Instead, he arose early, gathered his servants, and told them what had happened and what God had said. They, too, were afraid (v. 8).

The King of Gerar saw that Abraham's deception had brought a great sin on him and his nation. He did everything he could to set things right. He called

Abraham and confronted him directly. He fired three questions at him designed to lay blame on him and rebuke him. His first question was rhetorical: "What have you done to us?" It was to let Abraham know that he knew what Abraham had done and was holding him to account. No reply was offered or needed. The second question was "How have I offended you, that you have brought on me and on my kingdom a great sin? You have done deeds to me that ought not to be done" (v. 9).

Abraham did not reply here either. Both of these questions focused on Abraham's selfishness in acting only in his own interests and safety. It was a stinging rebuke, and Abraham probably felt a deep sense of guilt. The third question asked was "What did you have in view that you have done this thing?" (v. 10).

In reply, Abraham offered three rather weak excuses while acknowledging his sinful behavior. In all of these excuses, he was wrong.

- *He was wrong about Abimelech* and the people of Gerar when he presumed that they were as pagan as their neighbors. He said he was concerned that there was no fear of God in Gerar and that they would have killed him to take Sarah (v. 11).

- *He was wrong about himself* when he excused his deceit concerning his relationship with Sarah. He said "She is my sister," but the fact was, she was also his wife (v. 12).

- *He was wrong about God,* arguing that the reason he and Sarah had hatched the plan was because God "caused" him "to wander" from his father's house (v. 13). He was blaming God by reasoning that he wouldn't be in this mess if He hadn't called him in the first place. To sum up, he played the "blame game," much as Adam did in the Garden of Eden. The whole matter was a blot on Abraham's testimony and should stand as a warning to believers everywhere.

The Situation is Resolved (vv. 14-18)

After the confrontation was over, Abimelech restored Sarah to Abraham unharmed along with offerings designed to propitiate, that is, appease him and regain his favor. Despite Abraham's obvious failure, Abimelech had great respect for him and his God. He wanted to be sure to remove the threat of death that God had laid on him in the dream. When he restored Sarah, he made reparation for taking her with an offering of sheep, oxen, and servants, plus the offer to Abraham to live wherever he pleased in the land of Gerar.

Abimelech then told Sarah that he had given Abraham a thousand pieces of silver to vindicate her—literally a "covering of the eyes"—"before all who are with you and before all others" (v. 16). This may carry the idea of a justification of her honor in the eyes of those who knew the wrong that the king had done.

After the reparations were made, Abraham prayed for the healing of Abimelech and his household. Evidently Abimelech had been stricken with some physical ailment that hindered his sexual relationships. The women in his palace were also afflicted with inability to bear children. God answered Abraham's prayer for their physical healing. Isn't it remarkable that God allowed Abraham to be an intercessor for Abimelech even though Abraham's sin was greater than Abimelech's? It is significant that the term "LORD" is used for God in verse 18—the one who protected Sarah's purity so that the covenant with Abraham could be completed.

In Conclusion

In surveying chapter 20, we learn that Abraham's lack of trust in God was a besetting sin—despite the fact that he is commended for his faith in Hebrew 11 and other places. None of God's people are beyond falling while they live on this earth; the flesh does not "improve" with age. But God deals with us, as He did with Abraham, by bringing us to the place of confession and restoration. The root of Abraham's problem was really unbelief, which we can define as lack of trust in God's ability to fulfill His promises without our intervention. One commentator entitles his observations on this chapter "A Bit of the Old Nature." May we learn of the subtlety of these temptations and avoid them for the glory of our God.

The Fulfillment of the Promise

Chapter 21 is important *historically* because it records the fulfillment of the long-deferred promise to Abraham that he would have a son through whom the world would be blessed. It is important *theologically* because it illustrates the New Testament doctrine of the distinction between flesh and spirit, in particular that anything done "according to the flesh" (self-effort) is unacceptable to God and will never receive His approval. The two sons of Abraham illustrate the contrast between the works of the flesh (keeping the law) as a false basis for salvation and simple faith in Christ's work on the cross as the true grounds for salvation. Ishmael, conceived as a result of Abraham and Sarah's scheming, was rejected. Isaac, on the other hand, was born by God's power, will, and grace alone, and as such was heir to God's blessing.

The chapter is also important *ethically* as God was preparing Abraham for the great crisis to come when he would be asked to sacrifice Isaac as a burnt offering. God had to teach him to part with Ishmael, whom he loved so dearly, to prepare him for the greater test recorded in the next chapter. God was refining His servant, taking away the dross of his life so that he would trust in Him alone.

God Keeps His Promise (vv. 1-7)

The chapter begins with the assurance that God keeps His word. Verse 1 says, "And the LORD visited Sarah as He had said, and the LORD did for Sarah as He had spoken." Notice that it was the LORD, the covenant keeping God, who visited Sarah. The word *visited* carries the idea of a divine intervention to bless her. God empowered her to become pregnant, to carry the child, and to give birth. The same word will be used again in Genesis when Joseph prophesies about the future "visit" by God to the Israelites in Egypt to deliver them from bondage (50:24). Again, it would be by divine intervention.

Verse 2 tells us that God followed through on His promise right on schedule. It was "at the set time" of which He had spoken the previous year when He gave Abraham the covenant sign of circumcision. It was not Abraham's time, but God's time. It had been twenty-five years since he first entered Canaan expecting the fulfillment of the promise. He had to learn that patience and endurance are intrinsic elements of the life of faith. He also had to realize that what God said *would* certainly come to pass. Notice how this point is made three times in verses 1 and 2:

- "as He had said"
- "as He had spoken"
- "at the set time of which God had spoken"

What God had promised He performed at just the right time.

Sarah's Faith

Sarah, too, had become strong in faith. She had laughed in disbelief when she heard the Lord telling Abraham about her coming pregnancy (18:12). But she moved from disbelief to strong faith in God even before she conceived Isaac: "By faith, Sarah herself also received strength to conceive seed, and she bore a child when she was past the age, because she judged Him faithful who had promised" (Heb. 11:11). We are not told when this happened. Whenever it was, she accepted the truth that "He who promised is faithful" to keep His promise (Heb. 10:23).

God does not do things by halves. Sarah and Abraham were ninety and one hundred years of age respectively, yet Sarah's body was rejuvenated to the degree that she was able to conceive, carry, bear, and nurse her baby (v. 7), and Abraham's to the point that he eventually fathered six other sons by Keturah, whom he married after Sarah died (25:2).

The Birth and Naming of Isaac

Verses 1 and 2 emphasize the reliability of God's word. The next verses emphasize Abraham's obedience to God's word. Abraham did "as God commanded him" (v. 4). First, he was obedient in naming the child *Isaac*, meaning "laughter," just as God had told him to (17:19). Sarah's commentary on Isaac's name is remarkable, for her laughter of unbelief changed to joyous laughter (18:12-13). She now said, "God has made me laugh, so that all who hear will laugh with me" (v. 6). She was so happy about what God had done to her that she wanted all to hear about it. She would be reminded of God's faithfulness every time she spoke Isaac's name. The birth of Isaac, perhaps more than any other birth in the Old Testament, foreshadowed the birth of the Lord Jesus:

- it was specifically promised
- it was long awaited
- it was supernatural
- it was heralded with great joy

However, the birth of Jesus—the greater Seed—was accomplished by means of a far greater visitation from on high (cf. Luke 1:68; Gal. 3:19).

Abraham also obeyed God in circumcising Isaac when he was eight days old (v. 4; cf. 17:12). No doubt Abraham and Sarah carefully taught their son about God and the ways of righteousness. No doubt they rehearsed God's great covenant promises that He had made to Abraham. Isaac was, surely, a wonderful son to them and brought them great pleasure in their old age.

The Expulsion of Ishmael and Hagar (vv. 8-14)

There were now, however, two rival sons. When Isaac was born it became necessary for Ishmael to leave. In the expulsion of Ishmael, the Lord was reinforcing the concept that Isaac was the sole heir and the son of the bondwoman would not inherit the promises specifically made to Abraham. God was protecting the promise regarding Isaac.

Ishmaels Scoffs

When Isaac was weaned at about two or three years of age, Abraham made a great feast in his honor. It was a happy occasion—but not for Ishmael, who was now around sixteen-years old. His position as Abraham's firstborn had been superceded by the birth of his half-brother. He, Ishmael, was the child of a servant. The realization of this bred hatred and envy in his heart. At the feast, he did not conceal his feelings when Isaac was getting all the attention. He began to scoff at the young child with insult and mockery (v. 9). There is irony here because the word *scoffing* is the same word translated *laugh* in verse 6 when Sarah invited others to joyfully laugh with her.

The New Testament confirms the negative aspect of Ishmael's laughter in the letter to the Galatians: "He who was born according to the flesh then persecuted him who was born according to the Spirit" (Gal. 4:29). Ishmael was doing more than teenage teasing; he was maliciously scorning Isaac, whom God had so wonderfully brought into the family, by being disrespectful and disparaging of God's part in it. Sarah seems to have seen the potential for harm in Ishmael's attitude more readily than the patriarch did. However, we must also remember how angry she became when Hagar was pregnant with Ishmael (chapter 16). At that time, Hagar had scorned *her,* so it is understandable that she would be easily provoked by Ishmael's disposition. Sarah resented both Hagar and Ishmael. Her resentment, first seen in the tension between her and Hagar over Hagar's pregnancy, now explodes (16:5; 21:10).

Sarah Responds

Ishmael's mockery brought about a crisis of competition between the two women. Sarah could not endure it, so she said to Abraham, "Cast out this bondwoman and her son, for the son of this bondwoman shall not be heir with my son, namely with Isaac" (v. 10). These were harsh words against a personal servant of twenty years standing. Notice two things about her demand. First, Sarah spoke of Hagar as *the bondwoman,* whereas previously she was referred to as her *handmaid.* Second, she referred to Ishmael as *her (*Hagar's) *son,* while she referred to Isaac as *my son, even Isaac.* Thus the issue was over *sonship.* The text resolves the issue by identifying the "true" son as Isaac. God confirmed this by referring to Ishmael using the same word that Sarah had, that is, "the son of the bondwoman" (v. 13).

Abraham Acts

Abraham had developed a great love for Ishmael, who was for fourteen years his only son until Isaac was born. Sarah's demand caused him deep distress and displeasure, for he would have loved to see Ishmael honored in some special way (v. 11). God understood his feelings but had to speak to him sternly to get him to act responsibly in securing the inheritance for Isaac. He said to Abraham, "Do not let it be displeasing in your sight because of the lad." Abraham was allowing his human affection for Ishmael to blur his spiritual sense. There was only one solution: to send Ishmael away, as Sarah had demanded (v. 12). He had to comply out of sheer determination of faith and obedience even though it hurt him deeply to do so. He would have to clearly understand that only through Isaac could the promised Seed come. God had never intended to include Ishmael in His plan to redeem mankind. As students of the book of Genesis, we must see this incident in the light of God's exclusive choice of Isaac as the heir.

The Spirit and the Flesh

The apostle Paul used Abraham's two sons as illustrations of the spiritual man and the fleshly man. He spoke of Ishmael as the one "who was born according to the flesh" and to Isaac as the one "who was born according to the Spirit" (Gal. 4:29). Ishmael represents the spiritual descendants of Hagar who believe they can be saved by keeping the Law in the power of the flesh. According to Romans 8:8, "Those that are in the flesh cannot please God." God cannot and will not bless man's way of achieving righteousness. Isaac represents the spiritual descendants of Abraham who are saved through receiving God's promise by faith. The Law cannot grant eternal life for self effort, but God can give eternal life through the provision of a Savior to those who receive Him by faith. The covenant promise through Isaac looked forward to the coming Savior. Believers are children of faith and are no longer in bondage to the Law, which no one can fully obey. Those trying to keep the Law to gain salvation will always persecute those who trust in Christ. Law-keepers are in bondage like children of Hagar the "bondwoman"; believers are free like children of Sarah the "freewoman."

Despite the significance of what Ishmael represented in terms of theological truth, God did not abandon Ishmael the person. Even though he would be sent away from Abraham's home, God promised to provide for him. What God was doing was primarily protecting Isaac, the chosen seed. But God had plans for Ishmael, too. He told Abraham, "I will also make a nation of the son of the bondwoman because he is your seed" (v. 13), so Abraham did not need to fear in sending him away.

Ishmael and Hagar Leave

With a heavy heart, Abraham expelled Hagar and Ishmael the very next day, arising early in the morning to comply with God's command. He shines again as a worthy example of what it means to obey in that he set aside his human love for Ishmael out of love for God. It was one of the most difficult choices in his entire life. He was compelled to do what he understood to be God's will. God was further preparing him for an even greater test of obedience some years later that is recorded in the next chapter.

Abraham did what he could for Hagar and Ishmael in providing them with food and water. They took what they could carry, which was enough to meet their needs until they got to the next settlement. Archeological findings have revealed the existence of many settlements in that area at that time. Hagar left Gerar and "wandered in the wilderness of Beersheba" (v. 14).

God Preserves Ishmael and Hagar (vv. 15-21)

Hagar and Ishmael seem to have lost their way, and their provisions ran out. They became weak from dehydration and exposure, and Ishmael finally collapsed, exhausted. He had probably given most of the provisions to his mother. She moved him into the shade of one of the shrubs then sat down nearby to wait for him to die. "She said to herself, 'Let me not see the death of the boy,' so she sat opposite him and lifted her voice and wept" (v. 16). In her misery, she thought that they would both perish there in the wilderness. Ishmael was also crying, or he may have been praying, for God's attention was drawn to "the voice of the lad" (v. 17). The scene pictured is one of dramatic pathos: both mother and son were dying of thirst, all alone in the desert.

The Angel Rebukes Hagar

Just when everything seems hopeless, we reach the second crisis in the story (the first one being the clash between Ishmael and Isaac). As with the first crisis, God intervened here, too. While Hagar was waiting to die, the "angel of God" called out to her from heaven with a mild reproof: "What ails you?" or in other words "What is wrong with you?"

Sixteen years earlier, Hagar had been in desperate straits in the wilderness, and the Angel of the Lord had come to help her. He is not here called the "Angel of the LORD," the covenant-keeping God, but the "angel of God." Ishmael had no part in the covenant, so the term "God," associated with His life-sustaining power, is used. In the previous encounter, she had responded to God's promise about Ishmael growing up and having many descendants by acknowledging that He was "the God who sees me" (16:11-14). By now, however, she had either forgotten the way God had cared for her or was ignoring

His promise. Her spirit had reached a low point. Having rebuked her for unbelief, the angel then comforted her: "Fear not, for God has heard the voice of the lad where he is." Before he was born, God gave him the name of Ishmael, meaning *God hears*. At that time, He had heard *Hagar's* cry of affliction when she was mistreated and ran away (16:6-7). This time, God heard *Ishmael's* cry. We should remember in our own experience that God always hears our faintest cry and will respond at just the right moment.

God Provides a Well for Hagar

The moment of truth for Hagar came when the angel of God spoke audibly to her with a significant promise for the future. Not only would Ishmael's descendants multiply exceedingly, as God had said before, but they would become a great nation (cf. 17:20). God's prophecy was fulfilled when Ishmael's twelve sons became princes, ruling from Havilah to Shur. From them came many of the Arab peoples. At that point, God opened her eyes to see a well of water. Maybe He created it just for her, or perhaps it had been there and she just hadn't seen it. God met Hagar in her hour of need. Scripture does not reveal much about either Ishmael or Hagar's personal faith in God, but from the glimpses we have in Genesis 16 and 21 we find them crying to the Lord and God answering them. When it says in verse 21 that "God was with the lad," it indicates that God's blessing remained with Ishmael. We see God's compassionate nature in that He did not let them die in the wilderness.

Hagar and Ishmael settled in the wilderness of Paran, a desert region near Kadesh Barnea. There, Ishmael grew up and became an outstanding archer. In due time, he married an Egyptian girl obtained for him by his mother (v. 21).

Abraham's Covenant with Abimelech (vv. 22–34)

In the final section of chapter 21, Abraham makes a covenant with Abimelech the Philistine king of Gerar in Beersheba, which became Abraham's home for the final portion of his life. This was probably the same king who rebuked Abraham when he lied about Sarah being his sister. It was he who invited Abraham to live in the land wherever he pleased (20:15). Abimelech's territory was apparently quite extensive. With all his flocks and herds, Abraham needed considerable land on which to graze them. He seems to have settled about twenty-five miles east of Gerar in what came to be known as Beersheba. It was still considered to be Philistine territory. There was probably little more than an oasis at Beersheba in Abraham's time, although eventually a well-fortified city was built there, the ruins of which are just outside the modern city. There is also an ancient well in the vicinity that may have been originally dug by Abraham.

Abraham's wealth and influence became a matter of concern to Abimelech. Reasoning that wealth equals power, Abimelech took along his army general, Phichol, to meet with Abraham on a diplomatic mission. Abraham had not been altogether trustworthy in his previous dealings with him (cf. chapter 20), but peace would be advantageous to them both, of course. After acknowledging that God was with Abraham and had prospered him in all that he did (v. 22), Abimelech proposed a peace treaty with him.

The Treaty

Abimelech reminded Abraham of the kindness he had shown him during the incident over Sarah (cf. 20:14-15). In return, he wanted Abraham to swear that he would deal falsely with neither him nor those who would follow him in positions of authority and that he would not injure him or his people (vv. 23-24). Abraham readily agreed to all this and to live in peace. The student should note how God was progressively preparing Abraham during his contact with Abimelech for the great test of his faith in the next chapter:

- During the first contact with Abimelech (20:9-14), Sarah's purity was preserved, and Abraham's life was saved (albeit the threat to his life was only in Abraham's mind).
- The birth of Isaac took place at the time set for it (17:21; 18:14; 21:1).
- Following Isaac's birth, the rival son was expelled (21:10-14).
- Now, in this section, a covenant was made with Abimelech allowing Abraham to raise Isaac in a peaceful environment.

All of these events and responses were steps of faith and laid the foundation for the greatest test of all. God had put together all the pieces to emphasize that Isaac alone was the heir. Would Abraham's faith be strong enough to believe it in the face of the command to offer him as a sacrifice?

Abraham's Complaint

After Abraham swore to the peace treaty, he confronted Abimelech, complaining that Abimelech's servants had stolen his well (vv. 25-27). Abraham's servants dug wells and protected them as part of their shepherding duties. Living as they did in a marginally arid area, wells were of great importance for livestock. Abimelech's servants had seized a particular well that Abraham's servants had dug. The use of the word "seized" indicates that they took it violently. Abraham was wise to bring this up after the treaty was agreed so that the matter could be resolved peacefully. Abimelech protested his innocence and ignorance of the matter and indicated his willingness to return the well. Abraham immediately began the process of a covenant ceremony that would give him both the legal right to the well he had dug and permission to dwell peacefully in Abimelech's territory. These kinds of covenants were called parity covenants (i.e. between equals).

The Covenant Ceremony

First, he took sheep and oxen and gave them to Abimelech, and the two of them made a treaty that such disputes would not be repeated (vv. 27-31). The well he had dug, which would now be returned, was a symbol of God's blessing on him. Abimelech, in return, gained the promise from Abraham that he would not interfere with Abimelech's rule of the land or his subjects. There is a lesson for believers here: we should settle disputes with unbelievers peacefully and legally wherever possible (cf. Mark 9:50; 2 Cor. 13:11; 1 Thess. 5:13).

Abraham then took seven ewe lambs from the flock that he had given to Abimelech and set them aside. Abimelech asked why he did this. In accepting the lambs as a goodwill gift, Abimelech was conceding that the well did indeed belong to Abraham. There seems to be a connection between the Hebrew word for the number seven and the word for "oath," which are almost identical. Because of this, the number seven was incorporated into the ceremony of the oath.

Both Abraham and Abimelech agreed to the treaty, and they called the name of the place *Beersheba*, which can mean either "the well of the oath" or "the well of the seven." This ceremony would preserve the record of how the property was secured for the future generations.

It is interesting to observe that, in this chapter, God graciously provided a well for both of Abraham's sons. He opened Hagar's eyes to see the well in the wilderness that provided for her and Ishmael's needs. That well was a gift from God. The other well was at Beersheba, the "Well of the Oath," which Abraham recovered from the Philistines by means of a sworn covenant. His acquisition meant that he actually owned a well, a symbol of blessing, in the Promised Land.

The Planting of the Tree

Following the covenant ceremony, the Philistine king and his general returned home (v. 32). Abraham, however, remained and planted a tamarisk tree, or possibly a grove of them, near the well. A tamarisk tree is long-lived and evergreen and would be a symbol of God's enduring grace to Abraham. The tree was planted where there was a constant supply of water. It indicated Abraham's intention to stay in the region on a long term basis. The tree was a lasting landmark to God's provision of water and Abraham's first foothold in Canaan. It was only a well, but for Abraham it was a token of the land that God had promised him.

There Abraham "called on the name of the LORD" (v. 33). This was the third such occasion. The first was at Bethel where he built an altar and publicly worshipped God, thanking Him for the great promises of the land and the seed (12:8). Later, after he returned from Egypt, he went back to Bethel and again called on the name of the Lord in appreciation for God's protection from the mistakes he had made in Egypt (13:4). Now, for the third time, having been delivered from the consequences of his sin in Gerar and having sworn a covenant with Abimelech, he called on the name of the Lord in thankfulness.

"Jehovah El Olam"

When Abraham called on the name of the Lord it was by a special name, "the LORD, the Everlasting God" (*Jehovah El Olam,* v.33). The only other place it occurs is in Isaiah 40:28. Abraham was experiencing a taste of his coming inheritance. He now had Isaac (the first descendant in the line of his promised seed) and a well (the first small piece of the Promised Land), and he was able to look down the corridors of time and envisage God's plan to send a Redeemer becoming clear. He called on Jehovah the Everlasting God, the God of the Ages, in whose hands the future lies.

Abraham in the Land of the Philistines

The last verse tells us that Abraham "sojourned in the land of the Philistines" (v. 34). This detail may have been included to remind the readers that Abraham had not yet experienced the complete fulfillment of God's promises. Many Bible critics have claimed that the references to the Philistine people in this chapter are in error because the well-documented influx of sea peoples known as the Philistines from the Aegean area did not occur until around 1200 BC. Therefore, they argue, the use of the name "Philistine" in Abraham's day cannot refer to the same people. Evangelical scholars answer that Minoan traders were already active in Abraham's time, and a much earlier group of them probably had settlements along the Mediterranean coast in the Gaza area. Moses wrote Genesis more than two hundred years before the thirteenth century BC influx of Minoans. When he speaks of Philistines, we can be sure that at least some of them were already there.

In Conclusion

Chapter 21 has taught us that the flesh must go, pictured by Ishmael's expulsion from Abraham's home. It also teaches us that God is faithful to His word, in that He met the needs of Hagar and Ishmael in their extremity. We also learn the value of making peace with our unbelieving neighbors. And finally, we can be thankful that the future is in the hands of Jehovah, the Everlasting God.

The Test of Abraham's Faith

Genesis 22 contains the account of God testing Abraham by commanding him to sacrifice his son Isaac. As far as all Bible history is concerned, only the New Testament scene of God the Father sacrificing His well-beloved Son at Calvary exceeds it, being the fulfillment of what is pictured here in Genesis 22. In observing the patriarch ascending the mountain with Isaac toward the place of sacrifice, we are reminded of God giving up His Son for us. And when we read of Isaac carrying the wood for his own sacrifice we get a glimpse of the Lord Jesus Christ on His way toward Golgotha, carrying the cross on which He would be crucified.

Background

After Abraham made the covenant with Abimelech concerning the well at Beersheba we read almost nothing about his life until Isaac is grown. From Genesis 21:34 we know that Abraham "sojourned in the land of the Philistines many days" after planting a tamarisk tree in Beersheba. We also learn from Genesis 22:19 that following the mission that took them to Mt. Moriah, "they went together to Beersheba" and lived there. It is likely, therefore, that Abraham was encamped in Beersheba in the intervening years while Isaac was growing up.

Isaac was now a young man. Through him, all God's future promises concerning the land, his innumerable descendants, and worldwide blessing, would be fulfilled. Yet, at this critical juncture, the Lord asked Abraham to give Isaac back to Him by means of sacrifice. Before Isaac was born, it had been difficult for Abraham to believe that God would give him a son; the circumstances seemed insurmountable. But it was now far more difficult for Abraham to give that same son back to God, especially when it seemed so out of keeping with His previous promises.

Abraham's triumph of faith in passing the test is a fitting climax to the entire narrative. It is faith in action that is motivated by love for God—not love in the sense of affection, but self-sacrificial love. Although this premise is not stated in the text, it is implicit in that what he did was to sacrifice the greatest love of his life to please God. Only love for God could do that.

How Old was Isaac?

The next dated event in Genesis is the death of Sarah when she was 127 years old (23:1). She would have been about ninety-three when Isaac was weaned, so that leaves a period of approximately thirty-five years about which the Scriptures are silent. Isaac would have been thirty-seven when his mother died. We do not know at what point in the period between his weaning and Sarah's death the offering took place. He must have been at least in his teens, and quite possibly in his twenties because, although he is termed a "lad" in verse 5, the word used refers to a male of any age from a grown boy to a young man.

God's Command (vv. 1-2)

The "things" after which this event took place were the experiences that God had used to develop Abraham's faith. It is significant that what God was asking Abraham to do was a test of his obedience (v.1). It is not only Genesis which states that God "tested Abraham"; the book of Hebrews confirms that "Abraham when he was tested, offered up Isaac" (Heb. 11:17). The word *test* appears here for the first time in Scripture and, as is often the case, is most instructive. To test someone or something is to prove that he, she, or it can perform as claimed. God tested Abraham to prove that his faith and devotion were genuine. Abraham did this by giving up both his own will and his own wisdom in order to obey God concerning Isaac.

The word "test" is distinct from *tempt,* which means "to entice someone to sin." Satan is the great tempter. God never tempts us to sin, but He often tests us to prove our faith (James 1:13). Civil engineers test the structure they have built to assure potential customers that it will perform as promised, even though they themselves know it *will* withstand the rigors of the test. The Lord Jesus' experience of being tested for forty days in the wilderness is a good example of this. Satan may have been tempting Him, but God was proving Him so that everyone could see that, in spite of being subjected to the most difficult of tests, He would emerge spotless and blameless. It does not mean that He could have sinned, but that He was exposed to the full force of sin. He was like the one tree of the forest that is left standing after the hurricane, having withstood the full force of the storm.

God knew what Abraham would do when he was tested. The drama was, however, necessary for at least two reasons. First, Abraham sets the reader a wonderful example to follow of personal faith in action by the extent to which he went in obeying God. He proved that the Lord meant more to him than Isaac did. Second, throughout His written Word, God progressively reveals different aspects of Christ's work on Calvary, and this incident needed to be enacted to give a graphic advance portrayal of God's personal sacrifice in delivering up His very own Son.

One day, in the normal course of his life in Beersheba, Abraham heard the voice of God calling his name to get his attention. He responded simply by saying, "Here I am" (v.1), demonstrating a willing and open spirit. God then revealed to him exactly what He wanted him to do. Because Isaac was "the apple of his eye," every word was like a hammer blow to his heart:

- "Take now your son"—the one for whose birth he had waited in faith for twenty-five long years.

- "Your only son"—Ishmael was not even in the picture in God's eyes, as Isaac was the son of the promise.

- "Isaac"—meaning *laughter,* so-named by God because Abraham had laughed with joy in anticipation that God would do exactly as He promised.

- "Whom you love"—stressing the deep affection the patriarch had for the boy. Abraham also loved God, but every word of the instruction increased the tension between Abraham's love for God and his love for Isaac.

To the patriarch, this command must have seemed totally out of character with everything he knew about Jehovah God.

The Love of a Father for His Son

It is not insignificant that the word *love* is used here for the first time in the Old Testament. It may seem cruel to us, but at the very moment that God was requesting Isaac to be sacrificed, He reminded Abraham of his paternal love for his son. We have in Abraham's love for his "only son" a miniature of the love of God for *His* only Son. Jesus Himself gave testimony of the Father's love for Him in His great high priestly prayer when He said, "You loved Me before the foundation of the world" (John 17:24).

It is worth noting that in the New Testament—actually, in each of the three Synoptic Gospels—the first use of the word "love" also clearly expresses the love of the Father for the Son. Jesus was being baptized in the River Jordan when the Spirit of God descended on Him like a dove, and suddenly there was a voice from heaven saying, "This is my beloved Son, in whom I am well pleased" (Matt. 3:16-17; Mark 1:11; Luke 3:22). The first use of love in John's gospel is in chapter 3 verse 16. The love of God the Father for God the Son underlies His love for a lost world. He loved the world so much that He sacrificed His Son to redeem it. Thus, in both the Old and the New Testaments, love is first used, not in relation to a husband for his wife or to a mother for her children, but to a father for his son.

When Abraham lived in Haran, God called him saying, "Go ... to a land that I will show you" (12:1). He now uses similar language in saying, "*Go to the land* of Moriah, and offer him there as a burnt offering on one of the mountains *of which I shall tell you*" (emphasis added). The parallel phrases are so similar that Abraham would not have missed them. He would recall that his obedience on the first occasion was rewarded by God's faithfulness to him. With this in mind, he would be quick to respond to this call to obey. The two calls lie behind two references to Abraham's faith in Hebrews 11. His first call to go the land of Canaan is described like this: "By faith Abraham obeyed when he was called to go out to the place which he would afterward receive as an inheritance" (Heb. 11:8). His second call is described a few verses later: "By faith Abraham, when he was tested, offered up Isaac" (Heb. 11:17).

Skeptics view God's command in the light of human sacrifices that were the common practice of the Canaanites and Babylonians in those times. The Bible student should keep in mind that human sacrifice as practiced by pagan peoples (even up to modern times) was an early corruption of the animal sacrifices that God instructed believers to offer in faith as a picture of the coming Redeemer. Others are of the opinion that God never intended for Abraham to literally sacrifice Isaac. This view, however, would lead to some doctrinal confusion regarding the necessity for a sacrificial death. It is best to conclude that God meant for Abraham to understand the instruction to literally sacrifice Isaac to prove his *love* for God, as opposed to following the pagan mindset of sacrificing to *appease* their gods.

Even apart from the issue of God's asking him to do something that would nullify the fulfillment of His clear promises, we can hardly imagine the effect of the heavy blow of God's words on Abraham. God's directive touched Abraham at his most tender spot. Years before, he had found it hard to send his son Ishmael away because of his great love for him. So how could he comply with God's command regarding Isaac, which went far beyond merely sending him away and actually involved offering him as a blood sacrifice? Abraham's quandary was: "Is my love for God greater than my dearest human love?" That is a good question for us as believers. Our own Savior said, "He who loves son or daughter more than Me is not worthy of Me" (Matt.10:37). Could we willingly give up whatever is dearest and best to us if God should require it? An affirmative answer is easier to give when there is no such test in progress; it is much more difficult in the midst of trial, especially if the purpose of the trial is inexplicable in human terms.

Mount Moriah

The name Moriah is only mentioned in two places in the Bible: here and in 2 Chronicles 3:1, where Mt. Moriah is identified as the site on which Solomon built the Temple in Jerusalem. King David bought the ground from a Jebusite named Araunah (2 Sam. 24:16-24). That purchase would not take place for another one thousand years after Abraham. What happened on Mt. Moriah here in Genesis was to foreshadow the finished work of the Lord Jesus. For centuries, Jews and Christians have believed with good reason that the place where Abraham offered Isaac was the very spot where Solomon built the Temple in Jerusalem. Just outside the entrance to the Temple on the east was the brazen altar where the priests offered the sacrifices. More animals have been sacrificed on that altar than anywhere else on earth. The rivers of blood that have flowed from that multitude of sacrifices picture the one supreme sacrifice of the Lord Jesus Christ that would be offered to pay for the sin of all mankind.

Abraham's Amazing Faith (v. 3)

Abraham immediately obeyed the clear command of God even though it was so difficult. God had, perhaps, many ways by which He could have fulfilled His promises to Abraham, but Abraham had only one way by which he could please God, and that was to obey His word. It was not his business to reason out the matter, but simply to do God's will. He promptly did exactly as God had told him to do. In regard to the prospect of Isaac actually dying, the Bible tells us that Abraham believed "God was able to raise him [Isaac] up, even from the dead" (Heb. 11:19). He trusted the divine capability, even though he had absolutely no evidence that resurrection was feasible. He was putting his faith in God's integrity and ability to keep all the promises He had made, even if it meant He had to raise Isaac from the dead. Abraham's faith was amazing.

The Journey to Mt. Moriah (vv. 4-8)

The three-day journey is told in eloquently simple terms. Abraham traveled the forty-mile trip by donkey, probably because of his advancing years. He split the wood for the burnt offering, which presumably was carried by the two young men who accompanied them (v. 3). The party of four, including Isaac, set out from Beersheba. They traveled north for two full days and part of the third. As they approached Mt. Moriah, Abraham looked up and saw the place that the Lord had indicated for the sacrifice (v. 4). The little group halted, and the servants were told to stay with the donkey. No doubt they wanted to go all the way, but Abraham said, "Stay here ... the lad and I will go yonder and worship, and we will come back to you" (v. 5). These were remarkable words of faith in light of God's command to sacrifice his son. He was affirming his faith in the resurrection power of God.

It is important to note that Abraham was chiefly occupied with God, not with the human side of what would happen. He really believed that both he and Isaac would come back even though he fully intended to slay his son. His knowledge of God sustained him in the crucial moment. He had learned that God's promises were sure.

One of those promises was that Isaac would father a great nation; therefore, Isaac must live. What an example this is for us, that we be occupied with God rather than with the impossibilities with which our minds get engrossed. As far as Abraham was concerned, Isaac had been dead for the three days of the journey. It is vivid picture of the resurrection of the Lord Jesus Christ on the third day after he was crucified.

And what can we say about Abraham's statement that he and Isaac were going to "worship" (v. 5)? Could such an act as killing his son be considered "worship"? Yes indeed! It was a supreme act of worship because to worship God is to bow down to His will. We often think that worship is to sing hymns, say prayers, and listen to a sermon, but true worship is the acknowledgement of the surpassing worth of God as to who He is and what He has done in the light of our own unworthiness before Him.

The Ascent of Mt. Moriah

God had said, "*Take* now your son ... and offer him there as a burnt offering" (v. 2). The words of verse 6 echo that command: "So Abraham *took* the wood of the burnt offering ... and he *took* the fire in his hand, and a knife." The drama of the scene intensifies when Abraham lays the wood on Isaac's shoulders. It brings to mind that the Lord Jesus was forced to carry the wooden cross on which He would hang and die. This is what He endured along that terrible way of suffering, the *Via Dolorosa,* as He was led toward Golgotha (John 19:17). Abraham then took the brazier with the fire of coals in one hand and the knife in the other. In doing this, he pictured God the Father fulfilling Isaiah's prophecy: "Yet it pleased the LORD to bruise Him; He has put Him to grief" (Isa. 53:10).

Isaac's Willing Obedience

It then says of Abraham and Isaac that "the two of them went together" (v. 6). These words are deliberately repeated again in verse 8. We learn beyond question that Abraham was not compelling his son to go; Isaac willingly accompanied his father. He was a full-grown young man and could easily have resisted, but he willingly submitted to every detail of the ascent of Mt. Moriah. He pictures the willingness of the Lord Jesus Christ, who said when He came into the world, "I have come ... to do Your will, O God" (Heb. 10:7) and who prayed in the Garden of Gethsemane, "Not as I will, but as You will" (Matt. 26:39).

Abraham and Isaac walking together foreshadow the partnership of both the Father and the Son in the events of the crucifixion. "God was in Christ reconciling the world to Himself" (2 Cor. 5:19). Truly, only the Father and the Son could ever know the full pain of the penalty for sin that the Lord Jesus paid at Calvary. God did not force His Son to die on the cross. Jesus said, "My Father loves Me, because I lay down My life that I may take it again" (John 10:17). It was because both Father and Son went to the cross together that lost sinners can find forgiveness.

"Where is the lamb?"

As the two of them went together, Isaac said, "My father!" Abraham answered tenderly, "Here I am, my son." How eagerly he had said those same words—"Here I am"—just three days earlier when God spoke to him. But now, anticipating his son's question, he answered much more slowly and deliberately. Isaac asked, "Look, the fire and the wood, but where is the lamb for a burnt offering?" That question has echoed down through the centuries. Its answer is ultimately found only in Jesus Christ, the Lamb of God. Isaac must have known, as he walked up the hill, that he was the only possible sacrifice. What mental anguish he must have endured as he awaited his father's answer! His agony foreshadowed the questions in the human spirit of the Lord Jesus. In Gethsemane, Jesus recoiled from the prospect of the cross, sweating what became like great drops of blood (Luke 22:44). He petitioned God to remove the "cup" of suffering if at all possible. And later, on the cross, He cried out, "My God, My God, why have You forsaken me?" (Matt. 27:46).

"God will provide . . . the lamb"

Abraham's reply—"God will provide for Himself the lamb for a burnt offering"—is one of the great statements of the Old Testament. It was a promise that the provision of the lamb for Abraham's offering was to be the work of God alone. It looked forward to the greater Lamb, which God Himself would provide as a sin offering for you and me. Notice the use of the definite article—*the* lamb—not *a* lamb, which is what we would expect. The scene ends with the comment made for the second time: "And the two of them went together" (v. 8).

The theme of "the lamb" in this passage is found in many places between Genesis and Revelation:

- Abel's lamb pictures an acceptable sacrifice (Gen. 4:4).
- Abraham's lamb pictures a substitute sacrifice (Gen. 22:8).
- The Passover lamb pictures deliverance from wrath (Ex. 12:1-12).
- Isaiah's lamb pictures a willing and silent sacrifice (Isa. 53:7).
- John introduced Jesus as the Lamb who would take away sin (John 1:29).
- Peter spoke of the redeeming blood of the Lamb (1 Pet. 1:18).
- The throngs in Heaven extol the worth of the Lamb (Rev. 5:12).
- Heaven itself is adorned by the glory of the Lamb (Rev. 21:23).

The Sacrifice of Isaac (vv. 9-14)

We then read that "they came to *the place* of which God had told him" (v. 9, emphasis added). There is an ominous note in the use of the word "the place." In verse 3, we read the summary statement that he *went* to "the place." In verse 4 it says he *saw* "the place." Now in verse 9, we read that they *came* to "the place." We can only imagine the depth of emotion in Abraham's heart when he and Isaac arrived there. Most likely, "the place" was the flat outcrop of rock at the top of the ridge called Mt. Moriah. Muslim tradition has it that it was from this rock that Muhammad ascended to Paradise on his steed El Burak and later returned. Muslim tradition also says that Adam was created from this rock, that it was there that the ark came to rest, and that Jacob dreamed there of a golden ladder between earth and Paradise. Today, the Dome of the Rock is one of Islam's most holy places, called *Haram al Sharif,* which means "Most Noble Sanctuary."

What really happened at Mt. Moriah is revealed in the Bible. It was there that Abraham offered Isaac as a sacrifice and that God provided a ram that became a substitute for Isaac. In David's day, the same rock was the threshing floor of Araunah that David purchased as a site for the Temple that Solomon built. Many Jews maintain to this day that the most sacred part of the Temple, called the Holy of Holies, was built over the rock and that the sacred Ark of the Covenant stood on it. There the high priest sprinkled the blood of atonement on the most holy day of the Jewish year. It was the place of atonement and the place of meeting between God and man. Is it any wonder that the "Rock" is still the most politically sensitive spot on the entire planet?

The Altar and the Sacrifice

We may imagine Abraham selecting stones and slowly building an altar on the rock (vv. 9-10). As for Isaac, it is fascinating to consider what his thoughts were as he helped his father. Abraham had built altars at Shechem, Bethel, Hebron, and Beersheba and had offered lambs on all of them. But none of those places would do for this occasion. For the "true" sacrifice, the altar had to be on Mt. Moriah. Abraham did not have a lamb tethered nearby. He was not looking anxiously to the right or to the left for some sheep to appear. Nor did he storm heaven with his prayers. He simply completed the task that God had given him to do. The altar was finally finished, and the wood was carefully laid on it.

Isaac on the Altar

Abraham then "bound Isaac his son and laid him on the altar, upon the wood" (v. 9). God graciously draws a veil over the emotional aspect of this scene. There is no mention of the kisses of a heartbroken father or of the willing submission of a loving son looking up into his father's tear-stained face. Never was such a loving father and such an obedient son put to a test like this one. The Lord no doubt looked on with His own great heart throbbing with compassion at the faithful steadfastness of purpose displayed by both Abraham and Isaac.

At the climax of the test, the old man stretched out his hand, took the knife from its sheath, and raised it over the heart of his son (v. 10). At this point, Abraham's faith reached its pinnacle, for even as he was carrying out God's command he believed that somehow God would still make Isaac his heir. In the New Testament, James illustrated faith by the example of Abraham who "offered Isaac his son on the altar" (James 2:21). James went on to say that by works his "faith was made perfect," or complete. When his knife was poised in mid air, the genuineness of Abraham's faith was fully demonstrated.

God Interrupts Abraham

In God's eyes, Abraham passed his final exam. The voice of the Angel of the Lord interrupted him, calling out, "Abraham, Abraham!" In calling him by name twice, He conveyed the urgency of the message. For the third time in this chapter, Abraham answered, "Here I am" (v.11; cf. vv. 1 and 7). God then stopped Abraham from harming Isaac. "Do not lay your hand on the lad, or do anything to him, for now I know that you fear God, since you have not withheld your son, your only son, from Me" (v. 12). It becomes clear at this point that the command had been a test and that God was now satisfied with Abraham's response. As far as God was concerned, Abraham *had* given his son to Him.

The one who spoke is called the "Angel of the LORD"—none other than the second Person of the Trinity. The words "now I know" are important, for they reflect the happy response of someone who has benefited from someone's goodness to him. Jethro, Moses' father-in-law, for example, referring to God's deliverance of Israel from the Egyptians said, "Now I know that the LORD is greater than all the gods" (Ex. 18:11). In this passage in Genesis, it is God who joyfully exults in Abraham having loved Him to the point of sacrificing his own son.

Abraham's Faith is Proved

God, who knew Abraham's heart, acknowledged that he had acted out of fear of Him. Abraham had demonstrated his love for God, his faith in God, and his obedience to God. Now it is evident that he also acted out of fear of God. Fear was the foundation of Abraham's worship, as it is of all true worship. To fear God is to hold Him in awe and reverence and to do His bidding with unquestioning obedience. It is also to see ourselves as utterly unworthy in His presence and at the same time to find Him loving, gracious, and kind.

The Angel of the Lord said that Abraham's action proved that he really feared the Lord: "Since you have not withheld your son, your only son, from Me." The apostle Paul linked these very words with God's generosity in giving His Son: "He who did not spare His own Son, but delivered Him up for us all, how shall He not with Him also freely give us all things?" (Rom. 8:32). Abraham's offering clearly foreshadowed the sacrifice that God willingly made in giving His Son to die on the cross.

The Ram as the Substitute Sacrifice

Abraham then looked up and saw a ram caught in a thicket by its horns (vv. 12-13). In His own way, God had provided the "lamb." Abraham immediately untied the ropes that bound Isaac. He then took the ram and offered it up as a burnt offering instead of his son. The ram became Isaac's substitute. This is the first explicit example in Scripture of a sacrifice offered in place of another. The ram was killed, its blood was shed, and its carcass was burned on the altar until it was entirely consumed. Abraham and Isaac stood and watched the smoke of the offering ascending. Consider what Isaac must have thought as he witnessed the death of the ram on the same altar from which he had just been released. Isaac went free because the ram died in his place. Both Isaac and his father worshipped God that day with new insight. Believers today are like Isaac. We were on our way to an eternal death because of our sins, but God provided the Lamb, His Son Jesus, as a substitute for us. Jesus gave His life on the cross in our place. All we did was believe that He did it for us personally, as lost sinners, and accept our Substitute from God, who offers a full pardon on the basis of Jesus' sacrifice of Himself. Jesus Christ is the Lamb of God who takes away the sin of the world.

Many of the great truths of salvation at the cross of Calvary were pictured in what happened on Mt. Moriah. Consider them:

- The *voluntary nature* of the sacrifice. Isaac willingly gave himself to be the sacrifice, just as Jesus willingly laid down His life for us.
- The *substitutionary nature* of the sacrifice. As the ram was offered in the place of Isaac, so God's Son took our place.
- *God's satisfaction* with the offering, pictured by the smoke ascending, just as He was satisfied (propitiated) with the offering of His Son on the cross (1 John 2:2).

Jehovah Jireh

Having sacrificed the ram, Abraham named the place "The-Lord-Will-Provide," which is taken from the Hebrew, *Jehovah Jireh* (v. 14). In answer to Isaac's question, "Where is the lamb for the burnt offering?" (v. 7), Abraham had in faith replied, "God will provide for Himself the lamb" (v. 8). That God had provided the lamb is the central lesson of the story. Abraham wanted to preserve the memory of God's provision, so he declared Mt. Moriah to be a shrine and called it "The-Lord-Will-Provide." From this name grew up a saying among believers who looked forward to the coming sacrifice. This saying that was still known in the day that Moses wrote the book of Genesis, so Moses included it here: "In the mount of the Lord it shall be provided." It is a remarkable prophecy of confidence that God would ultimately provide the Lamb to die for man's sin.

There are two lessons here. The first is for the seeking sinner. God has provided the one great offering for sin in His Son's death on the cross. Anyone can, by faith, look at the cross today and say, "I believe Jesus died for me. I receive the gift of salvation that He offers to all who believe." The second lesson is for faithful worshippers who have devoted everything to the Lord.

They will find, as Abraham did, that God will provide; He will freely give them all things.

God Swears an Oath (vv. 15-19)

The Angel of the Lord called to Abraham once again from heaven. This time it was to affirm that God would bless him. He did so by an oath saying, "By Myself I have sworn, says the LORD" (v. 16). God swore by His own name to emphasize that, without a doubt, His word would be accomplished. The book of Hebrews comments on the meaning of this oath. It says, "Thus God, determining to show more abundantly to the heirs of promise the immutability [unchangeableness] of His counsel, confirmed it by an oath that ... we might have strong consolation [assured certainty that our salvation is secure], who have fled for refuge to lay hold of the hope set before us" (Heb. 6:17-18).

Just as God had told Abraham before he entered the Promised Land that in him all families of the earth would be blessed, so God affirmed that same promise on Mt. Moriah (v. 18; cf. 12:3). Note that the fulfillment of the promise was based on Abraham's obedience: "because you have obeyed My voice." This is the last recorded incident of God speaking to Abraham. He was now fully qualified to serve as a channel of blessing from God to the world. Therefore, God was ready to fully implement His plan, because Abraham had not withheld his son, his only son (v. 16).

Three times in these verses God used the word *seed*. Abraham's one seed, Isaac, would multiply as his descendants increased. It is significant, however, that God stressed the word "seed" in the singular rather than the plural. This points first to Isaac, not to Abraham's other children, but ultimately it points to the one Seed which is Christ, the Savior (Gal. 3:16). It is the same seed that was promised to Adam and Eve in the Garden of Eden (3:15). Here on Mt. Moriah, Abraham was impressed with the truth that one of his descendants would be the promised Anointed One. Jesus said, "Abraham rejoiced to see My day, and he saw it and was glad" (John 8:56). In His incarnation, Jesus fulfilled all that had been pictured in the offering of Isaac and the substitute lamb. God gave Abraham a glimpse of the atoning death of his Seed. Is it any wonder that Abraham was called the "friend of God" (Isa. 41:8)?

After God's affirmation, surely Abraham and Isaac returned to their waiting servants with a spring in their step, joy in their hearts, and smiles on their faces. The little party then returned to Beersheba (v. 19). Imagine the difference between what must have been strained silence on the outbound trip and their happy conversation on the way home!

The Family of Nahor (vv. 20-24)

With the testing of Abraham fully revealed, Moses now begins to prepare the readers of Genesis for the coming events in the life of Isaac. These few verses connect the history of God's dealings with Abraham to His continued dealings with Isaac. It contains a list of the twelve sons of Nahor, Abraham's brother, who still lived in Mesopotamia (possibly in the city of Nahor). Abraham probably obtained information about his relatives back in Mesopotamia by news from traveling caravans. Eight of Nahor's sons were born to his wife Milcah and four of them to his concubine, Reumah. One of Milcah's sons was Bethuel, who is singled out here as the father of Rebekah, the woman who later became Isaac's wife. Her role was most important because their children were to be the heirs of the promise. The lineage of Abraham's brother prepares the readers for the search for a suitable bride for Isaac.

In Conclusion

Genesis 22 is rich with imagery and insight for the Christian. We learn of the geographical importance of Mt. Moriah and the drama-filled history of Abraham's offering of Isaac. Christ is pictured as the substitutionary sacrifice and the Lamb of God. God is pictured in Abraham's love for his son and his willingness to give him up as a sacrifice. God provides for our salvation and every other necessity. We find wonderful lessons for believers here of supreme faith, willing obedience, and grateful worship.

The Death and Burial of Sarah

Some time after Abraham returned to Beersheba from Mt. Moriah he moved with his family back to Hebron where he had lived many years earlier. He was still an alien in Canaan, living in tents without any permanent home. Most of chapter 23 has to do with the negotiations between Abraham and the Hittites for a place to bury Sarah. There was some urgency because Sarah was already dead and Abraham needed to bury her immediately. This may indicate that her death was unexpected, leaving Abraham no time to arrange for this beforehand. He and Sarah had moved to Canaan at God's command and believed that God was going to give the whole land to his heirs, but as yet he did not own any of it. Abraham evidently felt it necessary that Sarah, as the mother of those who would eventually live in the land, be buried on legally held ground in the land.

Sarah Dies (vv. 1-2)

While in Hebron, Sarah died at the age of 127. She is the only woman mentioned in the Bible whose age at death is given. The apostle Peter cites her as the "mother" of all believing women (1 Pet. 3:5-6), and as such she sets an example for them to follow. She is listed among the heroes of faith in Hebrews 11 as one of those who "died in faith." By faith, she had received strength to conceive seed and bear a child "when she was past age"; by faith, she believed God to be "faithful who had promised"; by faith, she saw from "afar off" that all God's promises would be fulfilled (Heb. 11:11-13).

Abraham mourned deeply for Sarah. He no doubt recalled her partnership with him over the many years. They had listened to the voice of God and obeyed Him together. Despite their recorded failures, they had, as a couple, walked with God for nearly one hundred years. To Abraham, the loss of Sarah was great.

Abraham Purchases a Burial Site (vv. 3-18)

Even though he was still grieving, Abraham had to act quickly. He already knew the particular burial site he wanted. It was a field with a suitable cave in it, near to his encampment at Mamre (cf. v. 17), and it was owned by a Hittite named Ephron. The owners of the land around Hebron where Abraham was living as a "foreigner and a sojourner" were the "sons of Heth." Abraham probably rented living space from them and pastureland for his great herds. The sons of Heth were otherwise known as Hittites. They were one of the people groups in Canaan when the Israelites invaded it under Joshua (Josh. 1:4). The major clans of Hittites occupied much of present-day Turkey in ancient times, but at least one of the clans evidently settled farther south.

Abraham probably went to the gate of the city of Hebron (Mamre, cf. v.19) where, as in all ancient walled cities, all important city business was carried on. There he called a meeting equivalent to a city council (cf. v. 18). When it says that he "stood up from before his dead," it means that he rose up from where he was mourning Sarah's death to go and make arrangements for her burial. He acknowledged to the city elders that he was an alien among them and asked for a piece of property as a burial site for Sarah. The negotiations described seem strange to us, but they were carried on in accordance with their ancient customs and were fully understood by those involved. When Abraham asked them to "give" him property, he was not looking for a free gift. By saying that, he opened negotiations for a legal transaction that took the form of a public hearing.

The Hittite Generosity and Abraham's Request

The Hittites acknowledged that Abraham was a "mighty prince" (literally "prince of God"), indicating that they trusted him for whatever negotiations would follow. Abraham had a good testimony among the people; they held him in high regard.

This should be true of every believer with regard to living in the world. Then, they agreed that it was perfectly proper that he, as a "mighty prince," bury Sarah at any of their own burial sites or at any other site he wanted. They would not block his purchase, no matter who owned the property he desired. Abraham then, with all due formality, stood up and "bowed himself to the people of the land." He asked that they approach Ephron to negotiate the purchase of the cave of Machpelah (vv. 8-9). He promised to pay the full price for it. It appears that Ephron was present to answer for himself, with all the others as witnesses (v. 10).

Ephron spoke in the customary way of business dealings: "No, my lord, hear me: I give you the field and the cave that is in it; I give it to you in the presence of the sons of my people, I give it to you. Bury your dead!" Abraham understood that Ephron was acting according to custom when three times he said, "I give it to you" (v. 11). Ephron was not offering the land for nothing, but rather in exchange for the proper price yet to be agreed. Abraham then prostrated himself again and said that he would "give" Ephron money for the field. In their culture, this meant that Ephron's gift of the field was to be matched by Abraham's gift of money. Abraham said, "Take it [the money] from me and I will bury my dead there" (v. 13).

The Price is Agreed Upon

Ephron then stated his price, which seems to be more than the site was really worth (vv. 14-18). In setting the price at four hundred shekels of silver, he said, "What is that between you and me? So bury your dead" (v. 15). Abraham did not haggle, as would have been expected, but immediately weighed out the silver before the witnesses. Silver coins were not yet in use in Abraham's day, so precious metals were used as currency by weight. The legal transaction of the purchase confirmed that the cave and the field with the trees in it were deeded to Abraham as a "possession." As such, it now formally belonged to him and his heirs (vv. 17-18). It would be important for the children of Israel, for whom Moses was writing this history, to know that their original ancestor owned property in the land. It indicated that, in taking over Canaan, they were carrying out God's purpose already initiated through Abraham.

The Burial of Sarah (vv. 19-20)

The record then states that "Abraham buried Sarah his wife in the cave of the field of Machpelah, before Mamre (that is, Hebron) in the land of Canaan." At last, Abraham had established a tiny foothold in the land that God had promised him. He himself would be buried in that same place when he died, to be joined in the grave later by his son Isaac, Isaac's wife Rebekah, and still later by his grandson Jacob (Israel) and his wife Leah. The site where they all are buried is almost certainly the traditional site located beneath the modern mosque in Hebron. It can be visited to this day. The chapter ends with repeated statement about the sale (v. 20; cf. vv. 17-18). The importance of the purchase is also reaffirmed in the last chapter of Genesis (50:13). In this transition chapter in the Abraham story, even though the promise of possession of the whole land was unfulfilled as yet, the beginning of it was established with the purchase of one field and the burial there of the "mother" of Canaan's heirs.

In Conclusion

Sarah is one of the "cloud of witnesses" who testify to all believers today of God's faithfulness and who encourage us to "run with endurance the race that is set before us" (Heb. 12:1-2). Her experience reminds us that although God's promises are not necessarily fulfilled during our lifetime, we can live with the assurance of their future fulfillment. We also learn from Abraham's purchase of the field that, in times of grief over loved ones who have died in faith, we can demonstrate our confidence in God's future purposes.

A Bride for Isaac

Chapter 24 of Genesis, as a love story, has charmed the romantically-inclined for generations, only rivaled, perhaps, by the story of Ruth and Boaz (recorded in the book of Ruth). Its importance in the context of Genesis, however, far surpasses the romantic element. Chapter 23 tells how Abraham obtained a tiny piece of property in Canaan, looking forward to the time when the whole land would belong to his descendants. Chapter 24 tells how Abraham obtained a wife for Isaac, now a full-grown man, so that the seed of his family might be propagated and eventually fill the land in fulfillment of God's promise.

Moses' purpose in this chapter was to explain the underlying hand of God in the process of His supernatural oversight of Abraham's seed. From it would come the promised nation and the Savior. Abraham knew that it was God who had enabled Isaac's birth by Sarah. It was God who had preserved Isaac's life with a substitute offering at Mt. Moriah. Once again, the guiding hand of God in a supernatural way would be required to find the wife of His choice. Our chapter demonstrates the providence of God in bringing Isaac and Rebekah together.

Abraham Commissions His Servant (vv. 1–9)

Abraham himself is the focus in the first section of the chapter. He was still encamped near Hebron where Sarah was buried. He is described as "well advanced in age," being 140 years old. Isaac was forty (cf. 25:20). In addition to his age, we are reminded that "the Lord had blessed Abraham in all things" (v. 1). Ever since Abraham came to the land, he had prospered both spiritually and materially. It was clear to him that it was now time to seek a wife for Isaac. He realized that no one suitable was to be found in Canaan. The Canaanites were under God's curse because of their idolatry, violence, and immorality. Isaac's bride needed to be a believer in the one true God.

Abraham determined that the only way to find Isaac a bride was to make a trip to Haran, the home he had left more than sixty years earlier. Haran was nearly five hundred miles away, and news from passing caravans must have been sketchy at best. Some news had, however, evidently reached him, for he knew that his brother Nahor had a granddaughter named Rebekah (22:23). Perhaps there were others!

Abraham needed a trusted mediator because he himself was too old for such a venture. Wealthy people in his day often used intermediaries to arrange marriages for their family. He chose his oldest and most trusted servant for the task (v. 2). Although he is not named here, most students of Genesis think he was probably Eliezer, even though fifty years had passed since he was last mentioned (15:2). Whether it was indeed Eliezer is not important because his mission was not in his own name but in the names of Abraham, Isaac, and their God.

The Servant's Oath to Abraham

Abraham commissioned his servant to go to Abraham's "country" (Haran) and obtain a wife for Isaac from his "kindred" (vv. 2-9). Abraham's relatives were God-fearing people. The servant was concerned that, if he found the right woman, she might not be willing to come to "this land." If this happens, he asked, "must I take your son back to the land from which you came?" (v. 5). He reasoned that, if Isaac came with him, it would be much easier, humanly-speaking, to persuade a prospective wife to come back. But Abraham strictly warned his servant that under no circumstances should he take Isaac to Haran. Isaac needed to remain in the land of promise, for it was there that God's covenant purposes for His people would unfold.

With his mission clearly explained in detail, Abraham required his servant to swear a solemn oath that he would carry it out. The oath was taken in the name of the LORD (Yahweh), the covenant name for God, the "God of heaven and earth" (v. 3). Abraham went on to say that the Lord would "send His angel before you, and you shall take a wife for my son from there" (v. 7). Abraham's confidence that God would send His angel to help him find the right woman is remarkable. If the woman proved not willing to follow his servant, he would be released from his oath (v. 8).

The Oath

The form of the oath is strange to our thinking. The servant was to place his hand under Abraham's thigh and swear to him concerning his mission (vv. 2, 9). The word *thigh* refers to the loins or procreative organs, as it does in another significant passage (47:29). Jewish commentators understood the term to indicate the "source of posterity and the seat of power." Thus, the oath had enormous significance for the posterity of Abraham through his son Isaac. His servant would have been keenly aware of the importance of his promise.

The oath probably had even greater significance if the church fathers were correct in believing that it was administered in view of a *particular* descendant of Abraham—the coming Savior. The orthodox view is that Abraham anticipated the day when a Savior would come from his seed who would be the great substitute for sinners and a sacrifice for sin (John 8:56). Some liberals have suggested that this form of oath was the remnant of a pagan phallic cult. But the truth here is about an oath demanded by godly Abraham in the name of the covenant-keeping God. It looked toward his greatest hope, the coming Savior. Like Abraham and Sarah, Isaac and his chosen bride were to be the forebears of the whole Jewish race, and especially of the Messiah, the Lord Jesus.

The principle of taking a bride from among the people of God is a continuing biblical standard and should be carefully followed by God's people everywhere (cf. Deut. 7:3-4; 1 Kings 11:4; 1 Cor. 7:39; 2 Cor. 6:14).

The Servant and the Sign (vv. 10-14)

Abraham's servant made preparations to leave. He had ten camels laden with the provisions for the month-long journey. He also took valuable gifts for the marriage negotiations and servants to assist him. The probably route would have taken him across the Jordan and up the "King's Highway" to Damascus, then north through the Beqa Valley in Syria to Aleppo. From there, he would have gone northeast to the Euphrates River and on to Haran.

The story places special emphasis on the servant's faith in God as he sought guidance to find the right person. When he reached the gate of Haran, he rested his camels by the town well. It was afternoon, the time of day when women went out to draw water. He then prayed one of the most remarkable prayers for guidance in the entire Bible. He specifically asked the Lord to give him success and to "show kindness" to his master, Abraham. The word *kindness* is a covenant term and reveals that he expected the Lord to fulfill His promise to Abraham by leading him to the right bride for Isaac. She must be part of the believing family of Abraham who lived in this city. She must have the character and stamina for such a role. He was looking for a godly and virtuous woman, one who was both kind and industrious. She must also be healthy and strong.

The Test

To ascertain her character and ability, the servant devised a test for the women he might meet at the well. He told God that he would ask a woman who came out to draw water for a drink. Almost any woman would happily grant such a request from a traveler. However, if the woman not only granted his request, but then offered to water all his camels as well, he would take that as a sign that she was God's choice.

The condition he imposed was extraordinary in two ways. First, he was asking more than could be expected. Second, camels are notorious for the amount of water they drink—and there were ten of them!—so drawing water for them from a deep well would have been more than granting a simple favor. A woman who was kind enough, strong enough, and generous enough to offer that service to a complete stranger would be a remarkable woman indeed. Abraham's servant concluded his prayer, "And by this I will know You have shown kindness to my master" (v. 14). As well as being a great example of a believing prayer for specific guidance, it was a reasonable prayer because he was looking for the very person of God's choice. He was praying in the will of God (1 John 5:14-15). Yet, it was most unlikely to come to pass without the intervention of the "angel" of whom Abraham had spoken (v. 7).

The Servant and Rebekah (vv. 15-28)

The very next recorded words are: "And it happened...." The servant looked up to find Rebekah approaching the well with a pitcher on her shoulder. His prayer was answered before he had finished voicing it—although he did not as yet know it. How like our God (Isa. 65:24)! The fact that Rebekah was the first at the well says something about her attention to duties. The servant noticed that she was "very beautiful to behold" and a virgin. Maybe her beauty reminded him of Sarah's (12:11). The text describes her going "down" to the well (v. 16), from which we gather that the well must have been at the bottom of a pit with stairs leading down to it. The servant ran to speak to her, to see if she would respond according to the sign for which he had prayed.

Her answer to his request for a drink was "Drink, my lord," and she lowered her pitcher to provide it (v. 18). When he had finished she said, "I will draw water for your camels also, until they have finished drinking." Rebekah then made trip after trip, down the stairs to the well and back up to the trough with the water, while the camels drank gallon after gallon of it. The servant must have hardly been able to contain himself watching her, wondering how God could be answering his prayer so quickly. Rebekah was not only beautiful, she was showing that she was kind, energetic, and strong. But he did not rush to ask her about her family. It says that while he was "wondering at her," he remained silent, so as to know whether the Lord had made his journey prosperous or not (v. 21). He was, no doubt, excited, but he patiently waited for God to let the situation develop. There is a practical application here for us: we should not "get ahead of God" when we anticipate His leading in a certain matter, but patiently wait for confirmation.

When Rebekah had finally finished watering the camels, he presented her with a gold nose ring and two gold bracelets. He was rewarding her for her kindness, as God often does when His servants minister with a kind and generous attitude. It was then that he put the all-important question to her: "Whose daughter are you? Tell me, please, is there room in your father's house for us to lodge?" (v. 23). Her answer told him that she was the daughter of Bethuel and the granddaughter of Nahor, Abraham's brother. The servant's heart must have skipped a beat. She must be the Rebekah of whom Abraham had heard news back in Hebron! She went on to say that her home had plenty of straw and feed and room for the visitors to lodge.

The Servant Worships God

By this time, the servant was overwhelmed with gratitude to God, and "he bowed down his head and worshipped the LORD" (v. 26). For us, too, the only proper response to God when we recognize His acts of lovingkindness is worship. Note that Abraham's servant saw the answer to his prayer in relation to God first. He then responded with thanks on behalf of his master Abraham. Finally, as far as he himself was concerned, he thanked God for leading him to the house of his "master's brethren." It is always the proper order when God is first, others are next, and we are last.

As she stood by listening, Rebekah must have been amazed to hear the name of her great-uncle Abraham mentioned. No doubt her mind raced when she wondered why he had sent his servant to her city. As a believer, her heart must have been thrilled to see a spiritual man in prayer and worship, blessing God and thanking Him for His mercy and His truth. She turned and ran to her mother's house and reported the whole incident with high excitement (v. 28).

The Servant and Laban (vv. 28-54)

Rebekah's brother Laban seems to have been in charge of the family affairs. Perhaps her father Bethuel was getting old and was unable to manage the household. Laban heard his sister's news, saw the jewelry, and instructed the servants to prepare for guests. He ran to the well to invite the whole caravan to stay with them. Laban was certainly most hospitable, but he also may have had an eye for the financial possibilities. It was "when he saw the nose ring and the bracelets" that he began to act (v. 30). So he may have had mixed motives when he greeted Abraham's servant with "Come in, O blessed of the LORD! Why do you stand outside?"

After seeing to the traveling party's needs, Laban prepared a meal and set it before the servant, who said, however, "I will not eat until I have told my errand" (v. 33). It was not customary for the business of the day to precede the meal, but this business was so important to the man that he felt it necessary to break custom. It may be instructive for us to remember that the Lord Jesus had a similar zeal when He said, "I must be about my Father's business" (Luke 2:49).

The Servant and His Master's Business

Abraham's servant gave a remarkable testimony of the sovereign hand of God in all of the circumstances leading up to this point. It may seem redundant to us to repeat them. We should remember, however, that the repetition is deliberately designed to emphasize certain themes that Rebekah's family needed to understand in the light of the important decision they would have to make. With this in mind, let us consider them again and note parallels for each of us to apply to our own lives. The servant's explanation was remarkable:

- He spoke of *the blessing of God* on Abraham, who had become a great man and been enriched with great wealth in gold, silver, and huge flocks of domestic animals (v. 35).

- He told about *the inheritance* that Abraham had handed over to his son Isaac, according to God's covenant (v. 36).

- He explained *the solemn oath* that the servant swore before the Lord that he would not take a wife for Isaac from the Canaanites but find her among Abraham's kindred in Haran (vv. 37-39).

- He spoke of Abraham's *promise of the angel* to prosper his way in finding the wife of God's choice (vv. 40-41).

- He told them of *the prayer at the well,* in which he sought God's confirmation of the right woman by designating a particular sign (vv. 42-46).

- He mentioned the *identification of Rebekah* as the daughter of Bethuel, Abraham's cousin, and his response of bowing in worship to God (vv. 47-48).

Any discerning person could conclude that God was orchestrating all this for a purpose. The servant's impressive appeal was based on the obvious sovereign activity of God in bringing everything together for the climax of the present moment. Thus the servant's conclusion was "Now if you will deal kindly and truly with my master, tell me. And if not, tell me, that I may turn to the right hand or to the left" (v. 49). The expression "kindly and truly" was also used to describe God's favor to Abraham (v. 26). These two words appear often together as "lovingkindness" or "mercy and truth" in the psalms (cf. Ps. 117:2). They always indicate God's gracious activity toward man that is consistent with His holiness or truth. It was these two qualities that the disciples discovered in the Lord Jesus whom John described as "full of grace and truth" (John 1:14).

Rebekah's Family Agrees that She Should Marry Isaac

As a result of the servant's powerful testimony, Rebekah's family was convinced that God had ordered each of the steps and that Rebekah should become Isaac's bride (vv. 50-51). Laban and Bethuel said, "The thing comes from the LORD, we cannot speak to you either bad or good." The providence of God in the matter was so clear that it precluded any personal opinion or choice. The theme of "good or bad" in Laban's life will appear again, when God prevented him in a dream from doing either good or bad to Jacob (cf. 31:24). Both Bethuel and Laban said, "Here is Rebekah before you; take her and go and let her be your master's son's wife." Rebekah does not seem to have been consulted at this point, but neither did she object. She would do as the family directed, and her lack of expression probably indicated her willingness.

Worship, Gifts, and Celebration

When Abraham's servant heard the words of Bethuel and Laban, he knew the Lord had answered his prayer beyond his expectation (vv. 52-54). Rebekah was not only wonderfully suited to be Isaac's bride, her relatives had given their consent within a few hours of his arrival—and she was beautiful as well! Overwhelmed with gratitude to God, he fell to his knees and worshipped the Lord right then and there (cf. v. 27).

Having acknowledged God's gracious, omnipotent hand, he brought out gifts for Rebekah and for her brother and mother (v. 53). This was no slight to Bethuel, for gifts to her mother were, in effect, gifts to him also. The gifts of silver, gold, and clothing reflected the wealth of Isaac to whom she was betrothed. With the marriage arranged, the worship offered, and the gifts presented, it was time to enjoy the long-delayed meal. No doubt it became quite a celebration feast (v. 54).

Rebekah's Departure (vv. 54-60)

The next morning, Abraham's servant surprised the family by requesting that they leave immediately for Canaan. Rebekah's mother and Laban were reluctant to send her away so quickly and pleaded for a ten-day delay. After all, it was only one day since the whole matter had been raised! They wanted time to say their good-byes, but the servant insisted that they not delay because "the LORD has prospered my way" (v. 56). He believed that now that he knew the will of God, he should immediately act upon it. Any delay might give opportunity for a change of plans. In any case, Abraham and Isaac were keenly awaiting his return.

Rebekah's family then left the decision in her hands, asking, "Will you go with this man? And she said, "I will go" (v. 58). She, too, saw that God was at work, and she was willing to leave immediately. Her faith shines here. It did not shrink at the long miles to a strange country or at the prospect of never seeing her parents again. Like all people with genuine faith, she was ready to act immediately on what she believed was God's will for her life. Her decision, even in the face of family opposition, is an excellent example for all believers.

The family sent Rebekah away with their blessing (v. 60). Though they did not know it, their blessing was remarkably like that of the Angel of the Lord on Abraham after he offered the sacrifice on Mt. Moriah (22:17). The blessing came to pass when her descendants *did* number in the millions and *did* indeed possess the gates (the government) of the cities of Canaan in the days of Joshua.

Rebekah Meets Isaac (vv. 61-67)

No doubt Rebekah asked many questions about her husband-to-be on the five-hundred mile journey back to Canaan. From Abraham's servant, she would have learned of the faith of Abraham and Sarah, particularly as it related to their miracle son, Isaac. She would drink in every detail with delight, probably none more than the offering of Isaac on Mt. Moriah and the provision of the substitute ram. As she learned of him, her longing for him would have increased. As her longing increased, the more she looked for him.

Isaac had been living in Beer Lahai Roi, a good way south of Hebron where Abraham lived. He had come as far north as Hebron to meet his bride. It was there while he was meditating that her caravan drew near. Rebekah noticed in the distance a man coming to meet them. She asked, "Who is this man walking in the field to meet us?" When Abraham's servant said, "It is my master," she knew that it was Isaac. She dismounted from the camel and veiled herself in preparation for meeting him (v. 65), in accordance with marriage customs at that time.

Isaac brought Rebekah into his mother Sarah's tent, which had been vacant for the three years since her death. The Scripture says of Rebekah that "she became his wife, and he loved her." Their marriage was marked in the beginning with the love and respect for each other that God designed for marriage in the Garden of Eden. In being brought into Sarah's tent, Rebekah became the new *matriarch* of the family in Sarah's place. Isaac was the new *patriarch*, for the servant referred to Isaac, not Abraham, as his master (v. 65). Abraham is not even mentioned in this incident.

Isaac: a Type of Christ

There are so many parallels between the persons of Christ and Isaac that the Spirit of God obviously designed it that way:

- Isaac is a type of Christ, waiting to be united with His bride, the Church. Christ is preparing a place for her as He awaits her coming (John 14:1-3).
- Isaac was the promised son just as Christ's coming was promised time after time "as [God] spoke by the mouth of His holy prophets" (Luke 1:70).
- Both Isaac and the Lord Jesus were miraculously conceived, although Jesus' conception took place in a virgin womb (Luke 1:35).
- Isaac was born at the appointed time just as Christ appeared "when the fullness of the time was come" (21:2; Gal. 4:4).
- Both Isaac and Jesus were named before they were born (17:19; Matt. 1:21).
- Prior to their marriages, both were offered as sacrifices by their fathers (22:9; Rom. 8:32).
- Knowing what was before them, both submitted to being sacrificed (22:8; Phil. 2:8).
- Isaac and Christ were both brought back from the dead (Heb. 11:19; Eph. 1:19-20).
- Isaac's physical descendants (via his son Jacob), through whom all peoples would be blessed, are a picture of Christ's spiritual descendants by faith.

Rebekah: a Type of the Church

Rebekah is a type of the Church, the bride of Christ pictured as a chaste virgin (2 Cor. 11:2) who is anticipating being with Him at the marriage supper of the Lamb (Rev. 19:9). The Church, like Rebekah, was chosen when a long way from her groom (Eph. 1:4). Rebekah committed herself to Isaac before she saw him, even as believers in Christ do, one by one, when they are saved and leave behind their past life (1 Thess. 1:9). Rebekah learned of Isaac as she spoke to Abraham's servant—even as we learn of our Beloved from the Bible, the Holy Spirit's written revelation of Him. When she arrived, she would share the glory of her groom (v. 36; cf. John 17:22-24). She closely followed his servant until she and Isaac were united together. She longed to be with him, even at the cost of her closest earthly ties.

Rebekah foreshadows the Church as the bride of Christ who longs to be with her Bridegroom even though she has never seen Him. The apostle Peter put it well: "Whom having not seen, you love…. yet believing, you rejoice with joy inexpressible and full of glory" (1 Pet. 1:8). Rebekah became Isaac's wife, just as the Church will be the Lamb's wife in heaven (Rev. 19:7). Her marriage to Isaac is a picture of what is in store for the believer today as a part of the Church, the bride of Christ.

The Servant: a Type of the Holy Spirit

Abraham's unnamed servant is a type of the Holy Spirit whose ministry is to claim a bride for the waiting groom, to guide her toward her new life with Him, and to teach her of Him with whom she will one day be united (John 16:14). The Spirit is taking out from among the Gentiles a people for the Son (Acts 15:14). When the bride is complete, she (the Church) will be caught up to be united with Him forever (1 Thess. 4:17).

In Conclusion

Clearly, God ordained the marriage of Isaac and Rebekah. The sign to Abraham's servant had confirmed it; Rebekah's family recognized it; Rebekah herself stepped into it by faith. Their courtship and marriage should cause us as believers to worship God. It teaches us of the life of faith in dependence on God. It teaches us of the guidance of God for those who bathe their every movement in prayer. It teaches us to carry out the purpose of God with all diligence when we are assured of His will. It teaches us that God does have purposes and that there are distinct blessings in store for those who yield to them.

Abraham's Death and
the Birth of Esau and Jacob

The marriage of Isaac and Rebekah recorded in the previous chapter marks a turning point in the book of Genesis. Isaac and Rebekah now replace Abraham and Sarah as the focus of the story. Chapter 25 records Abraham's marriage to Keturah and the names of the sons she bore him. It also records Abraham's death, his burial, and the inheritance he left to his sons. With these events, Abraham's era draws to a close. The second half of the chapter commences the era of Isaac with the conception of twin sons (Esau and Jacob), their pre-natal struggle, the prophecy of their future relationship, and their remarkable birth. The chapter concludes with Esau selling his birthright to his younger brother Jacob.

Abraham and Keturah (vv. 1-6)

When Sarah died and Isaac moved away with Rebekah to Beer Lahai Roi (v. 11), Abraham married again. His wife's name was Keturah. Although verse 1 calls Keturah his wife, she is termed a concubine in verse 6 and again in 1 Chronicles 1:32. Neither she nor Hagar ever held the same official status in the household that Sarah did. It is possible that Abraham's marriage to Keturah took place prior to Isaac's (and even prior to Sarah's death) because the word "took" could just as well be translated "had taken." It is more likely, however, that Abraham married her after Sarah's death. Keturah bore him six sons. If Abraham did marry Keturah after Sarah died, it is testimony that the vitality that God restored to him before Isaac was born remained for many years.

Abraham's six sons by Keturah probably became the heads of clans. Midian's descendants (the Midianites) are mentioned a number of times in Scripture. They lived east of the Red Sea (cf. 37:25; Num. 25:1; Judges 6:3). Moses' wife and father-in-law were Midianites (Ex. 2:15). Two of Keturah's grandsons mentioned here, Sheba and Dedan, also had descendants mentioned in other places in the Bible. All of Keturah's sons appear to have settled on the Arabian Peninsula. For their benefit, Abraham left a legacy to them, as well one to Ishmael, the son of his former concubine, Hagar (v. 6). This would enable them to have a good start on their flocks and herds and to provide well for their mothers.

Abraham did not allow them to dwell in Canaan but sent them "away from Isaac his son to the country of the east," that is, Arabia (v. 6). Their removal was necessary for two reasons. First, to protect them from the curse and destruction that Abraham well knew was coming on the Canaanites owing to their growing iniquity (15:16). Second, to ensure that they could not contest the claims of Isaac's descendants for the land that God had promised to them alone. Above all else, Abraham wanted to be sure that there was a proper succession of the covenant blessings through Isaac, the covenant son. The strong and obvious point of these first six verses is to emphasize that Abraham bequeathed "all that he had" to his son Isaac as the sole heir of his fortune when he died (v. 5). Isaac was to stay in the land of the covenant. Abraham's astute foresight in estate planning for his family is a good example to us. Like him, we should strive to please God with what He has entrusted to us. We also see in Abraham's example a picture of God the Father giving all that He has to His glorified Son. The Church will share that bounty with Him in a coming day (Eph. 1:10-11).

Abraham's Death (vv. 7-11)

Abraham died at the age of 175 years. He had lived his first seventy-five years in the cities of Ur and Haran in Mesopotamia. For the next one hundred years he had been a pilgrim in the land of Canaan, living the life of a wealthy rancher—albeit without a "ranch"—and moving from one encampment to another. When Abraham died, Isaac would have been seventy-five years old (v. 7). Isaac's twin sons, Esau and Jacob, were born when Isaac was sixty, and were, therefore, fifteen years old when Abraham died, but they are not mentioned until later.

Abraham had outlived Sarah by almost fifty years. He died "at a good old age and full of years" (v. 8). He had enjoyed fellowship with God—just as it should be for all older believers who walk with God. And he died *full*, not literally full of years, but simply full or satisfied. He died in this condition because he was the friend of God and lived his life to the full. Abraham is one of the spiritual giants of the Bible. We ought to follow the faith of men like him. When it was God's time, he was "gathered to his people." This phrase indicates the continuance of his life in the presence of believers who had preceded him in death.

Both Isaac and Ishmael buried Abraham in Hebron beside his beloved wife Sarah in the only property he owned in the Promised Land. Ishmael was ninety years old. The old animosity between the brothers seems to have gone. After the burial of his father, Isaac lived in the Negev (south) at Beer Lahai Roi. The text says that God "blessed his [Abraham's] son Isaac." God had blessed Isaac by giving him a wonderful example of faith in his father and mother and a lovely God-given bride, Rebekah. Now, even though Abraham had died, God continued to bless him, as He does all those who trust in Him.

The Genealogy of Ishmael (vv. 12-18)

Moses inserts a genealogy of Ishmael at this point to record what became of him. Though he was not in the chosen line, his pedigree as Abraham's son is emphasized here. His mother Hagar's name is included. She, too, was a believer after her encounter with the Angel. God had promised to make Ishmael a great nation (16:10; 21:13). God had also promised Abraham that many nations and kings would come from him (17:6). Here is part of the fulfillment. Although the section is only seven verses long, it is seventh of the eleven sections of Genesis that begin with the phrase "This is the genealogy of," sometimes called the *toledoth* sections (from the Hebrew). The twelve sons of Ishmael that are listed became twelve princes, just as God had promised (17:20). Not much is known about them, though they seem to have settled in what is today northern Arabia "from Havilah to Shur" (v. 18). From those twelve tribes came many of the Arab peoples.

The short section ends with the record of Ishmael's death (vv. 17-18). Although it is out of chronological order, it concludes the matter of Ishmael so the story of Jacob and Esau can be related without interruption. He died aged 137 years and, like Abraham, was "gathered to his people." The phrase indicates to many commentators that Ishmael was a genuine believer in his father's God. It is used of only five other people in the Bible, all believers: Abraham (25:8), Isaac (35:29), Jacob (49:33), Aaron (Num. 20:26), and Moses (Deut. 32:26). Some commentators suggest that the phrase "in the presence of all his brethren" (v.18) could be understood as "to the east of all his brethren," which might imply that he lived apart from them. Others translate it "in hostility or defiance," which would fulfill the prophecy in Genesis 16:12.

Isaac, Sarah, and Family (vv. 19-28)

From this point to the end of Genesis, there are really two major sections. The first is the genealogy of Isaac (25:19-36:8), and the second, the genealogy of Jacob (37:2-50:26). Jacob is the dominant figure in both of them. This is the eighth occurrence of the key phrase "the genealogy of" in Genesis.

We read more about Jacob than any other person in Genesis. God took special delight in him. Even hundreds of years later, God said through Malachi, "Yet Jacob have I loved" (Mal. 1:2). The woman at the well could think of none greater when she asked of Jesus, "Are you greater than our father Jacob?" (John 4:12). At the end of his life, even the mighty pharaoh of Egypt bowed humbly before him to receive a blessing. This chapter records the beginning of his life and the remarkable circumstances surrounding it.

Isaac Prays for a Son

The story of the generations of Isaac begins with some background information about his wife, Rebekah (vv. 20-21). She was the daughter of

Bethuel the Syrian of Padan Aram and the brother of Laban. Syria is also called Aram in the Bible. Padan Aram is literally the plain, or flat land, of Aram. The man for whom the country of Aram was named was a son of Shem, which indicates that his descendants were Semitic. It was there in the city of Nahor that Abraham's servant found Rebekah. Her brother Laban still lived there. He would play a significant part later on in the Jacob story. At this point in time, Rebekah had been married to Isaac for twenty years (compare verse 20 with verse 26) but had borne him no children. Like Sarah before her, she had no son to carry on the seed of the promise and no heir to the land of the promise. The great tension here is that, once again, barrenness was an obstacle in the obtaining of the promise.

Isaac was sixty years old and getting concerned about having no family. Many years before, God had promised his father, "I will greatly multiply your descendants as the stars of heaven" (22:17). Isaac well knew that the descendants must come through him because he was the "only son." It may be that he assumed they would have a son right away. He may have wondered why his half-brother Ishmael had twelve sons, while he had none. After twenty years, he understood that if he and Rebekah were going to have a son it would be by God's power. Isaac prayed for Rebekah to conceive.

Waiting for God to Answer

God let Isaac and Rebekah wait because He wanted them to understand that their sons would be the result of His gracious intervention rather than through the ordinary course of nature (v. 21). Isaac did not repeat his father's mistake, that of demonstrating a self-sufficient spirit by procreating a child through a concubine. He prayed with great fervor, for it says that he "pleaded with the LORD for his wife ... and the LORD granted his plea." Prayer is the crucible out of which comes the blessing of God. Isaac did what all believers should do: he took the matter to God in prayer. God wants us to pray, to claim in faith the promises He has made. God wanted them to see that he, Isaac, a *miracle son*, and Rebekah, a *miracle bride*, were not adequate to become parents of the next heir without God. Now he prayed for another miracle in the birth of his own son.

Rebekah's Dilemma

The text says, "But the children struggled together within her" (v. 22). It is worth mentioning, in light of the current debate on abortion, that the unborn twins she was carrying were called "children" not fetuses. The word *struggled* indicates violent internal turmoil in her womb. When the sensation seemed extraordinary, perhaps even ominous, she took her concern to the Lord in prayer. The word *inquire* may carry the idea of seeking an oracle, a special word from God. She wanted to know: if her pregnancy was an answer to prayer, was this unusual struggle an indication of something significant? Indeed it was!

The Oracle Concerning the Unborn Twins

The Lord's answer *was* an oracle; it was an authoritative utterance that was also a prophecy (v. 23). He had allowed the struggle within her, so He could reveal His plan for the future to her. She would have two sons who would be founders of two separate nations. The struggle between them in her womb would continue after they were born and for as long as they lived. More than that, their descendants would form nations who would be antagonistic toward each other in subsequent history. In this prophecy lies the key to understanding the history of Israel and Edom through the centuries.

There were three elements to the prophecy. The first element was the fact that two nations would be founded, one from each child: the nation of Israel from Jacob, and the nation of Edom from Esau. The second element was that one of the sons had God-given priority over the other one. This was true in regard to Jacob's priority over Esau during his lifetime and the priority of Jacob's children, the Israelites, over Esau's children, the Edomites. Edom was subjugated by the Israelites in the time of David, as Balaam prophesied (Num. 24:17, 18; 2 Sam. 8:14). Its further subjugation was prophesied by a number of the prophets (see Isa. 34:5-6; Jer. 49:20; Ezek. 25:13; Joel 3:19; Amos 9:11:12; Mal. 1:4). The last Edomites recorded in Scripture were the family of Herod the Great. No doubt some of their ancestors are still in the area, but they cannot now be identified.

The third element in the prophecy to Rebekah was: "The older shall serve the younger." God was going to keep His covenant promise through Jacob, the younger of the twins. God said through Malachi, "I have loved Jacob, but I have hated Esau" (Mal. 1:2-3). God determined that Jacob was qualified spiritually and morally to transmit the seed in the messianic line. While still in their mother's womb, neither child had done anything either good or bad, but God sovereignly chose Jacob. The apostle Paul picks up on this theme in Romans to support the truth that God sovereignly works out His purposes, sometimes even against the natural order (Rom. 9:13). We see other examples of this biblical principle in relation to Mannaseh and Ephraim (Gen. 48:17-20) and Saul and David (1 Sam. 16:1). The phrase "I have hated Esau" does not mean that God disliked Esau or that he was condemned before he was born. It simply means that God chose Jacob, not Esau, to be the heir of the promise.

The point is that the sovereign God upset the natural order that always granted the inheritance privileges to the older son. Esau reacted against God's choice, with the result that there was conflict. The choice of priority had nothing to do with their personal eternal salvation. Both Esau and Jacob had the same opportunities to exercise faith in God. Rebekah clearly heard all three elements of the oracle and no doubt shared the entire revelation with Isaac and Abraham.

The Birth and Naming of Esau and Jacob

When the time for her delivery came, Rebekah bore twin boys (vv. 24-26).

They were given names to reflect the circumstances surrounding the birth of each. When Esau was born, his skin was unusually "red" and he was covered with hair. *Esau* means "hairy" or "shaggy." The red quality will reappear in his story years later when he gets hungry and demands that "red" stuff (vv. 28-34). His hairy features will play a significant role at the time he expects to receive his father's blessing (chapter 27). The two characteristics were also linked to the nation's name, *Edom,* meaning "red." The area of Edom was also called Seir or Mt. Seir, which had a very similar sound in Hebrew to the word used here for "hairy."

Jacob was born immediately after Esau with his tiny hand grasping Esau's heel so they named him *Jacob*, meaning "heel grabber." Abraham and Isaac would probably have linked this event with the prophecy about Jacob being the stronger, but at first it was a term of affection and had no negative connotations. With the passing of time and the events connected with the two brothers, the name came to mean "trip up," "defraud," or "supplant." Esau himself would later use Jacob's name in this way (27:36). Jacob's name came to be seen as symbolic of his life in striving or contending with Esau. The prophet Hosea seemed to interpret the name Jacob as evidence of spiritual power when he said, "He took his brother by the heel, and by his strength he had power with God" (Hos. 12:3).

The names of both twins ominously anticipated the nature and activities of their descendants. Before this chapter is concluded, the "red man" will display his appetite for "red stuff," and the "heel grabber" will gain the upper hand by buying the firstborn son's birthright from his brother.

Esau, the Sensual Man

Esau was a "skillful hunter, a man of the field" (v. 27). The only other hunter named in the Bible is Nimrod, the rebel against God whom we studied in chapter 10. Esau's actions will show that he was unconcerned about God. He was raised to be a shepherd like Jacob. He was an outdoorsman, a sportsman at heart, and he loved hunting. His life actually revolved around his five senses. He loved the adventure, the chase, the kill, and the aroma and taste of food. He was a man of the world and cared nothing for eternal and unseen realities. It is because of this that the author of Hebrews calls him a "profane person" (Heb. 12:16). There is no mention of him ever praying, meditating, or longing for God. He let spiritual things slide in order to enjoyed physical things. In contrast to Jacob, he did not want to be fenced in, either by the domestic life or by God's requirements.

Jacob, the Spiritual Man

Jacob, on the other hand, "was a mild man, dwelling in tents" (v. 27). The word for "mild" is used of Job but translated "blameless" (Job 1:8). The margin of verse 27 says the word literally means "complete," meaning that Jacob was spiritually, intellectually, and morally complete as a person. This is the right idea. In contrast to Esau (the man with no place or time for God), Jacob was a complete man with a special place for God in his life. He was basically a man of faith and wanted to enjoy all that faith could grasp. He was occupied with the future and invisible realities rather than the present and the visible. The great promises of God to Adam, Noah, and Abraham would have meant much to him. The description of him "dwelling in tents" indicates that he loved the domestic, pastoral life. The emphasis in the phrase is on the "dwelling," as opposed to Esau, the active man of the field. Jacob was domesticated, stable, and even tempered: a homebody. On the negative side, he was manipulative in getting what he wanted. He was shrewd and tended toward selfishness.

The Favoritism of the Parents

As the twin boys grew up, their parents allowed favoritism to develop (v. 28). "Isaac loved Esau because he ate of his game"—literally, because "his hunting was in his mouth." He loved the adventure stories and the venison that Esau provided. Esau pandered to his father's appetite—a weakness that Rebekah and Jacob would later exploit. The other side of the parental favoritism was that "Rebekah loved Jacob." Rebekah had married Isaac for spiritual reasons. Now, as Jacob was growing up, she discerned those same spiritual desires in Jacob, and because of it, she favored him. Isaac and Rebekah's sin of favoritism led to much unhappiness in the family. It serves as a warning for parents today. Favoritism can threaten God's blessing on the family. It most certainly damaged Isaac and Rebekah's marriage, though both early and later biblical testimony indicates they had an affectionate relationship (24:67; 26:8).

While Esau and Jacob were growing up, all three patriarchs were alive together. Abraham's spiritual influence was no doubt felt in the home when the boys were young. God Himself had said that Abraham would command his children to keep the way of the Lord (18:19). We can imagine the twin brothers sitting at grandfather Abraham's feet, listening to him telling the stories of his long life, especially about what happened on Mt. Moriah. The pilgrim patriarch would tell them of the future, that he was "looking for a city" (Heb. 11:10). It is not hard to envision Esau restless to leave and Jacob hanging on every word. When the boys were fifteen, Abraham died, still confident in God's promises and still looking for "the city."

The Sale of the Birthright (vv. 29–34)

The description of the two brothers sets the stage in the story for the sale of the birthright by the older to the younger. Maybe the two boys had discussed the birthright before this occasion. At any rate, Jacob had most certainly been thinking about its value, for it was the first thing that came to his mind when opportunity presented itself. Most of us are quick to criticize Jacob for taking advantage of his brother, but the Scripture places the fault at Esau's door.

The scene is described briefly (v. 29). Jacob had a meal of boiled red lentils cooking. Esau was famished and exhausted after returning from a hunting trip. As he drew near, he smelled the wonderful aroma of the cooked food and wanted it immediately. Seeing Jacob, he blurted out, "Please feed me with that same red stew, for I am weary" (v. 30). Literally what he said was, "Let me gulp down that red, red." He didn't even give it a name; the New American Standard Bible translates it as "red stuff." The way Esau repeated the word "red" emphasizes how desperately he craved immediate satisfaction for his hunger. The red man was overcome by his appetite for the red stuff.

Jacob perceived that his brother cared for nothing beyond his instant gratification. He had waited for a moment like this. Now he saw his opportunity to make a deal to gain the birthright. To Esau, the family birthright carried no immediate benefit. His low regard for it made him unfit to be the heir. Jacob, however, knew its value and that God had destined him to have it. He proposed the "deal" to Esau: the birthright for the lentil stew. He said, "Sell me your birthright as of this day" (v. 31).

Esau reasoned, "I am about to die." Literally, he said "on the way to meet death." What good was the birthright to him now? His reaction was like the Epicurean philosophy: "Let us eat and drink, for tomorrow we die" (Isa. 22:13). The truth was he was a young man and nowhere near death. Notice the predominance of personal pronouns in both his speeches: Esau was occupied only with himself (vv. 30, 32).

The Sale is Confirmed with an Oath

Jacob focused on persuading Esau to sell the birthright irrevocably. "Sell me ... this day.... Swear to me" (vv. 30, 33). Jacob demanded that Esau confirm the sale with an oath. There was to be no changing of his mind. Esau swore to the contract, and the sale was made. That one hasty decision by Esau had lifelong consequences. The story closes with a rapid succession of verbs describing what Esau did. He "ate and drank, arose, and went his way," demonstrating that he acted as a satisfied man without another thought about his lost birthright.

Esau Despises His Birthright

The chapter concludes by telling the reader that "Esau despised his birthright." We may sympathize with Esau, as many preachers do, but the testimony of Scripture is that he was at fault. The crux of the matter has to do with the value that each of the brothers placed on the birthright. Jacob was far from blameless in the way he obtained it. He acted precipitously—he should have waited for God's timing—but the point of the narrative is that Jacob regarded the birthright as worth having and Esau did not. The book of Hebrews calls Esau an immoral man, profane, godless, who sold his birthright for a single meal (Heb. 12:16). The word *profane* comes from the Latin word *profanum* meaning "outside the temple," that is, secular; there was no place for God in his life. Esau's life can be described in purely emotional terms: fainting, gasping, gulping, despising. Paul used the word "profane" in writing to Timothy: "Reject profane and old wives tales, and exercise yourself rather to godliness" (1 Tim. 4:7). The lesson of the sale of Esau's birthright is an important one: we should strive for the spiritual rather than the secular.

Understanding the Birthright

The birthright in ancient times was comprised of three privileges:

- The first privilege was that of *headship* of the family. Jacob became the "master" of his family (27:37; 43:33). In view of the covenant promises to Abraham (that his seed would be both the blesser and a blessing to all mankind), this was very significant.

- The second was that of *priesthood* (Num. 8:17-18; Deut. 21:17). As a priest, Jacob would assume the role of a spiritual mediator for the family, leading them in worship. We know that he built altars to worship God.

- The third privilege of the family birthright was that its owner would receive a double portion of the *inheritance* (Ex. 22:29; Num. 8:14-17; Deut. 21:17). We do not read specifically that Jacob inherited his father's wealth, but we can safely assume that he did.

Even if he had thought about it, Esau would only have been interested in the wealth, but he bargained that away in the deal. We should keep in mind that Esau's birthright had nothing to do with his sonship. Esau was always Isaac's son. His sale had everything to do with the privileges that he might have enjoyed as the firstborn son. There are lessons for believers from the sale of Esau's birthright. First, it teaches us to value our birthright as sons of God through the example Jacob gives us of desiring it so much. Second, it teaches us to beware of losing our birthright, that is, the privilege we have because we are sons. The key to the story and its application to us is in the *value* that the son places on the birthright.

The Birthright of a Believer

All believers are "born" into the family of God (John 1:12-13). They become children of God and heirs to wonderful blessings and privileges (Rom. 8:16-17). Believers in this age are all part of the "church of the firstborn" (Heb. 12:22-23), that is, they are a community of firstborn sons. Just as the firstborn Hebrews in Old Testament times had three great privileges, so Christian believers, all firstborn sons, have three parallel privileges:

- We are given a position of *authority*. God has made us to be a Kingdom (Rev. 1:6) in which we will one day reign with Him (2 Tim. 2:12), judging the world and the angels (1 Cor. 6:2-3).

- We have the privilege of *priesthood*. We are holy priests responsible to offer up spiritual sacrifices (1 Pet. 2:5). As priests, we mediate between man and God by means of intercessory prayer. We also worship God and witness for Him.

- The third privilege of Christian believers as firstborn sons is the possession of a spiritual *inheritance*. We are heirs to incredible wealth. While living in this world we are "blessed with every spiritual blessing in the heavenly places in Christ" (Eph. 1:3) and can look forward to more in the ages to come (Rom. 8:17; Eph. 2:7).

No true believer can ever lose his sonship, but it is possible, by being engrossed in present, worldly pleasures, to effectively lose the privilege and blessing of our birthright in terms of blessed spiritual experience now and future eternal rewards (1 Cor. 3:11-15; 2 Cor. 5:9-10).

In Conclusion

The overriding lesson of chapter 25 is drawn from Jacob and Esau's respective attitudes towards the birthright of their family. Eternal, unseen, spiritual things are the precious birthright of the Christian. If we are "Jacobs," we will value this possession, develop a mindset for it, claim it, and live in the light of it. If we are "Esaus," we will relinquish it in favor of what we can enjoy of the material "here and now," and thereby lose it. Our present attitude towards and use of our birthright determines our reward in the future. If we endure as sons now, we shall reign later (2 Tim. 2:12). If we exercise our priesthood now, we will be pillars in the temple of our God (Rev. 3:12). If we make good use of our riches in Christ now, we will have the greater eternal reward (Matt. 25:14-30; Luke 16:9-11). May we all place high value on our spiritual birthright as sons of God.

Isaac and Abimelech

The second half of Genesis is dominated by the life of one man, Jacob. Within the scope of Jacob's lifetime, the fulfillment of God's promise concerning Abraham's descendants increased from one man to twelve families. The nation of Israel emerged from those twelve families. In light of Jacob's own character and the negative circumstances surrounding him most of his life, few would think it possible that he could become such a key personage in the history of Israel.

Focusing on Isaac

A new section of Genesis called "the genealogy of Isaac" begins after Isaac's marriage to Rebekah and the death of his father Abraham. It deals with what became of Isaac's family until his own death. God's sovereign hand was clearly evident in the birth of Isaac's twin sons and in the tension regarding the birthright that Esau sold to Jacob. In this chapter, the narrative focuses specifically on Isaac. It is the only chapter devoted exclusively to his life. Though he lived longer than the other two patriarchs, he is overshadowed by them both. There is far less biblical narrative related to Isaac than to either Abraham or Jacob. Up to this point, we have learned several things about Isaac. We have observed that he was willing to be offered as a sacrifice on Mt. Moriah (Genesis 22), that he expressed faith and dependence on God when he prayed for Rebekah to conceive (25:21), and that he loved Esau more than Jacob (25:28).

It has been said: "Isaac was the ordinary son of a great father and the ordinary father of a great son." His whole life was far less turbulent that the lives of either Abraham or Jacob. We should consider, however, that it is often in the ordinary course of life that God's people have opportunity to please Him. As is the case with all believers, Isaac's life was marked by God's grace and blessing when his faith was strong and by God's mercy and discipline when his faith was weak. All of us can profit from Isaac's life as an excellent illustration of how to face some of life's difficulties and how to avoid others.

Comparing Isaac with Abraham

The similarities recorded in this chapter between Isaac's experiences and those of his father Abraham are remarkable. Both faced crises of famine in the land. Both encamped in Gerar in the land of the Philistines where they had confrontations with the reigning king of the time. (The reason the two kings bear the same name is because *Abimelech* was a Philistine term for king, much like *Pharaoh* was for Egyptian kings.) Both kings were attracted to their respective wives, and both Abraham and Isaac lied about their wives, saying, "She is my sister." Both were rebuked by the king for their deception. Because of these similarities, critics have suggested that the two stories are actually the same incident. We will see, however, that there *are* important differences that show that they relate to two separate events. The fact that Isaac failed to learn from his father's sin should warn us to carefully observe past sins and their consequences so as not to repeat them.

Isaac's experience in the land of the Philistines was not all negative. He emerged from his difficulties a better man. The story is built around three encounters he had with the king of the Philistines, first, in the city of Gerar (vv. 1-16), then in the Valley of Gerar (vv. 17-22), and finally at Beersheba (vv. 23-33). It begins with tensions over famine and violence, and it ends with an abundance of water and peace.

The Promise of God (vv. 1-5)

Isaac was at least eighty years old by this time, and Jacob and Esau were grown men. We do not know how much time elapsed between the occasion of Jacob bargaining to get the birthright from Esau and the events of this chapter, though by its end Esau is recorded as taking wives at the age of forty, so up to twenty years could have gone by. God allowed famine to come into the land to test Isaac. The author clearly distinguishes it from the famine that prompted Abraham to go to Egypt at least one hundred years earlier (cf. 12:10) and implies that no other famine had occurred in the intervening years. Isaac, therefore, had not experienced a famine before.

Isaac was presumably still living in Beer Lahai Roi, south of Beersheba. When the drought came to his area, he probably heard that the grazing was better nearer the sea coast. For the sake of his flocks, he went northwest as far as Gerar, evidently expecting some kind of assistance from the king of Gerar, for it says that he went to *him* (v. 1). He was probably thinking of continuing on to Egypt (cf. v. 2) by the coastal route. Note there is no mention of His asking God for help. His parents had once lived in the vicinity of Gerar for some time. Esau and Jacob, being grown men, probably did not go with him, but cared for some of the flocks in other places.

The Appearance of the Lord to Isaac

The Lord appeared to Isaac while he was in Gerar (vv. 2-4). This is the first time God appeared to him personally although he had witnessed the Lord's appearance to his father on Mt. Moriah. God had spoken to Rebekah before the twins were born, but this time He spoke directly to Isaac regarding guidance during the famine crisis. He warned him, "Do not go down to Egypt; dwell in the land of which I shall tell you" (v. 2). Isaac was to stay in Canaan, which included the lands of ten nations stretching from the River of Egypt to the Euphrates River (15:18-21). The land in which he was to sojourn (live temporarily) would be given to his descendants (v. 4). The Lord continued, "Sojourn in this land, and I will be with you and bless you." Egypt evidently attracted him because it offered immediate relief, but God warned him not to go there. God wanted Isaac to walk by faith, trusting Him, rather than by sight, trusting his senses. God would later allow Jacob to go to Egypt, but not Isaac. He promised Isaac that he would enjoy His presence and His blessing if he would stay there in the land. Then the Lord said, "for to you and your descendants I will give all these lands." Note that Gerar, which was in the land of the Philistines, was part of the promised inheritance.

God went on to say, "I will perform the oath which I swore to Abraham your father." He was referring to the oath given by the Angel of the Lord on Mt. Moriah in Isaac's hearing in which He had said, "I have sworn ... I will multiply your descendants as the stars of the heaven" (22:16-17). Now, many years later, God repeated the same promise (of innumerable descendants) to Isaac. To these descendants would also be given the lands promised to Abraham, and through them all the nations of the earth would be blessed (12:7; 13:15; 15:18). If Isaac were to enjoy those blessings, he would also need to exercise faith in God as a "fellow heir of the promise" given to Abraham (Heb. 11:9).

When God repeated the promises to Isaac, He added several new elements. First, God confirmed His oath to Abraham by appearing to Isaac (22:16-18). This is remarkable because God does not *need* to buttress His word with an oath; His word is His bond. Yet, He not only gave an oath to Abraham, He also repeated it to Isaac. Second, He affirmed the promise of the land to include "all these lands," meaning not only the land occupied by the Philistines where he then was, but the lands of other peoples who also lived in Canaan (15:18-21). Third, the promise now included the reality of God's personal presence when He said, "I will be with you and bless you."

God's Promise Based on Abraham's Obedience

The reason that God transferred the promises from Abraham to Isaac was "because Abraham obeyed My voice and kept My charge, My commandments, My statutes, and My laws." Those four terms all appear here for the first time in the Bible. This is a remarkable statement and echoes God's commendation of Abraham's obedience given on Mt. Moriah (22:18). Faith and obedience are always partners. To describe Abraham's obedience, Moses used the legal language of Exodus and Deuteronomy (Ex. 15:26).

Keep in mind that it was not Abraham's obedience alone that caused the promise to be fulfilled; it was his obedience *prompted by his faith* in the living

God. There, in offering Isaac, his obedience demonstrated his outstanding faith that God would fulfill His promise concerning Isaac, even if it meant raising him from the dead (Heb. 11:17). The point for Isaac was that he, too, should exercise faith by obeying God's instructions and awaiting the fulfillment of God's promises.

The Encounter at Gerar (vv. 6-16)

After the Lord had appeared to Isaac, he stayed in Gerar with the king's permission (v. 6). It was not long before the local men began to ask about Rebekah's marital status. She would have been about sixty at this time, but, like her mother-in-law Sarah, was "beautiful to behold" (v. 7, cf. 12:11). Isaac well knew that his father had been in a similar situation in the same location (20:1-3). He knew also that Abraham had lied to the then king, claiming Sarah was his sister. Isaac was afraid that he might be murdered on her account, and he fell into the same faithless trap that caught his father. It may be hard for us to understand how he could do it, but we should remember the deceitfulness of sin. What he did is perfectly consistent with what we know of human character. Sons often manifest the characteristics of their fathers. Isaac's failure here was a blot on *his* character. He failed because he was motivated by fear and self-preservation.

Isaac had been living there for some time when Abimelech happened one day to look down from his palace and see Isaac "showing endearment to Rebekah" (v. 8). He realized then that Rebekah was not Isaac's sister and that Isaac had lied to him. Abimelech summoned Isaac to reprove him (vv. 8-10). There is an obvious lesson for believers here. Whenever we disobey God, an unbeliever is probably watching from some "window." The result will be that our testimony will be damaged and that God's name will be dishonored. Isaac did not sin by living in Gerar, but he did sin when he lied. Likewise, we are to be "in the world" but not "of it." Isaac was candid in his answer to Abimelech, admitting he lied for fear of being killed on her account (v. 9). Abimelech then gave Isaac a lecture on the sanctity of marriage. Isaac might well have brought guilt on them if one of their people had taken Rebekah. He charged his people not to touch her on pain of death (v. 11). How sad, when a pagan king is more righteous than a man of God!

God Prospers Isaac

Isaac continued to live in the area around Gerar and he prospered (vv. 12-14). Not only did he keep his herds, but he obtained some land and became a farmer. It may be that the famine taught him that farming is a more reliable source of income than nomadic herding. The very first year he planted grain, he reaped one hundred-fold. He became a highly successful farmer. In this way "the Lord blessed him" (v. 12). The next verse tells us that he "continued prospering until he became very prosperous." It is interesting that Isaac's deliberate sin did not stop God from blessing him. We might ask how God could "reward" his unfaithfulness. The answer is that God often publicly honors His people while privately dealing with them in regard to their sins. This is how He dealt with Isaac: outwardly prospering him, but quietly disciplining him until he came back to the land. At the same time as God was prospering Isaac, He was setting him up to be forced out of the land by the envy of the Philistines. Note the disciplinary actions of God.

Isaac is Asked to Leave

Isaac's remarkable prosperity, as well as the special protection he had from their king, soon caused the Philistines to envy him. They saw him growing increasingly wealthy, and they wanted what he had. They knew their king would not sanction direct opposition so they began to stop up the wells that Abraham had dug many years before. They were obviously trying to force Isaac to leave even though they (though not them personally) had previously encouraged Abraham to live there.

Abimelech finally asked Isaac to leave Gerar because he was concerned at how powerful he was becoming (v. 16). Isaac did not resist, though he probably had a good case to claim the wells because his father had dug them. In the narrative of this chapter, wells were dug five times, and four of those occasions prompted opposition from the Philistines. Even in God's discipline of him, Isaac is a great example to us of submission and patient endurance.

The Encounter in the Valley of Gerar (vv. 17–22)

In those days, as in modern times, the hills of Judea that border with Philistine territory were very dry and subject to severe scarcity of water. Isaac was highly dependant on water for his large herds of animals. When the Philistines stopped the wells, he patiently responded by moving farther east up the valley of Gerar (v. 17). There he began opening other wells that had been stopped by the Philistines after Abraham died a few years before. Isaac emphasized his right to reopen these wells by giving them the same names that Abraham gave them (v. 18). One of the new wells was an artesian well, but the herdsmen of Gerar immediately claimed it. Isaac named it *Esek,* which means "quarrel," then let the Philistines have it (v. 20). Farther up the valley, Isaac dug another, but the Philistines quarreled over that one as well. Isaac called it *Sitnah,* which means "hatred," and he again moved further east.

The next time, he moved much farther away before he dug a well. The Philistines did not follow him there, and he called it *Rehoboth,* which means "the well of ample room" because no one quarreled over that one. In naming this well he declared, "For now the LORD has made room for us, and we shall be fruitful in the land" (v. 22). The reader will notice that although it was the Philistines who stopped up one well after another, Isaac recognized that it was the Lord who at last "made room" for him at Rehoboth. God's step-by-step discipline, forcing him to move eastward, brought him back to the Lord. And because the Philistines were no longer forcing his herdsmen out, Isaac left some flocks and herds there. He continued eastward until he arrived in Beersheba.

The Covenant at Beersheba (vv. 23-25)

Many years before, Abraham made a covenant with the Philistines at Beersheba and built an altar there (21:32-34). Isaac himself also lived there following the events on Mt. Moriah (22:19). Now, after the famine that drove him to Gerar and the difficulty that drove him away from there, he once again sensed the joy of fellowship with God. The first night he was back in Beersheba God wonderfully appeared to him, indicating the connection between his arrival there and his return into God's presence. It was God's second and last appearance to Isaac. When God spoke, He assured Isaac that He would be with him, that He would bless him, and that He would multiply his seed for his servant Abraham's sake (vv. 23-24). These promises were unconditional.

In response, Isaac built an altar in Beersheba. It is the only recorded time he did so. As the smoke of the sacrifices ascended, Isaac worshipped God. He also "called on the name of the LORD" (v. 25) as Abraham had done there (21:33). He proclaimed and extolled God's character and God's works. Isaac also expressed his thanks that God had delivered him from the consequences of his own sin. The altar itself spoke of the need for atoning sacrifice that Isaac, no doubt, saw clearly.

Notice the order in which he did these things. Isaac first *built* an altar, which speaks of worship. Then, he *called* on the name of the Lord, which speaks of public witness and thanksgiving. After that he *pitched* his tent. Pitching his tent at that spot speaks of dwelling in the place where God was present. The New Testament language would be "abiding" in Christ (John 15:4). Finally, Isaac *dug* a well. The well speaks of the refreshment and satisfaction found in Christ, the living water of life (John 7:37-38). How instructive this all is for us as believers.

The Encounter at Beersheba (vv. 26-33)

Isaac's men had just dug the new well at Beersheba when Abimelech appeared with a friend and the commander of his army. Isaac asked them, "Why have you come to me, since you hate me and have sent me away from you?" (v. 27). They answered that they recognized that the Lord was with him and wanted to remain on good terms. They were no doubt glad that Isaac was out of Philistine territory, and they had taken note of Isaac's policy of nonresistance. It made good sense for them to make a peace treaty with him. They also acknowledged how powerful Isaac was becoming by suggesting, "Let there now be an oath between us ... let us make a covenant with you, that you will do us no harm" (vv. 28-29). They reminded him that neither he nor

Rebekah had come to any harm in their land. It was at that very place where Abraham had made a similar agreement with the former Abimelech (21:31).

Isaac knew that God had just promised to bless him (v. 24), and he also understood that the Philistine pressure to leave the land had really been God's disciplinary action to move him back to Canaan. He did not argue with their claim of having done him "nothing but good" (v. 29). Thus he agreed to a non-aggression treaty and made a feast for them (v. 30). Isaac's action becomes a model for resolving conflict because he was more concerned with God's glory and peace with his neighbor than with maintaining his "rights."

Early the next morning, they "swore an oath with one another" before Abimelech departed. Abraham had named the place Beersheba, meaning "well of the oath," about seventy-five years earlier (21:31). Now Isaac made another oath at the same place. That same day, word came from his servants that water had been found in a new well that they had been digging. It is not certain whether this well was the reopened one that Abraham had dug or a different one. Isaac took the finding of the new well as confirmation that he had acted rightly and as God's timely assurance that He would take care of him. Isaac called it *Shebah,* which means "oath," the same name that his father had used. The city that grew up around that well is called Beersheba to this day (v. 33).

Esau's Wives (vv. 34–35)

The final verses in chapter 26 simply give us information about Isaac's son Esau. When he was forty years old, he married two wives, Judith and Basemath. Both of them were Hittites, which may indicate that Esau acted in defiance of the principle that Abraham had sought to follow when he sent his servant to find a believing wife for Isaac. Isaac always favored Esau, but there is no indication that he did much to encourage him to follow the Lord (24:3; 26:35). Evidently the two wives were thoroughly pagan, for it says "they were a grief of mind to Isaac and Rebekah." The record of Esau's marriages to pagan women is significant here as background for the next chapter. In the context of the escalating tension to come between Jacob and Esau, Rebekah used her fear that Jacob might follow Esau's example as reason to send Jacob away (27:4). Later on, Isaac did indeed cite Esau's pagan wives as motivation for sending Jacob back to Padan Aram to find a wife (28:1). Both chapters 26 and 27 close by mentioning Esau's marriages.

In Conclusion

Isaac's failure, as seen in this chapter, can be summarized as self-preservation in the place of spiritual progress. It led to his lies and his settling too long in Gerar. Isaac's experience is an example of how God deals with His children in grace. God rescued him when he failed and patiently disciplined him. He ordered Isaac's circumstances to bring him to the point when he acknowledged God's leading and blessing and publicly worshipped Him.

Though the Philistines were antagonistic toward Isaac the believer, they could not hinder the blessing of God. The more they tried to stop up the wells and seize the water supply, the more water Isaac's servants found. In the end, the only recourse for the Philistines was to ask for a peace treaty. It was a lesson for the nation of Israel in the years to come and also a good example for believers today in places where opposition is strong.

Isaac did not fight back; he trusted God, accepted His disciplinary hand in each situation, and moved on to receive another blessing. He ended up, as believers can today, with a good testimony in that the Philistines acknowledged, "You are now the blessed of the LORD." The words "bless" and "blessed" occur six times in chapter 26, indicating God's favorable regard to those who demonstrate, by a yielded heart, their trust in Him.

Jacob Obtains the Patriarchal Blessing

The events of chapter 26 spanned a period of about twenty years from the time Isaac left Beer Lahai Roi to live in Gerar until he was gradually forced to settle further east in Beersheba, where Abraham had once lived. When Esau was forty years old (and his father one hundred), he married two Hittite women named Judith and Basemath (26:34). Esau would have known how his own parents came to be man and wife: Abraham had stipulated that Isaac's bride was not to be chosen from among the Canaanites but from his God-fearing relatives in Haran (24:3-4). By marrying two pagan women, Esau showed that he had no interest in the covenant God made with the family or in his role in the line of the patriarchs. The two women became a "grief of mind" to Isaac and Rebekah (26:35), probably because they were idol worshippers. In the writing of Genesis, Moses wanted us to understand that Esau was unfit to inherit the blessing before we learn about Rebekah and Jacob's deceitfulness in this chapter.

What was the Blessing?

It is important that we understand the nature of the blessing that is so dramatically contested in this chapter. Isaac wanted to confer it. Esau wanted to get it. Rebekah wanted Jacob to have it. Jacob got it. As we noted in comments on Genesis 25, the birthright included family headship, family priesthood, and a double portion of the family inheritance. The birthright was originally Esau's by virtue of being born first, but he had sold it to Jacob many years earlier. The custom was for the dying father to *confer* the birthright and the blessing. He and Isaac now plotted to reverse the contract by means of a blessing that they assumed would take precedence.

To Esau, the birthright and the blessing were separate, as indicated by his complaint, "He took away my birthright, and now look, he has taken away my blessing!" (v. 36). However, God's Word declares that the birthright and the blessing were essentially the same thing. Note what the writer of Hebrews said in speaking of both the birthright *and* the blessing. Referring to Esau, he said, "Who for one morsel of food sold his birthright. For you know that afterward, when he wanted to inherit the blessing, he was rejected" (Heb. 12:16-17). By arranging the secret blessing, Isaac and Esau were trying to give back to Esau what God had sovereignly allowed Jacob to take away.

Six Scenes in Chapter 27

Between chapters 26 and 27, about twenty years pass without any comment. According to Genesis 36:6-8, the brothers were so successful that there was not enough grazing for them all in Beersheba. Esau, being more adventuresome, took his wives and went southeast to Mount Seir. Isaac was over 130 years old when the events in this chapter took place, and the twin brothers were in their 70s. The story line is built around Isaac's plot to give Esau the blessing and Rebekah's counterplot to ensure that it did not happen. The father's plot brought Esau into wrongful complicity, and the mother's counterplot did the same thing for Jacob. They are examples in themselves of the sinfulness of leading others into sin. The favoritism of each of the parents for one of the sons is clearly evident. There are six family scenes, all of which place two of the family together:

- Scene 1: Isaac and Esau (vv. 1-4)
- Scene 2: Rebekah and Jacob (vv. 5-17)
- Scene 3: Isaac and Jacob (vv. 18-29)
- Scene 4: Isaac and Esau (vv. 30-40)
- Scene 5: Rebekah and Jacob (vv. 41-45)
- Scene 6: Rebekah and Isaac (v. 46)

In none of the six scenes is the entire family ever together. It is an amazing commentary on the sinful potential of a dysfunctional family.

Isaac and Esau Plan for the Blessing (vv. 1-4)

Isaac was over 130 years old, and he thought he was about to die. His health may have been failing, and his eyesight was certainly impaired, but he was premature in his reckoning, for he lived another sixty years (35:28).

Isaac's "golden years" should be seen in contrast to Abraham's. Abraham kept his spiritual sights on the "city which has foundations" and the promises of the covenant right to the end. He made sure that Isaac married a believing woman and that other possible contestants for the blessing—Isaac's half-brothers—were sent away from the land that God had promised as an inheritance (24:67–25:6). He lived to see Esau and Jacob born and to learn that God had chosen Jacob to be the heir. As he aged, Abraham never lost his spiritual perception.

Isaac, by contrast, grew more and more distant from God. His spiritual sight became just as impaired as his physical sight. His family became dysfunctional because of his preference for Esau, and his wife's for Jacob. He loved Esau because he "ate of his game." His physical senses triumphed over his spiritual sense. How tragic when physical appetites affect the spiritual dimension! He is a warning to many older people today that they need to watch their appetites. It is hard to believe that this is the same man who allowed himself to be tied to an altar of sacrifice without a whimper. Isaac started out so well, but he became a self-centered old man with an appetite for the things of the flesh, resisting what he knew to be the will of God.

It is not certain as to why Esau happened to be in Beersheba at this time, but the likely reason is that when Isaac thought his days were numbered, he sent word to Esau asking him to come. Isaac was determined to honor his favorite son even though he knew full well that God had clearly revealed to Rebekah that the "older shall serve the younger" (25:23). He surely would have known that Esau had legally sold his birthright to Jacob. What God had revealed and the brothers had enacted, Isaac was now intent on reversing, but he would not and could not succeed against God.

In this first scene, note Isaac's self-centeredness in his request of Esau: "Hunt game for me…. make me savory food, such as I love, and bring it to me that I may eat" (vv. 3-4). There was no mention of God. Isaac stated his reason for his request: "That my soul may bless you before I die" (v. 4). Soul, or life, is the subject of the verb "bless" four times in this chapter (vv. 4, 19, 25, 31). It means that Isaac wanted to bless Esau with all the resources of his life. Esau was more than willing to cooperate in Isaac's plot. He didn't care for the spiritual aspects of the birthright and the blessing, but he did want the wealth and authority over his brother. Having heard his father's wish, he immediately complied (v. 5).

Rebekah and Jacob Counter with a Plot of Their Own (vv. 5–17)

The second scene features Rebekah and Jacob in a counterplot. Rebekah suspected something was up when she overhead Isaac and Esau's talking, and she immediately went into action to change their plan. She should have confronted Isaac, but instead she devised a plan of her own to preserve for Jacob what God already intended for him. Her goal was right, but she was mistaken when she assumed responsibility to do it her way and not God's. She did not have enough faith to believe that God would accomplish His will, no matter what Isaac schemed.

She immediately found Jacob and told him what she had overheard. She asserted her maternal privilege by commanding Jacob, "Now therefore, my son, obey my voice according to what I command you" (v. 8). Jacob was to fetch two young goats, and Rebekah would prepare them in such a way as to taste just like the savory venison that Isaac loved and craved, and capitalize on his inability to see what he was eating (v. 9). When the food was prepared, Jacob was to take it to his father, pretending to be Esau, "that he may bless you before his death" (v. 10). She believed that Isaac would fall for the ruse and pronounce the blessing on Jacob, thinking he was Esau. She couldn't wait for God's time. In her mind, it was now or never. We have no evidence that she ever learned the lesson of quietly waiting on God. Jacob would eventually learn this lesson, but it would not happen for another thirty years.

Jacob Fears He will be Caught

Jacob was afraid of being found out in his deception because, although he and Esau were twins, they greatly differed in the way they looked, felt, sounded, and smelled (vv. 11-17). What concerned him the most was his smooth skin: Esau had hairy skin, and his father would certainly notice the difference when they embraced. What he was *not* concerned about was deceiving his father and dishonoring God. Jacob only feared being found out and bringing a curse on himself rather than a blessing (v. 12). Rebekah had thought of that, too, and was willing to bear the curse herself should it come (v. 13). Neither she nor Jacob seemed to have any misgivings about how wrong their plan was—only whether they could get away with it. Rebekah's chief sin was that she did not trust God. She was very much like Sarah who, when she could not bear children, tried to help God by providing Hagar for Abraham. Her idea was devoid of godly wisdom or dependence on the Lord: she was a believer, but there was nothing of the "spirit" in her plan—her "flesh" was going against Isaac and Esau's "flesh." If fault is to be assigned, it lay more at Rebekah's door than Isaac's, for it was she who received the original direct revelation from God (25:23).

Jacob followed her instructions to slaughter two kids, and from them "his mother made savory food, such as his father loved" (v. 14). This is the third time that the food is described as "such as he loved," which indicates Isaac's fleshly craving for it (cf. vv. 4 and 9). After Rebekah prepared the meal, she took Esau's clothes "which were with her in the house" and had Jacob put them on. That she could do this confirms the fact that Esau must have been visiting from his home in Mount Seir; if he were living in Beersheba, his wives and children would surely have seen what was going on and raised objection. Then, she covered the backs of Jacob's hands and his neck with goatskins to make them feel like Esau's. She would have used the skins of a common breed of goat whose hair feels like human hair. Dressed in Esau's clothes and covered in goatskins, Jacob was now ready. Probably only about four hours had elapsed since Isaac had sent Esau hunting.

Isaac Blesses Jacob (vv. 18-29)

The third scene in this chapter portrays Jacob's meeting with his father Isaac. Jacob proved that it is possible to be successful through manipulation but also that there may be undesirable consequences. With the savory food and freshly baked bread in hand, Jacob entered his father's tent. Isaac expressed surprise regarding how quickly he had hunted game in the field, brought it home, and prepared it. Jacob answered with a series of lies. First he said, "I am Esau your firstborn," then, with respect to his filial obedience, "I have done just as you told me." Still pretending to be Esau, he reminded his father that he had come to be blessed (v. 19).

Jacob Lies to his Father

Old Isaac was still unsure and asked, "How is it you have found it so quickly my son?" (v. 20). An old saying goes "O what a tangled web we weave when first we practice to deceive." Jacob demonstrated its truth by replying with a deeper lie, bringing God into it. He said, "Because the LORD your God brought it to me." He was invoking God's name into that which was completely godless. It is worth noting that Jacob did not call the Lord "my God" but "your God." It was not until many years later, when he arrived back in the land, that he claimed God was *his* God (33:18-20).

Isaac was still not sure whether he was really Esau, so he said, "Please come near that I may feel you, my son, whether you are really my son Esau or not" (v. 21). Having felt the goatskin on his hands, Isaac was still bewildered. He said, "The voice is Jacob's voice, but the hands are the hands of Esau" (v. 22), yet he relied on his sense of touch rather than on his sense of hearing in his determination to bless Esau. He asked one final question for his own assurance: "Are you really my son Esau?" In saying "I am" (v. 24), Jacob told his fifth lie. Now that he was satisfied it was Esau, Isaac was intent on satisfying his gluttony. Jacob readily complied and served him the meat along with wine (v. 25). Here is the real scandal of the story: Isaac allowed his palate to govern his heart (see 25:28).

When he had finished eating and drinking, Isaac said to Jacob, "Come near now and kiss me, my son" (v. 26). It may have been his last attempt to resolve any lingering doubt. The kiss was part of Jacob's deception just as a kiss was part of Judas' betrayal of Christ. When they came together, Isaac smelled the scent of the field on his clothing, and he was finally ready to pronounce the blessing. We should observe that all five of the human senses were involved in the deception. Everything about the matter was sensual as opposed to spiritual. Only one of his senses, his hearing, gave Isaac a reliable reading. His sight was gone, and his senses of touch, taste, and smell all deceived him. Isaac's spiritual sensitivity was overwhelmed by his reliance on what is sensual.

The Significance of the Blessing

The blessing Isaac conferred on Jacob had four parts. The first part was connected to *God's blessing on the land.* It speaks of "the smell of a field which the LORD has blessed"—a field that was blessed with flocks and herds of domestic animals (v. 27). This blessing of field and farm assumes that Jacob was in the land that God had promised to Abraham and his descendants. The Promised Land was to be enriched with the dew of heaven and the fatness of the earth, which God would give to the heir (v. 28). Dew in Israel sustains the cropland and pastureland during the hot summer, and the fatness, or "oil," of the earth signifies the choicest of crops. Isaac's blessing speaks of the fertility of the soil to produce "plenty of grain and wine," picturing a loaded banquet table with more than enough for all. The blessing on Isaac's son is directly related to the blessing God gave to Abraham after he offered Isaac: "In blessing I will bless you" (22:17). In this way, Isaac conferred on Jacob the possession of the land.

The second part of the blessing had to do with the *authority in the family* bestowed on Jacob and his descendants over Esau and *his* descendants. There were to be peoples and nations who would serve him and bow down to him (v. 29). This will be fulfilled ultimately in the millennial reign of Christ when the descendants of Jacob, the nation of Israel, will be honored by other nations and peoples. Isaac thought that, in blessing Esau, he was overthrowing the purpose of God to have the older serve the younger (25:23), but in the sovereignty of God he was really blessing Jacob and giving him and his sons mastery over Esau and his sons. Even within the family, Jacob's "brethren" and "mother's sons" would come under his authority (v. 28). These terms have led some scholars to think that the language alludes to the existence of other brothers (27:37; 31:46). However that may be, the phrase "your mother's sons" is better understood as referring to Rebekah's descendants through Esau.

The third part of the blessing restated the *protection of God's chosen people* as first given to Abraham (v. 29c). There was to be a curse on those who cursed God's chosen people (12:3). This judgment on Israel's enemies has happened several times through the centuries. The final settlement of it is still in the future. The opposite of the curse comprised the fourth part of Isaac's blessing, reaffirming *blessing on those who bless God's chosen people.* In the direct link in the last two phrases to the original promise to Abraham (12:3), we see that Isaac was passing on the promises of God's covenant with Abraham.

Jacob, still kneeling before Isaac, did receive the blessing, but it was a long time before he received the benefits. God was not pleased with his deceitful tactics. For thirty years, he reaped a sad harvest from what he had sown (cf. Gal. 6:7). His brother wanted to murder him, and he had to run away. He never saw his mother again. Laban, his father-in-law, repeatedly deceived him, and after twenty years in his service he had to sneak away. Some of his sons were wicked. The greatest blow of all struck his heart when his own sons sold their brother Joseph into slavery.

Esau Claims His Blessing (vv. 30-40)

The fourth scene in chapter 27 shows Esau's dramatic meeting with his father after Jacob left Isaac's tent. We see Isaac's shock when he realized that God had overruled his selfish efforts to bless Esau rather than Jacob, and Esau's despair when he realized that Jacob had obtained the blessing by deceit.

Jacob had barely left the scene when Esau came back from the hunt with real venison. Without suspecting anything he prepared it in the way that his father loved and brought it to him, seeking his blessing (v. 31). "Bless" or "blessing" is the key term in this chapter, used twenty-two times. In this context, *to bless* means to bestow prosperity from God. Isaac was God's official representative in the family—the family patriarch—and he was perfectly correct in pronouncing these blessings. Biblical blessings might also be proclaimed by a priest (Num. 6:22-23) or by a king (2 Sam. 6:18). Some liberal commentators say that a blessing is a magical power bestowed on persons or things, but the Bible presents blessings as always under God's control. Isaac's blessing was related to the covenant, for he was "passing on the torch" to the son that would be the ancestor of the coming Messiah.

Isaac's Triumph of Faith

When Esau asked his father to eat of the food and then bless him, Isaac immediately suspected something was wrong. When Esau spoke, both his own stubborn resistance to God's will and Jacob's deceit suddenly became clear to Isaac (v. 32). God's Word declares, "Be sure your sin will find you out" (Num. 32:23). This is an important biblical principle. The effect on Isaac was immediate. He went into a state of violent trembling when he realized that he had blessed the "wrong" son. He made no attempt to revoke what he knew was irrevocable: "I have blessed [Jacob]—and indeed he shall be blessed" (v. 33). Isaac finally came to see that he had been pitting himself against God's purpose. But God had overruled, and Isaac humbly yielded to Him in saying "Indeed he shall be blessed." The fulfillment of the blessing was in God's hands alone now. This realization was probably the high point in Isaac's spiritual life. He understood that, although he had blessed Jacob unwittingly, it was done in the presence of the Lord, and he accepted His sovereign purpose by faith (cf. v. 37).

The New Testament confirms his faith at this point. "By faith Isaac blessed Jacob and Esau concerning things to come" (Heb. 11:20). In this great act, Isaac believed that God's way was best and joined the heroes of faith in Hebrews 11. It is remarkable that he ended his years of stubborn intent to thwart God's design in this spirit of acceptance. This encourages those who may have allowed much of their lives to slip away in faithless activity. For any who are willing to submit to Him, it is never too late to come back to God.

Esau's Godless Response

Esau, too, was deeply affected by the discovery of Jacob's deception—but in a very different way. "He cried with an exceedingly great and bitter cry ... bless me, even me also, O my father!" (v. 34). Isaac admitted that Jacob "came with deceit and has taken away your blessing" (v. 35). Esau retorted, "Is he not rightly named Jacob? For he has supplanted me these two times." The word *supplanted* is a play on the name "Jacob," sometimes called 'the supplanter" (cf. 25:26). Jesus made a similar play of the name when he spoke of Nathaniel as an Israelite "in whom there is no guile"—that is, no "Jacob" (John 1:47).

When Esau complained that Jacob took away his birthright, he "conveniently" failed to acknowledge his sworn agreement with Jacob over the matter. "And now look," he said, "he has taken away my blessing!... Have you not reserved a blessing for me?" (v. 36). It seems that this was the point at which Isaac saw that God had overruled the whole matter in favor of Jacob. Isaac's faith returns as the truth dawns on his soul. Isaac answered, "Indeed I have made him your master.... What shall I do now for you, my son?" (v. 37). Esau wept aloud, pleading for even a single blessing (v. 38). Esau's tears, however, were not based on spiritual values; he was not repentant, and nor did he seek God. He was upset because he could not change his father's mind (cf. Heb. 12:16-18). He spoke of "*my* birthright" and "*my* blessing," but they belonged to Jacob now.

Isaac's Prophecy about Esau

Isaac did prophesy over Esau, but what he said was more like a curse than a blessing. Some have called it an "anti-blessing" because it seems to repeat the blessing on Jacob. The actual word "blessing" is not even used. Several things should be noted. First, a better reading of verse 39 is "your dwelling shall be *away from* the fatness (that is fertility) of the earth." Edom, where his descendants would live, was, and still is, a most desolate and rugged part of the country. The second feature of the prophecy Isaac gave Esau was that he would live by his sword like a predator (v. 40). His descendants would hunt people, just as he had hunted game. Third, Isaac predicted that Esau would serve Jacob. Even living by the sword would not free him from this service. After King David's era, the Edomites were, for the most part, subjected to the Israelites. But service to Jacob was not destined to be their permanent state. Isaac concluded: "When you become restless ... you shall break his yoke from your neck" (v. 40). One day Edom would be free from servitude to Israel.

All these prophecies came to pass in subsequent history. The Edomites used the sword to take land from the Horites (Deut. 2:12). They encroached into Judah, but David subjugated them (2 Sam. 8:14). Edom made moves for independence, which they finally obtained when Joram, Ahab's son, was king of Judah (1 Kings 11:14-22; 2 Kings 8:20-22; 2 Chron. 21:8-10). Jeremiah and Ezekiel both prophesied against Edom (Jer. 49:10-19; Ezek. 35:3-15). Malachi made the final Old Testament reference to Edom, calling it "the territory of wickedness" (Mal. 1:4). The last known Edomites were members of the family of Herod the Great in New Testament times. As a people group, they have disappeared.

Rebekah Arranges for Jacob to Run Away (vv. 41-45)

The fifth scene of this drama finds Rebekah talking to Jacob again. Esau was, of course, furious. His grudge against Jacob grew into neurotic hatred (v. 41). It was more than he could bear to think of Jacob having dominion over him. His thoughts turned to murdering him, which he planned to do as soon as his father died. Evidently he thought Isaac was close to death as well.

Rebekah came to hear of his plan and immediately hatched another of *her* plans to help God out. She said to Jacob, "Obey my voice ... flee to my brother Laban in Haran. And stay with him a few days, until your brother's fury turns away ... then I will send and bring you from there" (vv. 43-45). She presumed two things: that Isaac's death was imminent and that Esau's anger would soon blow over. She thought she and Jacob could escape reaping what they had sown, but she was wrong. Actually, her "few days" lasted more than twenty years. She didn't reckon with Laban being as much of a schemer as she and Jacob were.

As far as the biblical record goes, Rebekah never saw Jacob again. Her loss of Jacob may have been God's discipline on her because of her role in deceiving Isaac. By saying "Why should I be bereaved of both of you in one day?" she was reasoning that if Esau killed Jacob, he would be executed for murder.

Rebekah Persuades Isaac to Send Jacob Away to Find a Wife (v. 46)

The last scene shows Rebekah talking to Isaac. Her scheming was never more sly than in the last verse of chapter 27. With her plan in mind to send Jacob to Haran, she reminded Isaac of the pain that Esau's two Hittite wives had caused them (cf. 26:34-35). She went on to speculate: "If Jacob takes a wife of the daughters of Heth ... what good will my life be to me?" She was hinting, of course, that Jacob should marry one of her own people in Haran, just as Isaac had done many years before. Rebekah did not want Jacob to marry locally, and she was afraid of the real threat that Esau had made. Her "suggestion" obtained the desired result in that Isaac did decide to "charge" Jacob to go and find a wife from among his mother's relatives (28:1).

In Conclusion

Isaac was not the only one who failed to walk by faith in this chapter. Rebekah sinned when she stepped outside her role as Isaac's wife and plotted against him. Jacob connived with his mother to grasp the blessing that was rightfully his by deceitful means. He clearly went about it the wrong way. Esau was guilty, too, although many see him as a victim. When he willingly and secretly cooperated with his father's plan to give him the blessing, he broke the solemn oath he had made to Jacob when he sold him his birthright.

All four characters in chapter 27 were guilty of something, and they all offer important lessons for us today. We should avoid Esau's worldly and godless ways. Isaac's stubborn resistance to God's will and his plans to out-maneuver God should teach us to bow in submission. Rebekah's scheming to outwit her husband teaches us of the error of helping God's plans succeed by ungodly means and of the dire consequences of such action. Jacob's complicity in deceiving his father only complicated a family crisis. We also should learn that, beyond all their scheming and deceit, God accomplished His sovereign purpose. We cannot win in a contest with God.

Jacob's Dream at Bethel

Isaac is the center of attention in chapter 27, but the focus shifts from him to Jacob for the next eight chapters of Genesis. In this chapter, Isaac sends Jacob away to find a wife. On the way, God gives Jacob a remarkable vision of a ladder connecting earth to heaven. The vision was a wonderful display of God's grace to him after he deceived his father regarding the blessing. We might expect God to strongly rebuke Jacob or punish him; instead, God gave him a stream of assurances flowing from the central theme "I am the LORD God of Abraham." In relation to time, these assurances extended from the distant past into the far future. In relation to space, they reached from the spot where Jacob stood out to the four corners of the earth.

The story of Jacob's progress toward greatness really begins here. He did not simply run away from home in fear, as we might imagine. He went to obtain a wife with the full blessing of his father and the assurance that he was the heir to the promises. It is true that Jacob fluctuated between depending on God, on the one hand, and maneuvering his circumstances slickly, using his own rationale, on the other. Little by little, however, God worked on him until he emerged at the end of his life as a spiritual giant. God honored his faith and changed his name to Israel because he believed God's promises concerning the land and the seed. He fathered the twelve tribes of Israel, and to this day, his name identifies both the people of Israel and the land of Israel.

Isaac Sends Jacob to Padan Aram (vv. 1-5)

After Esau's threat on Jacob's life, Rebekah suggested to Isaac that it would be a tragedy if Jacob married an unbelieving Canaanite woman as Esau had (27:41). Isaac had failed to make proper provision for Esau to marry a believing wife, and he had done nothing yet for Jacob. Rebekah's initiative opened the way for Isaac to take this step of faith. He had come at last to believe that Jacob was the son through whom the promises would be fulfilled. He now understood that Jacob needed a believing wife to continue the family line.

Isaac's Charge to Jacob

Isaac realized that for many years he had hindered God's plan, and he did not want to further delay or stand in the way of God's purposes. He called

Jacob and "charged" him, saying "You shall not take a wife from the daughters of Canaan" (v. 1). His words echo the orders Abraham gave his servant when he went to seek a bride for Isaac (24:3). We should note the difference between Isaac's word of faith—"go"—and Rebekah's word of fear—"flee" (27:43). Evidently Isaac knew from the "caravan telegraph" that Laban, Rebekah's brother in Haran, Padan Aram, had daughters among whom a bride might be found.

Isaac's Farewell Blessing on Jacob

At the same time as he commissioned Jacob to find a wife, Isaac favored him with a second blessing (vv. 3-4). In contrast to the patriarchal blessing (27:27-29), this one could be called a farewell blessing. Isaac enlarged on the earlier blessing that had been given in private and publicly acknowledged that Jacob was the rightful heir to the promises God gave Abraham. By doing this, he assured both Jacob and Rebekah that he fully intended the blessing to be on Jacob. The terms of the farewell blessing are much like those that Isaac himself received from God (26:2-4, 24). He used the name "God Almighty" (Hebrew, *El Shaddai*), the name by which God appeared to Abraham shortly before Sarah conceived Isaac (17:1, 19).

In that passage as well as this one, the name El Shaddai was connected with God's all sufficient power to bless (cf. 17:2, 6 and 28:3). It would encourage Jacob to know that the God who enabled his grandfather Abraham to bear children would also provide the blessing of a wife and children for him as he left home alone.

The blessing Isaac bestowed was strongly founded on God's promises to Abraham. When God first blessed Isaac at Beersheba, it was as the "God of Abraham" (26:24). God would multiply Jacob's children and ultimately make him an "assembly of peoples" through his descendants. He went on to say that they would inherit the Promised Land in which Isaac was a stranger. Isaac knew that, in order to begin the fulfillment of this process, Jacob must marry a believer, walk with the Lord, and enjoy His favor.

Isaac Sends Jacob to Laban

Isaac sent Jacob away to Laban in Padan Aram (v. 5). This was the last act of Isaac recorded in Scripture (though he lived for another fifty years), but it signified the deep change God had worked in him. As for Jacob, it would be twenty years before he would return to the land during which time he would learn some important lessons about walking by faith in God. The time he would spend minding sheep in Padan Aram would afford him plenty of time to meditate on God and His disciplinary ways. Stephen Charnock said, "We often learn more under the rod that strikes us than under the staff that comforts us." Take note of an interesting change in the word order of verse 5 where it speaks of "Rebekah the mother of Jacob and Esau." Jacob is mentioned first, affirming that Jacob was now "number one." Jacob's departure from his father and mother marked the beginning of Jacob's pilgrimage as a patriarch. Isaac's story was over; Jacob's was just beginning.

Esau's Marriage to Mahalath (vv. 6-9)

Esau knew that Jacob had left home—with his father's blessing and with the purpose of taking a wife from his mother's relatives. He also knew that his own Hittite wives displeased his parents because of their idolatry (v. 8). It had taken him a long time to come to this conclusion. Esau was exceedingly dull in his spiritual understanding. This clearly shows that he could never have been the man to inherit the promises and the blessing. It appears that Esau tried to improve relations with his family by going to the home of his uncle Ishmael in the wilderness of Paran, south of Beersheba (21:21) to obtain his third wife—his cousin Mahalath. Esau does not appear to have sought Isaac's advice in this, nor did he put away his Hittite wives. The sad fact is that, as far as the covenant promises were concerned, God had already rejected Ishmael's family, and Esau had disqualified himself by selling his own birthright.

Jacob's Dream at Bethel (vv. 10-17)

Jacob's journey from Beersheba to Haran was going to require him to travel over four hundred miles (v. 10). Jacob was not as familiar with adventure as Esau. The trip north was long and dangerous, especially for someone traveling alone. The important thing for him was to know that God was with him. The only thing we know that he took with him was his staff (32:10). No doubt he had many questions regarding the unknowns ahead of him and how God would fulfill the promises concerning the land. He certainly needed affirmation and confirmation from God, and God was about to meet that need.

The Place of Jacob's Dream

Jacob's first recorded stop was in the vicinity of a city called Luz (v. 19), about seventy miles north of Beersheba. We first read of it described as "a certain place," but by calling it *the place* no fewer than six times in the passage (vv. 11 [three times], 16, 17, and 19), its significance is emphasized. This was not just *any* place, but a place chosen by God. Jeremiah wrote, "It is not in man who walks to direct his own steps" (Jer. 10:23). Did Jacob know that he was near the spot where Abraham had built an altar (cf. 12:8, 13:3-4)? Might it be that he stopped to reflect at the ruins of Abraham's altar? From the context it seems he was caught by the oncoming darkness and had to camp in a lonely place.

He "took one of the stones of that place and put it at his head" (v. 11)—whether for a pillow or for protection, we do not know. In Israel today, tour guides show visitors a deep cistern with a stairway winding down the side to a rocky bottom and say, "Jacob slept down there and then dreamed of the stair"—

but this is highly unlikely. God had taken him away from the company of people and home to a special place so that He could speak to him. For many of us, it is when we are alone with God that we hear His voice most clearly. Jacob was about to witness the first of two night appearances of God that would mark the beginning and end respectively of his twenty years away from the land of Canaan. In both appearances, angels played a significant role.

The Ladder and the Angels

"Then he dreamed." God spoke to Jacob through a dream (v. 12). For the most part, dreams are natural and have no significance. This one was supernatural. It was one of the "different ways" by which "God spoke in times past to the fathers" (Heb. 1:1). The first feature Jacob noticed in his dream was a ladder or stairway. The phrase "behold, a ladder" indicates Jacob's obvious surprise. Twice more the word "behold" is used to give that effect (vv. 13, 15). The ladder was set up on the earth, and its top reached exceedingly high into the very presence of God in heaven. Its height was matched by its width, for it accommodated many angels ascending and descending between earth and heaven.

The angels were the ministers of God. They were coming to earth to carry out God's commands in caring for the needs of people and then returning to heaven to report on their work. The ladder signified their access to both God and human beings. There is nothing in the context of this passage that teaches about the function of angels, but other chapters of Genesis do give examples of the kinds of important tasks they are assigned:

- In chapter 3, we learn that they *guard;* they guarded the way to the Tree of Life.
- In chapter 18, they *communicate* with people, as in their telling Abraham of events to come.
- In chapter 19, they *protect* God's people; they protected Lot from the immoral Sodomites and from God's fiery judgment on them.

The fact is there is intense interest in heaven about what happens on earth. Angels bear man's needs to God and bring God's help to His people. God uses angels as "ministering spirits sent forth to minister to those who will inherit salvation" (Heb. 1:14).

God's Presence in the Dream

The focus of Jacob's dream was the Lord himself, Yahweh, who was standing above the stairway (v. 13). It was made obvious to Jacob that the source of the angelic ministry was God in heaven, and the object of it was man on earth. Think how awesome it was for Jacob to realize that God was using His mighty angels on behalf of ordinary people like him! Jacob would be assured that they were caring for him and protecting him. Many years later, Jacob told his son Joseph that the one who appeared to him was God Almighty (48:3). Not only did Jacob see the Lord, he also heard Him speaking. Jacob was encouraged by a direct message from God. It relieved his doubts and gave him confidence for his future.

The awesome character of Jacob's vision has given Jews cause for meditation down through their history. One such Jew was Nathaniel, who came with his brother Phillip to hear John the Baptist preaching near the Jordan River. Jesus greeted Nathaniel by saying, "Behold an Israelite indeed, in whom is no guile," or literally "no Jacob" (John 1:47).

Nathaniel understood that Jesus knew that he had been thinking about Jacob because he replied, "How do you know me?" Jesus told him that He had seen him meditating under a fig tree. When Nathaniel realized that Jesus knew his thoughts, he acknowledged Him to be the Son of God. Jesus went on to tell him that he, Nathaniel, would see even greater things than "these" (an obvious reference to Jacob's dream) because he would see "angels of God ascending and descending upon the Son of Man" (John 1:48-51). Jesus meant that the ladder on which Jacob saw the angels going up and down pictured Himself as the Mediator between God and man. It was through Him that God interacted with man and that man could approach God.

God's Promises to Jacob

God would speak to Jacob seven times, five of which were to be corrective in nature. If we make a comparison between God's communications to Abraham and to Jacob, we would see that in Abraham's case, each occasion was a step forward rather than a correction. In this, the first occasion, God revealed Himself to Jacob as the "LORD God of Abraham your father and the God of Isaac" (vv. 13-15). This is the first time that God identified Himself as the "God of Isaac." Once before (when speaking to Isaac), God referred to Himself as the "God of Abraham" (26:24). Now He was guaranteeing to Jacob that he would be the recipient of the blessings of the land and the seed first promised to Abraham and then confirmed to Isaac.

In the first part of the message, God promised Jacob that he would inherit the very land on which he lay (now called the West Bank). God went on to affirm, "I will give [it] to you and your descendants." Jacob's seed would be as numerous as the dust of the earth and would spread to the ends of the earth. Through these descendants, God promised that He would mediate His blessing so that "all the families of the earth shall be blessed." Thus far, Jacob had spent his life trying to *get* a blessing; in this dream, God emphasized that Jacob and his seed were to *be* a blessing. God's word was remarkable since at this point Jacob was still unmarried, yet God's promise was sure.

Assurance from God

The second part of the promises God gave Jacob contained four assurances:

- *Divine presence:* "Behold, I am with you" was a great promise that had special meaning for Jacob on the verge of leaving Canaan. Unlike the gods of the Canaanites, Jehovah was not a local deity who was only perceived as caring for people within a limited territory. Jacob's God, Jehovah, would be with him even when he was far away in Haran. We are reminded of the term *Immanuel,* meaning "God with us," first prophesied then confirmed as a name for the promised Messiah (Isa. 7:14; Matt. 1:23).

- *Divine protection:* "I will keep you." God promised to keep Jacob safe on his journey. No harm would come to him. The promise of God to "keep" His own is still claimed, as in the priestly blessing of Numbers 6:24: "The LORD bless you and keep you."

- D*ivine preservation:* "[I] will bring you back." Before Jacob even left the land, God promised to bring him back.

- *Divine purpose:* "I will not leave you until I have done what I have spoken to you." In saying this, the emphasis is on God's accomplishing His plan; God was not implying that He would leave him when He had done what He had promised.

There were no conditions for Jacob to complete. It was all of grace. Even Abraham had not had a vision like this.

Jacob's Response

The use of the conjunction "then" rather than "when" in relation to Jacob waking up implies that the intense nature of the dream wakened him (vv. 16-17). Jacob probably did not get much sleep the remainder of that night! He now realized the majesty of God in a new way. His spiritual sight had been sharpened. First, he had a new awareness of the presence of God. He said, "Surely the LORD is in this place, and I did not know it." Had he known it, he might not have gone there at all; if he had known God would visit him in this way, he would have at least prepared himself for it. He was surprised by God's presence. The glorious vision of God in heaven and the voice of God left him amazed. Abraham and Isaac had not been shocked by God's appearances, but Jacob was. He wanted God's blessing, but he had not realized that he could not have the blessing without God Himself.

The second way Jacob realized God's majesty was in his fresh awareness of God's holiness and his own sinfulness. "How awesome is this place!" he said. "This is ... the house of God." Jacob would have been familiar with pagan temples that housed idols; this experience was so real that it seemed to him that he was in God's house. He was afraid because he knew how far short of God's standards he had come. He realized that God was holy and that he was Jacob the deceiver. Jacob perceived that God in His grace was making Himself accessible to sinful man, of whom Jacob himself was an example. The "house of God" as "the gate of heaven" symbolized the way for man to go to God and a way for God to come to man.

The third realization was a general one, in that he had a new, personal awareness of Jehovah as the covenant-keeping God. He was the God of Abraham and the God of Isaac who had now confirmed the covenant to him, Jacob, that in his seed all the families of the earth would be blessed (v. 14). If it were possible to pinpoint Jacob's conversion, this may be it.

Jacob's Vow (vv. 18-22)

In the morning, Jacob took the stone that had been at his head and set it up as a memorial pillar, a single upright stone. It was to remind him of his spiritual experience with the Lord and especially to commemorate His appearance and promises to him. As such, it was a stone of witness (cf. 31:45) that certainly did not resemble the pillars the Canaanites built, which were used as fertility symbols or to be inhabited by spirits. When Jacob poured oil on the stone, he was making an offering to the Lord. He was demonstrating his devotion to God and consecrating the place, setting it apart as holy (cf. Ex. 30:25-29). This is the first mention of oil in the Bible.

After Jacob consecrated the stone, "he called the name of that place Bethel," which means "House of God." The name was the expression he used in verse 17 when he was struck by how awesome the place was and said, "This is none other than the house of God," implying it was where God dwelt.

In view of his dream and the memorial he had just erected, Jacob made a vow (v. 20). It is the longest vow in the Old Testament. It was not a bargain with God; Jacob was not saying that, if God did certain things, he would respond in a certain way. Jacob was expressing his thankfulness to God for the promises He had made to him in verse 15. On the basis of those promises, Jacob declared his commitment to God. He said, "Then the LORD shall be my God." It was a reorientation of the whole purpose for his journey. Instead of it being an escape from the anger of his brother Esau or a trip to find a suitable wife, it was now a pilgrimage. The person of God was its focus, and the glory of God was its purpose. For the first time in his life, Jacob became an active partner with God to accomplish His will. He said, "This stone which I have set as a pillar shall be God's house" (v. 22). He vowed to come back there to Bethel, the House of God, and present thank offerings. His encounter with God had changed him into a worshipping believer.

Finally, Jacob vowed that he would "surely give a tenth to [God]" (v. 22). He believed that God would bless him materially. Of that blessing, he would return a tithe to God in appreciation for all God had done. His giving was to be an act of worship. This vow to God was a significant step forward in Jacob's transformation. He who had been the heel grabber, grasping after all he could get his hands on, now promised to become a giver. If he gave one tenth, he would be following in the steps of his grandfather, Abraham, who gave tithes to Melchizedek the priest-king (14:20). Later in Bible history, tithing became a legal obligation for God's people (Lev. 27:30), but here, Jacob promised to give a tithe of his possessions to God as a worshipful, voluntary expression of heartfelt thanks. In this he is an example to all God's people.

In Conclusion

Believers today do not usually dream of God's majesty and the ministry of angels, as Jacob did. We do, however, have the constant assurances of the Word of God that He will protect and care for His people, even using angels to do so. We can appreciate that the way to God is open to all, and we can certainly respond to the majesty of God as Jacob did, in worship and in consecration.

Jacob's Marriages in Haran

After his remarkable encounter with God at Bethel, Jacob continued his journey northeast to Haran. Here in this chapter, we learn of his meeting with Rachel at the well, the invitation to stay with her family, and his subsequent marriages to both of Laban's daughters.

Jacob's twenty years in Haran were to be years of discipline in the school of God. Here he would learn to be a servant. To accomplish this, God would allow him to suffer keen disappointment. He would come to discern that God's training was for his good. It was all evidence of God's careful design for him personally, and it would also make him fit to be used to fulfill God's greater purposes.

The world-famous family who grew into the nation at the centerpiece of God's purpose in world history had its humble beginnings right here in Haran. The story begins with romance and courting but culminates on the wedding night when the deceiver is deceived. Our chapter does not make great theological statements, but it does reveal theological lessons throughout. Biblical narrative is always living and powerful—it is never simply neutral. Just as God's providence and God's discipline followed Jacob, so His goodness and mercy follow us all the days of our lives (Ps. 23:6).

Jacob Arrives in Haran (vv. 1-6)

The chapter begins with Jacob's arrival at the well outside the city of Haran. When we compare the arrival of Abraham's servant in Haran (24:10-16) with Jacob's, there are some obvious similarities. In both instances, God had arranged for the travelers to be at the well at the right time and for the bride-to-be to come on the scene at the strategic moment. However, the arrival of Abraham's servant at Haran was bathed in prayer, while Jacob's was marked by self-seeking without any reference to God.

Abraham's servant came with a train of camels loaded with goods, while Jacob arrived alone and presumably empty-handed. Abraham's servant accomplished his mission within hours and was on his way back with Rebekah the next day, whereas Jacob was beginning a twenty-year contest with Laban over the right to marry Rachel, the right to fair wages for his work, and the right to take his family to the Promised Land.

The story of Jacob after God appeared to him at Bethel begins with "So Jacob went" (literally "Jacob lifted up his feet"), a unique phrase meaning that he put his plan into action. It indicates he had a new spring in his step because of the assurance God gave him at Bethel. His long and dangerous journey is not even mentioned. Like all believers who claim God's promises, he found joy in the obedience that such belief spawns. He was confident that God would guide him into the unknown. Having "lifted up his feet," he came to the "land of the people of the east," a general phrase that may indicate that he was not quite sure where he was.

Suddenly Jacob was aware of three things, indicated by the triple use of the word "behold." The original text says:

- "Behold a well" (NKJV "He looked, and saw a well") in verse 2
- "Behold, there were three flocks of sheep" in verse 2
- "Behold Rachel is coming" (NKJV "look ... Rachel is coming") in verse 6

Jacob's attention was first captured by the well, then by the flocks of sheep, and finally by Rachel. These three "beholds" parallel three uses of the same word in the vision of the ladder where Jacob's attention was attracted by:

- "a ladder" (28:12)
- "the angels," literally "there the angels," (28:12)
- "the Lord" (28:13)

In both passages, the third "behold" gives the point of the incident. At Bethel, the ladder and the angels brought *the Lord* into view. Here, in the field of Haran, it was the well and the shepherds that brought *Rachel* into view.

The well appears to have been the primary watering place for the flocks in the field, and it was managed by shepherds, not the townspeople. On learning that the shepherds waiting at the well were from Haran, Jacob asked, "Do you know Laban the son of Nahor?" (v. 5). Laban was Jacob's uncle and Rebekah's brother. Nahor had been her grandfather. Nahor had stayed in Ur when Abraham and Terah left but had evidently come to live in Haran after Abraham went to Canaan (cf. 11:27-31; 22:20). Nahor's son Bethuel was Laban and Rebekah's father, but he is in the background in this story; he may have died by this time. The shepherds told Jacob they not only knew Laban but that his daughter Rachel was even then on the way with her sheep to that very well (v. 6). Rachel became the centerpiece of the story even before she arrived on the scene. Jacob could hardly believe his good fortune, and no doubt his heart began to beat a little faster. God's providence was in operation, though Jacob gave Him no credit at this point.

Jacob Waters Rachel's Sheep (vv. 7-14)

Remember that Jacob was a skilled shepherd, as were all the patriarchs. He could not understand how shepherds with three flocks of sheep were just waiting at the well. From experience, he knew they were wasting time: they should be watering the flocks so the sheep could go on with feeding (v. 7). The shepherds explained that others were still to come who would remove the stone. The reason for waiting was probably to protect the water in the well from evaporating. They did not want to risk having it exposed too long, so their local custom was to wait until all the flocks arrived, then remove the large stone and water them all at one time. The drama in the story is building towards Rachel's arrival.

While Jacob was talking with the shepherds, Rachel came to the well with her father's sheep. The comment that "she was a shepherdess" indicates that it was unusual for her, as a woman, to be doing this work (v. 9). When Jacob saw her, he could restrain himself no longer. His generous, active spirit was stirred, and he single-handedly rolled away the stone and watered Rachel's sheep. As an experienced shepherd, he knew exactly what to do. The other shepherds seemed to respect his skill and authority. They made no protest even though he was a stranger. Then Jacob, in a high state of emotion, kissed Rachel and "lifted up his voice and wept" (v. 11).

Surprised by Joy

Jacob could hardly believe how everything was coming together so quickly. He knew that the angels he had seen on the staircase were doing their job directed by God. Yet we should observe with care that Jacob's response is purely emotional here; it was not toward God. How different from the response of Abraham's servant who, in similar circumstances, prayed with great faith before Rebekah appeared and then "worshipped" the Lord when he met her (24:12-15, 26). There is nothing about prayer or worship in Jacob's actions.

Like Mother, Like Daughter

Maybe Jacob noticed a family resemblance between Rachel and his mother. Note in verse 10 how the word "mother" is mentioned three times. When Jacob finally composed himself, he told her that he was her cousin, the son of Rebekah and Isaac. As soon as Rachel heard that, she "ran and told her father" (v. 12)— no doubt in a state of great excitement. When Laban heard her news, he ran outside to meet Jacob. He greeted him both warmly and enthusiastically. Jacob explained the circumstances of his coming. The phrase "all these things" (v. 13) indicates that he gave Laban a fairly full account of all the things that led up to his arrival in Haran. Laban might have been surprised that he arrived all alone, especially if he remembered the richly-laden camel train that had accompanied Abraham's servant many years before.

Laban welcomed Jacob as a relative, saying "Surely you are my bone and my flesh" (v. 14). He was echoing Adam's response when he exulted over Eve whom God had made from his rib and given to him as his wife (2:23). Jacob and Laban would have talked very late that night. Jacob knew that he had found the family of which his mother and father had spoken. He knew that he was to look for a bride here and that perhaps he had already met her. Note there is no mention of Laban's wife. It may be that she had died, leaving the family that included the two daughters. Jacob stayed with Laban for a month, during which time he fell deeply in love with Rachel.

Jacob's Marriages to Leah and Rachel (vv. 15-30)

Having arrived in Haran and met the right people at the right time in the right place, Jacob could be certain, if he thought about it, that God had kept His promise to be with him. He probably anticipated that the various pieces in the puzzle of his life would continue to come together easily and that he would soon be traveling back to Canaan with his new bride to set up his own household in Beersheba. There were, however, things in Jacob's life and character that needed attention, and God was going to see that several of these things were corrected during his stay there.

Laban's Negotiations with Jacob

Jacob proved himself to be a master shepherd. Laban did not fail to notice this and figured that he could profit from Jacob's expertise. He was in no hurry to send him back. After the first month, Laban talked to him about the conditions under which Jacob might stay in Haran and serve him (vv. 15-17). Working as a servant would be quite a comedown for Jacob, but he had no other good options. Laban was crafty enough to manipulate Jacob into becoming indebted to him while advancing his own business enterprise at the same time. But, in the wisdom of God, Jacob would learn a valuable lesson by submitting himself to Laban's mastery.

Laban had two daughters, the "elder" and the "younger" (v. 16). There is an ominous note here when we think back to Isaac's twin sons, Esau the elder and Jacob the younger. At that time, Jacob had abused the honor of the firstborn. Now he would suffer abuse by Laban over a similar issue: he would have to learn to respect the firstborn. For Jacob, it was going to be a time of reaping the seeds he had sown when he had gotten the better of Esau.

The narrative interrupts the dialogue to describe Laban's two daughters. "Leah's eyes were delicate, but Rachel was beautiful of form and appearance" (v. 17). The margin gives an alternate rendering that Leah's eyes may have been "weak." Some commentators suggest that she had blue eyes, which the Syrians considered to be a blemish. Both women were probably attractive, but Rachel's beauty was outstanding by comparison; maybe she had dark, sparkling eyes. Jacob was definitely drawn to her by her physical charms.

Jacob's Love for Rachel

Because of his love for Rachel, Jacob responded to Laban's question by offering to serve him seven years for her (v. 18). Note that he specified Rachel, his "younger" daughter. Rachel does not seem to have been consulted here as Rebekah had been (24:57-58). Laban agreed that Jacob was a good prospect as a son-in-law and said, "It is better that I give her to you than that I should give her to another man. Stay with me" (v. 19), meaning, of course, that Jacob would stay as his servant. Laban's strategy of getting Jacob to name the terms of the contract paid off handsomely: he would get seven years of free service from a skilled breeder and shepherd. We do not know whether he was already planning to trick Jacob regarding the coming wedding. He might have been hoping that Leah would find a husband during those seven years. Jacob happily served the term, which "seemed but a few days to him because of the love he had for her" (v. 20). No doubt he believed Rachel to be more than just the girl of his dreams: he presumed she was the woman God had chosen to be the mother of those who would inherit the promised blessing.

Jacob Deceived by Laban

Jacob was about to learn that he must reap the same kind of crop that he had sown (vv. 21-30). When the seven years were complete, Jacob asked for the marriage according to the agreement. He had to remind Laban, who was to be in no hurry as he was profiting from Jacob's skill in animal husbandry. Laban arranged for the wedding and a week of feasting for all his male friends, following Syrian custom. On the first night of feasting, presumably when Jacob was in high spirits, the bride was brought in for all the wedding formalities. Jacob had no idea that the veiled woman presented to him was Leah and not Rachel. At the end of the ceremony, Jacob and his bride went off to the prepared chambers to consummate the marriage. "So it came to pass in the morning, that behold, it was Leah" (v. 25). The use of the word "behold" here can be contrasted with "behold" in verse 6 (NKJV "look"), when Jacob was very pleasantly surprised by his first sight of Rachel!

One commentator describes Laban's deceit as a "masterpiece of shameless treachery." We wonder how he obtained the cooperation of both sisters. Perhaps Rachel was forcibly held against her will. Perhaps she agreed that the older should marry first. Whether Leah secretly loved and wanted Jacob or whether she was forced to cooperate is not stated. Laban no doubt thought it a hilarious public joke, and we can almost hear the raucous laughter as he related it all to his friends. He had nothing to lose, for he had found a husband for Leah and almost certainly would have Jacob in his grasp for another seven years to work for Rachel.

Jacob's Outrage

There are still unscrupulous people in the world like Laban. Occasionally, God's people are entangled in their plans. It is good if we remember that God is sovereign and has a purpose in the end for what is beyond our control. Eventually, Jacob would come to that conclusion as well. The fact that he did not repudiate his marriage to Leah right away is probably evidence that he saw God's disciplinary hand at work in him.

Jacob confronted Laban the next day in outrage. "What is this you have done to me? Was it not for Rachel that I served you? Why then have you deceived me?" (v. 25). The answer to his question may have dawned on him the moment he used the word "deceived." Laban's trick mirrored what he did to his own father when he dressed up like Esau to deceive him. In meeting Laban, Jacob had met his match. But in time, he would come to appreciate the lesson God was teaching him about reaping what he had sown.

Other Lessons Jacob Learned

Two more things happened that night that echoed Jacob's own past, and they taught him valuable lessons. The first was from Laban's well-rehearsed explanation as to his actions. He said it was local custom to give the firstborn in marriage before the younger (v. 26). The word "firstborn" must have resonated in Jacob's mind, just as the word "deceived" had (27:19, 35). He was not the firstborn in his family, yet he had abused his brother's rights as the firstborn to obtain the position for himself. It was a stinging reminder. Laban then proposed to Jacob that after completing the week-long wedding celebration, he could also marry Rachel—but he would have to serve him another seven years to fulfill the contract.

The word "serve" must have struck another familiar note in Jacob's mind, for had not his father blessed him with the words "Let peoples serve you, and nations bow down to you" (27:29)? Now he would have to humble himself. Before God would allow people to serve him, he would have to learn the lesson of serving others. This is what Jesus taught His disciples (Mark 10:45). Through Laban's trickery, Jacob learned three important lessons from his past: he learned about the pain of being the one who is deceived; he learned to submit to the unscrupulous acts of others; and he learned of the necessity of humble service. Without any further complaint to Laban, he accepted the situation, surely recognizing in his heart that God had orchestrated it. God's providence and God's discipline often go together.

Jacob's Marriage to Rachel

Seven days after marrying Leah, Jacob married Rachel as well (vv. 28-30). No details of the second wedding are given. With the giving of his daughters to Jacob, Laban also gave each of them a personal maid. To Leah, he gave Zilpah, and to Rachel, he gave Bilhah (vv. 24, 29). These two maids became intimately involved in the struggle over motherhood that developed between Jacob's two wives. Together, the four women became the mothers of the twelve tribes of Israel. It is worth noting that polygamy was not uncommon in those days, though it was never God's plan for mankind at the beginning (2:24). Multiple marriages certainly did not bring any joy into Jacob's life. Jacob's marriages may make for a captivating love story, but it is a tale more easily set in Hollywood than among believers. We read nothing of God, or prayer, or seeking wise counsel. In fact, there is no word at all about Jacob's spiritual aspirations during the early years in Haran. He was away from the place of blessing and did not seem to seek it.

The passage about Jacob's marriages ends with a statement that he loved Rachel more than Leah (v. 30). Jacob's favoritism of Rachel set the stage for a great deal of unhappiness in their home in the years to come; evidently he had not learned from the experience in his own family. But God's providence was still, and would continue to be, at work.

Jacob's Prosperity

Jacob was about seventy-three years old when he arrived in Haran and, therefore, about eighty when he married Leah and Rachel. He spent thirteen more years in Haran, seven of them for Rachel and the final six working for wages from Laban. The Lord blessed him there in two ways: he quickly gained a large family, and he became wealthy in flocks and herds. In both these areas of wealth, it was really God who enriched him.

There are lessons for us in both his family life and his business life. Both began under difficult circumstances, and both were blessed by God as Jacob's faith increased. What God did for Jacob's immediate family in Haran was a foreshadowing of what He would do later for his descendants in Egypt. Just as the family grew and prospered before Jacob eventually returned to the land of promise so, as a nation, they would multiply numerically and materially in Egypt by the time the Lord called them back to Canaan. At that time, they numbered two million strong and were also materially rich.

The Children of Leah and Jacob (vv. 31-35)

Many of us can easily identify with Jacob in his passiveness and his hope that things would improve at home. He gradually learned to honor God in it and to escape Laban's economic clutches. These verses begin a section that is primarily a record of the births of eleven sons and a daughter (29:31-30:24). For the Bible student, it is genealogical information of great importance to the rest of the biblical narrative because these were the children on whom the tribes of Israel were founded. God was blessing Jacob by giving them to him. God's blessing, however, does not always arrive like a gentle summer breeze. Sometimes it moves in like a storm.

Tense Relationships

The human drama that was being played out in Haran has some profitable lessons for us. They surround two tense relationships. One was between Jacob and his uncle Laban over fair compensation for Jacob's service. The other was between Leah and Rachel and their rivalry for Jacob's affection. Jealousy and friction divided the family and tarnished those thirteen years. As the two wives competed for Jacob's affection, they used the names of their children to express their feelings.

The tension and rivalry between them was a symptom of immature faith and lack of submission to God. Nor had Jacob himself fully submitted to God's sovereign hand. He had partially submitted to the discipline by serving sly Laban and unwittingly marrying Leah, but he had not yet submitted to the fact that *God* had given Leah to him as his wife, and because of that she deserved and needed his love. He had no idea when he contracted to marry Rachel that these complications were just over the horizon. He thought that marriage to Rachel was going bring all the happiness he could want. He found out that successful marriages need a stronger foundation than romantic moments. They are built on the totality of the stuff of life, and husband and wife must learn to thrive in it.

God was at work overseeing the childbearing capabilities of the mothers as to which mother would bear her child at just the right time. God had orchestrated the exact timing of the births of Jacob and his father Isaac, so it should have been no surprise to Jacob that God took an active role in the births of those who were going to father the twelve tribes of Israel that would become His chosen people.

Leah's Plight and God's Response

Jacob did not hide the fact that he loved Rachel more than Leah. Obviously, he was chafing against God's allowing him to be married to Leah. The immediate result was a dysfunctional home, and the long-term one, ingrained bitterness among the family members. He allowed competition to develop between the two wives and grow into a serious family situation. It took a long time for him to appreciate Leah as the great woman she really was. There is a lesson here for us in our marriages. Too often, even Christians come to the place where they wish they were not married to the spouses that God gives them. The results have led to needless tragedy in thousands of our Christian homes.

God was aware that Leah was "unloved" by Jacob. The original word means "hated." God's response was to open Leah's womb and to close Rachel's (v. 31). God gave Leah four sons in a row, and the names of each one reflect her longing for Jacob's love and her recognition of the blessing of Jehovah. We should not miss the spiritual side of her reason for naming each of them. These boys were born in quick succession, possibly in less than four years. Leah named them with two things in mind. On the emotional side, she was looking for Jacob's loving response; on the spiritual side, she was looking to God for an answer to her prayer for Jacob's love.

Notice her references to God in the reasons for using the names she gave her four sons. The first son was Reuben, whose name means "see a son," for she said, "the LORD has surely looked on my affliction. Now therefore, my husband will love me" (v. 32). The second was Simeon, meaning "heard," and she said, "Because the LORD has heard that I am unloved. He has therefore given me this son also" (v. 33). The third son was Levi, whose name means "attached," for she said, "Now this time my husband will become attached to me, because I have borne him three sons" (v. 34). The fourth she named Judah, which means "praise" or "Now I will praise the LORD" (v. 35). Her faith had grown, from acknowledging that the Lord has seen her need and heard her prayer to praising Him for four sons. There is no sign of competition or superiority in Leah during this time. When these four sons were born, Leah ceased bearing children.

In Conclusion

Two major lessons stand out in Genesis 29. The first is that we reap what we sow, a principle referred to a number of times in Scripture (cf. Job 4:8; Ps. 126:5; Prov. 22:8; 2 Cor. 9:6; and Gal. 6:7, 8). The second great lesson is that God providentially orders the affairs of His people for their own good and for His glory. God ordered the affairs of Jacob's life to mature him and to accomplish His purposes.

Jacob's Children and Jacob's Prosperity

Leah and Rachel had now been married to Jacob for three to four years (allowing the minimum time period for Leah to conceive and give birth four times). Leah the "unloved" was blessed with four sons, while Rachel the "loved" had no children (29:30-31). The resulting tension in the household affected it negatively for two generations. None of the key characters dealt with the discord in a godly manner, as we shall see. Jacob appeared to be passive towards the tension, failing to either lead his family or work for harmony between his wives. This chapter records how—despite the dysfunctional family situation—God enriched Jacob with eleven sons and a daughter.

Rachel Responds to Leah Bearing Children (vv. 1-8)

The chapter opens with Rachel allowing her envy of Leah to cloud her reason. She was desperate to have children. There is no mention of her praying to God or expressing any dependence on Him. She took the matter into her own hands and demanded of Jacob, "Give me children, or else I die!" She seemed to blame Jacob for her barrenness. He was taken off guard. He was suffering the effects of his own favoritism toward her, and he became angry with her. He understood that it was not in his hands to provide her with a child, for he said: "Am I in the place of God, who has withheld from you the fruit of the womb?" However unwise and insensitive his reply may have been, he was absolutely right in discerning that it was God who controlled such things. Rachel had left God out of the equation.

Rachel Gives her Maid to Jacob

Rachel would have known that Sarah had used her maid Hagar to obtain a child by Abraham. (16:3). She would also have been aware of the trouble that this union had brought into Abraham's home through the resulting birth of Ishmael. Nevertheless, she devised a plan of her own to get what she wanted without any reference to God. She said to Jacob, "Here is my maid Bilhah; go in to her, and she will bear a child on my knees, that I also may have children by her" (v. 3). This was a symbolic ritual carried out by parents and grandparents to welcome and legitimize a new child into the family (cf. 48:12; 50:23). Rachel was not walking by faith, but by scheming.

To please Rachel, Jacob "went in" to Bilhah with the result that two more sons were born. Rachel named them, as Leah had done to her own, but unlike Leah, the names she chose did not demonstrate faith in Jehovah, the covenant-keeping God. They revealed, instead, her bitter feelings against Leah. When Dan (meaning "Judge") was born, Rachel said, "God has judged my case … and given me a son" (v. 6). She assumed that, when Bilhah gave birth, it was God vindicating her plans by that means. When Bilhah bore Jacob a second son (Naphtali, meaning "wrestling"), Rachel said, "With great wrestlings I have wrestled with my sister, and indeed I have prevailed" (v. 8). The emphasis in the naming of Dan and Naphtali was on herself. Note her words: "… *my* case … God has given *me* a son…. *I* have wrestled … *I* have prevailed." She viewed herself from the perspective of winning the competition with her sister.

Leah Responds to Rachel's Action (vv. 9-13)

Leah, having stopped bearing children herself, was not to be outdone. Although she had demonstrated a spiritual, God-ward attitude when she was carrying her four sons, her "flesh" now responded to Rachel's "flesh." Leah entered into the rivalry by offering her maid Zilpah to Jacob. Jacob seems to have been unwilling or unable to intervene in the conflict between the sisters. Maybe he was just pleased to be fathering so many sons. Zilpah bore Jacob two more sons, both of whom were named by Leah. The first she called Gad, whose name may mean "troop" or more likely "fortune," as in the marginal reading (v. 11). She sensed that fortune had smiled on her. Leah named Zilpah's second child Asher, meaning "happy," for she said that other women would call her blessed or happy (v. 13). By this time, Jacob had eight sons: four by Leah, and two each by Bilhah and Zilpah.

Rachel's Bargain for Mandrakes and the Birth of Issachar (vv. 14-18)

One day, at the time of wheat harvest, Reuben, Leah's eldest son found some mandrakes in the field and brought them to his mother. The roots of this small-orange colored fruit have been considered as having medicinal value and the flesh as having aphrodisiac qualities. Even today, mandrakes are said by the Arab world to promote child-bearing. Rachel wanted to have the mandrakes; she hoped they might solve her problem of barrenness. Leah was hesitant, for she had stopped having children (29:35), and evidently she and Jacob had not had conjugal relations for a long time, perhaps at Rachael's insistence. Tension between the sisters was obviously still high. Leah said to Rachel, "Is it a small matter that you have taken away my husband? Would you take away my son's mandrakes also?" (v. 15).

Rachel wanted the mandrakes badly enough to propose a bargain: Leah could have Jacob for a night in exchange for the mandrakes. Rachel was still showing her lack of dependence on God to provide her with children. The deal was made. That very evening Leah met Jacob returning from the field, no doubt looking as attractive as possible. She told him that she had "hired" him with Reuben's mandrakes. Jacob passively complied, as usual. We should not miss the fact that Leah had been praying, taking her burden to the Lord. The text says, "And God listened to Leah, and she conceived and bore Jacob a fifth son" (v. 17). She called him Issachar, which means "hire." We may be surprised by her reason for naming him so, however. She perceived him to be a reward from God "because I have given my maid to my husband." We would assume her reason to relate back to her trading the mandrakes (vv. 16, 18). Perhaps both reasons played a part in her thinking. However that may be, she acknowledged that it was God who had enabled her to bear Issachar.

The Births of Zebulon and Dinah (vv. 19-21)

Following the birth of Issachar, Jacob paid more attention to Leah, and soon she bore him a sixth son, Zebulon, whose name means "dwelling." She again praised God for giving her a "good endowment" and believed that at last her husband would "dwell" with her. She was still yearning for Jacob's love and companionship.

Leah's seventh and last child was a daughter—Dinah—whose name means "judgment." Later, Jacob had other daughters (37:35; 46:7, 15), but neither their names nor the identity of their mothers are given, presumably because these details were not relevant to the history of the Israelites that Moses was writing.

Reflecting on the bizarre family situation surrounding the births of these eleven children, it is hard to think that it did not have a very negative influence on the boys as they grew up. Young as they were in the period of time covered by this chapter, they would have observed the strife between Leah and Rachel. In addition, the poor leadership their father displayed undoubtedly set them a bad example, putting them at a disadvantage.

Rachel Gives Birth to Joseph (vv. 22-24)

As time went on, Rachel still had no child, but she stopped scheming and, like Leah, started praying. Then, "God remembered Rachel" as He had "remembered Noah" when he was in the ark (8:1). This means that He began to act on her behalf. God also "listened to her, and opened her womb." It was God, without either mandrakes or handmaid, which brought her the joy for which she had been waiting since her marriage six years earlier. In her joy, she declared that God had removed the reproach of barrenness that she had endured (v. 23). She named her son Joseph, which can mean either "may he add" or "taken away." Rachel used both meanings, for she said first, "God has taken away my reproach," and then, "The LORD shall add to me another son" (v. 24), expressing faith that she would provide her husband with another male child. God honored her faith but also tested it: at least fifteen years passed before Benjamin was born.

It appears from verse 25 that all twelve children were born during the seven years between Jacob's marrying Leah and Rachel and his request to leave. For that to be possible, it was necessary for at least two of the women to have been pregnant at the same time.

The Prosperity of Jacob's Animal Husbandry (vv. 25-43)

Having described Jacob's acquisition of a large family, the author of Genesis now describes how he acquired large herds of livestock. The two sections of the chapter complement each other. In both parts, the key factor is God's sovereign hand. It was God who enlarged Jacob's family, and it was God who multiplied his animals. What happens in this next portion of Scripture is summarized in Jacob's later words to his wives: "God has taken away the livestock of your father and has given them to me" (31:9). How it happened is interesting.

No doubt Jacob was a master breeder of livestock, much better than Laban. Many commentators see Jacob here as an unscrupulous genetic engineer, outwitting Laban at his own game of deception. However that may be, the point of this section is that God was blessing Jacob by enriching him in livestock, just as in the previous section He had blessed Jacob by enriching his family with eleven sons and a daughter. There may be some question about the propriety of Jacob's activities, but there is no question that God was at work on Jacob's behalf in a remarkable way. Laban, not Jacob, is the conniver here who reaped what he sowed.

Jacob Agrees to Stay in Haran

Verses 25 to 34 form a dialogue between Jacob and Laban that took place after Joseph was born. It begins with Jacob's request for release from Laban's service (having completed the fourteen-year contract) so that he could return to his homeland with his wives and family. After all these years, he still had no flocks or herds of his own, and he was, after all, heir to all the wealth of his parents, Isaac and Rebekah. Laban, however, wanted Jacob to stay—not because he liked Jacob but because Jacob had made him wealthy.

Laban Recognizes God's Power

Laban's reply is interesting in light of his pagan leanings (v. 27). He had discerned what many commentators have failed to see—that God was at work in Jacob's life. He said, "Please stay, if I have found favor in your eyes, for I have learned by experience that the LORD has blessed me for your sake." Under Jacob's capable management, his herds of domestic animals had multiplied in extraordinary ways. Laban was not a godly man, but he recognized that Jehovah God had blessed him financially on Jacob's account. The phrase *learned by experience* means "to divine," as in acquiring knowledge by divination or through some kind of soothsayer. In this context, he may have been applying a familiar expression to say that he had come to see by close inspection that God had been directly responsible for Jacob's success. Alternatively, it may mean he actually learned it from the spirit world. Apparently Jacob had not openly confessed his faith in God to Laban, who seems, at best, to have compromised his faith in the true God with idolatry and, at worst, to have been a polytheist. There are many "Labans" among professing Christians today; they are the ones who compromise their faith by dabbling with false religion.

Jacob's Obligation to His Family

Laban replied to Jacob's plea to let him go by trying to persuade him to stay. He asked Jacob to name his price. He no doubt thought he would outsmart Jacob somehow (v. 28). Jacob reminded Laban that he had been a good servant and that Laban had profited handsomely. Laban's "little" had become a "great amount" with Jacob as chief herdsman. He emphasized his "service" to Laban twice (vv. 26, 29); He agreed that it was Jehovah who had blessed Laban through his service (v. 27). However, he went on to say, in effect, "My obligation to you is finished. Now I must take care of my dependents" (v. 30). He was almost ninety years old and recognized his obligation to provide for his large family.

Jacob's reply illustrates a solid biblical principle: the head of the household must provide for his family. It is a work ethic that should characterize all God's people. It is the responsibility of those who are able to work for their living and to support their dependents. The Bible says, "If anyone will not work, neither shall he eat" (2 Thess. 3:10). Able-bodied Christians should not be relying on government welfare assistance unless absolutely necessary and should certainly not exploit it to their advantage.

Jacob's Proposal for Wages

Laban asked, "What shall I give you?" Jacob proposed that his wages would be the multi-colored goats, sheep, and cows in Laban's flocks plus any that would yet be born from his flocks (vv. 31-34). They would be kept separately and be managed by Laban. He went on to say that if a single plain-colored animal was found among his own, it would be considered stolen and returned to Laban's herds. Jacob said, "My righteousness will answer for me in time to come, when the subject of my wages comes before you" (v. 33). He expected that God would vindicate him in every single dispute they might have. Jacob's plan was easy to manage with integrity because any observer could easily distinguish plain-colored animals from multicolored ones.

The whole arrangement seemed highly favorable to Laban, for the laws of genetics would indicate that, if Jacob's plan were followed, fewer than ever of the odd-colored animals would be born. Laban stood, therefore, to gain handsomely with Jacob managing his flocks. Laban, shrewd man that he was, immediately accepted the offer. As for Jacob, it was an act of faith. If he were to prosper, it would be God's doing. Jacob was now trusting God and declared that his honesty (righteousness) would answer for him (v. 33). Like many Christians, he was competing in a dishonest world. The answer was not to try to compete with the world on its own terms but to work honestly and have confidence in the fact that God would honor his faith. While that attitude did not guarantee he would be rich, it did guarantee that God would be pleased.

Jacob Prospers

Laban tried to make sure that he would have the advantage. That very day, he separated out all the oddly-colored animals and sent them three days journey away to be looked after by his own sons (vv. 35-36). This was to insure that no additional multicolored animals would breed among his own herds. If Jacob were to gain more such livestock, they would have to be born to those that were plain-colored. True to his crooked nature, Laban didn't trust Jacob.

We come now to Jacob's curious tactic of his use of the rods of green poplar, almond, and chestnut trees. He peeled some of the bark off in strips so that the rods were striped. He put these striped rods in the watering troughs of Laban's herds "so that they would conceive when they came to drink" (v. 38). The next verse tells us, "The flocks conceived before the rods, and the flocks brought forth streaked, speckled, and spotted" (v. 39). We do not have biological answers to the questions raised by this section. Jacob was a highly skilled breeder with many years of experience. Whatever he did, he knew what he was doing.

Rods in the Water Troughs

Some view Jacob's putting the rods in the water trough as "cheating," but if that is true, God was his partner. No—only Laban was cheating. The next chapter tells us that Laban changed the rules about the spotted and speckled ten times, but, said Jacob, "God did not allow him to hurt me" (31:7-8). His testimony was that God, by this means, took Laban's livestock and paid him the wages he deserved (31:9). It was God who told Jacob in a dream what to do and God who accomplished it (31:11, 12).

Science is still learning about DNA and genetics today. We don't know what pre-natal chemical or psychological effects on the genetic process, if any, may have worked here. Maybe Jacob knew some things that modern biologists have yet to find out, but it is doubtful that either chemistry or psychology provides the answer.

Jacob's Advantage

During those six years, the large majority of all the flocks and herds that were born profited Jacob enormously (vv. 34-43). He couldn't lose, because God was on his side, and Jacob was trusting Him. Laban couldn't win, because God was paying Jacob's wages with Laban's property. Jacob's flocks had grown so large that he employed many servants and became a prosperous rancher.

And Jacob's faith allowed him to say, "So my righteousness will answer for me in time to come" (v. 33). God had responded to his faith.

In Conclusion

In the remarkable ways recorded in each half of this chapter, God enriched Jacob with a large family and a large fortune. In both areas of Jacob's life, it was God who orchestrated his prosperity—in an environment where others were trying to manipulate the process to their own advantage. We have observed the use of some mysterious elements (mandrakes and peeled and striped rods in animal water troughs). In both scenarios, Jacob was more passive than active. It was God who was active, sovereignly controlling the situations, preparing Jacob's family for their role as God's chosen people and for their inheritance in the Promised Land. Jacob's experience has much to teach us in terms of family responsibility, reliance on God, and the willingness to accept what we cannot change.

Jacob's Flight from Haran

It was time for Jacob to leave Haran and return home. On his way to Haran twenty years earlier, God had encouraged him at Bethel with wonderful promises. Now God was calling him back there. While he had been waiting for the opportunity to return to the land, God had enriched him with both family and livestock.

When it came time to leave, God announced it to him in clear and certain terms. Just as an eagle stirs up its nest and pushes the eaglets out to force them to fly, so God stirred up Jacob's "nest" in Haran so that he might "mount up with wings" (cf. Deut. 32:11; Isa. 40:31). The growing tension between Jacob and Laban that had marked those years in Haran reaches a climax in this chapter, then suddenly resolves into a peaceful agreement.

Time for Jacob to Leave (vv. 1-3)

As Jacob became more and more prosperous, Laban's sons looked on with growing concern. Jacob's herds were increasing at a faster rate than their father's, giving them cause for worry about their own future inheritance. Jacob overheard them saying, "Jacob has taken away all that was our father's, and from what was our father's he has acquired all this wealth." It was natural for them to think like that. They did not understand that it was God, not Jacob, who was causing it to happen to make up for Laban's not sharing with Jacob, according to custom, the proceeds of his fourteen years of labor. During that time he had not given Jacob a single goat. His sons were blind to the fact that justice had now been done, and Jacob was astute enough to see that their rising anger and bitterness would give him good reason to leave Haran.

A second reason for Jacob to consider leaving was Laban's own resentment toward him. Hypocritical smiles had given way to dark looks. Every time Laban pulled another of his tricks to outwit Jacob, God caused it to backfire in Jacob's favor. The way Laban saw it, Jacob's blessing was at his own expense. Laban's "countenance" or face was no longer favorable toward him (v. 2). His attitude gave Jacob good reason to fear what Laban might do, and thus good reason to leave. Laban saw his livestock falling into Jacob's hands, but, like his sons, he did not realize that God had engineered it. Laban's resentment continued to grow—and along with it, potential danger to Jacob.

The third and most compelling reason for Jacob to leave Haran was God's direct command to do so. At the right time, the Lord said to Jacob, "Return to the land of your fathers and to your kindred, and I will be with you" (v. 3). Circumstances may be indicators of God's guidance to believers, but decisions based solely on circumstances are never as well founded as those based on a direct word or command from God or the Bible.

Twenty years previously at Bethel, God had promised Jacob, "I am with you and will keep you where you go, and will bring you back to this land; for I will not leave you until I have done what I have spoken to you" (28:15). It gave Jacob assurance when God repeated that promise. Before he left Beersheba, his mother Rebekah had promised to send for him, but no such word had come. It was God Himself who commanded Jacob to return. The lesson for us is clear: just as God directed Jacob by both the circumstances and His spoken word, so He guides and directs His people by circumstances and His written Word today.

Jacob Confers with Rachel and Leah (vv. 4-16)

Although Jacob knew he must leave Haran, he needed to convince his wives that it was the right thing to do and the right time to do it. He was in the field with his flocks and called his wives out to him. The subject of leaving was exceedingly sensitive, and they needed complete privacy while they talked. This is the first recorded occasion of Jacob taking the spiritual leadership of his family, and he acted with concern for the best interests of both Rachel and Leah. They were about to make an important decision with far-reaching consequences, and they must act as one. Jacob's willingness to include his family in the decision-making process stands as a good example to all husbands. He was going to reason that it was both necessary and wise for them to leave Laban. He built his sound argument in three stages, each one of which highlights his faith in God and gives all the credit for his material success to Him.

God's Presence

First, Jacob argued that God was still favoring him, even though Laban was not (v. 5). He expressed his faith by saying to his wives, "The God of my father has been with me." When Laban was profiting from Jacob's breeding and herding, he had been happy. Now that the livestock business was not benefiting him as before, he only grunted and growled at Jacob (vv. 2, 5). While Laban was frowning at him, God was smiling on him. There is a contrast here between *your* father, Laban the deceiver, and *my* father Isaac, whose God is trustworthy, the God whose presence was real to Jacob. In the storm of Laban's wrath, Jacob found an anchor in God's presence. The conscious presence of God is an important key to maintaining sanity in a confusing world. No wonder the promise that God is with us is the most often repeated promise in Scripture!

God's Protection

The second argument Jacob used was that, in his service to Laban, he had been diligently faithful, while Laban had been deceitful. "You know that with all my might I have served your father," he said. Rachel and Leah would have been well aware of his conscientious labor. Jacob had nothing to be ashamed of, whereas Laban had cheated him and changed his wages ten times (v. 41). Jacob's response had been to keep on faithfully fulfilling his end of the contract and to trust God for the outcome. Jacob's clear testimony to his wives was "But God did not allow him to hurt me" (vv. 6-7). God had protected Jacob's interests and orchestrated everything to accomplish His greater purposes in Jacob's life. In saying what he did, Jacob implied that even Laban's first deceitful act of substituting Leah for Rachel was actually designed by God for his good. When Jacob responded to God's discipline, God did not allow Laban to hurt him. He was making a significant statement about God's faithful care.

God's Provision

The third argument Jacob used in persuading his wives to leave Haran was that, despite Laban's deceitful tactics, "God has taken away the livestock of your father and given them to me" (v. 9). God had not only been present with and protective of Jacob, He had also provided for him. Jacob gave all the credit to God. It was God's power operating on Jacob's behalf while he was maturing spiritually.

Jacob recounted to his wives a dream he had had in which the male animals were streaked, speckled, and spotted, even though they were actually, in real life, plain-colored. The meaning of the dream was that God was going to produce calves that were streaked, speckled, and spotted from Laban's plain-colored herds. These young calves had all become Jacob's. Then in his dream he heard "the Angel of God" address him personally saying, "Jacob," to which he answered, "Here I am." It is clear from Genesis 22 that "the Angel" was none other than the Lord Himself (v. 11; cf. 22:11). The Angel told him to pay careful attention to what he saw in his dream, "For," He said, "I have seen all that Laban is doing to you" (v. 12). God had not only acted to make up for Laban's unfair treatment of him, He also wanted to convey to Jacob His personal concern and compassion to prompt Jacob to deepen his trust in Him. God's involvement helped Jacob objectively, in providing for his physical needs, and subjectively, in fostering Jacob's relationship with Himself.

The God of Bethel

Jacob told Leah and Rachel that the Angel in the dream identified Himself as "the God of Bethel, where you anointed the pillar and where you made a vow to Me" (v. 13). The Angel was reminding Jacob that He was the One atop the ladder in the dream vision at Bethel twenty years earlier. At that time, Jacob had vowed that if the Lord would provide for him while he was away—

and bring him back—then the Lord would be his God, and he would give back to God one tenth of all that He gave him (28:20-22).

Jacob then went on to tell his wives that God had clearly told him to return to his homeland. (Verse 3 was probably a summary statement of God's words recorded in verses 11 and 12.) God's personal call of Jacob here lifted the whole idea of moving to Canaan out of the realm of expediency and into the realm of obedience. It was not just a good idea; it was God's command. This was the climax of Jacob's three persuasive arguments to Rachel and Leah. Jacob had experienced God's presence, God's protection, and God's provision. Then he heard God's clear call: "Arise, get out of this land, and return to the land of your kindred."

God held Jacob accountable to his commitment at Bethel. He also calls *us* to fulfill the commitments we have made to Him. If we, like Jacob, have sensed God's presence, protection, and provision, we must then obey Him when He makes His will known. Leah and Rachel had now reached a crucial juncture spiritually. They needed to respond to the God of Bethel—and so should we.

Rachel and Leah Agree to Leave

After hearing Jacob's reasons for leaving Haran, Rachel and Leah answered him in unison (vv. 14-16). For the first time since their marriages to Jacob, there was agreement between them. They saw clearly that Laban had used them from the outset for his own material gain. He now treated them as foreigners and no longer as part of the family. With the profits from Jacob's service, he should have provided a financial base for their future, but he had not. He had not only taken all Jacob's earnings; he had also withheld their inheritance. They admitted that their father had not been fair. He had sold them and "completely consumed" their money (v. 15).

Leah and Rachel's reasoning was not on the same high plain as Jacob's, but they did acknowledge God, and they were ready to go. They confessed that it was God who had "taken" from their father, transferring his wealth to Jacob. The word "taken" is the same word used concerning the Israelites fleeing from Egypt when it says that the Israelites "plundered" the Egyptians to provide for their trip to the land of Canaan (Ex. 12:36). In the same way, Rachel and Leah claimed that the wealth Jacob had rightfully earned really belonged to them and their children anyway. Together, Leah and Rachel said to Jacob, "Whatever God has said to you, do it" (v. 16).

Jacob's Flight from Haran (vv. 17-21)

Jacob immediately "rose" and prepared to leave with all his possessions, servants, flocks, and herds. It must have made an impressive convoy as they set out with heavy-laden camels, oxen, and donkeys, and thousands of cattle, sheep, and goats. In terms of the history of Israel, it was a momentous occasion. Jacob was officially on his way to the Promised Land where he would assume the role of patriarch of God's chosen people, following in the steps of Abraham and Isaac. Through him and his sons, God's promises of a Savior and international blessing would be fulfilled. He was finally going home, but there were unanswered questions. He probably did not know whether his parents were still alive. He certainly did not know how his brother Esau would react. However, he went in faith and obedience to God.

Two things clouded the occasion. One was that Laban knew nothing of it. He was three days journey away, shearing his sheep and enjoying the celebrations that usually accompany this happy activity. Jacob deliberately kept his departure hidden from Laban, wary of his shifty character and the strong likelihood that he would expropriate all of Jacob's possessions and send him away as poor as he had come. They traveled south and had crossed the Euphrates River before Laban knew anything about it. The whole entourage was traveling southwest toward the mountains of Gilead, a distance of about three hundred miles (v. 21). Jacob knew that Laban would likely be angry when he found out what happened and that he might pursue them. He needed all the lead-time he could get.

The other fact that marred this important milestone in Jacob's life was that, unknown to him, Rachel had stolen the household idols from her father's tent (v. 19). These idols were probably a pair of figurines called *teraphim*. There has been much debate as to their significance and why Rachel would want to take them. Teraphim were certainly associated with pagan beliefs. In Bible times, they were used as household idols (Judges 17:5). During the revival under King Josiah, they were put away because of their pagan connections (2 Kings 23:24). The King of Babylon used them for divination to reveal the unknown (Ezek. 21:21). Teraphim were believed to be able to protect a household. Some expositors think that they were used to lay claim to the family inheritance because of an instance mentioned in extra-biblical writings. We can only surmise that Rachel took them because of incomplete faith in God. The teraphim were part of her old life, and they should have been left behind. There is no place in a believer's life for anything connected with the pagan world of evil spirits. Rachel's act of taking along the teraphim can be compared with a believer today who reads the horoscope in the daily paper or consults with spiritualist mediums.

Laban's Pursuit and His Dispute with Jacob (vv. 22–23)

On the third day after Jacob departed, Laban was told that he had fled and was by this time across the Euphrates. Laban guessed immediately where Jacob was going. He also knew that traveling with flocks and herds would really slow him down. Even though Jacob had a good head start, it would be possible for Laban and his men to overtake him traveling by camel and unhindered by herds of livestock. By the time Laban was able to break away from his responsibilities and begin his pursuit, it was seven days before he caught up with Jacob in the mountains of Gilead (v. 24). There is no doubt that his furious chase accompanied by armed men meant that he planned to take back all the possessions by force if necessary. He may even have intended to kill Jacob.

God Intervenes to Protect Jacob's Family (vv. 24-25)

We reach the crisis of the story at this point. Laban and his small army caught up with Jacob, but he waited until the next morning to confront him. Jacob undoubtedly knew that Laban was there and that he had no way to defend his family and flocks. Knowing Laban as he did, he must have spent an anxious night. But God was true to His promise, and that same night, He intervened by visiting Laban in a dream. Notice that Laban is now called "Laban the Syrian," no longer Laban the son of Nahor, Abraham's brother.

God warned Laban not to speak to Jacob either "good or bad." It is interesting that Laban had used the same phrase more than one hundred years earlier to Abraham's servant when he had come to ask if Rebekah could accompany him to Canaan to marry Isaac (24:50). On that occasion, God prevented Laban from interfering with divine purposes. Now God was echoing the phrase to Laban in order to prevent him from interfering with His purposes for Jacob. Laban had intended at the very least to claim all Jacob's animals, but God stopped him in his tracks with this warning. Laban was no believer, but he had witnessed enough of God's power in Jacob's life to fear Him. He dared not harm Jacob.

Laban's Confrontation with Jacob (vv. 26–42)

The next morning Laban overtook Jacob for his confrontation. The dialogue between Laban and Jacob is the center of the section. It brings an end to Laban's part in Jacob's life. Jacob was in his nineties by now. Laban must have been around 120. The tension between them was high. Jacob was fearful, and Laban was furious. It was to be a stormy interview. The dialogue runs like a legal dispute, starting with Laban's complaint and Jacob's response as to his innocence. Laban laid a claim, and Jacob a counterclaim. The language is military in nature—note words like "fled," "overtaken," "pursuit," and "captives."

First, Laban claimed that he was hurt as a father—his daughters had been taken away like captives. How sorry he was, that he had not been informed and given the opportunity of sending them away with "joy and songs, with timbrel and harp" (v. 27). He blamed Jacob for not allowing him to kiss his grandsons and his daughters (v. 28). In all of this, he was a hypocrite, having sold his daughters out of a purely mercenary spirit and provided nothing for their future wellbeing. Second, he admitted that he had come as an avenger to harm them but that "the God of your father spoke to me last night saying, 'Be careful that you speak to Jacob neither good or bad.'" Third, he accused Jacob of stealing the teraphim. "Why did you steal my gods?" he wanted to know (v. 30).

Jacob Responds

Jacob told Laban the truth. The reason he had left Haran secretly was because he was afraid of him—and with good cause (v. 31). Laban knew this was true. Jacob then declared his innocence in the stealing of the teraphim. He did not suspect anyone in his family, and he challenged Laban to find the gods himself. Anyone discovered responsible for taking them did not deserve to live, and he, Laban, could reclaim any of his own property that he found. Unknowingly, Jacob was putting Rachel's life on the line. Laban took up the challenge and made a personal search through Jacob's tents. When he came to Rachel's tent, he found nothing, and she explained that her menstrual period did not permit her to rise from the camel saddle on which she was sitting. The saddle contained the stolen teraphim, but Laban never dreamed that she would ceremonially contaminate gods in this way, and he departed without finding them.

Two things stand out in this compromising incident. First was Rachel's weak faith in having taken the idols. Her action became a hindrance to Jacob, not a help. Jacob did not want them. We are reminded that the weakness of our faith can often affect our spouse. If she had talked to Jacob before she took them, things would have been very different. The second weakness here is that of the idols themselves. They were quite incapable of protecting themselves or of communicating with Laban to reveal their own whereabouts. The true and *living* God of Abraham, Isaac, and Jacob is not like that!

Jacob's Rebuttal of Laban's Charges

When Laban returned from searching Jacob's belongings, he was empty-handed. At that point, Jacob's pent-up emotion erupted. In his anger, he leveled a countercharge at Laban. "What is my sin?" (v. 36). In effect he was saying, "I am innocent. Show me a single thing that I have taken from you!"

Jacob then told Laban that he should consider his treatment of his son-in-law during the previous twenty years. He gave Laban a "history lesson" about how well he had cared for his sheep (vv. 38-41). Not only did the animals not suffer miscarriages under his care, he did not even use them for food. What was more, he had personally borne Laban's losses. Jacob went on to say, "There I was! In the day the drought consumed me, and the frost by night, and my sleep departed from my eyes" (v. 40), indicating the difficulty and discomfort of the work, as well as his personal sacrifice. Obviously, Laban had never commended Jacob for his conscientiousness over the years.

The third thing that Jacob told Laban was that *he* was the guilty one. "You have changed my wages ten times…. You would have sent me away empty-handed." In saying this, Jacob showed that he understood that Laban intended to take back all his flocks, and that when God rebuked Laban in the dream of the night before, He had effectively prevented Laban from carrying out his intentions.

Jacob's Treaty with Laban (vv. 43-55)

Laban had no grounds for defense. Jacob was right, and all those standing around knew it. However, like most hypocrites, he would not acknowledge his guilt, so he changed the subject. He expressed surprise that Jacob would even *dream* that he would harm his own daughters! He never referenced his own culpability. He tried to shift the attention away from himself and suggested a treaty of separation that would involve a boundary between them and an agreement to stay apart. When Laban asked for a "witness" between him and Jacob, he was implying that Jacob was the slippery one and needed to be watched. Actually, Jacob did not need the treaty at all because God was protecting him. He welcomed it, however, because such a plan would keep Laban away from him while also allowing Laban to "save face." Jacob set up a single stone at the point where the line was to be; then, they piled other stones around it and called it "Heap of Witness" in two languages; Aramaic and Hebrew (v. 47).

Laban also called the place of the treaty *Mizpah,* which means "watch," saying, "May the LORD watch between you and me" (v. 49). The word Mizpah has been used on jewelry and cards to signify comfort, concern, and friendship. The sentiment "May God keep you safe while you are away from me" has often been used between couples when one goes off to military service for an extended period, but such use of this passage is well out of context. Its actual meaning here is flavored with hostility and mistrust; it is a warning to stay apart, not an expression of care while separated. To Jacob, the monument was a memorial to God's faithfulness in bringing him safely back to the land. To Laban, it was a means by which he could assert his dignity and report what a kind and generous man he was in making an agreement with that "rascal" Jacob.

In his response, Laban called on the God of Abraham (Jacob's grandfather), the God (better "god") of Nahor (his own grandfather), and the God (or "god") of "their father," that is, Terah. Terah was the great-grandfather of both Jacob and Laban and an idolater (Josh. 24:2). Laban did not claim the true God as his own God, but he did call on the God (god) of his ancestors to judge between them (v. 53). Jacob made three responses. First, in response Laban's polytheistic statement, Jacob swore to keep the treaty "by the Fear of his father Isaac," that is, in reverence before his father's awesome God, the one true God. Second, in commemoration of the agreement, Jacob offered a sacrifice to God to seal the agreement. Third, Jacob hosted a meal from the sacrifice to celebrate the agreement in the customary way (v. 54).

In Conclusion

Laban went home to Haran a defeated man, but it was not Jacob who had defeated him—it was God. Laban tricked Jacob into marrying both his daughters, but God used that act to give Jacob a large family. He tricked Jacob in his wage contracts, but God used it to make Jacob rich at Laban's expense. He pursued Jacob to steal his honestly-earned wages, but God stopped him. Laban could not win against God. Jacob returned to Canaan a better man and growing in his faith. Again, it was God who accomplished this, and in the process of disciplining Jacob to walk more by faith and less by sight, He had protected Jacob from his enemy.

Jacob's Wrestling with the Angel

After Jacob and Laban had parted in Gilead, Laban returned to Haran and Jacob continued toward Canaan. The two men agreed that each would permanently stay on their own side of the treaty line. The effect of the treaty for Jacob and his wives was that there was no turning back. There would be no more interaction with the family of Nahor in Haran. The pillar that Jacob and Laban erected at Mizpah marked their separation, and the sacrifice he offered there sealed it.

Having just come through one crisis, Jacob did not realize that he was about to face a bigger one with his brother Esau, who had once vowed to kill him. Was reconciliation with Esau possible? In this chapter and the next, we will see that it was, but only by God's doing, not as a result of Jacob's careful planning. Before he met Esau again, Jacob met God twice in ways that would change him forever. He would be forced into a situation where God was his only resource. He had come to realize that God had been at work behind his struggle with Laban; he would find that, behind his struggle with Esau, God was accomplishing not only His own purposes, using those purposes for Jacob's own good. We, too, may discover that God uses troubling situations to draw us closer to Him and to fulfill His purpose in us. Like Jacob, we need to allow God to take control of our lives.

Jacob ought to have been moving confidently into Canaan, trusting in the faithfulness of God who had assured him many years earlier that he would return there safely (28:15). He had nothing to fear from God, for He had only recently instructed him to go home, promising His continued presence (31:3). Jacob had nothing to fear economically, for he was now a wealthy man with a large family and thousands of animals. He was on his way to be with his father, also wealthy in his own right. The opening verses of chapter 32 reveal that what Jacob *did* fear was Esau's reaction to his return.

"Two Companies"

The narrative in this section surrounds the phrase "two companies":

* Jacob used the word first in *awe of God*, when he named the place where the angels met him *Mahanaim,* meaning "double camp," signifying God's camp of angels and his own camp of people (vv. 1-2).

- He employed the term a second time in *fear of Esau* when he separated his whole caravan into "two companies" (v. 7). He heard that Esau was coming with a sizeable army and thought he might save one of his groups if Esau attacked the other.

- The third time he used the phrase was in *thankfulness to God*. In his prayer, he gratefully acknowledged God's faithfulness and blessing during the previous twenty years. He said that he had crossed the Jordan then with nothing but a staff; now his entourage was large enough to be made into "two companies" (v. 10).

Jacob Meets the Company of Angels (vv. 1-2)

God knew Jacob needed some personal assurance because of his fear of Esau. He graciously sent a "camp" or host of angels to meet him before Jacob knew Esau was on his way to meet him (v. 1). It must have been one of the most awesome events in Jacob's experience. His eyes were suddenly opened to see a large company of angels coming toward him. The angels met him as if they had come from the direction of Canaan especially to escort him there. The sight must have reminded him of his dream at Bethel, of angels going up and down the ladder from earth to heaven (28:12). Both times, Jacob interpreted what he saw and gave the place a new name (vv. 1-2; cf. 28:17). On each occasion, Jacob witnessed the heavenly world of angels making contact with him on earth. It is interesting that the term "angels of God" is not used anywhere else in Scripture other than in these two instances.

Jacob's response to the experience was to say: "This is God's camp." He and his large caravan of people and livestock certainly comprised a host, but when he saw that a larger "host" was nearby and working for his good, he realized that his own large company was not alone. God's "host" was available, come what may. With these two hosts in mind, he called the name of the place Mahanaim, as mentioned above.

Unseen angelic hosts surround God's people today. We should not fear our enemies, real or imagined. The Bible says that God has provided His angels as "ministering spirits sent forth to minister for those who will inherit salvation" (Heb. 1:14). Thus, we may confidently say "The Lord is my helper; I will not fear. What can man do to me?" (Heb. 13:6).

Jacob Faces the Threat of Esau (vv. 3-12)

Even after seeing God's host of angels, Jacob couldn't resist the temptation to "play it safe." He wanted to assess Esau's mood before he actually crossed into the land. He planned to camp by the river Jabbok for a few days while he sent messengers ahead to Esau, whom he supposed was home in Mount Seir, eighty miles away in the land of Edom. Jacob instructed the messengers how to approach Esau: they were to call him "lord" and refer to Jacob as Esau's "servant." They were to explain that Jacob was returning peacefully from Haran and sought Esau's favor or agreement. He hoped that, in announcing his coming, Esau would see he had only peaceful intentions. He had no desire to assert the family authority over Esau that his father had conferred upon him (27:29). Jacob probably expected the messengers to take a week or more to travel the distance between Seir and his camp.

Imagine Jacob's surprise when the messengers came galloping back into camp within a day or two! They had seen Esau approaching with four hundred men only one day's journey away (v. 6). Esau had already learned by "caravan mail" of Jacob's return with his family, flocks, and herds. Esau didn't know what to expect from Jacob, so he had mustered a small army and was now almost on Jacob's doorstep. Neither brother knew for sure the other brother's intentions.

The messengers said nothing about having delivered the message as they had been instructed. We may assume that they were so surprised that Esau was on the way that they did not stop to ask questions. They had turned around and ridden back with all speed. When Jacob heard the messengers' news, he was "greatly afraid and distressed" (v. 7). With the events of Mizpah behind him, there was no turning back. With the rugged wilderness around him, there was no escaping with his large number of people and animals. And with Esau's army fast approaching ahead of him, he was desperately afraid.

Jacob forgot the host of protecting angels that God had revealed to him. What he did do was two things, one *not* necessary and the other *always* necessary. First, he carried out a common defense strategy: he divided his group into two so that if one were attacked, the other might have a chance to escape (vv. 7-8). The second and more vital thing he did was to pray (vv. 9-12).

Jacob's Prayer for Deliverance

Jacob prayed as a desperate man. It is sadly true that many believers, like Jacob, hardly pray at all unless they are desperate. It is often the case that we only reach out to God in prayer when we are convinced that no human resources remain on which to call. Despite Jacob's agitated state, however, it is a wonderful prayer. It reveals his growing faith. Note several features that should be instructive to us:

- *He acknowledged the power and character of God* (v. 9). Jacob used the same titles for God by which He had first revealed Himself at Bethel (28:13). The *God of Abraham* had led Abraham to enter the land of promise. The *God of Isaac* had protected and blessed Isaac while he resided there. Like Abraham, Jacob was conscious of his need to be guided into the land and, like Isaac, of the need to be protected once there. He also called God "the LORD," Jehovah, the covenant name of God.

- *He obeyed the command of God* (v. 9). In his prayer, Jacob reminded the Lord that he was simply obeying His command to "return" to his country.

- *He claimed the promises of God* (vv. 9, 12). He reminded the Lord of His promise that when he got back to the country, He would "deal well" with him. Jacob also quoted back to God a portion of the covenant promise. God had said to his grandfather Abraham, his father Isaac, and Jacob himself: "I will surely treat you well and make your descendants as the sand of the sea, which cannot be numbered for multitude" (v. 12; cf. 13:17; 22:17; 28:14). Jacob was claiming the promises that God clearly made to him. Promises provoke prayer; to claim God's promises is a timeless principle of prayer.

- *He recognized that he was the object of the grace of God* (v. 10). He confessed he was "not worthy of the least of all the mercies and of all the truth" that God had shown him over the past twenty years. He referred to himself as God's "servant," indicating a humble spirit. He thanked God for showering him with blessings when he said, "I crossed over this Jordan with [only] my staff, and now I have become two companies (v. 7)." We Christians should recognize that God has dealt with us in grace also; none of us is worthy to receive His abundant spiritual and material blessings.

- *He made a specific request of God* (v. 11). Jacob prayed, "Deliver me, I pray, from the hand of my brother, from the hand of Esau, for I fear him." He confessed his fear and implied his inability to help himself. It is important to see here that Jacob was concerned about deliverance from Esau, whereas God was concerned about Jacob's deliverance from *himself.* Often the biggest obstacle to victory in the Christian life is our spiritual condition rather than our external circumstances.

This prayer of Jacob's is the longest prayer in the book of Genesis. It is a wonderful model because it includes the important elements of all true prayer: worship, confession, humility, thanksgiving, candor, petition, and confident trust in God.

Planning by Human Wisdom (vv. 13-23)

Despite all that he had just said, instead of quietly trusting God to do what He had promised, Jacob resorted to trying to pacify his brother with gifts of livestock. He quickly selected five droves of a variety of domestic animals from among his herds, 550 in all. He spaced the droves apart to create a cumulative impression as they arrived one by one. Each drove leader was to say,"They are your servant Jacob's. It is a present sent to my lord Esau; and behold, he also is behind us" (vv. 18-19). Jacob's insecurity is evident in how he justified his strategy: "I will appease him with the present that goes before me, and afterward I will see his face; perhaps he will accept me" (v. 20).

During the early part of the night, Jacob did one more thing. He took his whole family and crossed the Jabbok River, which flows westward through canyons into the Jordan River. This was a step of faith, for retreat would have been very difficult from there. It would also be apparent to Esau that Jacob was not preparing for battle. Having moved his loved ones across to the south side, Jacob seems to have returned to the north side of the Jabbok to spend the rest of the night alone.

Jacob Wrestles with the Angel (vv. 24-30)

Jacob must have hoped for some rest after putting into motion his scheme to placate Esau. The text emphasizes that he was alone (v. 24). What was his state of mind? He might have been in prayer, crying to God for strength and deliverance. Maybe his own fears were hindering him from fully trusting God, or perhaps he was more concerned with his own physical protection than the progress of God's purposes. Suddenly he found himself in a wrestling match with a "Man." It was dark. Who was Jacob's mysterious assailant? The prophet Hosea revealed hundred of years later that Jacob had "struggled with the Angel" (Hos. 12:4). Notice the use of the definite article. The Man who wrestled with Jacob was the second person of the Trinity in one of His pre-incarnate appearances (cf. 22:11). Jacob acknowledged that it was the Lord when he said, "I have seen God face to face" (v. 30).

The Lord took the initiative in wrestling with Jacob. His purpose was to expose Jacob's weakness and to bring him to the point of depending only on God. Jacob struggled desperately to stay in control for the rest of the night, refusing to yield. Hosea made the point that he "struggled with *his* strength" (Hos. 12:4, emphasis added). Jacob's experience here illustrates many believers who resist giving God the full control of their lives. "Self" does not want to yield to God. To resist His control is to assume that things will be better if *we* are at the helm. The truth is, we will only experience God's rich blessing when we fully submit to Him (Rom. 12:1-2).

The Turning Point

The turning point came when the Angel touched Jacob's thigh in such a way as to leave him with a dislocated hip. Jacob was helpless. By disabling him in that pivotal joint in his body, He made it impossible for him to continue wrestling. God "touched" him where Jacob thought he was the strongest in order to teach him to depend on God, not on himself. Then Jacob did the only thing he could do: he just clung to his opponent, having finally realized that He was supernatural.

As morning dawned, the Angel said to Jacob, "Let me go, for the day breaks." But, in his desperation, Jacob replied, "I will not let You go unless You bless me" (v. 26). Jacob made spiritual progress when he realized that he could not prevail against his opponent and sought to have His blessing instead.

This was just where God wanted him. In clinging to the Lord, Jacob was never stronger in his whole life.

Jacob's New Name: Israel

Jacob's opponent asked him, "What is your name?" This was not the first time Jacob had been asked that question. His blind father had once asked him the same thing when Jacob wanted the blessing. On that occasion, he answered, "I am Esau" (27:32). He was able to deceive his father then, but he could not deceive God now. He had to answer, "I am Jacob." In saying he was Jacob, he was calling himself the "heel grabber." He was admitting to being Jacob, the deceiver. In effect he was saying, "I am the one who contended for what he wanted and got it. I am the one who contended with my brother and my father for the blessing and prevailed. I am ashamed of myself as an unworthy sinner. I am Jacob."

God then said, "Your name shall no longer be called Jacob, but Israel; for you have struggled with God and with men, and have prevailed." There is a link between the meaning of Jacob and the blessing. As the prophet Hosea said, "In his strength he struggled with God. Yes, he struggled with the Angel and prevailed; He wept, and sought favor from Him" (Hos. 12:3-4). But in what sense had he prevailed? Not physically, for he was crippled, and he probably limped for the rest of his days. Nor had he prevailed regarding Esau, whom he currently feared as an immediate threat to his life.

The answer is that he prevailed *spiritually*. God had crippled the "old" Jacob to the point that he could only hang on and cry out to God for blessing. The old Jacob had given up his old ways. As a humbled and changed man, he clung to the Angel of the Lord until he was assured of God's blessing. It was at this point that God gave Jacob his new name of Israel. The name change was most significant. Jacob had risen to a new level in his life as a man of faith and received a new name to match, but it was not his until he confessed that he was only "Jacob" and that he could not obtain blessing by his own means and strength, only from the gracious hand of God.

Jacob's desperate prayer for blessing was in line with God's will. On the surface, the name of Israel is taken to mean *One who prevails with God* because of the explanation in verse 28. However, there is disagreement among commentators on this interpretation in view of the uncertainty about the root of the Hebrew word. Some render it *Prince with God,* and still others *God prevails.* The latter would fit the situation well in that it focuses on God's action in bringing about Jacob's spiritual advancement. God, therefore, is the One who actually prevailed in Jacob's life when Jacob steadfastly clung to Him in faith. Jacob's life would no longer be marked by "grabbing heels" but by trusting God. We all need to come to the same point in our lives that Jacob did: confess our own weakness, ask for God's help to deal with our independent spirits, and express our utter dependence on God for His blessing and strength.

The Memorial Name

Jacob then asked the name of the One who had wrestled with him. Jacob had already discerned that his opponent was divine. His unwillingness to release His name may have been to disassociate Himself with pagan ways of manipulating the names of their gods. The Angel said, "Why is it that you ask about My name?" as if to say, "Don't you see who I am?" Jacob should have known that it was Jehovah, the LORD, who had revealed Himself to him at Bethel twenty years earlier, the same God who had instructed him to leave Haran. We then read that "He blessed him there" (v. 29). Having seen the Angel "face to face," Jacob named the place *Peniel,* which means "Face of God." How often we, too, catch a glimpse of the Lord in the middle of our struggles. When we see the Lord in His Word, the blessing we gain from the comfort in those written pages is often the answer to life's perplexities. Jacob now realized that his encounter with God was actually the answer to his prayer for deliverance from his brother Esau (v. 11). First, he met God face to face; then, he learned his own weakness and the power of prevailing prayer. Jacob no longer needed to fear Esau.

The Dawning of a New Day (vv. 31-32)

"The sun rose on him." A new day dawned, and he would never be the same again. What a day it was going to be! As the sun rose, Jacob crossed the Jabbok and made his way up the south bank limping. He was a changed and humbled man, having seen the Lord face to face. We, too, may have close encounters with God that should bring us to humbly realize how weak we are and how mighty God is. May it be that, as we hand over the control of our lives to Him, we shall see Him and long to be more like Him! Then, a "new day" will dawn for us as well in which we will see His power working His perfect will.

There is an interesting and curious editorial comment at the end of the chapter about the children of Israel not eating "the muscle that shrank, which is on the hip socket" (v. 32). Moses was obviously drawing attention to the origin of this Jewish tradition for the sake of his original readers. God did not stipulate this dietary restriction, and it was not included in the Levitical laws set in place during Moses' lifetime. It does indicate, however, that the Israelites recognized the significance of Jacob's encounter with God and desired to remember it.

In Conclusion

The experience Jacob had in wrestling with the Angel was one of the great victories of his life. To him, it amounted to what the experience on Mt. Moriah was for Abraham. It was there that Abraham offered to sacrifice his dearest treasure and found blessing from God. In this passage, Jacob gave up his ability to contend by his own strength and found blessing in clinging to God instead.

The sinews of the old Jacob were shriveled up so that the new Jacob, under God's control, could live by faith. At last, Jacob was ready to meet Esau and then move back into the Promised Land. God's preparation of Jacob is a great illustration of the spiritual exercise every believer needs to experience to enter the place of blessing that God has prepared for us.

Jacob's Return to the Land

Genesis 33 brings the issues between Jacob and Esau to a conclusion and marks the end of Jacob's absence from Canaan. The story of his wanderings began with his fear of Esau and his leaving the land. It ends in this chapter with their reconciliation and his return to the land. Jacob was surprised to find that God had changed Esau's heart such that he was eager to be reconciled. In spite of Jacob's failure, the narrative describes this incident as an answer to Jacob's prayer (32:11). It goes on to record Jacob's purchase of a plot of land near Shechem where he settled and built an altar to God.

The Old Jacob Lives On

Although Jacob had a new name, he did not always live up to all that it implied—especially when he met his brother. The Bible acknowledges Jacob's tendency to fall back into depending on his "flesh" by continuing to use his old name, Jacob, much more frequently than his new name, Israel. After Abram's name was changed to Abraham, his old name was never used again. Not so with Jacob. For the remainder of Genesis, the Holy Spirit moved Moses to refer to him as Jacob forty-five times, compared to twenty-three times as Israel. He is rightly called Jacob in this chapter because, following his blessing at Peniel, he failed when God tested him. He met the test with panic instead of faith. He almost groveled in the dust at Esau's feet, as if Esau were his lord. However, although he continued to fail from time to time it is also true that, from this point on, Jacob constantly reached ever higher levels in his spiritual experience.

So it is with us. We, too, tend to fall back by relying on ourselves rather than living consistently in dependence on God. F. B. Meyer comments, "It is one thing to step up to a level like that. It is quite another to keep it.... Yet it is well to have stood there for even a moment. For once they have caught sight of a new ideal they will never be satisfied to live as they have lived." Let us arise from every failure of faith to increasingly new heights of spiritual attainment.

Arranging the Family for Meeting Esau (vv. 1-2)

When Jacob "lifted up his eyes," he saw what his lookouts had previously reported—that Esau was approaching with four hundred men (v. 1, cf. 32:6).

He had prayed desperately the previous evening to be delivered from the hand of his brother (32:11); now, the moment of truth had arrived—Esau was coming. But as was so typical of him in the past, Jacob was still trying to figure things out on his own without depending on God. He divided up his children and their mothers in a particular order. The most "expendable" ones were placed first in line, while the ones dearer to him were positioned nearer to the back. In this way, he put the concubines with their children in the first group: Bilhah and her sons Dan and Naphtali together with Zilpah and her sons Gad and Asher. Next came Leah with her seven children: Reuben (Jacob's firstborn), Simeon, Levi, Judah, Issachar, Zebulon, and Dinah. Last, and most protected, came his favorite wife, Rachel, with Joseph. The children would have ranged in age from thirteen to six. Rueben, at the very least, was old enough to observe how his father favored Rachel and Joseph. Certainly, Jacob's action must have hurt and humiliated Leah. Jacob's conduct here must have contributed to the jealousy and hostility that Joseph's brothers evidenced when they later sold him as a slave to the Midianites (37:2-11). Jacob's actions in this incident set a negative example for fathers to heed.

Jacob's Meeting with Esau (vv. 3-4)

To Jacob's credit, he preceded his wives and children in the procession and met Esau first. His bowing down seven times was more suited to that of a vassal approaching a king than one twin brother greeting the other—especially considering that Jacob had been given the blessing and patriarchal status. Esau paid no attention to Jacob's formal manner but responded with a warm embrace. Jacob's actions betrayed his personal fear and sense of guilt over the past. Esau's actions, on the other hand, were friendly and forgiving; he ran to Jacob and embraced him. What a contrast! Their embrace marked their reconciliation. The Lord Jesus Himself used the phrase "fell on his neck and kissed him" to convey how the father gladly received his wayward son in the Parable of the Prodigal Son (Luke 15:30). It must have been a touching scene to see Jacob and Esau weeping together.

We are not told the reason for Esau's change of heart. Clearly, he had forgiven his brother and held no grudge against him. Maybe his own prosperity had effected a mellowing in his attitude towards Jacob over the years since he had first threatened to murder him. Perhaps the gifts that Jacob had sent ahead had convinced him that *Jacob's* attitude had changed. He also realized that Jacob was no military threat. Esau's reason for bringing an army with him may be attributed to his initial assumption that because Jacob was coming with a large retinue, he was also armed for an attack.

Esau Meets Jacob's Family (vv. 5-7)

Esau, open and friendly, asked "Who are these?" referring to the company of women and children behind Jacob, to which Jacob replied, "The children whom God has graciously given your servant." He gave God the glory for prospering him. But note how he still referred to himself as "your servant." He then introduced his wives and children to Esau, each group taking turns to bow before him. All this ceremony revealed Jacob's hesitant formality in contrast to Esau's warmth—more evidence of Jacob's fear and guilt. Instead of standing tall in the dignity of his God-given rightful position, he was still wary and insecure, dependent on his fleshly efforts to handle the situation.

Jacob Explains the Gifts (vv. 8-11)

Esau asked Jacob the meaning of the herds of animals he had received (cf. 32:13-15). Jacob's original purpose for the gift was to "find favor" in Esau's eyes (32:20). Note the emphasis on favor, or grace, in the whole passage. Jacob now realized that Esau had already accepted him. He had already found grace. Looking into Esau's face was like seeing the face of God (v. 10). Jacob must have been thinking of his experience the previous night when he had seen God "face to face" (32:30). It was *God* who had dealt graciously with him then. Now he was looking in Esau's face, and he, too, was dealing with him in a way that he did not deserve. Jacob was seeing in Esau's face a reflection of God's favor to him.

The situation prompted Jacob to build on the grace he had found. He designated the gift as his "blessing" (v. 11)—provisions from God's hand. No doubt both men were recalling another "blessing," one that could only ever belong to *one* person—the blessing that Jacob had stolen from Esau (27:27-29). Esau would infer from Jacob's use of the word that he was trying to make restitution for his wrongs. Jacob could not give that particular blessing back, but he could share the fruit of it with his brother. Note how Jacob took advantage of the opportunity to give God the glory (v. 11)—this time for His kindness to him.

Jacob knew that Esau's reception of him had been accomplished by God, so he now invited Esau to take the gift as a guarantee of acceptance. By not offering a gift to Jacob in exchange, Esau was conveying that he received Jacob's gift in reparation for the wrong done to him twenty years earlier. Reconciliation between them was now complete.

There is a word study here that is worth noting. In verse 9, Esau said, "I have enough," referring to his material wealth, his prosperity. The word means "I have *much.*" But in verse 11 when Jacob said, "I have enough," a different Hebrew word is used: Jacob actually said, "I have *all,*" meaning everything. Esau's material possessions may well have exceeded Jacob's, but Jacob had an inexhaustible resource in God. God had blessed him beyond measure. We, too, can say that "we have everything" because we have been blessed with "every spiritual blessing in the heavenly places in Christ" (Eph. 1:3).

Jacob and Esau Separate (vv. 12-17)

We can rightly imagine the two brothers spending the rest of the day sharing with each other their personal histories of the previous twenty years. Jacob would especially want news about their parents. Esau no doubt told him, but the book of Genesis does not record anything other than their deaths and burials (35:27-29; 49:31). In all likelihood, Rebekah was already dead. Isaac, though still alive, would have been over 150 years old at this time and both blind and incapacitated.

The brothers separated peacefully. There are commentators who see some deception on Jacob's part in this section. Esau first offered to travel with Jacob for protection. Jacob declined his help, citing the need of the children and the herds with their young to travel slowly (v. 13). He was still using formal language, calling Esau "my lord." He promised to "come to my lord in Seir" (v. 14) but, as far as we know, he never did that. One likely reason might be Seir's location outside of Canaan (bearing in mind Jacob's intention to complete his mission from God and return to the land). Another reason might have been some residual mistrust of Esau. Jacob may also have been cautious about associating with family members again, bearing in mind his recent dealings with Laban. There is, however, no hint of any latent ill-feeling on Esau's part when the brothers met to bury their father some years later; it was accomplished without any incident between them (35:29).

Esau then generously offered to leave some of his people with Jacob to help, and again Jacob declined, citing no need. Jacob's parting statement, "Let me find favor in the sight of my lord," may have been a diplomatic way to part peacefully because he did not want to insult Esau by refusing his offer (v. 15). Why he did not simply tell Esau that he was committed to obeying God in returning to Canaan, and to Bethel in particular, we do not know. Maybe he chose diplomacy to avoid a possible confrontation; old wounds might have been opened if he had actually said he was fulfilling the role God had once designated for him (25:23). We can learn from the incident, however, that just as Jacob did not need to use any form of deception in following the Lord, neither should we. When the world entices believers to follow, they should make their intention to obey God perfectly clear and not compromise in any way.

Verses 16 and 17 tell us that Esau returned home to Mt. Seir in the south and that Jacob turned north towards Succoth, east of the River Jordan, a few miles to the northwest of Peniel. Jacob built a house for himself there and booths for his livestock—in fact the place took its name from his doing this, as *Succoth* means "booths." How long Jacob lived in Succoth or why he halted there before crossing the Jordan into the land, we are not told.

Twenty years before, when God spoke to him at Bethel on the west side of Jordan, God promised to bring him back to "this land" (28:15). Later, when God directed him to return to the land, He said, "I am the God of Bethel where you anointed the pillar and where you made a vow to Me. Now arise, get out of this land, and return to the land of your kindred" (31:13). Jacob stopped short of complete obedience to God and settled at Succoth. Perhaps the grazing was good there, but to stop short of the land when he was so near seems strange. His delay at Succoth here is a lesson for believers who understand the will of God but stop short of completely fulfilling it. It is all too easy to neglect the Word of God and to make decisions based on our own security and expediency.

Jacob at Shechem (vv. 18-20)

Jacob eventually left Succoth and moved westward across the Jordan to Shechem. Finally, he was back in the land. The wording is that "Jacob came safely to Shechem." Many years before, Abraham stayed in Shechem when he first came into the land (12:6-7). Perhaps Jacob was trying to follow in his grandfather's steps. He entered the land and camped in the same place. It is probably in this sense that he came safely to Shechem.

The text reminds the alert reader that Shechem was in "the land of Canaan," a name synonymous with wickedness. The text also ominously implies the possible defilement of being there when it says, "He bought the parcel of land where he pitched his tent before [in plain view of] the city." We are reminded of what happened to Lot when he moved close to the wicked cities of the plains (cf. 13:12; 14:12; Genesis 19). Finally, the name of the owner's son, Shechem, is mentioned. These three observations—the wickedness of the Canaanites, the close proximity of Jacob's camp to the city of Shechem, and the naming of Hamor's son, Shechem—foreshadow the sin against Jacob's daughter Dinah that we will study in the next chapter.

Jacob bought a piece of land there from the children of Hamor. It was likely a good-sized property because the exact price is noted ("one hundred pieces of money [silver]") to show that the sale was genuine and final. It was only the second piece of property obtained by Abraham and his descendants in the Promised Land. The first was the burial site Abraham bought for Sarah at Hebron (23:20). Jacob no doubt looked forward to the day when his children would own the whole of the land. Jacob dug a well there, though we do not learn that it was Jacob who dug it until the time of Jesus (John 4:6). That well can still be identified on the shoulder between Mt. Gerazim and Mt. Ebal. Joseph's bones would be brought back from Egypt and buried here at Shechem (Josh. 24:32).

The Altar called "El Elohe Israel"

After Jacob purchased the property in Shechem, he built an altar on it. It was an act of worship in which he acknowledged that God had faithfully brought him back to the land. He knew, no doubt, that Abraham had built an altar near that very spot when he first entered Canaan (12:7). This was Jacob's first altar and marked a significant step in his life of faith. He named the altar *El Elohe*

Israel which means "The God of Israel is El," that is, He is the strong God, the mighty One, and the God of Israel. Notice how he was identifying his new name (and new self) with God. In building the altar, he was establishing a place of worship and witness among an unbelieving and idolatrous people. He was, in a sense, claiming the land for his descendants in God's name.

There was, however, a negative side to all of this. Jacob and his family had stopped short again—this time of Bethel, where he had vowed he would return (28:21-22). He was living very near a city filled with pagan people and pagan ideas. His maturing family could hardly help but be negatively influenced by them. He should have recognized the danger into which he was placing them. Unfortunately, Jacob did not realize the danger until his daughter was raped and two of his sons had retaliated by committing mass murder. When this trouble came, we will see how Jacob returned to responding remarkably passively to his family in crisis situations (29:31-30:24), which had to reflect a spiritually low state again. He would learn the hard way that "friendship with the world is enmity with God" (James 4:4).

In Conclusion

The narrative in this chapter has told us of Jacob's dramatic meeting with Esau and the surprisingly warm welcome he received. As a practical example of how reconciling parties should conduct themselves—showing attitudes of humility, forgiveness, and acceptance—the incident is a worthy one to follow. We see Jacob setting us a good example in that he gave God glory for his blessings (his wives and children, his peaceful meeting with Esau, and his wealth in livestock) but also a poor one in not being completely honest with Esau as to his plans.

We have also learned of Jacob's unexplained delay at Succoth, where he paused on the verge of entering the Promised Land, and of his first settlement in the land at Shechem, where he built an altar to the God of Israel who had brought him safely back. Believers can identify with Jacob's ups and downs as he faced his own fears and failings, the complexities of his family, and the unknowns in Canaan, while trying to relate his growing faith in God to them.

Treachery in Shechem

Jacob was, at last, back in Canaan—with the family and livestock that God had prospered him with in Haran. They had crossed the Jordan and settled just outside the city of Shechem. Jacob would no doubt have visited his father Isaac in Beersheba while they were living there. There is no record of these visits in Genesis, probably because they were not relevant to Moses' purpose for writing.

What *was* relevant to his purpose was the family history of Israel that occupies this chapter and the very important issue of intermarriage between the descendants of Abraham and the Canaanites. Chapter 34 deals with the rape of Jacob's daughter, Dinah, and the subsequent massacre of the men of Shechem that was committed by Simeon and Levi. The emphasis is on the brothers' violent deed because it had far-reaching consequences for the family, but it was Dinah's seduction that triggered it.

The Violation of Dinah (vv. 1-4)

About ten years must have passed since Jacob and his family left Haran in order for Dinah to now be in her mid-teens and old enough to marry. Several verses refer to her as a "young woman" (vv. 3, 4, 12). Her brothers Simeon and Levi would have been in their early twenties. In the first verse, the narrator identifies Dinah as Leah's daughter. This fact is important because it reminds us that she was the full sister of Simeon and Levi who later acted on her behalf. We are not told if she had other sisters or half sisters by this time. Even if she did, she was certainly the oldest (30:21), so it is understandable that she would seek the company of other girls her age.

Like all Canaanite cities, Shechem was morally decadent and already marked out for judgment by God. Assuming that Dinah had been warned of the moral dangers of visiting the city, she paid little attention. She "went out to see the daughters of the land." Marriageable girls would not normally go alone into an area outside their clan's territory. Like many young people in every generation, when she ventured into "the world," she became vulnerable to its enticements and exposed to its dangers. While visiting with the "daughters of the land," the young prince of the city, Shechem, became strongly attracted to her.

The Scripture says, "[Shechem] took her and lay with her, and violated her." The words "took" and "violated," together with the word "defiled" in verses 5 and 13, indicate that he used force. We would call it rape. It appears from verse 26 that he then kept her against her will in his house.

Shechem was an influential prince, and Dinah a gullible teenager. Who was to blame? Most certainly, Dinah placed herself in harm's way. Jacob also shared some blame for he chose to settle with his family close to the wicked city. Shechem was personally responsible for his violent and immoral act. As a pagan raised in a pagan society, he offered no apology and showed no remorse for violating her physically, yet verse 3 indicates that he did have emotional feelings for Dinah in that he loved her, he spoke kindly or tenderly to her, and he wanted to legally marry her. He went to his father Hamor and demanded, "Get me this young woman as a wife."

Jacob's Failure (vv. 5-7)

The striking aspect about Jacob's reaction to the rape of Dinah is his lack of reaction. The emphasis in the text is on her brothers' active response, not her father's. Verse 5 says that "he held peace [kept silent] until they [his sons] came." However, the impression given from the dialog between the two families in verses 8 to 17 is that he *remained* silent. His passivity is hard to understand. It may reflect indecisiveness or perhaps guilt due to his part in the compromise of exposing his family to the city of Shechem. Jacob shows none of the leadership expected of a patriarch. His behavior is reminiscent of the way he ignored the strife between Leah and Rachel in their early family life (29:31-30:23). Certainly, he was neglecting his responsibilities as head of the household that God ordained in the Garden of Eden. Meanwhile, Hamor, Shechem's father and the mayor of the city, took the initiative to come to Jacob's camp to make his proposal about intermarrying.

Jacob's sons were "grieved and very angry" by the news of Dinah's rape. Shechem had committed a "disgraceful thing" (v. 7). It was especially abhorrent because it was done "in Israel." Moses was emphasizing for his readers that "Israel" was more than a new name for Jacob; it stood for a people with whom God had made a covenant. Simeon and Levi seem to have discerned that the offence was against not only Dinah but the God to whom they were now related. Their family was distinct from any other people on earth—especially the idolaters of Canaan. It is significant that this first mention in the Bible to Israel, referring to the chosen people of God, emphasizes the difference between them and all other peoples.

Hamor Negotiates for Intermarriage (vv. 8-12)

Jacob left all the negotiations to his sons, whereas both Hamor and his son took part in the discussion. Hamor began by saying how Shechem longed to marry Dinah and courteously asked that they give her to him. He made no apology for the crime committed against her nor did he even refer to it. He did not offer any reparations (v. 8). Hamor went on to make a broader proposal that his people, the Canaanites, intermarry with Jacob's family. He listed the advantages to them: "The land shall be before you. Dwell and trade in it, and acquire possessions for yourselves in it" (vv. 9-10). Peace and prosperity—it sounded like an appealing offer!

Some commentators view Hamor as a generous man trying to make the best of an awkward situation. This interpretation is far from the truth. He was really proposing the assimilation of the Israelites into Canaanite society. The Canaanites would thus acquire all the Israelite livestock and property and get richer at their expense (cf. v. 23). The effect of that on Israel would be the loss of their identity as God's covenant people and increasing defilement by Canaanite wickedness.

Hamor was crafty and deceitful in his offer. He had no intention of letting the Israelites prosper as a separate people. It was because of these very dangers that Abraham had commanded his servant not to take a bride for Isaac from among the Canaanites (24:3).

Genesis was being written for the children of Israel who were poised to enter the Promised Land, and the lesson of this story was vitally important for them. Moses knew the dangers and wanted to prepare them to withstand the great temptation to intermarry with the Canaanites still living in the land. He commanded them not to intermarry in Deuteronomy 7:3: "You shall not give your daughter to their son, nor take their daughter for your son." The nation's spiritual livelihood was at stake. Beyond that, the purity of the line of Messiah was threatened. If Jacob and his sons had accepted Hamor's proposal, it would have had far-reaching consequences for the Israelites and, effectively, the messianic promise.

After Hamor's proposal, Shechem spoke up. He was only interested in getting permission to marry Dinah as soon as possible. The larger and long-term issues were of no interest to him. He wanted to gain the favor of Dinah's family, pay whatever they demanded as a dowry for her, and even add a gift over and beyond that. He concluded, "But give me the young woman as a wife" (vv. 11-12). He was only thinking of pleasing himself, not of her honor.

Jacob's Sons Make a Proposal (vv. 13–17)

Jacob's sons, meanwhile, were hatching a plot of their own to even the score (v. 13). They responded to Hamor's offer of free intermarriage by making a deceitful counter-offer. To intermarry with uncircumcised Canaanites would be a "reproach" to them (v. 14). They reasoned that if all the males in the city of Shechem were circumcised, like the Israelite men, they then would agree to intermarriage and becoming "one people." Of course, Shechem would then be free to marry Dinah (v. 15-16). If the Canaanites did not agree, the brothers would take Dinah back and leave (v. 17).

Dinah's brothers were being as deceitful as the Canaanites, They were using the rite of circumcision, the sign of their covenant relationship with God, to lure the men of Shechem into a murderous trap. There was absolutely no warrant for them to abuse circumcision by using it as a cover for premeditated murder. The Shechemites did not worship Jehovah; they were not God's covenant people, and they did not appreciate the special significance that circumcision had to these descendants of Abraham. They may have been familiar with the practice, though, in its connection with the religions of other people.

Hamor Accepts their Proposal (vv. 18-24)

Hamor did not suspect any foul play on their part. In fact, he believed they were playing into his hands. All that would be required, he thought, was that the men of the city undergo a small surgical procedure. The end result was worth it: intermarriage that would soon absorb the whole community of Israelites.

Hamor, as mayor, persuaded the men of the city to accept Jacob's sons' demand that every male of the city be circumcised (vv. 20-24). He appealed to their covetousness, saying, "Only let us consent to them, and they will dwell with us." He pointed out that eventually their livestock and property would all belong to the Canaanites (v. 23). With this gain in mind, and apparently because Hamor's son was well respected among them (v. 19), the townsmen agreed to act immediately upon the plan. The phrase "all who went out of the gate of his city" is repeated to emphasize that there were no men left to defend it (v. 24).

The Treachery of Jacob's Sons (vv. 25-29)

On the third day after the circumcision when the men of Shechem were "in pain," Simeon and Levi attacked the city with swords. With the Shechemites so incapacitated, their strategy worked exactly as planned. They killed every male, including Hamor and Shechem. Dinah was rescued from Shechem's house and taken back to Jacob's camp. Beyond that, they were joined by the rest of Jacob's sons who plundered the city of its valuables and took all the livestock from both inside and outside the city (vv. 27-29). They also captured all the women and children.

It was an inhumane atrocity of enormous proportions that never should have occurred. It was a blot on the reputation of God's people; they acted no better than their pagan neighbors and, like many appalling barbarities since, it was committed in the name of religion. It was a crime that embarrassed Jacob and one that he never forgot to his dying day. On his deathbed, in the final words he ever spoke to his sons, Jacob remembered their brutal act and said of them, "Simeon and Levi are brothers; instruments of cruelty are in their habitations" (49:5). They were both passed over for special blessings from the old patriarch, and Genesis 34 explains why.

Jacob's Rebuke (vv. 30-31)

Jacob finally broke his silence and reproved Simeon and Levi for their actions. He seemed more concerned at this point, however, about the marring of his reputation with the Canaanites than with their atrocity. "You have troubled me by making me obnoxious among the inhabitants of the land" (v. 30). He made no reference to their excessive force, nor any comment about Dinah's honor or the Lord's. It seems that Jacob sinned not only in his silence before the massacre but also in his speaking out after it. Notice the stress on the first person pronouns "me" and "I"; they occur eight times in verse 30. The overriding thrust of his speech was self-centered. The fear he expressed for his household's safety, however, could be construed as a concern for God's covenant purposes. He might have thought that, if the Canaanites retaliated and wiped out his family, the messianic promise could not be fulfilled. Thinking along *this* line, however, would demonstrate his lack of faith in God's power to protect them.

Simeon and Levi had the last word, which is the climax of the story. They said, speaking of Shechem, "Should he treat our sister like a harlot?" (v. 31). They scolded their father for his lack of moral outrage and tried to justify their actions. It was a rhetorical question. Their point was, all they really wanted was revenge for the rape of their sister. They sought to judge an evil but went about it in an evil way, for which there was no justification. Apart from the carnal satisfaction of revenge in their hearts, all their action accomplished was the need to flee. Jacob, for the second time in this chapter, had nothing to say. As a spiritually-compromised man, Jacob was incapable of making proper moral judgments.

In Conclusion

The Shechem story shows the extremes of response to moral evil. On the one hand, Jacob displays a paralyzing fear of standing up for righteousness and does nothing at all. On the other hand, Simeon and Levi allow justifiable anger over the offence to express itself in excessive and cruel retribution. It is sad that neither side took God into account or walked by faith.

The great lesson of this sordid story to the Israelites waiting to enter Canaan was to be prepared to encounter the Canaanites with faith in God rather than with their own ingenuity. God was going to use them as instruments of judgment on the Canaanites, but this judgment was to be carried out at His directive and to accomplish His divine purposes. It was unthinkable, therefore, that they would entertain the idea of intermarriage with the Canaanites; they were to remain pure, completely separate from them (Lev. 18:24; 20:5; Num. 5; Deut. 7:1-5). They were neither to vent their anger improperly nor allow fear to stop their progress. The great keys were the foundational ones of faith in God and obedience to God. Sad to say, their later history in the land showed how often they failed to trust and obey. Believers today should pay close heed to the truths and warnings illustrated so clearly in this chapter.

The Renewal of the Covenant at Bethel

Chapter 35 is the final episode in this section of Genesis called the "genealogy (or generations) of Isaac" (25:19 to 35:29). It is a chronicle of Isaac's family from the time of his father Abraham's death to his own (25:8; 35:29). The focus of the section is particularly on Isaac's son Jacob and how God disciplined him, prepared him, and changed him until he became worthy of his new name, Israel. Shechem had been a place of compromise for Jacob and his family. He allowed Dinah to keep company with the Canaanites there and reaped the seeds of family neglect that he had sown: Dinah was raped, and Simeon and Levi took revenge on the inhabitants of Shechem. With his reputation in shambles, Jacob and his family had to leave the area in disgrace.

In this chapter, we read of Jacob's belated obedience to return to Bethel and of God's second appearance to him there to reconfirm the promises made to Abraham and Isaac (28:15). This occasion was one of the high points in his spiritual life. The completion of the patriarch's family is recorded with the birth of Benjamin to Rachel. Along with these victories, however, we learn of the moral defeats with which he had to deal. These included idolatry and the incestuous sin of Reuben. The chapter ends with three deaths in the family, those of Deborah, Rachel, and Isaac.

The Command to Go to Bethel (vv. 1-7)

Bethel was an important place in the life of Jacob. God had first revealed Himself to Jacob at Bethel when he was leaving the land (28:19). Later, while he was in Haran, God referred to Himself as the "God of Bethel" and told Jacob to return there (31:3, 13), but Jacob went to Shechem instead. Now, when Jacob was still consumed with concern about the possibility of Canaanite retaliation because of his sons' brutal massacre of the Shechemites, God again spoke to Jacob. He commanded him to "Arise, go up to Bethel" (v. 1). Jacob still had not fulfilled his vow to go there. Bethel was only thirty miles away, but his spiritual journey would not be complete until he did this. Many Christians are like Jacob: they take far too long to reach the spiritual high ground of "Bethel." Like Jacob, they become smug in their spiritual compromise. He thought that building an altar in Shechem was good enough, but he was wrong. It was necessary for him to separate himself from the world and go back to the place where he had first discovered communion with God.

The command from God to go to Bethel marked the third time God told him to return to the land. The first time was when he was in Haran (31:3), the second, when he was on the border of the land (31:13), and the third, when he was in Shechem (v. 1). Shame on us if God needs to speak more than once with a clear command to do His will! There is strong emphasis on the words "Arise, go up to Bethel and dwell there." Jacob offered no resistance. He knew he couldn't stay in Shechem. God reminded him that the last time he went to Bethel he was on the run from Esau and had seen that wonderful vision of God's presence and protection. This reminder would have caused Jacob to realize how far he had fallen from his first Bethel experience. God was humbling him, causing him to see that he had left his first love, like those in the New Testament Ephesian church (cf. Rev. 2:4-5). If we know that we need to spiritually "retrace our steps" to Bethel, we, too, may hear God reminding us "from where [we] have fallen." May we humbly accept God's reproofs and yield to Him. Jacob knew that when he came to Bethel he was to "make an altar there." He needed to become a worshipping man once again.

Jacob had grown accustomed to the worldliness of the Shechemites. He had lost his vision of God, left God out of his reckoning, and neglected his worship of Him. This is a constant danger for us all; we are so prone to being distracted by the world. God had to use a heavy hand on Jacob until he woke up to his spiritual condition (chapter 34). Jacob should have gone directly to Bethel from Peniel ten years earlier. Perhaps the answer lies in the fact that he knew he had not kept at least two of the vows he had made there thirty years before (28:21-22). He had said, "The LORD shall be my God" but had allowed idolatry in his family. He had promised that the pillar he had set up in Bethel would be "God's house," but he didn't go there until God commanded him. He had promised to give one tenth of his possessions to God, but we do not know that he ever did. He evidently had not even visited Bethel during this time, which seems strange because Bethel is almost en route from Shechem to Hebron, and Jacob must certainly have gone to Hebron from time to time to visit Isaac.

Jacob had taught his family about God, but they were obviously not truly following Him. Jacob had failed in his spiritual leadership of them. It is interesting to note that passivity and neglect had characterized some areas of his life, just as purposeful planning and scheming had characterized other areas. Jacob now knew that his family's lifestyle of idolatry had to be put away and that God had to be brought into focus. It is a good lesson for all of us.

Jacob's Preparation for Worship (vv. 2-4)

With a humbler heart, Jacob responded to God by living up to his new name of Israel and taking leadership in the family. He prepared them for worship with three commands: he told them to "put away the foreign gods that are among you, purify yourselves, and change your garments" (v. 2). These three commands summarize the preparation for worship in every age:

- *Put away:* True worship of the Lord will permit no rivals.
- *Purify yourselves*: True worship of the Lord will permit no sin.
- *Change your garments:* True worship of the Lord will permit no unholy testimony.

Jacob also gave them the reason for his call: as a family, they would go up to Bethel where he would "make an altar there to God, who answered me in my distress and has been with me in the way which I have gone" (v. 3). In saying this, he must at last have been recalling his vow when he had said, "If God will be with me, and keep me in this way that I am going ... then the LORD shall be my God" (28:20-21). He was recognizing and testifying that God had indeed been with him and kept him in "the way" he had gone.

The people in his household—even his favorite, Rachel—immediately handed over their idols because Jacob was now speaking as the spiritual leader of the family and with God's authority. Jacob hid the idols beneath a terebinth tree near Shechem before they went to Bethel. Perhaps it was the same tree noted by Abraham when he first entered the land (12:6). The word for *hid* literally means "dumped unceremoniously," indicating that they no longer feared the idols. Removing false gods and the earrings associated with them was their first step of preparation for worship. *Our* "idols" must go too. Idols for us can be anything that takes the place of God in our hearts, be it pleasure, sports, relationships, or material goods.

The second step was moral and spiritual inner cleansing. Paul told believers to examine themselves before partaking of the Lord's Supper (1 Cor. 11:28). The apostle John explained how the filth of sin can be cleansed: "If we confess our sins, He is faithful and just to forgive us our sins and to cleanse us from all unrighteousness" (1 John 1:9). And in the context of dealing with worldliness, James exhorted Jewish believers to purify their hearts and humble themselves before the Lord (James 4:8, 10).

The third step was to exchange their soiled garments for clean ones. The new clothing refers to outward appearance and acts that reflect the inner cleansing that has taken place. It is what others see. The old clothes must be exchanged for new. That is, we must be clothed in garments befitting salvation rather than the filthy rags of our old life. We are to "put off ... the old man ... and put on the new man which was created according to God, in righteousness and true holiness" (Eph. 4:22-25; cf. Rom. 6:6).

These three acts prepared Jacob and his family for the worship of God at Bethel, the house of God.

God Protects Them (v. 5)

Jacob's active determination to please the Lord and to lead his family in worship is instructive to all of us. As they journeyed from Shechem to Bethel, the Lord protected them from attack by the inhabitants of the Canaanite cities they passed. Normally speaking, these cities would have come to Shechem's aid after such an incident as the massacre. God caused the cities to become paralyzed with supernatural fear: "They did not pursue the sons of Jacob." With the sovereign God in control, the enemies of His people can do nothing. We can be sure that God will do more than "meet us halfway" in any efforts we make to encourage our families' worship of Him.

Jacob's Altar at Bethel (vv. 6-7)

The memories and thoughts of his vision thirty years before must have flooded Jacob's mind when he and all his retinue arrived at Bethel. How thankful he would now feel to be in God's will at last. In coming to Bethel, Jacob did what God had told him to do (v. 1) and what he had promised his family he would do (v. 3). The name of the altar means "The God of Bethel," or more fully "The God of the house of God," or still more fully "God over all in God's house." The altar back in Shechem was called El-Elohe Israel meaning "God, the God of Israel," that is, the personal God of Jacob who was now called Israel. But here in Bethel, the altar is called God-of-the-House-of-God because He is the God of all Israel's children. We who are in the family of God can also rejoice in the communal sense in God's name, El Bethel, the God of us all. The New Testament says that we are built up as a spiritual house to offer up spiritual sacrifices to God (1 Pet. 2:5). In returning to Bethel, Jacob was returning to the joy of his salvation that he had lost when he deceived his father and fled from his brother Esau (cf. Psa. 51:12; Isa 12:1-3).

The Death of Deborah (v. 8)

Deborah had been Rebekah's nurse and a lifelong handmaid. She had come with her from Haran when Rebekah had left home to become Isaac's wife (24:59). It is interesting that her death is recorded but Rebekah's is not. She had no doubt been with Rebekah until she had died and had then come to live with Jacob after one of his visits to see Isaac. She might have become a grandmother figure to Jacob's children. She would have been around 180 years old (as was Isaac when he died). She was buried under a terebinth tree near Bethel which was called Allon Bachuth, meaning the "Oak of weeping." Obviously Deborah was a much-loved and revered member of the household. This special tree was to be a shrine and a memorial for the old nurse. Her life bridged two patriarchs, Isaac and Jacob.

The Confirmation of the Covenant at Bethel (vv. 9-15)

After Jacob built the altar at Bethel, God appeared to him for the fifth time and "blessed him." In this revelation, God confirmed the covenant He had first made with Abraham, had later repeated to Isaac, and now reiterated to Jacob, along with final details (cf. 12:1-3; 15:1-21; 17:1-27; 22:15-19; 26:24-25). Note that this revelation came "when he came from Padan Aram" (v. 9). Nothing is said of Jacob's disastrous stay in Shechem or of his living in Succoth. Jacob is given credit for his obedience to God's call to return to Bethel, even though it was delayed (cf. 31:3). Jacob's life paralleled Abraham's here: Abraham was called to go to Canaan but wasted many years in Haran (cf. 11:31; 12:5). There is no excuse for partial obedience, but God is gracious when we make a new start to obey Him—even when we have faltered along the way.

The first thing God did was to affirm the change in Jacob's name (v. 10). The change of Jacob's name to Israel parallels Abram's to Abraham, the "father of many nations." It was a sign of the surety of God's promise (17:5-8). God had told Jacob of his name change about ten years earlier, but Jacob had not appropriated the meaning of it (32:28). A few commentators see the two mentions of the name change as a mistake or perhaps an unnecessary repetition. The second naming is not a problem if we discern that God was simply ratifying it.

The name change to Israel was a confirmation of the promises that included seed, land, nationhood, and royalty. Every time the name Israel was used, Jacob could be assured of the promises. God gives believers new names as well. When we put our trust in Christ for salvation we can rightly be called by such new names as "saints" and "sons of God," but sometimes it is years before we appropriate the meaning of these names in our daily lives. Note an additional phrase in this passage: after saying "Israel shall be your name," God added, "So He called his name Israel" (v. 10c). God saw and acknowledged signs of change in him.

God Declares His Name: El Shaddai

After God affirmed Jacob's new name, He declared His own name to be God Almighty, *El Shaddai*. When Jacob had asked His divine assailant for His name at Peniel, God had refused to tell him because he was asking more out of curiosity than spiritual interest. Jacob had now reached a point in his life when God was prepared to reveal Himself to him by one of His names. The only way *any* of us know God is by self-revelation.

El Shaddai had been first revealed to his grandfather Abraham (17:1), and Isaac later used it in blessing Jacob before he left home (28:3). Now God used El Shaddai in blessing Jacob (v. 11), referring to His power in the face of man's weakness and frailty. Jacob must have been encouraged to hear El Shaddai confirm the promises to him in almost the same words He had used with Abraham and Isaac. God, as expressed in the name El Shaddai, made a lasting impression on Jacob (cf. 43:14; 48:3; 49:25).

Also included in the prophecy was the fact that Israel's future would include "a nation," "a company of nations," and "kings" (v. 11). The kings of Israel and Judah could look back directly to this promise. The promise of the coming kings was to appear next in the Davidic covenant (2 Sam. 7:12). All of these things were going to happen in the land that God had reiterated would belong to Jacob descendants and in which Jacob was currently standing (v. 12). It is from this point forward that the family of Jacob began to increase and eventually became a nation. The promise is not yet completely fulfilled. And although wars are still being fought over the Promised Land, the promise remains.

God then "went up from him in the place where he talked with him" (v. 13). We recall that the first time Jacob was at Bethel, God said, "I will not leave you until I have done what I have spoken to you" (28:15). Neither that phrase nor the statement that "God went up from him" implies that God's presence with Jacob would be limited to his absence from the land. Instead, God was emphasizing the fact that He would accomplish a specific work in and through him during that time. Genesis 35:13 confirms that God had indeed completed that particular task.

A Memorial Stone

Jacob's love for memorials is again seen in this incident. Thirty years earlier, he had reared the stone on which he had slept and anointed it with oil, naming the place Bethel (28:18-19). Now, here he was again, erecting a pillar, pouring oil on top of it, and once again naming it Bethel. It could have been the same stone of his first visit. Almost certainly he would have looked for it. This time, he did not go back to his old ways but continued in faith. The term "drink offering" is used for the first time here. These offerings were usually wine poured out, signifying the worshipper's devotion and consecration to God. Later, they were used in addition to other offerings as personal expressions of devotion. Jacob's pillar became a memorial stone much like the tombstones of loved ones. It was a place of reflection for Jacob; it was where he had recovered his faith, or seen from God's perspective; it was where God had recovered His wayward child. We may be tempted to assume that, from here on Jacob's life was free from trouble. Actually, Jacob's life was dogged by trouble for many more years. We shall see some of it even before the end of this chapter.

The Death of Rachel and the Birth of Benjamin (vv. 16-21)

After his spiritual experience at Bethel, Jacob and his family moved south to Hebron where Isaac lived. It appears that he did not completely obey God by *dwelling* at Bethel (v. 1). Three incidents marked his journey and brought to a close the "genealogy of Isaac": his favorite wife, Rachel, died in childbirth; his firstborn son committed incest with one of his concubines; and his father, Isaac, died.

As the family with all their flocks and herds neared Bethlehem, Rachel went into labor with her second child. She had prayed for a second son when Joseph was born. In naming Joseph, she had shown her faith that the Lord would make this second pregnancy possible (30:24). About fifteen years had passed; her age might possibly have contributed toward the difficulties of giving birth, though she was likely a good deal younger than Jacob, who was about 105 at this time. In the midst of her birthing process and close to death, the midwife assured her that she had a son. Even in her final moments, Rachel was comforted in knowing that her prayer had been answered. With her dying breath she named him Benoni, which means "son of sorrow." Many have suggested that her untimely death had to do with her stealing the idol gods from her father Laban (31:32). There is not even a hint in the story to indicate this. Rachel's death is the first recorded death-in-childbirth in the Bible.

Benjamin is Named

Jacob was no doubt stricken with grief when Rachel died because he loved her dearly. However, he did not allow her choice of name to stand. He changed it from Benoni to Benjamin, which means "son of my right hand" (v. 18). One name conveyed despair of the here-and-now, the other, hope and strength for the future. Benjamin is the only one of Jacob's sons that he named. Perhaps this demonstrates again that he was asserting leadership in the family now that they were back in the land. The name indicates a particularly honored position in the family.

Rachel was buried on the way south to Bethlehem, and Jacob set up a pillar over her grave in memory of his love and sorrow (v. 20). He remembered Rachel till the end of his life (48:7). The pillar marking her grave could still be seen in the days when Moses wrote Genesis (v. 20). Rachel had seen her share of sorrow. She was replaced by her older sister on her wedding night. She was involved in rivalry and jealousy in the home. She deprived herself of spiritual blessing by clinging to idols and superstition instead of clinging to the living God (30:14). She prayed long and longingly for another son and, in the end, gave her life in giving him birth.

We read that "Israel" journeyed on south (v. 21). This is the first time that Scripture refers to Jacob as Israel, suggesting that he journeyed on in the will of God. The next campsite named is just to the south of the city at a watchtower for shepherds called the Tower of Eder (2 Kings 17:9).

Reuben's Disgrace (v. 22)

The next recorded family incident was of Reuben who, now about thirty, disgraced himself and his family by sleeping with Bilhah, Rachel's maid (v. 22). Bilhah was very much older than he and was the mother of two of his half brothers, Dan and Naphtali. We do not know why he committed this sin. Jacob no doubt put a stop to it, but no punitive action is recorded. It certainly caused Jacob a great deal of grief. He seems to have found strength in God and quietly accepted what he could not change. However, in time, the sin cost Reuben the privilege of leadership as the firstborn son in the family (49:3-4; 1 Chron. 5:1-2). His brothers Simeon and Levi had already forfeited their right to it by their massacre at Shechem. It is for this reason that, ultimately, it was Leah's fourth son, Judah, who assumed the leadership of the family and through whom Messiah came.

Jacob's Twelve Sons (vv. 22-26)

The author of Genesis here inserts a record of Jacob's twelve sons with an emphasis on the number twelve. Significantly, the list begins with the sons of Leah followed by the sons of Rachel. The list concludes with the record of the sons of Bilhah and Zilpah, the two concubines. This record is a witness to God's blessing on the family and evidence that they would continue in spite of sin and death. These sons were due to become the clan leaders of the twelve tribes of Israel.

The Death of Isaac (vv. 27-29)

From the Tower of Eder, Jacob continued on his southward journey to Hebron, where Isaac was living. His pilgrimage had finally brought him home to the place "where Abraham and Isaac had sojourned" (v. 27). It had been more than thirty years since he had fled for his life from the family home. Genesis 28:10 says that "Jacob went out from Beersheba" when he left for Haran, so Isaac and Rebekah must have moved again to Hebron in the intervening years. Isaac was, by this time, very old and feeble.

When Isaac died, he was "gathered to his people," a phrase which indicates his life after death in Sheol, the place of the dead. Old Testament believers like Adam, Shem, Noah and Abraham were there awaiting the coming redemption. Although his death and burial are recorded at this point in time, the fact that he was 180 years old when he died indicates that he was still alive when Joseph was sold into Egypt.

Esau was notified of his death and joined Jacob in burying him. Their joint cooperation here gives evidence of their full reconciliation. Isaac was buried in the sepulcher of the patriarchs there in Hebron with his wife Rebekah and his parents, Abraham and Sarah. Later, Leah and Jacob would be buried there as well. The sepulcher is still in Hebron to this day. Think again of the three loved ones Jacob buried in this chapter. He buried Deborah, his mother's maid. He buried Rachel, his favorite wife. Finally, he buried his father, Isaac. Death is written over the whole scene. In this way, the "genealogy of Isaac" is ended.

In Conclusion

Some lessons stand out for us in the experience of Jacob. We learn something of the dangers of a spiritual letdown, even after great experiences with God. We also learn that even in times of sin, death, and disappointment, God is faithful. A third lesson is that restoration to fellowship with God does not guarantee a life without grief or sorrow. In Jacob's case, God disciplined him by weaning him away from self-reliance and affection for the things of earth so that he could cast himself wholly on God. He began to live up to the new name of Israel.

The Family of Esau

A new section of Genesis begins here after the death of Isaac reported in the last chapter. The rest of the book focuses on the story of Isaac's two sons. A brief account of his older—but rejected—son Esau is given in our present chapter. The much longer account of his younger—but elected—son Jacob fills the remaining chapters of Genesis, ending with his death (37:2–49:33). It is the same structural pattern Moses used in recording the "generations" of Abraham's sons: after the death of Abraham, Moses first gave a short report of the genealogy of Ishmael the older, rejected son (25:12-18), followed by the much fuller record of his younger, elected son Isaac (25:12-18; 25:19–35:29).

Contrasting the Covenant and Non-Covenant Brothers

The repetition of this pattern heightens the sharp contrast between the older sons who did not obtain the promises of the covenant and the younger sons who did. Nevertheless, this chapter will clarify that as far as the older non-covenant sons were concerned—as actual persons, not just biblical pictures—God blessed them in other significant ways. While the covenant sons had their own noted descendants who issued in the nation of Israel, the non-covenant sons had descendants worth mentioning as well. Ishmael fathered a large and legitimate family. He became the father of twelve princes (17:20). Esau had five sons and ten grandsons (36:10-14). Both these non-covenant sons of the patriarchs received a blessing from God in terms of their descendants, or seed.

The contrast between the covenant sons and the non-covenant sons is not only seen in their relationship to the promised seed of Abraham, but also to the land of Canaan. Both Ishmael and Esau established their families *outside* the land of promise and separate from any ties to it. Ishmael moved east to Arabia, and Esau moved south to Edom. But the younger covenant sons, Isaac and Jacob, lived *inside* the land and maintained close ties to it. Ultimately, it was to be the inheritance of their descendants (36:8; 37:2).

The Family of Esau (vv. 1-8)

Esau was also known as Edom, meaning "red," signified by the red stew for which he sold his birthright. His descendants were known as Edomites (v.

1; 25:29-30). Three times in this chapter we are told "Esau is Edom" (vv. 1, 8, 19). The record of Esau's family is important because Moses, the author of Genesis, wanted the Israelites to understand their common ancestry with these people: they were *all* descended from Isaac. The Israelites would pass through Edom on their way to Canaan, but although they were "brothers," the Edomites became their most subtle enemies during their wilderness journey. Edom's military strength, moral depravity, and religious apostasy would strongly oppose them on the way. Moses was preparing them for that by explaining how the Edomite nation became powerful.

Esau and his twin brother Jacob were 120 years old when Isaac died (cf. 25:6 and 35:28). Esau had been married for eighty years, while Jacob had only been married forty years or less (26:34). It is not surprising, therefore, that Esau had many more descendants than Jacob at this particular point in time. It may be that Jacob obtained many of these records of Esau's family when the two men met to bury Isaac. At some later period, Moses must have obtained additional data, which may explain why some of the information is stated twice (cf. "This is the genealogy of Esau," vv. 1 and 9).

It is also helpful for the Bible student to know what happened to the Esau branch of the family, as it is introduces the record of the Jacob branch that is predominant in the remainder of Genesis. It demonstrates God's faithfulness in multiplying Abraham's seed as "the dust of the earth" (13:16): Abraham's descendants included the Edomites and the Amalekites (vv. 8, 12). The details of Esau's descendants should alert the Bible student to the importance of the Edomites and their relationship to Israel—a theme that appears throughout Old Testament history.

Esau's Wives and their Children

The account of Esau's descendants begins with his marriages to three Canaanite women and the sons who were born to those unions (v. 5). We can contrast Esau's Canaanite wives with Jacob's wives, who came from the covenant family. Esau's three wives were Ada (a Hittite), Aholibamah (a Hivite), and Basemath (an Ishmaelite). There is a textual problem when we try to harmonize these names with the names given in Genesis 26:34 and Genesis 28:9 and to clearly determine the time and place of their marriages and the births of their children. However, we do learn from this chapter the names of the five sons that Esau's wives bore him (in verses 4 and 5) and the fact that he had at least one daughter (v. 6).

Esau's Move to Mount Seir

Verses 6 through 8 give credence to Esau's having moved away from the family home prior to Isaac's call to bless him and Jacob's deception that led to his fleeing from Esau's anger (chapter 27). Because he had sold his birthright, Esau understood that Jacob would be the principal heir of Isaac's possessions.

There was not, in any case, enough pastureland for all their flocks and herds, so he relocated his own family and herds farther south. Esau is reminiscent of Lot, who had moved away from Abraham "because of their great substance" (cf. 13:6). Even beyond the overgrazing problem, the significant reason for the move was to get "away from the presence of his brother Jacob" (v. 6). He eventually settled in an area south of the Dead Sea called Mount Seir (v. 8). We read in Deuteronomy that Esau conquered the peoples who lived in Mount Seir known as the Horites (Deut. 2:12, 22). As time went on, the area became known as Edom and was protected by the fortress city of Petra. Its red rock cliffs only added to the significance of the name Esau had acquired when he had sold his birthright for the "red stuff" and had become known as Edom himself.

Esau's Sons and Chiefs (vv. 9-43)

The author now turns his attention to how Esau's descendants became a nation. The record deals first with his family, particularly his sons and his grandsons. Then, it describes the transition from a family clan to a tribal arrangement with chiefs heading each tribe. The new tribal organization may be another reason for the repetition in verse 9 of the phrase "This is the genealogy of Esau."

Esau's five sons are named again (vv. 10, 14). Eliphaz had seven grandsons, and Reuel had four, making eleven in all (vv. 11-13). These grandsons were all named "chiefs."

There is a question about Korah, who was certainly a chief, but perhaps the son-in-law of Eliphaz and not his actual son. He is included in verse 16 but not in other lists (cf. v. 11: 1 Chron. 1:36). To these eleven chiefs were added the three sons of Esau by Aholibamah. Thus, there were fourteen tribal chiefs altogether. Added to these chiefs were the seven sons of Seir, the Horite, who were also called chiefs (vv. 20-30). When Esau conquered the Horites, they were obviously allowed to manage their clans under his rule. The main point is that Esau's family had developed into a number of tribes with Esau as their powerful overlord.

After listing Esau's sons, grandsons, and the chiefs, verses 31 to 39 record eight kings who successively followed Esau, extending from Esau's time until the time of Moses (the last king's death not being mentioned). Moses shows us that Esau's family became a nation ruled by kings long before Israel had a king. All this was in fulfillment of Isaac's prophecy to Esau that he would dwell with the fatness of the earth, live by the sword, and shake off the yoke of his brother from his neck (27:39-40).

The chapter closes with another list of the chiefs, or perhaps chiefdoms, of Esau, the "father of the Edomites" (vv. 40-43). The names probably refer to geographical areas (like counties) that were named after certain chiefs, rather than to a succession of chiefs themselves.

In Conclusion

While chapter 36 is perhaps the least likely chapter in the whole book of Genesis from which commentators might draw spiritual lessons, there are some. We see the divine Author, through Moses, conveying the fact that God is interested in all people, even those outside of the covenant. He cared for Esau's family as well as Jacob's. We also learn that God keeps careful records concerning people. One day the books will be opened (cf. Rev. 20:11-12). Third, there is the contrast between Esau, the man of the world, and Jacob, the man of faith. That contrast carries over into the New Testament where we are warned of falling short of the grace of God "like Esau," who sold his birthright and was rejected (Heb. 12:16). We can also appreciate that God was faithful to His promises, both to Jacob and to Esau.

Joseph's Dreams and Betrayal

The final fourteen chapters of Genesis, apart from comprising the eleventh and final *toledoth* ("the generations of"), form the climax of Genesis. They bring to a conclusion the themes that have been developing since God first spoke to Abraham: the promised *seed* grew from one old man and his barren wife into an extended family of at least seventy within the bounds of the promised *land.* God was now putting into effect His master plan to relocate the whole family temporarily to Egypt. By the time they would reenter the land, Canaan itself would be ripe for God's judgment and ready for the *nation* of Israel to occupy it.

God was Preparing His People

One feature of these chapters is to explain *why* God moved them from Canaan to Egypt. *Numerically,* they needed a place where they could multiply in relative peace. They did this by living in a choice location under Pharaoh's favor. *Spiritually,* they needed to be separated from the idolatrous influence of the wicked Canaanites so that they could worship God with less distraction and be confined to marrying within their tribes. *Socially,* God wanted to teach them to overcome their intra-family rivalry and hatred and to learn to live with one another in peace.

Another feature of these final chapters is that they explain how the various inheritance rights of the twelve sons of Jacob came about. We learn how and why Judah, the fourth son, gained authority in the family and became head of the kingly line from which David, and ultimately Messiah, would come. We also learn why Joseph received the double portion of the inheritance.

The Genealogy of Jacob

The genealogy of Jacob begins with the death of Isaac and continues until the death of Jacob. It is, in large part, the story of Joseph and is certainly one of the most captivating narrative sections of the entire Bible. But, beyond its literary value, there are several reasons why it is well worth a detailed study. One reason is that Joseph's story is a direct fulfillment of prophetic revelation. God had told Abraham that his descendants would be strangers in a foreign land where they would suffer affliction. Eventually, God would judge that nation, and Abraham's descendants would come out with great possessions (15:13-14). Joseph's betrayal by his brothers, slavery in Egypt, rise to princely power, and bringing of the whole family there to live fulfilled the first part of this prophecy.

The Joseph Story

Another reason for studying these chapters in depth is that Joseph's story is a wonderful illustration of God's providence: God does indeed work all things together for good for those who trust Him (Rom. 8:28). God's sovereign work, even when it seems to be in conflict with His people's welfare, is designed to accomplish His perfect will. Joseph experienced much evil at his brothers' hands, but his eventual testimony was that what they intended for evil, God meant for good (50:20).

Joseph's life also powerfully illustrates many features of the life and work of Christ that we will highlight throughout the story. See also the comprehensive comparison chart at the end of this chapter. Though Joseph is not directly linked with Christ in the New Testament, there are so many parallels between them that God's intent in providing Joseph as a reflection of His Son is unmistakable.

Trouble in Jacob's Family (vv. 1-4)

Chapter 37 begins by reminding us that Jacob, like Isaac and Abraham, dwelt in the land as a "stranger" and a *sojourner,* a temporary resident (Heb. 11:9). God's promises still awaited fulfillment. Joseph lived in Hebron with his father Jacob and his grandfather Isaac, whose death was chronicled earlier in order to bring his story to completion (35:29). Joseph was born in Haran around the year 1745 BC, the youngest of the eleven sons born to Jacob there. Now, at seventeen years of age, his story begins to unfold.

Like his brothers, Joseph grew up as a shepherd, which necessitated traveling extensively to find pasture for their livestock. The combined factors of large herds and shortage of pasture meant that sometimes the brothers had to divide themselves and their flocks into separate groups and go in different directions. We find Joseph in a group with the sons of Bilhah and Zilpah (v. 2). It may be that Joseph was with them because Bilhah, his mother's maid, had taken a special interest in caring for him after Rachel's death. Thus, it would be natural for Joseph to accompany her sons in the field to learn the skills of animal husbandry. Joseph's brother Benjamin, still a toddler, was probably at home under Bilhah's care.

We immediately sense a growing tension between Joseph and his brothers, Dan, Naphtali, Gad, and Asher. They had done something dishonorable—we do not know what—while they were away shepherding the flocks. Joseph was concerned enough about it to tell his father. It was not the first time he had witnessed their evil deeds. The reader will recall the wholesale plundering of

Shechem, in which we have to assume Joseph took no part if his later exemplary conduct is anything to go by.

It is hard to say if Joseph was right to make this report, but we can assume that the brothers were guilty. Some commentators view him as a bratty talebearer, wanting to distance himself from the evil they were doing and curry favor with his father. Others believe he acted as a trusted son because he was concerned for Jacob's name. The thrust of the context leads us to best see him as the faithful son among unfaithful brothers. Whatever his motive, it most certainly angered his brothers because their evil was being exposed. The Lord Jesus Himself was hated because He pointed out the wickedness of the religious but unbelieving Pharisees. He said, "[The world] hates Me because I testify of it that its works are evil" (John 7:7). Joseph, like the Lord Jesus, was being faithful to his father, even though he knew his brothers would not like it. It is the first time we see Joseph exercising leadership and moral integrity. He is a good example to all would-be leaders.

The Tunic of Many Colors

Jacob, here called Israel, was no doubt embarrassed by his sons' evil behavior. Other sons, including Reuben, Simeon, and Levi, had brought dishonor on him in the past. Scripture says that he "loved Joseph more than all his children" (v. 3). Joseph was the first son of his favorite wife. His moral and spiritual standards were obviously higher than the others. He was called the "son of his old age," a phrase meaning he was a "wise son." In our idiom, we would say he was mature for his age. The phrase does not mean that there was a large age gap between him and his older brothers; all eleven had been born in a seven-year period (29:31-30:24).

Israel then gave Joseph a special tunic, familiarly known as a "coat of many colors" (KJV). Its Hebrew meaning is not certain. It was possibly a long-sleeved coat; perhaps it had been specially decorated. The same word indicates a regal robe in 2 Samuel 13:18. What Joseph's new coat meant to the family, however, was that he was being publicly recognized as having authority and position over his brothers. That coat heralded Joseph's changing fortunes: first, it was the symbol of his father's love and his status in the family; then, it was the object of his brother's hatred and rejection when he approached them at Dothan; and finally, it was the "proof" of his supposed death when it was flung at Jacob's feet.

Although it was their father who had given Joseph such honor, the brothers poured out their resentment on Joseph himself, a common reaction in this kind of situation. It was the coat especially that infuriated them. Israel may have had good reasons for his actions, but he was showing favoritism, which always creates resentment among those not so favored. Evidently, he had not learned from his boyhood experience when his own parents had played favorites with Esau and himself with terrible consequences. Now, all of Joseph's brothers perceived their father's favoritism and hated Joseph. They could not even bring themselves to greet him (v. 4). It would not be long before their bitterness led to a sinful reaction.

Joseph's Dreams (vv. 5-11)

The tension between them escalated when Joseph related his first dream to his brothers (vv. 5-7). The word "behold" in verse 7 occurs three times in the original text, which adds to the impact of recounting it. It would sound something like this: *"Behold* my sheaf arose and also stood upright; and *behold* your sheaves stood all around; and *behold* they bowed down to my sheaf." To their ears, Joseph was boasting. His brothers understood the meaning and immediately reacted with envy and heavy sarcasm saying, "Shall you indeed have dominion over us?" (v. 8). Their envy is understandable from a human perspective, but viewed in the light of Joseph's faithfulness, it demonstrates why their father did not favor them.

In Joseph's second dream, he saw the sun, moon, and eleven stars bowing down to him. The sun and moon stood for his father and mother and the eleven stars for his brothers. He related this dream to his brothers also, and they grew angrier than before. Even Jacob rebuked Joseph this time. "Shall your mother and I and your brothers indeed come to bow down to the earth before you?" (v. 10). He did understand that the dreams were to be taken seriously, however; instinctively, he sensed some purpose of God in them. Jacob "kept the matter in mind" (v. 11).

Dreams Without Words

These dreams are the first revelations recorded in the Bible where God's voice is not heard. Up to chapter 35, God revealed Himself by appearances, dreams, and visions, in all of which He spoke audibly. But Joseph's dreams, as well as those of the butcher and the baker and later those of Pharaoh, were simply visual revelations. In all three instances, the dreams came in pairs, probably for emphasis. In these final chapters of Genesis, with the exception of His appearance to Jacob in chapter 46, God communicated *visually* through symbolic dreams and *providentially* through circumstances.

Why did Joseph relate these dreams to his brothers when he knew they already resented him deeply? We do not know. He was wise to tell his father, but to tell his brothers seems unwise except in the light of the future events that would unfold in Egypt. Those brothers would eventually come to realize that the dreams had been prophetic revelations from God. God's intention and design was for the dreams to give Joseph personal comfort and hope in view of the suffering he was to endure before long.

The dreams announced Joseph's future glory. The Lord Jesus, likewise, awaits a day when every knee will bow before Him (Phil. 2:10-11). Joseph's brothers would bow once when they first met him in Egypt. Later, they would bow twice, and ultimately they would throw themselves at his feet (42:6; 43:26-28; 50:18). Just as Joseph had this dream to comfort him during his suffering, so the Lord Jesus anticipated "the joy that was set before Him" while He endured the Cross. Both were rejected by those closest to them. Jesus' Jewish brothers cried out, "We will not have this man to reign over us" (Luke 19:14; cf. John 19:15). In both Joseph and Jesus' sufferings, we see further evidence of the enmity between the "seed of Satan" and the "Seed of the woman."

Joseph is Sent to His Brothers (vv. 12–17)

It is likely that Jacob's sons had largely taken over responsibility for the business and made their own decisions about where to graze the animals. But why, of all places, would they take their flocks to Shechem? It had only been a few years since they massacred the men of the city. Maybe it was the memory of that horrific episode that increased Jacob's routine concern for the welfare of his sons and his livestock and prompted him to send Joseph to check on them. Shechem was probably still in ruins with few people living in the area, but even a few could have made trouble for them.

Jacob probably did not know how intensely his sons hated Joseph, or he would never have sent him. Joseph responded immediately to his father's request with "Here I am." What marks Joseph here is his obedience, no matter what prospect of danger lay ahead of him. Jacob explained his mission: "Please go and see if it is well with your brothers and well with the flocks, and bring word back to me" (v. 14). The phrase "if it is well" is interesting because it is the common word of greeting—"Shalom"—still used by Jews in Israel. The word as used here has an ominous note because, in verse 4, the brothers could not speak *shalom,* or peaceably, to Joseph.

The fifty-mile journey to Shechem would have taken Joseph two days, but after not finding them, he sought them farther afield and finally met a man who told him that they had moved on to Dothan, another fifteen miles north. In all of this, Joseph's obedience to his father reflects something of the obedience of the Lord Jesus Christ who came to do His Father's will, even in hostile circumstances. Just as Joseph went looking for his brothers, so the Lord Jesus "came unto His own" (John 1:11)—but they, too, "received him not."

Joseph's Brothers Plot to Kill Him (vv. 18-24)

It would have taken Joseph another day to reach Dothan and locate his brothers with their herds. The sight of him approaching from a distance brought back to their minds his dreams about ruling over them, and their pent up resentment boiled over. Before he came close, they began plotting to kill him. They said, "Look, this dreamer is coming!" (v. 19). *Dreamer* means literally "master of dreams;" we can almost hear the derision in their voices. They wanted to make sure that Joseph's dreams did not come to pass, and here was a perfect opportunity. They said to one another, "Come therefore, let us now kill him and cast him into some pit" (v. 20). The plan was to cover up their crime by saying "some wild beast has devoured him." So much for Joseph's dream predicting he would rule over them one day! It is significant that Joseph's dream bothered them even more than his tunic. Their plot to kill Joseph reflects the plan of the Pharisees who looked for opportunities to kill the Lord Jesus (Matt. 26:3-4; Mark 3:6).

Reuben's input is interesting. He was of a mild disposition, but he was up against the impetuous spirits of Simeon and Levi, at least. As the oldest, he was the one who would have to give account to their father. Instead of killing Joseph, he suggested simply throwing him into a pit. He was hoping to quietly "rescue" Joseph later (v. 22). The brothers accepted Reuben's plan, but he appears to have left Joseph in their "care," perhaps to go look after the herds. He did not exert or sustain his leadership role to see his secret plan through. This incident sets a negative example for all leaders today; constancy and consistency are essential characteristics of good leadership.

Having taken hold of Joseph and stripped him of that despised robe (in effect taking away the title of the "royal son"), they roughly threw him into a dry pit. The word "cast" indicates that they used some force. They left him there without food or drink then callously sat down to eat within earshot of Joseph's cries. Many years later, when they were sensing their own guilt over this occasion, they admitted that they were aware of his distress, yet they would not listen (42:21). Similarly, the Lord's own brethren despised and rejected Him; one day they will confess that they hid their faces from Him and did not esteem Him (Isa. 53:3).

Judah Plots to Sell Joseph as a Slave (vv. 25-30)

With no apparent concern for Joseph, his brothers sat down to eat. They saw a camel caravan approaching made up of a group of spice traders from Gilead (east of Jordan) on their way to Egypt. They were called both Ishmaelites and Midianites (vv. 25 and 28) because the group was probably made up of some of each nationality. Both groups were descendants of Abraham. Judah came up with a third plan for what to do with Joseph. He said, "What profit is there if we kill our brother and conceal his blood? Come and let us sell him to the Ishmaelites, and let not our hand be upon him, for he is our brother and our own flesh" (vv. 26-27). His brothers agreed to this scheme. By selling Joseph as a slave, they were not only getting rid of him, but they were also going to profit in the amount of twenty shekels of silver.

In the end, the only difference between their original plot and this one was the sale. They had captured him, taken his coat, rid themselves of him, and still planned to lie about him to their father. Like Joseph, the Lord Jesus was betrayed by a "Judah"—Judas, one of his close companions. He, too, was sold into the hand of His enemies—"valued" at thirty pieces of silver, the price of a slave that had been gored by an ox (Ex. 21:32; Matt. 26:15).

When Reuben returned to the pit to release Joseph, he was gone. Although he tore his garments as a sign of grief, his words indicate his concern was for himself as much as for Joseph (v. 30). There is no record of him confronting his brothers, and there was nothing he could do at that point to help Joseph. In his weakness, the only thing he did do was join with them in plans to deceive their father. Reuben was a total failure as a family leader.

The Deception of Jacob (vv. 31-36)

For their cover-up, they slaughtered a goat and dipped Joseph's long coat in its blood to give the impression that Joseph had encountered a wild beast. They brought the coat to Jacob, saying, "We have found this. Do you know whether it is your son's tunic or not?" (v. 32). They did not directly lie, but they did deliberately deceive him. Predictably, Jacob said, "It is my son's tunic. A wild beast has devoured him. Without doubt Joseph is torn to pieces." The wicked brothers all let him make these wrong assumptions; they all became part of the deception.

This is the most pitiful part in this chapter. Jacob mourned deeply for his favorite son. All his family tried to console him, but he refused to be comforted (v. 35). Their treachery had not only caused Joseph to be sold into slavery, but it had also brought terrible pain to his father. Joseph was the eldest son of his beloved Rachel; the only son who was faithful and honest. Jacob had given him the robe of authority in the family, but now all his hopes were dashed. He believed his son was dead because he left God out of his reckoning. Little did he know that God's providential hand was in it all and that one day Joseph would save the whole family from starvation. We can learn from this that, no matter what seemingly terrible things happen to us, God's program will not be put off track. This was true for both Joseph and Jacob in their respective distressing situations.

The chapter ends with a postscript as to where the Midianites had taken Joseph. When they reached Egypt, they sold him to Potiphar, an officer of the Pharaoh and the captain of the bodyguard. Although there is no comment as to Joseph's emotions, he must have been afraid, disappointed, homesick, and perhaps resentful as well.

In Conclusion

We have seen that Joseph pictures the person and experiences of Christ. There are so many similarities between them in this chapter that it may help us to compare some of them in detail. They are remarkable and worthy of our meditation as we conclude this chapter.

Joseph, the son of Jacob	Jesus Christ, the Son of God
Was a shepherd (v. 2)	Is the Good Shepherd (John 10:11)
Stood for truth and righteousness when he reported the evil of his brothers (v. 2)	Lived a perfect life in contrast to that of His brethren (Heb. 7:26)
Was the beloved son of his father (v. 3)	Is the beloved Son of God the Father (Matt. 3:17)
Was given a coat of distinction by his father because he always pleased him (v. 3)	Always pleased His Father (Matt. 3:7; John 8:29)
Was hated by his brothers (v. 4)	Was hated by the Scribes and Pharisees (John 15:24-25)
Was aware of his coming glory (v. 5-9)	Was aware that He would return in glory on the clouds of heaven (Matt. 26:64)
Was envied by his brothers (v. 11)	Was envied by His enemies (Matt. 7:17-18)
Was sent on a mission by his father (v. 13)	Was sent on a mission by His Father (1 John 4:10)
Sought the welfare of his brothers who did not want him (vv. 13-14)	Came to His own but they received Him not (John 1:11)
Left home and came to Shechem, a place of sin and sorrow (v. 15; cf. Gen. 34)	Left heaven to come to a sin-cursed world (Phil. 2:5-7)
Looked for his brothers until he found them (vv. 15-17)	Looked for and found the lost sheep of the tribe of Israel (Matt. 10:6)
Was plotted against by his brothers (vv. 18-22)	Was plotted against by the ruling Jews (Matt. 12:14)
Was stripped of his coat (v. 23)	Was stripped of His garment (Matt. 27:28)
Was sold as a slave for twenty pieces of silver (v. 28)	Was sold for the price of a slave, thirty pieces of silver (Matt. 26:15)

We can only marvel at these many similarities and thank God again that His beloved Son was willing to suffer reproach, shame, and dishonor (Ps. 69:19) to accomplish our salvation.

The Family of Judah

After Joseph's brothers betrayed him into the hands of the Midianites, the story of Joseph is interrupted by an extraordinary episode in the life of Judah, Jacob's fourth son by Leah. The chapter extends from the time of Joseph's betrayal to his family's removal to Egypt, about twenty-three years. Judah, like all Jacob's sons, would have known that one of God's covenant promises was to create a nation from them as numerous as "the dust of the earth." The sons' response and responsibility was, of course, to obey God's command to Jacob to "be fruitful and multiply" (35:11). However, this chapter recounts how Judah's line struggled to survive owing to their being in a state of spiritual weakness and moral bankruptcy.

The Significance of this Chapter

Not only is this story itself strange, but its inclusion in the Bible seems odd until we understand why.

- The Israelites in the wilderness would need to know why Judah became the leading tribe. This chapter provides the family history that establishes Judah's line and the beginning of his spiritual transformation that opened the way for his leadership.

- It was important for them to know how the sons of Tamar the Canaanite became the leaders of the clans of Judah.

- It records what prompted Judah's change of heart; it was, after all, he who initiated Joseph being sold into slavery.

- The overtly evil nature of Judah's sons, raised by a pagan mother in a pagan environment, illustrated the terribly corruptive power of Canaanite society. God removed the covenant family to Egypt until they were a large enough force to be able to fight and destroy the Canaanites.

- It explains how Tamar's son, Perez, rather than his twin brother, Zerah, came to be in the line of Messiah.

Though God is hardly mentioned, the story does display His providence in a wicked society, working out His will amid circumstances that were ruled by pride and lust.

Judah's Marriage (vv. 1-5)

Shortly after the wicked betrayal of Joseph and the grief it caused Jacob, Judah wanted to get away from Hebron. Perhaps he was feeling his own guilt. He left the family home and "went down" (from the hills to the lowlands) to Adullam to stay with his Canaanite friend Hirah. He did not, however, abandon his family connections in Hebron, for when it was necessary to go to Egypt for food, he accompanied his brothers. Nor did he go far: Adullam lies only fifteen miles northwest of Hebron.

Evidently part of Judah's reason for leaving was to look for a wife, and before long he found one: the daughter of a Canaanite named Shua. We never do learn her name. The Scripture says, "He saw ... he married her and went in to her." There is no indication that he consulted with Jacob or that his wife was interested in following the true God. In that pagan cultural setting, she bore Judah three sons, two of whom are described as "evil." Judah's marriage to a Canaanite was not in harmony with the plan of the patriarchs. Isaac and Jacob had both taken believing wives from Abraham's family in Haran (28:1). It is wrong for a believer today to even consider marrying an unbeliever. The Scripture makes it plain that an "unequal yoke" is sin and leads to disharmony and tragedy in the home (2 Cor. 6:14-18).

The three sons, Er, Onan, and Shelah, were born in quick succession (vv. 3-5). By the time that Shelah was born, they had moved to the nearby town of Chezib that was later settled by his descendants (v. 5; 1 Chron. 4:21-22). The boys evidently grew up knowing little of their father's God.

Er Marries Tamar (vv. 6-7)

Judah knew it was crucial that his sons marry and bear him grandchildren for the fulfillment of God's promise to Abraham, Isaac, and Jacob. When his son Er was old enough to marry, Judah took the lead and obtained a wife for him named Tamar. Though she was a Canaanite, he probably discerned some spiritual quality in her. Er, however, was "wicked in the sight of the Lord." In the context of the whole passage, God's assessment of him probably had to do with his refusal to consummate his arranged marriage. If so, he was rebelling against God's purpose both for marriage generally and for Abraham's descendants specifically. God judged him by taking his life. Judah knew that and the reason for it.

Onan Marries Tamar (vv. 8-11)

Judah then instructed his son Onan to marry Tamar, telling him to "raise up an heir to your brother." The custom of all the peoples of that day was that when an older brother died without an heir, his younger brother would marry his brother's widow and their son would inherit the older brother's estate. Later, this custom was accepted into the Mosaic Law and was called levirate marriage (Deut. 25:5-10; Matt. 22:24). Much later, Boaz married Ruth under the laws of levirate marriage (Ruth 1-4). The name *levirate* comes from the Latin *levir* which means "brother-in-law."

Tamar agreed with Judah's goal to produce an heir. Onan, for his part, complied with marrying Tamar and presumably consummated the marriage but must have consistently seen to it thereafter that his "seed" spilled on the ground to ensure that Tamar never conceived. In this way, he demonstrated his own rebellious spirit in not wanting to produce an heir for his brother and was therefore going against God's purposes. His sin was not in wasting his seed but in refusing to enable Tamar to have children and effectively nullifying his father's plan. He thus rebelled against God, so God took his life too (v.10). Of both Er and Onan, it says that "the LORD killed him" (vv. 7, 10).

Judah had one more son, Shelah, who was evidently just too young to marry, in the sense of not having quite reached puberty. The boys must have married in their youth for the complete story to have taken place in the twenty-three year time frame. Judah wanted an heir, but he also feared for his only remaining son's life. Tamar, as Er and Onan's widow, was Judah's responsibility, but Judah was afraid that she would bring more bad fortune on the family. Although he had no intention of giving Tamar to Shelah, he told her to return to her home until Shelah was old enough to marry her (v. 11). Perhaps he thought that time and distance would prompt her to start a new life. Her presence was an irritation and embarrassment to him.

Judah's Wife Dies (v. 12)

It was not long before another blow fell on Judah: his wife died. Judah would have been about forty-two years old. Her untimely death may have been a stroke of the Lord's discipline on him. After a time of mourning, he returned to his shepherding duties and joined the sheep shearing festivities at Timnah with his friend Hirah (v. 12). Contrary to Judah's hopes, Tamar had *not* given up her right and desire to provide an heir for Judah's family. We can infer that she longed to do her part in God's plan that Judah had explained to her and that she no doubt resented being back at her pagan home. She belonged in Judah's home, where she had an opportunity to follow Judah's God. She showed a persevering spirit by devising a plan that was both bizarre and dangerous.

Tamar's Desperate Plan (vv. 13-23)

Judah had brought Tamar into the family and successively promised her his three sons in marriage. However, he had reneged on giving her to Shelah, though he was now past puberty. Tamar believed in the promises about God's future for His people and His land, so she enacted her plan, trusting that God would enable her to produce a son. She exchanged her widow's clothing for something attractive and wore a veil to hide her identity. She then presented herself as a temple prostitute in the gateway of Enam. Temple prostitutes were "a step above" the usual kind and an accepted part of Canaanite culture. She selected a place where she knew Judah would pass by. She hoped he would notice her and seek her "services." In doing, this she was not pursuing a life of prostitution. She was deliberately trying to get pregnant by Judah and force him to fulfill his promise to her when she married his sons, that of providing him with a son and heir. The risks to both her and Judah were enormous, but she took them, believing it was the only thing she could do.

Judah did notice her and said, "Let me come in to you." The author wants us to know that he did not intentionally commit adultery with his daughter-in-law, for he did not recognize her. Nor, when he left home, had he planned this action, for he had nothing with him with which to pay her. Nevertheless, we do see him giving in to the pagan practices of the day. When she asked, "What will you give me?" he promised a kid from the flock. She was careful to seek a pledge for his payment: his signet, which was a mark of authority that he wore around his neck, and his staff that would have been etched with his name marked on top. When their act was completed, she departed and resumed wearing her widow's garments. Even after all this, Scripture does not cast moral judgment on Tamar. In fact, her daring plan to address Judah's sin is commended (38:26; cf. Ruth 4:12). Her one aim was to raise up seed for her deceased husband.

Judah's Hypocrisy Revealed (vv. 24-30)

Judah did honor his commitment by sending Hirah with the kid hoping to retrieve the pledge. Hirah, of course, could not find her. Judah decided to keep quiet for the sake of his reputation. He thought that the matter would end there, and no one but himself and Hirah would ever know what he did. After all, what good were his seal and staff to a prostitute? Little did he know!

God's sovereign hand was in the situation in that Tamar did conceive by means of that one time act. Three months later, Judah was told that Tamar had "played the harlot" and was pregnant. She was, in theory, still betrothed to Shelah, and it was Judah's responsibility to see that justice was done. His reaction seems harsh: he immediately called for her to "be burned." Privately he may have been relieved that this opportunity to get her out of the way had presented itself. His responsibility to her would be over. She was brought to the place of judgment, usually the gate of the city, and accused of harlotry; at this point, she produced the seal and the staff and declared, "By the man to whom these things belong, I am with child" (v. 25). Judah recognized them and immediately confessed his part in the affair. He also understood her motive and said, "She has been more righteous than I, because I did not give her to Shelah my son" (v. 26).

Judah's reputation had been hurt once more, but it brought him to his senses, and he admitted that he had been immoral, hypocritical, and negligent of his family responsibilities. He realized that it wasn't Tamar who had brought ill fortune on the family; it was he who had been the root cause of his sons' death by marrying into the Canaanite culture in the first place. Having confessed his sins, we can assume that God forgave him. From this point on, Judah began to rise in his life of faith. Judah could no longer give Tamar to Shelah as a wife, but neither did he marry her himself. What he did do was to accept her offspring as his legitimate child with the plan to raise it as his own.

The Birth of Perez and Zerah

When Tamar's time for delivery came, "behold, twins were in her womb" (v. 27). She had not expected twins. During the birth process, one of them put his hand out, and the midwife tied a red thread on it because she presumed this was the child that would be born first. However, he pulled his hand back, and the other twin was born first. Once again in Genesis, a "younger" brother prevailed in a struggle with his "older" brother—though in this case, the child actually born first was the one intended to be in the line of blessing. The firstborn was called Perez, meaning "to break out." His name also signified the end of Tamar's struggle to bear "seed" for the line of Judah. Perez was the father of the Perezites, the leading tribe of Judah and the kingly line through which David was born, and ultimately the Messiah (Matt. 1:3). The twin with the red thread around his hand was named Zerah. He became the head of the Zerahites. In the course of time, Judah's third son, Shelah, must have married, for we later read that one of Judah's clans was called the Shelahites (Num. 26:20).

In Conclusion

There are some lessons for us in this bizarre story. In the first place, sometimes God's people do rebellious things that tend to complicate God's program, as Judah did when he married a Canaanite. Second, God *will* discipline and humble His children when they disregard His will for their own selfish reasons. In Judah's case, he "humbled himself in the sight of the Lord," and God eventually "lifted him up" by endorsing his tribe as the head tribe of Israel and as the one through whom the Messiah was born.

Even Tamar might offer us a lesson from the risks she took to accomplish what she believed to be God's purpose. We cannot, however, sanction the methods she used. Tamar has the honor of being one of the few women named in the official genealogy of Jesus (Matt. 1:3). Like the other three Gentile women listed there (Rahab, Ruth, and Bathsheba), she came from a pagan background. All four had unsavory things in their past, and all became strong believers in the Lord. These women give powerful testimony to the grace of God.

Joseph in the House of Potiphar

In chapter 39, the narrative of Genesis returns to the story of Joseph that was interrupted by the account of Judah and Tamar. Chapter 37 marked the end of Joseph's life in Canaan. This chapter takes up the story of his life in Egypt that continues through most of the rest of Genesis. In Canaan, he was the favored son, honored above his brothers, only to be betrayed and humiliated by them. The pattern will repeat itself in Egypt where Joseph held an exalted position in Potiphar's house, only to be betrayed and humiliated by Potiphar's wife. It was all part of the training process through which God was preparing Joseph for his great responsibility in the future. The purpose of God's discipline is not always to punish or correct; sometimes it is to strengthen by giving opportunities to "pass the test." What is always true is that God's intent is to mature His people spiritually by purifying and refining them, both for their good and His glory.

There are three distinct sections to this chapter:

- Verses 1-6: Joseph's success and prosperity in Potiphar's house.
- Verses 7-20: Joseph's refusal to yield to sexual temptation from Potiphar's wife.
- Verse 21-23: Joseph's success and prosperity in prison.

In the first and third sections, the Lord's presence with Joseph is emphasized because it led to his prosperity in both Potiphar's house and the prison. In both places, Joseph earned a high reputation with his masters, Potiphar and the jailor. The two sections about Joseph's success frame the center section regarding his being tempted to sin. Joseph's great victory over temptation becomes one of the classic passages on the issue in all of Scripture.

Egypt, Land of Joseph's Imprisonment

Egypt, where Joseph would spend the rest of his life, was an ancient, highly civilized nation that was ruled by a strong government. Its religion was polytheistic (they worshipped many gods), and its culture was morally degraded. It was ruled at this time by conquerors from the East called the Hyksos who invaded Egypt in about 1720 BC. The Hyksos were of partially Semitic stock. It may be for that reason that they looked more favorably on allowing the

Israelites to live within their boundaries (45:18), as they, too, were Semitic. It may also explain why Potiphar is called the "Egyptian" three times in the chapter to distinguish him from the Hyksos rulers (vv. 1, 2, 5). They in turn were expelled before the time of Moses and replaced by Egyptians. Their expulsion explains why the Pharaoh in Moses' day "did not know Joseph" (Ex. 1:8).

Potiphar is called by his full title, "the captain of the Pharaoh's bodyguard" (literally "chief of the executioners"). He held one of the more important political positions in Egypt. He is also called an "officer of Pharaoh." The Hebrew word for *officer* means "eunuch" (cf. 2 Kings 20:18; 23:11; Jer. 39:13). This may indicate that Potiphar was compelled to submit to the custom of many rulers whereby they ordered their high officers to be castrated to thwart any ambition they might have to take over the kingdom and establish dynasties of their own. Daniel is an example of this practice in the Babylonian kingdom. If this was true in Potiphar's case, he must have consented to the procedure in order to gain high office. It may also explain why Potiphar's wife made such bold sexual advances toward Joseph.

The Character and Person of Joseph

Joseph was a highly intelligent, capable, and personable young man. He was of exceptionally high moral integrity and trustworthiness. Joseph's character led to his rapid advance among the many servants of Potiphar. It is often true that unbelieving employers like to employ believers because they benefit from their personal integrity and honesty. It is an incentive for believers to live and work as God's representatives so that opportunities may present themselves for speaking of their faith in Christ. Joseph's experience can be contrasted here to that of the Lord Jesus, whose exemplary character had the opposite effect on the authority figures of His day.

Joseph's Prosperity in Potiphar's House (vv. 1-6)

The first verse repeats the information given in Genesis 37:36, except it is recounted from the Egyptian viewpoint: Potiphar, one of Pharaoh's officers, bought (as opposed to "the Midianites sold") Joseph from the Ishmaelites (not the Midianites). As we noted in chapter 37, the trading caravan consisted of some from both peoples.

We also learn that "the LORD was with Joseph" (v. 2). Although his brothers had betrayed him and sold him into slavery, the Lord was with him. The promise of God's presence is one of Scripture's most repeated promises and the essence of one of the Lord Jesus' names, *Immanuel,* which means "God with us." God's presence with Joseph was the key to his prosperity in Potiphar's house. Even as a slave in a foreign land, he was aware of the presence of God.

Joseph's prosperity pictures the Lord Jesus Christ, of whom Jehovah said, "He shall see His seed, He shall prolong His days, and the pleasure of the LORD shall prosper in His hand" (Isa. 53:10). Prosperity to the Hebrews meant that of body, mind, and soul. It was certainly not limited to material possessions. By it, Joseph could see beyond his circumstances to the Lord and the future.

Joseph's Promotion in Potiphar's House

Joseph's immediate circumstance placed him "in the house with his master the Egyptian" (v. 2). Thus he began life as a slave in Potiphar's house. Very quickly, Joseph's excellent work caught his master's attention. Potiphar was astute enough to see that it was Joseph's God who gave him success in all he did. Having found favor in Potiphar's eyes, he was soon promoted to the position of overseer of Potiphar's house and industry. While Joseph was in charge, "The LORD blessed" everything Potiphar owned. It is an outworking of God's first promise to Abraham that whoever blesses the seed of Abraham would himself be blessed (12:1-3).

Joseph's success should encourage all employees, whether of high or low status, to have a high work ethic. Paul encouraged the Colossians in this way: "Whatever you do, do it heartily, as to the Lord and not to men, knowing that from the Lord you will receive the reward of the inheritance" (Col. 3:23-24).

We have seen Joseph's prosperity in terms of his enjoyment of God's presence and his promotion by Potiphar in verses 3 to 6. All this comes to a climax in the last phrase of verse 6: "and Joseph was handsome in form and appearance," that is, he was handsome in face and figure. The same description is used of his mother Rachel (29:17) and of King David and his son Absalom. The assessment of Joseph's physical appearance prepares us for the next section about the sexual advances of Potiphar's wife.

The Temptation of Joseph (vv. 7-19)

Scripture deliberately dishonors Potiphar's wife by not naming her (as with Lot and Judah's respective wives). By means of the role she played in Joseph's life, however, God was further testing Joseph in secret to prepare him for service in public. Unlike the test of his betrayal, this test gave him the choice to submit to temptation or to flee from it. He was far from home, in complete privacy, with an attractive proposition; it would have been so easy to submit and so hard to resist. Joseph chose to resist under the eye of God. He was well aware of God's original design for marriage. God ordered that sexual intimacy between man and woman was to be confined to the marriage bond (1:27-28; 2:22-24). Though this principle had been violated—even within his own family—Joseph resolved to personally honor and defend it.

The temptation to sin came in three cycles, each more severe than the last, and ended in the false accusation of the very thing he had refused to do.

The First Temptation—Direct Proposition

The first is recorded in verses 6-9. Joseph's manliness obviously attracted Potiphar's wife. She deliberately tried to seduce Joseph into bed with her.

Joseph was a healthy young man and was no doubt flattered by her attention as she "cast longing eyes at [him]." Her body language was a prelude to her blatant verbal invitation: "Lie with me." Her appeal to Joseph's legitimate passions doubled the force of the temptation.

Joseph's response was a polite refusal, and he explained the reasons why such sexual intimacy between them was wrong. First, it would violate the trust that Potiphar had placed in him. He said, "My master ... has committed all that he has to my hand" (v. 8). To breach that trust would display ingratitude to him. The second reason (assuming Joseph was not aware that Potiphar may have been a eunuch) was that it would violate her husband's marital rights. He said, "Nor has he kept back anything from me but you." Potiphar's wife belonged to him alone. Joseph's final reason for refusing his temptress's overtures was the overriding one. "How then can I do this great wickedness, and sin against God?" (v. 9). Such a sin would offend God's authority; it was He who set the bounds of marriage. It would also offend God's holiness; it was He who placed moral standards on man whom He made in His own image. For Joseph to deliberately sin against his God was incongruous to him as a believer.

Therefore, Joseph's reasons for refusal were his clear *responsibility* to his master's trust, his *obligation* to the exclusiveness of the marriage bond, and his *faithfulness* to God's moral standards. He would not consent to her request.

The Second Temptation—Constant Pressure

But Potiphar's wife did not take "no" for an answer (v. 10). She kept after Joseph day after day, even though he was unresponsive to her sexual charms. No doubt she tried all the subtle ways she could think of to get him into a compromising situation: being constantly near him, praising his work, his appearance, and his manhood with flattery and endearments. She hoped that what she had failed to achieve by direct means she could accomplish by wearing down his resistance, but Joseph "did not heed her." Rather than revisit the issue with her, he simply closed his ears and eyes to her. Continual pressure can be harder to resist than a sudden proposition. Many committed believers have been worn down by persistent "attack" until they yield to the temptation. The same people would have resisted the more overt kind of temptation that Joseph experienced at first. Joseph stood firm, however, against both kinds of pressure.

The Third Temptation—Sensual Attack

Potiphar's wife tried one more tactic (vv. 11-12). What she had failed to accomplish by direct proposition and constant pressure, she now tried by sensual attack. She took advantage of a time when all the other servants were out of the house. Catching Joseph unawares, she grabbed hold of his garment (obviously a loosely-worn robe) and forcibly pulled him close. She hoped that passion would overcome reason and that she would succeed in seducing him. Joseph realized the danger and pulled himself away. He ran outside, leaving his garment in her hands. He did the only thing he could do in the circumstances—he ran. He had been faithful to God, and all he could do now was to trust himself to the One who was "with him"—no matter what the consequences might be.

Potiphar's Wife Retaliates

The woman's pride was sorely wounded by Joseph's refusal, and she wasn't going to let him get away with it (vv. 13-19). Shakespeare well said, "Hell hath no fury like a woman scorned." She first called the men of the household and blamed her husband for employing Joseph. She told them, "See, he has brought in to us a Hebrew to mock us. He came in to me to lie with me, and I cried out with a loud voice" (v. 14), and she produced Joseph's clothing as evidence. When Potiphar came home, she again claimed to be the victim and blamed her husband to his face with the same prejudicial language against Joseph. Twice she cast slurs on Joseph by calling him a *Hebrew* and a *servant,* and twice she implicated her husband in the "crime" by blaming him for bringing Joseph into the house in the first place (vv. 14, 17, 19).

Joseph Imprisoned (v. 20)

Potiphar had no choice but to dismiss and punish Joseph. The text says that "his anger was aroused." Curiously, it does not say that his anger was directed against Joseph, simply that he was angry, perhaps because he was going to lose Joseph's outstanding service and the profit that Joseph had brought him. It is quite feasible that Potiphar trusted Joseph more than he did his wife and that he really did not believe her. What Potiphar did with Joseph seems to confirm this: he did not commit him to the criminal prison or have him executed as he could have done (being the king's executioner), but he put him in jail with the king's prisoners over whom he had charge. All of this indicates that God was overseeing what was happening to Joseph.

It may be that Potiphar hoped to employ Joseph again one day but God was placing him in the prison near the palace where one day he would be exalted. It is easy to forget that only a few walls separated Joseph in the prison from Pharaoh on the throne.

How often it is that believers who have suffered injustice end up where they would not choose! But it may well be that injustice done to us is part of God's plan for something wonderful to come.

Joseph Did Not Defend Himself

There is no indication in the text that Joseph tried to defend himself. He may have sensed relief that God had removed him from that sphere of temptation and that no matter where he was sent he could hold his head high before his God. He knew that Potiphar could not publicly take a servant's word over that of his wife. Thus, he accepted his plight as one more step in God's will for him. The lack of any recorded protest prefigures the Lord Jesus Christ who, like Joseph, was falsely accused and, like Joseph, did not open his mouth (Isa. 53:7; Matt. 27:12-14; 1 Pet. 2:19-23). The apostle Peter's observations emphasize the Lord's quiet acceptance of His suffering as an example to all of us when we endure injustice to "commit" ourselves "to Him who judges righteously."

Overcoming Temptation

Joseph's victory over sin sets a classic example as to how to overcome temptation. Note three important aspects about him:

- He lived in the conscious presence of God. "The LORD was with Joseph" (v. 2).

- He was more concerned with the holiness of God than with gratifying his flesh. He said, "How can I do this great wickedness, and sin against God?" (v. 9).

- When "fighting" the temptation did not bring him relief, he fled to separate himself from it. The New Testament also instructs us to flee: "Flee ... youthful lusts" (2 Tim. 2:22). Running from overwhelming temptation is not a sign of weakness but of wisdom and strength.

Joseph in Prison (vv. 21-23)

Joseph's fortunes were still in decline. He had suffered betrayal at the hands of his brothers, humiliation at being sold into slavery, and injustice at being falsely accused of a serious offence. God had allowed these downward steps for a purpose. In each step, Joseph was faithful to God and sound in character and work.

There in the prison, God rewarded Joseph's faithfulness as He had rewarded him in Potiphar's service. Three parallel things happened in both situations:

- Just as "The LORD was with Joseph" (v. 2) in Potiphar's house, so He was with him in prison (v. 21). When Joseph sensed God's presence, he knew God approved of his character and behavior.

- Just as Potiphar recognized him as extremely capable and worthy of greater responsibilities, so the prison warden noticed him because of these same traits. He "committed to Joseph's hand all the prisoners who were in the prison." This did not mean that Joseph was living in luxury. The Psalmist declared that they "hurt his feet with fetters" (Ps. 105:18). Whether this means literal iron chains or simply that he was in prison is not clear, but it certainly does not indicate that he had an easy time.

- The third parallel with his experience in Potiphar's house was that "whatever he did, the LORD made it prosper" (v. 23; cf. v. 3).

Prosperity in Adversity

Joseph's experience in both situations illustrates the principle of prosperity in adversity: spiritual blessing is available for all believers who faithfully live in the light of God's presence, no matter how bad the circumstances. The poise and peace that result from living righteously in trials is the consequent blessing of God. His active presence—sovereignly controlling events and providing the strength to endure—is the key. Seventeen hundred years later, when Stephen was giving a sweeping review of Israel's history, he deliberately mentioned that even though Joseph's brothers sold him into Egypt, "God was with him" (Acts 7:9).

Joseph's trust in God, even though he was unjustly treated by his brothers and by Potiphar's wife, is in pointed contrast to Jacob's lack of trust in God when he ran away to Haran and relied on his own wisdom and strength. Joseph's confidence that God was in control gave him strength to resist temptation and remain faithful even in prison. His success in prison indicated God's approval. All the while, Joseph probably remembered his prophetic dreams about his future glory and was able to hope in the future despite the stormy clouds of the present.

We, too, live in the light of coming glory. We can follow Joseph's wonderful example by being faithful to our earthly masters and our God, no matter what the circumstances.

In Conclusion

In a number of ways, this chapter is rich with incidents in Joseph's life that picture similar incidents in the life of the Lord Jesus. Listed below are some of the parallels. A study of these will be most profitable for the believer.

Joseph was a servant (v. 1)	Jesus took the form of a bondservant (Phil. 2:6-7)
Joseph prospered (v. 3)	It was prophesied of Jesus: "The pleasure of the Lord shall prosper in his hand" (Isa. 53:10)
Joseph was strongly tempted, yet he did not sin (vv. 7-12)	Jesus was tempted by Satan yet did not yield (Matt. 4:10)
Joseph was tempted three different ways (vv. 8-11)	Jesus was tempted three different ways by Satan (Matt. 4:1-11)
Joseph was falsely accused by Potiphar's wife (vv. 14-18)	Jesus was accused by false witnesses (Matt. 16:59-60)
Joseph did not defend himself (vv. 14-18)	Jesus did not defend Himself (Isa. 53:7)
Joseph was cast into prison (v. 20)	Jesus was arrested and imprisoned during his trials (Luke 23:1-25)
Joseph suffered at the hands of the Gentiles (Egyptians)	Jesus was condemned by Gentiles (Acts 4:12)

Joseph in Prison

Joseph had been unjustly accused of attempted rape and then cast into prison and left there to languish. It was the lowest point in the long downward spiral of his fortunes from being his father's favored son to being Potiphar's forgotten prisoner. Beyond the appearance of his misfortunes, however, the larger picture shows that Joseph was exactly where God wanted him at exactly the right moment in history. Every negative circumstance in Joseph's life was really within the realm of God's providence. God was using his misfortunes to mold his character and strengthen his faith for the greater purpose of saving Egypt from famine. Beyond that, God's purpose was to preserve Jacob's family for its worldwide role in fulfilling the great promises God had given them through Abraham.

Joseph's brothers betrayed him when he was seventeen, and he was thirty when he was finally elevated to be the second ruler in Egypt (41:46). During those thirteen intervening years, Joseph must have wondered when the prophetic dream of his family bowing down to him would be fulfilled. Although his faith was being severely tested, he showed no hint of bitterness toward God. This chapter gives us the only details we have of what happened during the years he spent in Potiphar's prison: two of Joseph's fellow prisoners had prophetic dreams that Joseph correctly interpreted. The incident gave Joseph fresh hope for the future when the prisoner who was released promised to "remember" him, only to have that hope dashed when, in fact, he forgot him.

Pharaoh's Butler and Baker are Sent to Prison (vv. 1-4)

Joseph would have been in prison for as many as eleven years by now (cf. 41:1 with 41:6), continuing to be faithful to his increased responsibility there as a kind of warden's assistant caring for other prisoners. One day, Pharaoh's butler and baker were summarily ushered in to the prison and placed under Joseph's charge. They had somehow "offended" Pharaoh (v. 1). Because both men were directly connected to Pharaoh's food service, one commentator suggests that they may have been under suspicion of being involved with a plot to poison Pharaoh.

An investigation was probably being conducted while the two men were awaiting their fate, and Joseph was charged by the captain of the guard (possibly still Potiphar) with taking care of them. "He served them" for the duration of their imprisonment (v. 4). These were influential high officers in the court by reason of their frequent contact with the king. Note that both held the "chief" positions (v. 2). Because cupbearers served the king's wine and because bakers were in charge of the king's food, they were important political figures.

The Dreams of the Butler and the Baker (vv. 5-8)

One night both these men had dreams. The dreams were mysterious enough, but when they related them to each other in the morning, the mystery grew as both dreams were connected with Pharaoh as well as with their former official positions. The men became dejected and worried; they wondered if the significance of the dreams carried ominous interpretations. Had they still been in Pharaoh's court they would have sought out the court astrologers for answers, but here they were, locked in prison.

Dreams that have been recorded in the Bible *do* have significance. In addition, down through history, many people have had vivid dreams that clearly revealed subsequent events. Certainly, God has the ability to influence dreams, and demonic powers do as well, to a limited extent. Psychologists and mystics today rush to offer their interpretations—for a price—but believers ought to be very cautious in seeking after the possible meaning of any dreams they have. Joseph was right when he said, "Interpretations belong to God" (v. 8). When Joseph came to Pharaoh's officials' cell in the morning, he immediately detected something was wrong. He asked them, "Why do you look so sad today?" (v. 7).

The men told Joseph, "We each have dreamed a dream, and there is no interpreter of it." Joseph sensed immediately that their dreams might contain a message from God in the same way that his own dreams had. It was then that he said to them, "Do not interpretations belong to God?" Joseph was implying that not only does God sometimes give dreams for His purposes but also that the Egyptian magicians would be unable to interpret the dream because God would not reveal it to them. He went on to say, "Tell them to me, please." He knew God well enough to believe that He would give him the meanings because of his own experience with dreams (37:5-11).

Joseph Interprets the Cupbearer's Dream (vv. 9-13)

The Cupbearer volunteered to tell his dream first, perhaps, as some commentators suggest, because he was sure of his innocence in the plot against Pharaoh. Verses 9 to 11 describe the dream. The cupbearer might have assumed that the fact that he placed the cup into Pharaoh's hand in the dream could mean that he would return to his job, but the three branches that were so prominent in his dream were a mystery to him.

God gave Joseph the assurance of the dream's meaning immediately. With confidence he said, "This is the interpretation of it; the three branches are three days. Now within three days Pharaoh will lift up your head and restore you to your place, and you will put Pharaoh's cup in his hand according to the former manner, when you were his butler" (v. 13). How relieved the cupbearer must have felt, not only to have the prospect of being cleared of guilt, but to be restored to his high position in the court.

Joseph Asks to be Remembered (vv. 14-15)

Joseph asked a simple favor of the cupbearer: "But remember me when it is well with you, and please show kindness to me." His restored position so close to Pharaoh would afford him opportunity to plead Joseph's case to him and "get [him] out of this house." Joseph explained how he had been kidnapped from his homeland and sold as a slave and that he had committed no offence in Egypt for which he should be imprisoned. This was a rare moment of self-defense by Joseph. He was careful not to mention his brothers' guilt or implicate Potiphar's wife as to the reason for his being in prison. His discretion and restraint here is admirable.

Joseph was an accused innocent, as was the cupbearer, and he hoped to find a sympathetic ear. No doubt the cupbearer intended to speak to Pharaoh. We can all identify with failing to carry out good intentions. Joseph's plea to be remembered here is the preparation for the time when the butler, in God's perfect time, *would* finally remember him.

Joseph Interprets the Baker's Dream (vv. 16-19)

The baker was encouraged by the positive interpretation of the cupbearer's dream and no doubt hoped that the interpretation of his own would be as good. The number three was prominent in his dream as well in that he saw himself with three baskets of bread on his head, one on top of the other. In the top basket, there was a selection of all sorts of baked goods for Pharaoh. But unlike the cupbearer's dream, he was not serving his baked goods to Pharaoh. Instead, birds were eating the bread out of the top basket because the person carrying the bread had not protected it. This was a sign of serious negligence, whether intentional or not. Perhaps the baker knew he was guilty, and the dream reflected this.

God gave Joseph the interpretation of the baker's dream as well. He probably hesitated to speak, but he faithfully gave it, even though the baker's future was to be so different from the cupbearer's. The three baskets represented three days just as the three branches had in the cupbearer's dream. The significant difference was that the breads were not set before Pharaoh as the cup had been (cf. v. 11). The baker would not be restored to his office. Instead, as Joseph told him, Pharaoh would "lift up your head from you and hang you on a tree; and the birds will eat your flesh from you" (v. 19).

The devouring of his dead flesh, just as the birds ate the bread in the dream, spoke of the loss of his life and the public shame of not being assigned to a grave. There is a little irony in the phrase "lift up your head" that Pharaoh would do to both the butler and the baker. The phrase usually means to be raised up to favor (cf. v. 13). The butler's head would be lifted up to serve again, that is, he was to be restored to Pharaoh's favor. The baker's head would be lifted up *"from"* him, meaning that the favor he had had with Pharaoh would be taken away.

The Dreams are Fulfilled (vv. 20-23)

The final segment of chapter 40 reports what actually happened to the cupbearer and the baker. On the third day, just as Joseph had said, both men were summoned. It happened to be Pharaoh's birthday, and during the feasting, Pharaoh "lifted up the head of the chief butler and the chief baker," that is, he brought them before the crowd. When the butler appeared, Pharaoh restored his position to him again, but when the chief baker appeared, he hanged him, as God had revealed through Joseph.

The fulfillment of the dreams must have strengthened Joseph's faith in God and been a great source of encouragement regarding his own situation. Surely God was still working in his life, and the fulfillment of his own dreams given eleven years earlier was as certain as ever. Like the cupbearer, he also had to wait for the realization of his dreams—although in his case he had to wait considerably longer. There is a lesson here. Sometimes we compare the way God deals with others with how He deals with us. Maybe others don't endure such lengthy trials as we do. We must guard against making such comparisons and rest in the confidence that God knows the best way to raise each of His children to spiritual maturity.

Joseph was not bitter. God had used him in the butler's life, so he could be confident that God would continue to use him. He would need this added personal encouragement because the last verse of the chapter tells us that the cupbearer "did not remember Joseph, but forgot him." If Joseph's faith was in the cupbearer, he was doomed to disappointment. He knew, however, that God would not forget him. God was molding Joseph into a leader whose faith would not falter because of circumstances. He would soon entrust Joseph with much greater responsibility.

Be Patient!

In today's world, there are many would-be leaders who aspire to responsible positions in churches and ministries before they know enough of God and His Word and without much experience in God's disciplinary ways. They tend to become impatient when older, seasoned leaders with much more experience do not step down to allow them to take over. They are often unwilling to wait for God to open doors for them to implement their own ideas as to how a particular ministry should be carried on. Joseph's story in this chapter might be a help to impatient believers today. They, like Joseph, need to wait for God to act in His own way and time. Joseph may have thought that he was ready to be the leader that God had revealed he would be one day, but God knew that thirteen hard years as a slave and as a prisoner were needed to prepare him for that job at the age of thirty.

In Conclusion

God often purposed for some of His best servants to wait before taking on important positions of leadership. David was thirty before he became king, although he had been anointed fifteen years earlier (2 Sam. 5:4). Paul spent years in God's school of discipline in Arabia and Tarsus before Barnabas called him to come to public service in Antioch. Joshua spent forty years in the role of Moses' servant before the Lord called him to lead His people (Josh. 1:1). Moses himself spent forty years in the desert herding sheep before God called him at the burning bush. The Lord Jesus did not enter His public ministry until He was about thirty years of age (Luke 3:23). The key to all of these, like Joseph, was that they were faithful in little responsibilities before God gave them bigger ones. The Lord said to the good and faithful servant, "You have been faithful over a few things. I will make you a ruler over many things" (Matt. 25:23).

Pharaoh's Dreams and Joseph's Exaltation

Three pairs of remarkable prophetic dreams mark Joseph's story, all of which he interpreted. When he was still at home in Hebron, he himself had twin dreams that foretold how his family would one day bow down to him (37:5-11). He believed the future glory they conveyed, and that hope sustained him when he was betrayed and sold into Egypt. While he was in the Egyptian prison, Pharaoh's cupbearer and baker had twin dreams which foretold that Pharaoh would "lift up their heads" within three days, one to his restored position and the other to the gallows (40:9-19). The immediate fulfillment of those dreams assured Joseph that God was still in control and would, therefore, bring about the fulfillment of his own dreams.

In this chapter, we read of a third pair of prophetic dreams, experienced this time by Pharaoh. Joseph's interpretation of them to Pharaoh was the means through which God exalted Joseph in Egypt. All three pairs of dreams that Joseph interpreted proved true in his lifetime, but more than that, God used them all in Joseph's life to encourage him to continue to trust Him.

God's Sovereign Control

This chapter is also an excellent example of how God controls nations to accomplish His purposes. It is God who sets rulers up and brings them down (Dan. 2:21). Here He turned the economy of Egypt upside down and brought it under the control of a Hebrew slave for the immediate good of Egypt and for the long term development of the people of Israel into a nation. It is interesting to note that Joseph's experience parallels the prophet Daniel's (recorded in Daniel 4) in that they were both slaves, they were both summoned before the reigning king to interpret a dream, the "wise" men of the court were unable to interpret the dreams, it was God who revealed to His servants the correct interpretation, both were rewarded with high office, and both affected the destiny of their nations.

Pharaoh Has Two Dreams in One Night (vv. 1-8)

Two full years had passed since Pharaoh's cupbearer had been restored to his former position in the court. He had forgotten Joseph's appeal to "remember" him before Pharaoh. Joseph, meanwhile, continued to endure life and service in prison, no doubt longing to be free and yearning to see his father and brother Benjamin again. He no doubt found comfort in meditating on all he had learned from his father concerning the ways of God, the words of God, and the promises of God passed down from Adam to Jacob. Joseph had become a much wiser man during his years of testing, and it was now God's time to elevate him to greater responsibility. Pharaoh's dreams were the turning point in his life.

One night Pharaoh had two extraordinary dreams. In the first one (vv. 1-4), he saw himself standing by the River Nile. The Nile was the key to Egypt's economy; not only did it provide fertility to the soil with its annual flooding, but it was also Egypt's source of irrigation to keep the crops and pasture land watered. Of course the Nile and its flow were not under Pharaoh's control, but God's. It was common for cattle to stand in the river in the heat of the day to remain cool while grazing on the grasses by the river's edge (v. 2). In his dream, he saw seven plump and healthy cattle coming up out of the river followed by seven "ugly and gaunt" cows. Suddenly, the seven thin cows turned on the seven plump cows and proceeded to devour them. It could only happen in a dream, but it so disturbed Pharaoh that he woke up.

He soon fell back to sleep and dreamed again, this time about Egypt's grain fields, the "bread basket" of the whole region (vv. 5-7). The unusual feature he observed was a stalk of wheat with seven heads of grain instead of the usual one. The heads with their "plump and good" kernels indicated an unusually wonderful harvest. Then, a similar thing happened to the plump heads as had happened to the plump cattle. (Notice the word "behold" in both verses 3 and 6, indicating Pharaoh's surprise at the sight.) Beside these full heads grew up seven thin heads of grain that had been blighted by the heat of the sun and the blast of the east wind off the Arabian Desert, which swallowed up the seven full heads. Again Pharaoh woke up. He realized that his dreams were so vivid, so real, that they must contain an exceedingly important message for him.

Pharaoh's Concern about His Dreams

By the morning Pharaoh was doubly concerned (v. 8). There was something ominous about his twin dreams—something very significant—and because it troubled him to the point of deep agitation, he summoned the magicians and wise men of his court to advise him.

These advisors to the king were usually associated with the local gods. Many of them were actually controlled by occult powers. It is necessary in the Joseph story to know that these prominent counselors had no ability to interpret the message from the living God because they had no relationship to Him. Demonic forces have, at times, been allowed some limited power to influence dreams and predict their outcome, but they are powerless to either understand them or change what God determines to do. They are always subject to God's will and purposes (Ex. 7:11, 22). Thus, they were frustrated this time because Pharaoh's dream came from God. Pharaoh rehearsed the two dreams to all these magicians, "but there was no one who could interpret them for Pharaoh."

The Cupbearer Remembers Joseph (vv. 9-13)

With all the magicians coming and going before Pharaoh, his cupbearer finally remembered Joseph and the fact that he had interpreted his own dream. He realized that he had failed to keep the promise he had made to speak to Pharaoh on Joseph's behalf (v. 9). He now spoke up and related the occasion of his own dream and its fulfillment (vv. 10-13). He told Pharaoh of the dreams that he and the baker had on the same night in prison two years earlier and of the Hebrew youth, a servant of the captain of the bodyguard, who had correctly interpreted their dreams such that they had come to pass exactly as Joseph had said (Genesis 40). No doubt Pharaoh clearly remembered the incident. Although the butler had certainly been guilty of neglecting Joseph (and rightly confessed his shortcoming), in the context of God's sovereign ways, it was exactly the right time, strategically speaking, for Pharaoh to hear about Joseph and to be eager to seek his help. If the butler had mentioned Joseph any earlier, Pharaoh would probably have paid no attention. God can use even peoples' failures to accomplish His perfect purposes. What a wonderful encouragement to us all about the wisdom of God's timing!

Joseph Before Pharaoh (vv. 14-24)

Pharaoh, in his intense desire to understand the dreams, immediately sent for Joseph to be brought from the dungeon. Before he could approach the king, however, Joseph had to make himself presentable (v. 14), but the moment came when the Hebrew slave from Canaan was brought before the Pharaoh of Egypt. Pharaoh told him frankly, "I have dreamed a dream, and there is no one who can interpret it. But I have heard it said of you that you can understand a dream, to interpret it" (v. 15). Most people would have been flattered by the compliment. At this point, Joseph might have selfishly made a bargain with Pharaoh—a proper interpretation in exchange for his freedom.

Joseph's answer, however, is remarkable. He corrected Pharaoh about his own interpretive or prophetic abilities by saying, "It is not in me; God will give Pharaoh an answer of peace" (v. 16). He claimed no credit for himself, and by assuring Pharaoh that God would give him "an answer of peace," Pharaoh was to infer that, although he must prepare for the troubles that were about to afflict his kingdom, they would result in peace from God Himself.

The key to all that Joseph said in this portion was his insistence that it was God who was the Revealer of dreams and the Sovereign of the world and that all the glory belonged to Him. Note carefully what Joseph said:

- Before he started interpreting, he said, "God will give Pharaoh an answer" (v. 16).

- When he heard the dreams, he said, "God has shown Pharaoh what He is about to do" (v. 25).

- After interpreting the dreams, he said the same thing: "God has shown Pharaoh what He is about to do" (v. 28).

- In explaining the dreams further, he said, "The thing is established by God, and God will shortly bring it to pass" (v. 32).

When Joseph had given all his counsel, Pharaoh himself acknowledged that "God has shown you all this" (v. 39). All through his conversation with Pharaoh, Joseph gave God the glory and took none of it for himself. In doing this with a sincere heart, Joseph sets a wonderful example for all God's servants whom He uses to accomplish His will.

Pharaoh Relates His Dream to Joseph

Pharaoh included a few more details in the retelling of his dreams to Joseph. He described the thin and gaunt cows as "very" ugly, such as he had "never seen in all the land of Egypt" (v. 19). He also added that even when they had eaten up the fat and healthy cows, they were just as ugly as before (v. 21). The dream had made an unforgettable impression on Pharaoh. He went on to recount the second dream, adding that the seven thin heads also looked "withered." He ended by lamenting that none of his magicians (soothsayer priests) had been able to interpret the symbolism in the dream (v. 24). The gods of Egypt had been shown up to be helpless in making sense of the dreams that had come from the living God.

Joseph Interprets Pharaoh's Dreams (vv. 25-32)

Whether Joseph paused to pray and reflect or whether God instantaneously gave him the meanings is not told. His initial, categorical statement was that Pharaoh's dreams were, most certainly, "one"; they both conveyed the same thing. By means of those dreams, God was telling Pharaoh what He was going to do in Egypt over the next few years. This was probably Pharaoh's first encounter with any representative of the living God. Though he considered himself something of a god, he had no choice but to listen and respond to what the Creator God said to him through Joseph.

The "sevens" indicated years. The seven fat cows and the seven full heads of grain both spoke of seven years of abundant and unparalleled prosperity in Egypt's economy. The seven lean cows and the seven thin heads foretold a severe and unprecedented famine of another seven years, which would follow the seven bountiful years. During the famine, Egypt's former prosperity would "deplete [ravage] the land." It would dwindle to nothing and be all but forgotten because of the famine's severity (v. 30). Joseph added that the reason it was given twice, with two different symbols, was to convey both its certainty and its imminence. God was going to bring about the whole succession of events very quickly (v. 32). Evidently Pharaoh and his whole court immediately discerned that Joseph's interpretation was true and that it needed to be addressed in an extremely urgent nature.

Joseph's Advice to Pharaoh (vv. 33-36)

Joseph did not stop with the bare interpretation of the dream. He went on to advise Pharaoh as to what he thought Pharaoh ought to do in light of it. It was wise counsel on how to prepare for the coming crisis. First, Pharaoh should find a "discerning and wise" man to direct a government-enforced program over the whole land. Individuals in the country could not be trusted to prepare and provide for themselves for the famine. The administrator should then delegate to a group of supervisors a program to start saving the grain: one fifth of all the produce was to be collected during the seven plentiful years and stored in new granaries to be built all over Egypt. Not only was it to be carefully stored, but it was to be guarded and reserved for use during the coming famine, as Joseph said, "so that the land may not perish [be cut off] during the famine" (v. 36). The administrator would be in charge of the fair distribution of the grain to the people of Egypt when it was needed. The right man would be a savior; the wrong man could be a tyrant. The success of the whole project would depend on the wisdom and integrity of the man Pharaoh chose.

This grain collection may or may not have effectively been a twenty-percent tax. It is possible that the central government bought the grain with money, but it seems more likely that it was a tax that the people contributed during the really good years. They would still have as much grain to live on as they usually had. In view of the fact that a scheme like this might generate some resistance, the program would need a persuasive and diplomatic administrator. In advising Pharaoh like this, Joseph did not have an ulterior motive; he did not manipulate the situation to guarantee that they would select him as the administrator. After all, he was young, a foreigner, and without any political or governmental experience. Even though we know that God had prepared Joseph for this very thing, Joseph knew nothing of it.

Joseph is Promoted as Administrator of Egypt (vv. 37-44)

Joseph's rapid rise to power in Egypt began with Pharaoh's response. Pharaoh and his court had perceived that the interpretation of the dreams was from the living God even though they did not know Him. They also heard Joseph's exceedingly wise counsel as to how to handle the coming years of prosperity and famine for the good of Egypt. "The advice was good in the eyes of Pharaoh and all his servants" (v. 37). No one could be better suited for the position than Joseph himself. "Can we find such a one as this, in whom is the Spirit of God?" Pharaoh asked (v. 38). Though he would have known nothing of the existence or ministry of God the Holy Spirit, what he literally said was that in Joseph was the spirit of God.

Pharaoh reached an immediate decision and made the pronouncement, "You shall be over my house, and all my people shall be ruled according to your word; only in regard to the throne will I be greater than you" (v. 40). He went on, "See, I have set you over all the land of Egypt" (v. 41). With just a sentence or two, Joseph was elevated from the status of a prisoner to becoming the second most powerful man in the nation. He had full authority to do anything he thought wise. Everyone in the kingdom, except Pharaoh, would be required to give Joseph absolute obedience. It is amazing that he was promoted so far so fast. Only at this point do we understand that the years of suffering and humiliation Joseph had endured prepared him for the great responsibility he would now assume. Other men would have succumbed to pride, but Joseph had passed his tests in God's school of discipline and was ready.

Pharaoh gave him his own signet ring to endorse the official documents with royal authority and dressed him befitting his royal position. Joseph now rode in a royal chariot while servants proclaimed "Bow the knee!" before him everywhere he went. Pharaoh was still the final authority in the land, but Joseph's dominion was such that it was said of him that without his permission no one could raise hand or foot throughout Egypt (v. 44).

Joseph's exaltation is often compared to the exaltation of the Lord Jesus Christ. At His incarnation, He took the form of a servant. He humbled Himself by becoming obedient to the point of death, even death on a cross (Phil. 2:6-8). After His humiliation, God highly exalted Him (Phil. 2:9-10). Joseph's exaltation from the prison to the palace foreshadows Christ's exaltation from His death on the cross to His glory with the Father.

Joseph's Marriage (v. 45)

Pharaoh further honored Joseph with an Egyptian name that would give him status as an Egyptian and make it easier for the people to accept him. His new name was Zaphnath-Paaneah, which is generally taken to mean "God Speaks, He Lives" but has also been rendered as "Savior of the World," "Revealer of Secrets," and "God's Word Speaking Life." We cannot be certain, but all of these meanings together may anticipate "the name above all names" that was given to Christ in His exaltation to the Father's right hand.

Pharaoh also provided an Egyptian wife for Joseph whose name was Asenath. She was the daughter of Poti-Pherah, an Egyptian priest of On, or Heliopolis. We know nothing more about her. In view of the depth of Joseph's commitment to the Lord, however, we can be sure that he would not have married her unless she left her pagan background and became a true believer in the God of Israel and His promises. Because she was to become the mother of Joseph's children, he would want her to bring them up in the fear of the Lord his God. Another point of comparison between Christ and Joseph is his marriage to a Gentile bride (albeit the Church consists of believing Jews also). God is today claiming a bride from among the nations for His exalted Son. It will culminate in the marriage supper of the Lamb when the Church is taken to heaven to be with Him forever (Rev. 19:7-9).

The Prosperous Years (vv. 46-49)

It had now been thirteen years since Joseph had been betrayed by his brothers. He was thirty years old and ruler over Egypt. He began his administrative work by traveling all over the land to ensure that his program was in place. The prosperous years began just as God had revealed with greater harvests than had ever been experienced. The earth brought forth "abundantly" or literally "by handfuls." The imagery is that of the earth showing her bounty with full hands. Joseph began collecting and storing twenty-percent of the harvest in various cities around the country. The people living near each city would have confidence in the plan as they saw it being carried out. Joseph, through all his officers, saw to it that it was done fairly and correctly. With each superabundant harvest, the stores of grain became so vast that it became impossible to keep an accurate accounting. It was "without number" or beyond measure (v. 49).

Joseph's Sons (vv. 50-52)

During the seven years of plenty, Joseph's wife Asenath gave birth to two sons. The firstborn was Manasseh, which means "forgetting," because, as Joseph said, "God has made me forget all my toil and all my father's house." Joseph had been able to put aside all the bitterness that had been caused by betrayal and injustice. He discerned that God had allowed the troubles in his life for his own good. Very likely he was also beginning to see the possibilities for the deliverance of his family from the coming famine. Another son was born whom he named Ephraim, which means "fruitfulness," for he was now thankful to God for providing him with two sons. His first, Manasseh, had marked his turnaround in fortunes. His second marked his family prosperity. Later his father Jacob announced that Joseph was a "fruitful bough" (49:22; cf. Deut. 13:13-17; Hos.13:15). Both sons were given Hebrew names, a fact that confirms Joseph's continuing faith.

The Years of Famine (vv. 53-57)

As surely as God had revealed it through the interpretation of Pharaoh's dreams, the years of plenty ended and the years of famine began. Joseph had been in Egypt for twenty years by this time. The Nile was running low, and the annual floods failed. The famine affected all the surrounding lands as well as Egypt. The difference was that only in Egypt was there "bread" or food. Joseph waited to sell food as long as possible to conserve the grain. When the people of Egypt needed food, Pharaoh told them, "Go to Joseph, whatever he says to you, do" (v. 55). Joseph then carefully sold grain to the people, probably on some kind of ration system, just as he had planned. People in the surrounding countries were unprepared for the famine. When they heard that there was grain for sale in Egypt, they came to buy it.

In Conclusion

There are some wonderful lessons for us in this chapter. We can learn to patiently wait for God's sovereign actions even when we are being unfairly treated. In His time, He exalted Joseph and put him in charge of the whole economy of Egypt to accomplish His purposes. Second, Joseph's continuing faithfulness to God is a lesson to us in his testimony before Pharaoh and in his integrity in the task he was given. He never let his sudden rise to power affect his relationship with God. Finally, in the naming of his two sons, he acknowledged that God had given him victory over past bitterness and fruitfulness in his life. Many believers today need to get past old hurts and wrongs and make the most of the life God has given them, as Joseph did. Some reflections of the Lord Jesus, as seen in the life of Joseph, are found in this chapter as well: his exaltation to glory (vv. 40-43), his new name, (v. 45), his Gentile bride (v. 45), and his provision for the needs of the people (v. 55).

Joseph's Brothers' Journey to Egypt

While Joseph was ruling the economy in Egypt, his father Jacob continued to rule his household in Canaan, presumably in Hebron. Jacob and his sons reappear here in the story line for the first time since chapter 37. Joseph had been away from home twenty-one years. His older brothers were now married and in their forties, and Benjamin was in his early twenties. This chapter tells how God used the widespread famine to bring Joseph's brothers back into his life to set the stage for the removal of Jacob's entire family to Egypt. The focus of the chapter is on the realization by the brothers that their betrayal of Joseph all those years earlier was somehow causing the strange events that were happening to them.

The famine prompted Jacob to do something about his family's physical welfare. Behind the scenes, however, God was doing something about their *spiritual* welfare by working in their hearts to enable them to be the channel of the blessing promised through Abraham. God planned that they would become a nation in Egypt, but first they needed to be tested. God used Joseph to lead them through a series of tests designed to awaken their consciences regarding their sin, so they would recognize it, acknowledge it, confess it, and repent of it. The drama takes place in four scenes in this chapter:

- Verses 1-5: Canaan, from where Jacob sends his sons to Egypt to buy grain.
- Verses 6-24: Egypt, where Joseph accuses his brothers of being spies and makes a deal.
- Verses 25-28: The road home to Canaan, where one brother finds his payment returned.
- Verses 29-38: Canaan, where they report to Jacob about their trip.

Jacob Sends the Ten Brothers to Egypt (vv. 1-5)

The famine was taking its toll on Canaan. Jacob's large family was already feeling its effects; finding sufficient pasture for their vast herds was becoming increasingly difficult. Caravan "telegraph" would have brought news that Egypt had grain to sell. The old man, obviously frustrated by his sons' helplessness and lack of initiative, reprimanded them: "Why do you look at one another...."

go down to that place and buy for us there, that we may live and not die" (v. 2). Jacob was still in charge; he sent all his sons except for Benjamin to Egypt. He would not allow his youngest son to go because he doted on Benjamin as the surviving son of his favorite wife Rachel. He had never gotten over losing Joseph, so the fear that "some calamity [might] befall [Benjamin]" kept him from allowing Benjamin to join his brothers (v. 4).

Joseph Confronts His Brothers (vv. 6-24)

In Egypt, Joseph was the "governor over the land" and at the zenith of his power and influence. He was directly in charge of all the stores of grain and seemed to take personal charge of the foreign sales. Perhaps he was waiting for the arrival of his brothers, knowing that the famine would eventually touch Canaan and that there was no other source of food to which they could turn. When his brothers arrived to present themselves for the purchase of Egyptian grain, they kept protocol before the ruler in charge by bowing themselves down with their faces to the ground. Little did they guess that it was their brother Joseph to whom they were showing deference!

Despite the passage of time, Joseph recognized them—but they did not recognize him. Of course, they were not expecting to see Joseph, and his Egyptian appearance and attire enabled him to keep his identity to himself. In addition, he spoke through an interpreter (v. 23); they had no reason to believe this man was anything other than a native of Egypt. His speaking another language here gives us insight into the trial of Joseph's early days in Egypt when he would have had to learn that new language.

Joseph had good reasons for not wanting his brothers to recognize him just yet (v. 7). He knew that there could be no true reconciliation between them without true repentance. He planned, therefore, to help them to face their sin and confess it in order to bring them to the point of realizing the enormity of their offence against him and against God. Meanwhile, he longed for news of his family at home, particularly his father and brother Benjamin. Thus, he played the part of a stern officer suspecting them of a crime. His harsh manner was not meant to be vindictive; Joseph never had any vindictive feelings against his brothers. Out of this comes one of the most dramatic scenes in all of Scripture.

Joseph Remembers His Dreams

When Joseph recognized his brothers and saw them bowing down before him, he "remembered the dreams." He realized for the first time the full extent of what God had been saying through those dreams about the future. Twenty-one years earlier he had been the younger and despised brother. Now he was governor of Egypt, and their "sheaves" and "stars" were bowing themselves before him, asking him for help. It is typical of Joseph that he remembered *his dreams,* not their betrayal of him. He did not plot how he could avenge their crime. What he wanted was genuine reconciliation between them based on confession and forgiveness. No doubt he had thought often about what he would do when they came to Egypt. That time had come.

To gain further opportunity to talk with them, Joseph accused them of being spies. Literally, he accused them of "footing it," that is, walking through the land as travelers but secretly observing the fortifications and "undefended parts" of the land with a view to giving sensitive information to their own government (v. 9). This may have been a legitimate concern of Egypt's, but Joseph knew his brothers were not spies. Joseph's detractors have accused him of violating what he knew to be the truth. However, in making his accusations, he was outwardly playing his part as the governor of the land. In terms of his relationship to his brothers, he was really leading them to confess to the truth for their good, not for his own advantage.

The Brothers Protest Joseph's Accusation

The ten brothers protested their innocence, of course (vv. 10-11), but Joseph did not let up the pressure. He kept repeating the charge. In their efforts to defend themselves, they gave Joseph more information: their number actually included two other brothers. The youngest, they said, "is with our father today;" the other "is no more," implying that he was dead. Appearing to still not be convinced of their innocence, this time Joseph said they would be tested as to whether they were spies or not (v. 15). He commanded "by the life of Pharaoh" that they would not be allowed to leave Egypt until their younger brother came. To prove they were honest men, they would need to send one of them to bring him from Canaan while the rest remained in prison in Egypt (vv. 15-16). Joseph then had them all confined in prison for three days to consider his terms.

What did they think about during those three days? No doubt their consciences were working overtime. The fact that they were "all together" meant they had plenty of opportunity to talk things out, as well as to meditate and face their own individual part in their past guilt. What follows (vv. 21-22) indicates that they were certainly aware that God's justice was catching up with them. They had sold their brother to be a slave in Egypt. Now they themselves faced spending the rest of their lives imprisoned there. Those three days must have been full of self-examination and recrimination among the brothers.

Conscience Haunts Joseph's Brothers

On the third day, Joseph called them, knowing they had been thinking and talking. He now wanted to show himself to be a reasonable and just man, not a capricious tyrant (vv. 18-24). He said that he, too, feared God (v. 18). He modified his demand, tempering it by mercy for their families as well as for the men themselves. He stipulated that only one would be held in prison while the others could take the food they purchased to Canaan to ease the famine in their households. After that, they would have to return with their youngest brother in order to secure the release of the one. Then, not realizing that Joseph could understand their conversation, they admitted what was on their consciences: "We are truly guilty concerning our brother, for we saw the anguish of his soul when he pleaded with us, and we would not hear; therefore this distress has come upon us" (v. 21). After all these years, the incident was still a vivid memory. It is one of the most striking instances of the power of a guilty conscience in the whole Bible.

Reuben went on to say, "Did I not speak to you saying, 'Do not sin against the boy'; and you would not listen? Therefore behold, his blood is now required of us" (v. 22; cf. 37:21-22). Reuben had tried to save Joseph from the pit in Dothan; he was still agonizing over his failure to do that. He was recognizing that they were not just guilty of selling him as a slave but of causing his assumed death as well. Whether or not they truly believed him dead, they accepted that they were responsible for his fate. Joseph heard all this and could not contain his emotion as he heard them verbally confessing their sin (v. 24). He had to excuse himself.

When he returned, he chose Simeon to be the one to stay in prison while the others went home with the supply of corn. Joseph did not pick the oldest, Reuben, because he now knew he had tried to help him escape. Simeon was the second oldest. He had been a ringleader in the massacre at Shechem and may have been an instigator in the outrage against Joseph. If so, he would now have plenty of time in prison to reflect on his sin. The others were probably surprised that Simeon was chosen; maybe they thought that God's justice was finally being served. By binding him "before their eyes," Joseph may have intended to further stir their memories and consciences: they had no doubt watched *him* being bound by the traders who bought him and took him to Egypt (37:28).

The Brothers' Money is Returned (vv. 25-28)

Evidently each of the brothers, as heads of families, paid individually for the grain they bought because, when the sacks were filled with grain and Joseph commanded their payment to be returned, it was apportioned between their sacks. Given Joseph's character, it is likely that he financed their purchase personally. Joseph also gave them provisions for the trip (v. 25). He was treating them with kindness they did not deserve. His action was not only going to show them how generous a man he was, but it would also serve as another test for their softening consciences. They began the two-week journey back to Canaan by way of either Gaza or Beersheba. At one of their campsites, one of them opened his sack and discovered that his money had been returned. "Their hearts failed," or sank. Instead of reacting with appreciation for the governor's kindness, they were consumed with fear that he now had some hold over them. Their new dilemma threw them all into perplexity; they believed (rightly) that

God was behind all that was happening to them (v. 28). There was no doubt that their consciences were increasingly holding them accountable to Him.

The Brothers Report to Jacob (vv. 29-38)

When they returned to Hebron, they gave Jacob a full report of their experiences in Egypt: their being treated like spies by the harsh ruler, the demand to bring Benjamin back with them, and the mystery of the money in one of the sacks (vv. 29-34). It was not until now, as they began to unload, that they discovered *all* their monies had been returned. Once again, they responded not with delight but in great dismay. For the second time, it says they were afraid (v. 35; cf. v. 28). Sometimes we, like Joseph's brothers in relation to Joseph, need to be humbled still further before we can accept the grace that God freely offers and can truly appreciate Him for it.

Jacob jumped to the wrong conclusion as well. He assumed that the return of the money was part of some mischievous design by the governor in Egypt. Then, he assumed that the governor would now charge them with stealing in addition to spying. He also assumed that Joseph was dead, and the implication is that he thought the brothers had something to do with that. He did not seem to fully trust them. He further assumed that Simeon would never return home from prison in Egypt. In putting all these assumptions together in his mind, he could only come to one conclusion. He responded in utter frustration, "And you want to take Benjamin away. All these things are against me" (v. 36). Of course, he was wrong on all counts. Joseph was not dead; he was alive. The ruler of Egypt would not charge them with stealing because the money was returned by Joseph partly out of kindness to his family. Simeon would be released from prison, and Benjamin would never be safer than when he was in Joseph's care.

Assumptions are Dangerous

When Jacob made all his assumptions, he was neglecting the principle of faith. He was making judgments by the appearances of things from his limited perspective. He was forgetting the promises that God had already kept, and he was leaving out the clear promises that El Shaddai, the All Powerful Provider, had made to him concerning the future of his family. A nation would come from him, as God had promised, and the land would be given to his descendants (35:11-12).

Even though he could not see the physical evidence of the promises working out, Jacob should have simply believed what God had said. There is no record of him praying to the Lord about his fears and concerns. Because he fretted, he put himself through unnecessary distress. Jacob added up the negative factors and therefore reached the wrong conclusions. Although it is not easy for God's people to submit to the discipline of God's providence, this is a powerful lesson for us who are prone to evaluate outward factors and make wrong assumptions rather than take God at His word and rest in faith until He chooses to bring the pieces together.

Reuben tried to allay his father's fears by offering his two sons as surety for Benjamin. He said that Jacob could put his two sons to death if he did not bring Benjamin back from Egypt. Jacob, however, rejected Reuben's proposal because he knew Reuben to be weak and unstable, no matter how well-intentioned. Further, he did not know what unforeseen circumstances might intervene to thwart Reuben's good intentions. Jacob was at the place where he trusted neither God nor Reuben. He said emphatically, "My son shall not go down with you." He went on, "If any calamity should befall him ... then you would bring down my gray hair with sorrow to the grave" (v. 38). Jacob was more concerned with his personal welfare and happiness at home than in trusting the disciplinary hand of a wise and kind God (cf. Heb. 12:7-8). Let us beware lest we fall into the same trap that ensnared Jacob.

In Conclusion

There are some other good lessons for us in this story. There is the lesson of the progress of the purpose of God that included the famine, the confrontation, the prison, and the demand for Benjamin. All these were factors in what would be revealed as God's providential design. Then, there is the lesson of confession and repentance that the brothers were learning. Genuine repentance was their pathway to future blessing. God was dealing with them as He does with us: softening hard hearts little by little. In the phrase "Thus he did for them" (v. 25), we see in Joseph's gracious provisions for his brothers a picture of what God did for us in Christ before we ever appreciated it (Rom 5:8). Finally, we observe how foolish it is to make assumptions based on incomplete information. Jacob thought everything was against him when the truth was that, when God was for him, no one could be against him (Rom. 8:31).

Joseph's Brothers Return to Egypt

The Joseph story continues in chapter 43 with the record of his brothers' second visit to Egypt. There is a similarity between this chapter and the preceding one. Both are arranged around a journey of Jacob's sons to Egypt and their dealings with Joseph when they arrive there. In both chapters, it is the intensity of the famine that drives them there to buy food. In both chapters, they are confronted by Joseph, who is anxious to bring about reconciliation. There is great tension on both visits because the brothers are unaware that "the man" is Joseph. He, on the other hand, both knows and tests them. In this chapter, Joseph specifically tests them as to their possible jealousy of his full brother Benjamin. The chapter is in two parts: Jacob's reluctant agreement to send Benjamin on this second journey (vv. 1-14), and Joseph's reception of his brothers, including serving them a grand feast (vv. 15-34).

The famine was in its second year (cf. 45:6) and continuing to worsen. The supplies they had obtained on the first visit had run out, and the family was in real danger of losing not only their extensive flocks but their very lives. Jacob, still in control of the home and household, instructed his sons again to "Go back, and buy us a little food" (v. 2). Note the two tensions that run parallel in the first half of the chapter. The first is Jacob's resistance in allowing Benjamin to accompany them. The second tension derives from the brothers' fear of meeting the governor of Egypt again. The overarching theme of the whole story is how God sovereignly orchestrated all the circumstances. God was doing two things: He was saving Jacob's family from extinction, and He was providing a place for them where they could grow to become a united nation.

Jacob Commands His Sons to Return to Egypt (vv. 1-7)

When Jacob instructed his sons to return to Egypt for more supplies, they were filled with consternation because they well remembered the conditions that "the man" had imposed. Judah, the fourth son, took the lead in speaking with Jacob because Reuben, the oldest, had proved to be ineffective. Second-born Simeon was being held for ransom in Egypt, and Levi, the third son, had been out of favor since his part in the Shechemite slaughter twenty years earlier. Thus Judah reminded Jacob of the Egyptian governor's warning that they would not even see his face unless they brought their younger brother with them. (Although not recorded in chapter 42, Joseph probably made this threat when he "talked with them" while Simeon was being shackled [42:24].) Judah put it gently but plainly to his father: "If you send our brother with us, we will go down and buy you food. But if you will not send him, we will not go down" (vv. 4-5).

Jacob knew deep down that he really had no choice but to comply. However, he reacted irrationally by venting his feelings on his sons. He reproached them unfairly for having revealed to "the man" the fact that they had a younger brother (v. 6). The brothers responded that they had had no option. The ruler had questioned them specifically about their family, and they had seen no reason not to answer him truthfully (v. 7). Jacob had no choice but to trust God. The careful reader of Genesis should note that his new name of Israel is used in this chapter for the first time since he had sent Joseph to look for his brothers (vv. 6, 8, 11; cf. 37:13). "Israel" is never used of Jacob when he was acting in unbelief. In assuming Joseph was dead, he had ceased to trust in God, choosing instead to rely on his own ability to protect Benjamin. Now he was exercising faith in God again by trusting Him to protect Benjamin in Egypt, so the name Israel is used once more because he was proving himself worthy of it. We, as God's New Testament people, have several new names to live up to: "believer," "saint," and "Christian" are just three of them.

Judah Offers to Stand as Surety for Benjamin (vv. 8-14)

Judah then took the initiative again as a good leader by reasoning with his father in two ways. First, he explained that it was a life and death issue for them all. If they did not get food, they would all die of starvation (v. 8). Survival depended on going to Egypt without delay. He then coaxed his father to allow Benjamin to go by saying that he would be surety for him. If anything happened to Benjamin, he would bear the blame forever (v. 9). It is good to see that Judah's conscience had brought him to the point of taking full responsibility for Benjamin, especially in light of the fact that it had been Judah's idea to sell Joseph as a slave (37:26-27). Judah was beginning to emerge as the leader among the brothers; eventually his tribe would become the head of the twelve and be honored with bearing the messianic line.

Jacob (again called Israel) finally agreed that it "must be so." He set his mind to practical matters by offering some wise counsel that they should appease "the man" in Egypt with gifts (vv. 11-12). Obviously some of the products of Canaan were not yet affected by the famine. He urged them to take the "best fruits of the land," a phrase that literally means the "song of the land." So they took balm, honey, gum, myrrh, pistachio nuts, and almonds which were exports of Canaan and scarce in Egypt. He also told them to take twice as many funds as before. That way they could replace the bundles of money from the first trip in case the return of them had been a mistake. It is interesting the ten brothers each took twenty *bundles* of money to buy from Joseph, whom they had sold for 20 *pieces* of money (37:28).

Finally, their father gave a benedictory prayer saying, "And may God Almighty [*El Shaddai,* the all-sufficient God of the Abrahamic covenant] give you mercy before the man, that he may release your other brother and Benjamin" (v. 14). He was committing them in faith to God's care for the journey. Israel simply put his trust in God, believing that God would work things out according to His will. Israel's faith was well justified; God did answer his prayer. As for his paternal love for his youngest son, he would submit to God's will. He said, "If I am bereaved, I am bereaved!" Thus, accompanied by Benjamin and laden with gifts, the brothers went to Egypt the second time.

The Brothers' Reception in Egypt (vv. 15-25)

When they stood before him, Joseph immediately saw that Benjamin was with them. Instead of conversing with them at that time, he ordered his steward to take them to his own home and prepare a meal. He planned to dine with them at noon. His instructions implied preparations for grand entertainment (cf. 31:54). The brothers were afraid, not only because it was highly unusual for foreign traders to be treated like this, but also because they suspected that it had something to do with the money in their sacks. Maybe they were to be charged, and they would all be made slaves (v. 18). Joseph had no doubt noticed that no harm had come to Benjamin along the way. They did not know it, but Joseph was planning for their good. He had seen the seeds of repentance on their first visit and was actually preparing for a full reconciliation.

Before they even entered the house, they tried to head off the accusation that they had stolen the returned money. They approached the steward and explained how they had found it. They told him that there must have been some mistake and that they had brought the money back. They had also brought other money to buy grain this time. They wanted to make their case before they were charged to show that they had no evil intentions. The steward put them at ease, telling them not to fear. Obviously their God had given them "treasure" in their sacks, and they should thank Him. He, the steward, had received full payment for their supplies. The implication was that someone else had paid for the grain, probably Joseph himself (v. 23).

It would seem from his language that the steward himself had come to know God, perhaps through Joseph. He then restored Simeon to them, which must have helped them to shed their fears and begin to relax. The eleven brothers were then escorted into Joseph's house where the steward washed their feet as honored guests. They were given a chance to bathe and dress for the luncheon while their donkeys were fed. While they waited, they prepared the present for the ruler. They must have been awed by the opulence, accustomed as they were to living in tents as shepherds. They must have also been apprehensive about meeting "the man" again.

Joseph Entertains His Brothers (vv. 26-34)

When Joseph arrived home, the brothers presented him with their gifts from Canaan (v. 26). This is the second time they bowed down in fulfillment of Joseph's prophetic dream, and this time all eleven brothers were on their knees, just as the dream indicated (cf. 42:6). They did not, however, realize the significance of their posture as yet. Joseph, as a gracious host, asked about their well-being and that of their father. They told him he was still alive and well. Once again, they "bowed their heads down and prostrated themselves" to Joseph for the third time. The dream of the sheaves must surely have flooded his mind.

For the second time in this chapter (cf. v. 16), Joseph saw Benjamin, or as it is beautifully put in modern versions, "his mother's son." This time he really looked at him (v. 29). He had not seen Benjamin since he was about two years old. Savoring the moment, he asked his older brothers, "Is this your younger brother of whom you spoke to me?" and then impulsively pronounced a blessing on Benjamin (v. 29). Joseph could not hide his emotions. Being deeply stirred, it says "his heart yearned for his brother." He had to leave the dining hall and retreat to his own chambers where he could weep unseen. They were tears of tenderness and affection, and they reveal something of the heart of this great man. Having washed his face, he returned to his brothers and ordered for the meal to be served, determined to contain his feelings this time (v. 31).

Three separate tables had been set: one for Joseph, one for his brothers, and one for the Egyptian guests. Egyptian protocol would not allow Hebrews to sit with Egyptians, for they considered themselves much superior to foreigners, especially shepherds. Joseph, as an Egyptian official, could not eat with the Hebrews and risk offending the Egyptians when he was trying to reconcile with his brothers (v. 32).

Benjamin is Shown Special Favor

The Egyptian's snobbish attitude toward foreigners, especially Hebrew shepherds, made Egypt the ideal place for Jacob's family to grow into a nation. Egypt's elitist attitude and unwillingness to interact socially would work to the Hebrews' advantage by allowing them to not be influenced by the Egyptians' idolatry and paganism. Isolation from that kind of environment could only foster a pure faith in God while they looked for the promises to be fulfilled.

When Joseph's brothers sat down, they realized with amazement that they were all seated according to their birth order, from Reuben the firstborn to Benjamin the youngest. They wondered how he could have known. The arrangement must have made them uneasy.

Joseph then sent "servings" from his own table to honor his Hebrew guests. In serving Benjamin five times as much as the others, he was treating Benjamin with an exceedingly high and distinguished honor. A double portion would have been a special honor. Joseph was deliberately showing his brothers that Benjamin was his favorite. The brothers feasted and drank freely with their host, but they showed no hostility or resentment to Benjamin when Joseph honored him. Joseph watched their reaction very carefully because it had been Jacob's favoritism for him that had led to his brothers selling him as a slave. His brothers passed this crucial test. The meal proceeded happily to the point of becoming festive (v. 34), and the brothers' concerns evaporated. One further test was necessary in Joseph's mind. Provided that they passed *that* test, Joseph planned to proceed with fully reconciling with them. That test is explained in the next chapter.

In Conclusion

We can learn some good lessons from Genesis 43. First, it is frequently necessary for God to push us into crisis situations before we will submit to His will. Jacob was stubbornly irrational in his insistence that Benjamin not go with his other sons to Egypt until Judah reminded him that, if he would not allow it, they would all starve to death. Many believers need to let go of their own stubborn wills and yield to the will of God.

Second, Jacob's example teaches us a lesson about recovering faith and trust in God when the situation is out of our control. Not only did Jacob let go of his stubbornness, but he also refocused his faith on God and lived up to his new name, Israel. It is not right to make trusting God our last resort, however. Third, God's continued discipline and training of Jacob show us that there is always room for spiritual growth, even in one's later years; it is encouraging to know that God never gives up on us. A lesson from the brothers' experience in this chapter is that God may be testing us in life's most ordinary activities, even though we are not conscious of it. Joseph's brothers had no idea that their eating, their attitudes, and their reactions were going to have an effect on the rest of their lives. May we take advantage of even the routine activities of our lives to grow spiritually.

The Testing and Confession of Judah

Joseph had not yet finished with his plan of making his brothers see the enormity of their sin in betraying him. This was especially true of Judah, their rising leader, who had cold-heartedly turned a deaf ear to Joseph's cries from the pit and initiated the plot to sell him to the Midianite traders many years before. The brothers had passed the first test, the test of jealousy over Joseph's displayed favoritism of Benjamin (chapter 43), but one further test remained in Joseph's mind concerning the betrayal itself. The brothers had sold him as a slave without regard to the cost to him or to his father. For Joseph, the cost included separation from his father, certain suffering, and physical hardship at risk to his life. For Jacob, it was the loss of his favorite son, now presumed dead, and the loss of trust in any of the ten sons who had brought back the varicolored coat stained with blood. At that time, nothing had mattered to Judah and his brothers except their desire to eliminate Joseph from their lives.

The Bigger Picture

The narrative of this chapter amounts really to an interruption in the brothers' return journey to Canaan. When they set off for home, they thought that their problems with the ruler in Egypt were over; after all, he had treated them to a fine meal in his own home, had sold them more grain, and had let Simeon go free. Joseph, however, had much broader insights into the situation. He knew the famine would last another five years. He also knew that God had exalted him for the purpose of both saving the family from the ravages of famine and furthering God's purposes concerning the land and the Seed. He knew that, to fulfill this purpose, the family would have to be brought together and brought to the point of trusting God.

Joseph was in a position to help in this process by getting them to acknowledge their sin and to humbly confess it. Only then could they be reconciled to God and to him. Thus, the events of this chapter unfold. Joseph set in motion a brilliant scheme designed to put before the brothers a clear moral choice. His eyes would have been on Judah particularly, because he was their leader; Judah represented his brothers. If Judah were to show to Joseph that that he was willing to suffer, even to give his life to save Benjamin, Joseph would then be convinced that Judah's repentance, and that of his brothers, was real, and then they would pass the test.

Joseph's Plan to Endanger Benjamin (vv. 1-5)

The morning after hosting a feast in honor of his brothers—and especially in honor of Benjamin—Joseph sent them away with their donkeys loaded with grain. But before they left the Egyptian capital, Joseph instructed his steward to again return each man's money in the mouth of his sack and to put his personal silver cup in the mouth of Benjamin's sack. Before they had gone far, Joseph told his steward to pursue them, and when he caught up with them, to demand why they had "repaid evil for good" (v. 4). He was to tell them that a special silver cup belonging to Joseph was missing, and they were under suspicion of stealing it—a crime worthy of the death sentence.

The cup would have been exquisitely made and of very high value. Cups like this one were used for divination, that is, for determining information from the Egyptian gods, often about identifying those guilty of a crime (v. 5). It is highly unlikely that Joseph, as a strong believer in the true God, would have ever used his cup for such a purpose. The divination cup played a necessary part in Joseph's plan because it would reinforce the brothers' concept that they were dealing with a pagan Egyptian ruler who worshipped his peoples' gods. The more convinced they were of that, the greater would be their surprise when Joseph revealed himself to them. However, the brothers had had good relations with the steward who had overseen the filling of their sacks, and they would have had no reason to fear that any deception would come from him, any more than they would have expected it from Joseph. They did not yet understand the disciplinary ways of God, and certainly did not yet know how much they needed to.

The Cup is Discovered in Benjamin's Sack (vv. 6-13)

Joseph's steward caught up with the eleven men just outside the city and followed his master's instructions to the letter. The brothers were dumbfounded that such an accusation could be made, and they denied any part in it. They argued that as they had offered to return their money from their previous visit, it proved they were honest men. They reasoned, "How then could we steal silver or gold from your lord's house?" To them, it was unthinkable. Confident that it was impossible that any of them could be implicated, they said to the steward, "With whomever of your servants it is found, let him die, and we also will be my lord's slaves" (v. 9). They did not suspect that they had been set up to make just such a statement. The steward accepted their bargain and said it was sufficient for "he with whom it is found" to be the governor's slave; the rest could go free (v. 10).

The brothers were only too glad to prove their innocence. They unloaded the sacks for the steward's inspection, beginning with the oldest. All went well until they came at last to Benjamin's sack in which, of course, the missing cup was found (v. 12). The brothers were caught off guard by this; in utter dismay, they tore their clothes. They had no choice but to reload all the donkeys and return to Joseph's house. Note that Judah's leadership is taken for granted. They are described as "Judah and his brothers" (v. 14). Joseph, of course, was anxiously awaiting their return. Before they said a word, they "fell before him on the ground." This was the fourth time they had bowed down to Joseph (although this time as much from fear as from respect), bearing out the dreams of his youth, and this time it was Judah leading his brothers in the act.

Judah's Confession (vv. 15-17)

Joseph said to them, "What deed is this you have done? Did you not know that such a man as I can certainly practice divination?" In reply, Judah again took the lead without even pleading innocence. He said, "What shall we say to my lord? What shall we speak? Or how shall we clear ourselves?" Then, he said what Joseph was waiting to hear: "God has found out the iniquity of your servants; here we are, my lord's slaves, both we and he also with whom the cup was found" (v. 16).

Judah's statement was a remarkable confession. He admitted that it was God, not the steward, nor the lord of Egypt, who had found them all guilty and that they deserved to be punished by becoming his slaves. Judah knew that none of them had anything to do with stealing the lord's silver cup, but he also knew that God had been working on his conscience regarding the sin they had committed twenty-two years earlier. What he was saying was that, if they were all made slaves because of that sin, it was a righteous punishment they deserved from God.

But Joseph was not yet finished. He replied to Judah that enslaving them all would not be necessary. Justice would be served by taking only the man in whose sack the cup had been found and making *him* a slave. As if to drive the point home, he told Judah and the rest, "As for you, go up in peace to your father" (v. 17). This was Joseph's great test for Judah who had taken the lead in selling him as a slave. Would he leave Benjamin as a slave and return home, or would he make good on his promise to their father to be a surety for Benjamin and bear the blame for whatever might happen (cf. 43:9)? An even bigger matter was also at stake for the children of Israel for whom this story was written. Was Judah qualified to be the leader of the twelve, and his descendants qualified to lead the Israelites in their invasion of the land of Canaan? Judah's reply would supply the answer.

Judah's Magnificent Plea for Benjamin's Life (vv. 18-34)

Judah's speech in Genesis 44 is second in length only to Jacob's speech of blessing on each of his twelve sons in Genesis 49. In this scene, Joseph's eleven brothers stood accused before the man they only knew as the powerful lord of Egypt who was "even like Pharaoh" (v. 18). Benjamin had been "caught red handed" and was without defense for a capital crime of which he was entirely innocent. At this point in the drama, Judah approached Joseph as Benjamin's surety in order to take Benjamin's place and keep his promise to his father. He who had been so cruel and heartless when he had heard Joseph crying for mercy in the pit and had then exchanged him for money, now offered himself as a ransom for Benjamin to be a slave in Egypt. Though he did not yet know who the lord of Egypt was, he offered himself as a slave to the very man he had sold into slavery.

The content of Judah's plea to Joseph is remarkable. His whole appeal demonstrates humility. He called Joseph "my lord" seven times, his brothers "your servants" four times, he himself "your servant" four times, and even Jacob "your servant my father" four times. He approached Joseph and pled with him to not be angry but to allow him to "speak a word." He made numerous tender references to his aged father and called Benjamin "the lad" repeatedly to appeal to the governor's heart.

Judah Pleads for His Father

Judah began his speech by reminding his accuser that, when they met a year earlier, he had asked the brothers if they had a father or another brother. They had told him of Jacob, of Benjamin, and of the only other child of his mother, now dead. Speaking of Benjamin, Judah said, "He alone is left of his mother's children, and his father loves him" (v. 20). Judah then also reminded his accuser that it was he who had commanded them to bring this younger brother with them so that he could see him. At that time, they had pleaded that, if the young boy were to leave his father, his father would die (v. 22). The lord of Egypt had then clearly told them that, unless their brother came with them, they could not see his face, implying they would not be allowed to buy more grain. But when their father had instructed them to return to Egypt because the food had run out again, they had told him that they could not go without Benjamin. He went on to share with Joseph why their father had resisted allowing Benjamin to go: he was still grieving for his other son, whom he described as "the one [who] went out from me," who had been "surely ... torn to pieces," and whom he had not seen since (v. 28).

Judah went on to quote his father in saying that, if any harm came to Benjamin, "You shall bring down my gray hair with sorrow to the grave." He further stated that their father's very life was "bound up in the lad's life." If he failed to bring Benjamin back, it would be such a terrible grief to his father that he would probably die as a result. Judah now came to the climax of his impassioned speech. He offered himself as a substitute for Benjamin to bear the punishment that would be his. He told Joseph that he had promised his father that he would become "surety for the lad." He had told Jacob, "If I do not bring him back to you then I shall bear the blame before my father forever" (v. 32). Judah's climactic statement was "Now therefore, please let your servant remain instead of the lad as a slave to my lord, and let the lad go up with his brothers. For how shall I go up to my father if the lad is not with me, lest I see the evil that would come upon my father?"

Summary of Judah's Plea

Notice three things that Judah did in his extended plea for Benjamin:

- He confessed his guilt before God for the sin which was really bothering his conscience (v. 16). He did not even try to maintain his innocence regarding the silver cup, though he well knew that neither he nor any of his brothers had stolen it. He did, however, admit his guilt before God for the larger sin of betraying his brother.

- He demonstrated sincere compassion for his aged father. Jacob had grieved over the "death" of Joseph and the "cover up" following it. Judah wanted to spare him further grief (vv. 25-32). He pled with the lord of Egypt to show special favor so that his father would not have to suffer more grief.

- He made a sincere offer to give up everything he had in life and take Benjamin's place so he would be free to return home (vv. 32-34). This, for him, was the hardest part of all: to pay a life-long penalty for Benjamin's sake.

Joseph was at last convinced that all the trouble he had gone to in trying to bring Judah to the place of repentance had been used by God to humble him to the point where he admitted his sin and took full responsibility for it. Judah's faithfulness to Benjamin in the crisis led to a strong bond between the families of the two brothers that continued into the succeeding generations. The tribe of Benjamin stayed with Judah when the other ten tribes broke away from the kingdom under Jereboam. Judah's courageous stand for Benjamin prepared him for the leadership position that he would have in the patriarchal family. And from this point on, Judah and the tribe called after his name would be the leader of the nation of Israel.

In Conclusion

An application for believers can easily be found in Judah's open confession of his longstanding sin: "If we confess our sins, He is faithful and just to forgive us our sins" (1 John 1:9). It can also be found in Judah's compassion for his grieving father that was well overdue but finally demonstrated in his plea before Joseph. The honoring of father and mother is basic to Christian living. A third application is in Judah's commitment and self-sacrifice for the sake of his brother. Though that, too, was a long time in coming, it was the crux of the whole story. Our sacrificial commitment to our brothers and sisters for the Lord's sake is equally important (1 John 3:16-18).

The Reconciliation of Joseph with His Brothers

The reconciliation of Joseph with his brothers is not just a surprising and delightful twist that brings this human life drama to a happy conclusion. It is also directly related to the theme of Genesis and the line from which the Seed of the woman would come (3:15). God "cultivated" a godly line to establish a special, chosen people destined to live in a special, chosen land. The One who would bruise the serpent's head would descend from this people. God chose Abraham and called him to the land of Canaan. From Abraham's sons, God chose Isaac. From Isaac's sons, God chose Jacob, whose twelve sons would be the first leaders of the coming nation. To preserve Jacob's family from famine, idolatry, and self-destruction, God chose Joseph to become the ruler of Egypt so that he would be in a position to provide his family with the time, space, and means to develop into a nation. They would then be strong enough to invade and capture the Promised Land, to freely worship God, and to be a witness to surrounding nations.

Joseph's part in the Egypt segment of their story is, therefore, crucial. But before he could provide for his family to live and prosper there, the issue of his brothers' sin against him needed to be confronted. Joseph longed to be reconciled with them, so he planned three tests to bring that about. They had failed all three tests in the past.

Three Tests

The first test, relating to their callous treatment of him, prepared them for reconciliation: *Did they feel guilty about betraying him?* To arouse their consciences, Joseph falsely accused them of spying, jailed them, and demanded to see their younger brother. They passed that test when, in Joseph's hearing, they linked the governor's harsh treatment with their twenty-year old sin of ignoring Joseph's pleas from the pit (42:21). The second test had to do with family unity. When Jacob showed favoritism towards Joseph, the brothers decided to do away with their brother as a way of dealing with the issue and effectively broke up the family. Joseph tested them by favoring Benjamin more than the others at the feast. *Would they become jealous of Benjamin and again break the unity of the family?* They did not. "They drank and were merry with him" (43:34). The third test concerned respect for their father. They had not cared for his feelings when they got rid of Joseph. *Would they rate their own well-being higher than their father's now?* Joseph accused Benjamin of theft and threatened to make him a slave. Judah protected his father from suffering life-threatening heartbreak by offering to take Benjamin's place (44:32-34). From Joseph's perspective, they passed the three tests that related to himself, to Benjamin, and to his father respectively, and he was satisfied that their repentance was genuine.

Joseph Cries Tears of Compassion (vv. 1-3)

After hearing Judah's moving speech on Benjamin's behalf, Joseph could no longer restrain his emotions. He sent all his servants out of the room, including "those who stood by him," probably bodyguards. He did not want what would happen next to be witnessed by anyone other than those who were personally involved. Once they were all alone, Joseph broke down and blurted out to his brothers in their own language, "I am Joseph." His sobbing and crying were loud enough for all outside the room to hear it, and news of it even reached Pharaoh. His high emotion showed how intensely he wanted to heal the breach between them.

But his brothers did not respond by jumping up and down for joy; rather, they froze as if they had been struck dumb. Small wonder—the revelation that the lord of Egypt was their brother Joseph terrified and confused them. The word "dismayed" (v. 3) carries with it the idea of fear. They didn't know if he would take advantage of the moment and have them all killed on the spot. Joseph's three words were as dramatic a confrontation as any in all history and literature. Not only was it a moment of high drama, but it was also a milestone for Jacob's family. From this moment in history emerged the nation of Israel and, through its people, the Scriptures and the Messiah.

Joseph broke the stunned silence by asking about their (and his) father. Once, as ruler of Egypt, he had asked about Jacob's welfare. Now he asked as a loving son, "Does my father still live?" He was looking for the intimate details only shared among family. He immediately diverted the guilty feelings that his announcement had awakened because he was satisfied with their confession and actions and had already forgiven them in his heart. What they needed to hear now were reassurances. He wanted to focus their attention on the family and the future.

Joseph Forgives His Brothers (vv. 4-8)

To dispel their fear, Joseph urged them to approach him. When they did, he said again, "I am Joseph your brother, whom you sold into Egypt." There could be no mistaking who he was. This man could not be a pretender. He wanted to tell them how God had been with him and brought him to this point and place, so he counseled them not to be grieved or angry at themselves for what they had done. They had repented of their sin of despising and betraying him. The matter was now behind them. We, too, should never fear approaching God who has freely forgiven us as a result of Christ's payment for sin on the cross. We stand accepted in the Beloved (Eph.1:6; 1 John 4:18).

Long ago, Joseph had realized that God was working out His sovereign purposes and plans. From Joseph's perspective, it was God who had made the moves. Three times Joseph told them it was God who masterminded all that had happened to him after they sold him (vv. 5, 7, and 8). When they betrayed him, God overruled their evil designs; by their wicked deeds, He accomplished what He had already decreed: that Joseph would be their savior. He made three statements about God's part in the whole series of events:

- Concerning the past, it was God who sent him "before" or ahead of them to "preserve life" through the seven-year famine that had five years still to run (v. 5).

- Concerning the distant future, it was God who had sent him to "preserve a posterity for you in the earth and to save your lives by a great deliverance" (v. 7). The word for "posterity" is the usual word for "remnant." Both this word and "deliverance" are words commonly used in prophecy to look forward to the expectation of salvation for the people of Israel (cf. Ezra 9:14; Isa 10:20; 15:9). God was using Joseph as part of His plan to ensure the survival of His people in crisis situations.

- Concerning the immediate future, it was God who had made him lord of all Egypt, thus putting him a position to control resources and make them available to his family (v. 8).

Thus, God not only gave the promises to the patriarchs but also engineered everything for their fulfillment.

"Not You Who Sent Me Here, But God"

When Joseph told them not to be angry with themselves for selling him into slavery, he did not mean his brothers were free of responsibility. Nor was he implying that God caused them to commit sin because He had masterminded events. They had sinned willfully and had already paid a high price for it in their fractured family, their stricken consciences, and the trouble that followed. Their lives in the past twenty-two years would have been very different if they had not committed so significant a sin. Every sin carries a cost, but some carry a higher cost than others. God, in his sovereignty, is able to bring good out of evil, as He did with Joseph. Joseph suffered more than his brothers during those years, but very differently. His brothers suffered as a result of their sin. They reaped what they sowed. Joseph's suffering, however, was the means for his greater usefulness in line with God's purposes. Both of them needed to see God's hand in it. The brothers needed to see God's hand of discipline that brought them to repentance and restored harmony in the family, and Joseph needed to see God's hand preparing him to be a channel of blessing.

Joseph Instructs His Brothers (vv. 9-13)

In pursuing the reconciliation process, Joseph gave his brothers urgent instructions. They were to return at once to their father and tell him that "God has made [him] lord of all Egypt." He was not to delay in coming down to him; Joseph was going to provide for all the family's future needs in a place called Goshen (v. 10). Their removal was necessary for the family to survive in view of the five years of famine still to come.

In caring for them, Joseph would fulfill his destiny as his family's deliverer: "I will provide for you" (v. 11). In Joseph, we see a picture of the Lord Jesus who was willing to be our Savior and has all the resources at His disposal to meet the needs of His people.

Once more, Joseph assured his brothers that their eyes were not deceiving them. Everything was true. He was Joseph, and he had the ability to save them all. Even Benjamin, with little more than a dim childhood recollection of Joseph, could be sure that he was Joseph (v. 12). They were to tell their father of all Joseph's glory and splendor, to convince him of the truth of it all, to testify that they themselves had seen it. Joseph's glory would convince him that it was all true. Finally, he said they were to "hasten and bring my father down here" (v. 13).

Reconciliation at Last (vv. 14-15)

It had been a long day for those eleven men: they had ridden away from the Egyptian capital in triumph "as soon as the morning dawned" (44:3) with their supplies; they had crashed in despondency with the accusation against Benjamin of stealing the cup; they had humbled themselves in confession, especially when Judah offered himself as a slave in place of Benjamin, and then they had heard that the Egyptian lord was none other than their brother Joseph whom they had betrayed. Joseph and Benjamin embraced each other, weeping, then Joseph kissed and embraced each of his brothers in reconciliation. Each one of his brothers was completely forgiven. All that had divided them for more than twenty years was removed. The family was unified, and peace was restored.

Joseph was a man of tears. This is the fourth of six occasions where Joseph is portrayed as weeping. He wept when his brothers expressed their guilt (42:24) and again when Judah confessed his sin and offered to take Benjamin's place in prison (45:2). He wept for joy over being reunited with his younger brother Benjamin (43:30; 45:14). He wept when his father died and over his brothers' mistrust of him (50:1, 17). It is hard not to compare Joseph with the Lord Jesus, whom Isaiah described as a "Man of sorrows" (Isa. 53:3). Scripture specifically records Jesus weeping in Luke 19:41-44 and John 11:35.

The reconciliation of Joseph and his brothers vividly foreshadows a greater reconciliation in the future between the Lord Jesus Christ and His brethren, the people of Israel. In that day, God will "pour on the house of David and on the inhabitants of Jerusalem the Spirit of grace and supplication" (Zech. 12:10). Christ will appear in power and glory and His people will mourn "as one mourns for his only son" when they realize that they were the ones who betrayed Him. And when they mourn for Him in repentance and understand the shame they brought upon Him, God will forgive them for their rejection and betrayal. At that time, they will also realize that the One they had despised and rejected had suffered on their behalf. They will say, "Surely He has borne our griefs, and.... He was wounded for our transgressions" (Isa. 53:3-5). What a day that will be!

Pharaoh's Command to Joseph's Brothers (vv. 16-20)

When Pharaoh heard that Joseph's brothers had come from Canaan and had been reconciled with him, he was glad for Joseph. There is no doubt that Joseph had earned the respect of Pharaoh and his court by his wise administration of the country's economy. It was common knowledge that Joseph's family comprised of wealthy and free nomads, a class of people who were held in high regard. Pharaoh was delighted with Joseph's idea of bringing his family to Egypt. He sent word to them via Joseph that they should travel back to Canaan and return with Jacob and their families to live in Egypt. He promised to give them the "best of the land of Egypt" to live in and "the fat of the land" for food (vv. 17-18). Later, when the children of Israel were in the wilderness, they were still raving about the richness of the land (Num. 20:5). Pharaoh's invitation to live in Egypt fulfilled the first part of the prophecy given to Abraham that his descendants would be "strangers in a land that is not theirs." Eventually, they would "come out with great possessions" (15:13-14).

Pharaoh expanded on his invitation by telling Joseph that his brothers should take "carts out of the land of Egypt for your little ones and your wives" (vv. 19-20). Most commentators think these were two-wheeled carts, but there are existent terra cotta models of four-wheeled wagons from that era. Whether two-wheeled or four-wheeled, they were the latest in Egyptian transport technology. Jacob's family was not to worry about bringing heavy household items such as clay pots, furniture, or the like. These things could be left behind. Pharaoh assured them that in Egypt there was plenty of everything to meet their needs.

Like many material blessings, however, the blessing of living in Egypt had its dangers for Jacob's family. The chief one was in becoming so satisfied with Egypt that they would not want to return to the Promised Land. The love of Egypt in the Old Testament equates to the New Testament love of "the world." A worldly attitude is one that leaves God out of one's thinking. The danger comes when we lose our vision of God and focus on the things of this world (1 John 2:15-16), allowing it to shape our priorities and lifestyles.

Joseph Provides for their Journey to Canaan (vv. 21-24)

In addition to the carts for transportation and provisions for the journey to Egypt, Joseph gave them clothing, probably Egyptian clothing for festive occasions. The brothers had shown their hostility towards Joseph by stripping him of his coat, but Joseph honored them by giving them several sets of quality clothing. The clothes spoke of their new situation and prospect; it signaled that everything they would need in Egypt to be provided. But to Benjamin, his full brother, he gave five changes of clothing and three hundred pieces of silver. Benjamin's special status shows up again, and Joseph doesn't need to explain it. Joseph's large monetary gift to Benjamin stands in contrast to the twenty pieces of silver that all the brothers except Benjamin received in selling Joseph into slavery. Joseph also sent a special gift to his father which was loaded with personal gifts that more than matched the gifts Jacob had sent to "the man" (v. 23, cf. 43:11).

Joseph's final instruction was "See that you do not become troubled along the way." Literally it meant "don't get excited," and its intent was that they should not quarrel. Joseph knew that they would have to explain to their father their deception about his fate. The potential for blaming one another as they discussed it on the way home was enormous. The journey would have taken them two or three weeks. Joseph had forgiven them—how much more should they forgive one another! Every one of Joseph's promises had proved true, and they could look forward to a prosperous life in Egypt—but they would need to cooperate with one another.

The Brothers Return, and their Report to Jacob (vv. 25-28)

Their caravan must have made quite a scene. The many wagons drawn by oxen or horses, plus the twenty donkeys laden with gifts, the dozens of Jacob's donkeys that the eleven brothers had brought to carry back grain, and all the servants and gear, all contributed to an impressive sight.

Jacob, waiting in Hebron, was no doubt scanning the southern horizon for his sons' return, especially Benjamin's. The best he could hope or expect was to see both Benjamin and Simeon and enough food for another few months. What must he have thought at that splendid sight? As they drew near, he heard the excited and almost unbelievable words: "Joseph is still alive." And not only that, he was governor "over all the land of Egypt." Old Jacob could hardly take it all in. In fact it says that "Jacob's heart stood still, because he did not believe them."

The Bible closes the door discreetly on the scene of the brothers' confessing to their father how Joseph came to be in Egypt in the first place (vv. 27-28). But in relating "all the words which Joseph had said to them," they must have told him Joseph's account of his life in Potiphar's house, his unjust imprisonment, and his exaltation to Pharaoh's court, along with his testimony of how God had been with him working out His purposes. Then, they would have explained how Joseph had led them to confess their sin of betrayal and brought them to the point of demonstrating their repentance when Judah offered to become a slave in Benjamin's place. We can only imagine Jacob's feelings on hearing not only of his sons' enormous offence against their brother, but of how Joseph had kissed them and forgiven them all. And now he was providing for them and offering to save them from the ravages of the famine!

The reality of what his sons were telling him began to sink in when Jacob saw the wagons that Joseph had sent to bring the family to Egypt. Only a king could do that. The effect on Jacob of seeing those wagons would be like refugees living in a humble cottage reacting to the sight of a presidential jet landing nearby to carry them to a wonderful new country. It was when the old man saw the wagons that his spirit revived. Not only did his spirit revive—his faith and joy did as well. The next verse says "Then Israel said, "It is enough. Joseph my son is still alive. I will go and see him before I die" (v. 28). The twenty years of sadness and doubt that had marked the "old" Jacob vanished, and we see again how his name of Israel reflects a healthy spiritual state (v. 28). It was to Israel that God opened the door to all He had planned for his blessing in Egypt and beyond.

Israel exemplifies for us three aspects of biblical faith in verse 28:

- He said, "It is enough." Although Joseph was not there in the flesh, he *believed* that what he had been told was true (cf. John 20:29).

- He said, "I will go." He *acted* on his faith by agreeing to move to Egypt with his whole family as Joseph had instructed (cf. 1 Thess. 2:13-14).

- He said, "I will … see him." He *expressed confidence* that he would see his beloved Joseph before he died (cf. 2 Tim. 1:12).

Note that Jacob's personal focus was on Joseph now—not on the preservation of his family or on his future prosperity, but on being with his son Joseph. Jacob's restored faith now energized the rest of his life as he rose higher and higher in his walk with God. He ended his life on that rising plane. His faith is a good example to us all. We have observed how, even when his faith was weak, God cared for him and watched over every detail of his life. During that time, however, Jacob missed much of the joy that might have been his had he fully trusted God. As his faith rose during the last seventeen years in Egypt, so did his joy in God. The story of Jacob has long been an encouragement to believers who have questions about their own unexplained sufferings.

In Conclusion

For us, this passage has several valuable lessons. The most obvious one is that forgiveness is both necessary and possible, even for the worst of sins. If Joseph could forgive those who betrayed him and sold him as a slave to a foreign country without cause, surely we can forgive one another for the sins that so easily fracture our fellowship (Col. 3:12-13). We also learn that, before reconciliation can take place, there needs to be genuine confession of wrongs committed. It was Joseph's careful guidance of his brothers that led them to see their sin and repent of it.

We learn, too, that a dysfunctional family can be reunited when all the members humble themselves before God. Joseph was humble even in his exalted office, not using his power to crush his brothers, but rather to forgive them. Judah and his brothers humbled themselves by confessing their sin and responding to Joseph's acceptance of them. In Joseph's testimony, we see by example how we should recognize God's hand in our circumstances. And in Jacob, we see an example of depression, despondency, and self-pity giving way to renewed faith in God after discerning God's hand in his family's life.

Israel's Journey to Egypt

Jacob's eleven sons had returned safely from Egypt with news that Joseph was not only alive, but ruling Egypt. Jacob's initial reaction was to not believe them (45:26), but his faith overcame his unbelief and he said, "It is enough, Joseph my son is still alive. I will go and see him before I die" (45:28). Jacob saw that God's hand had clearly been on Joseph for the good of the family. He is rightly called "Israel" as he journeyed in faith towards Egypt (v. 1) accompanied by his whole family as well as household servants, shepherds, and others who had associated themselves with Jacob's clan. They packed up all that they needed and set out from Hebron on the last and happiest journey of the aged patriarch's life.

Israel's Sacrifice at Beersheba (v. 1)

The first stop on Israel's journey south was Beersheba, twenty miles from Hebron. Beersheba had been a significant place in Jacob's ancestry. His grandfather Abraham had "called on the Everlasting God" there after he made a covenant with a Philistine king over water rights; he had lived there for a considerable time too (21:33-34; 22:19). The Lord appeared to his father Isaac in Beersheba confirming the patriarchal promise, and Isaac had responded by building an altar there (26:23-25). Beersheba became Isaac's home; he raised his twin sons Jacob and Esau there. It was from Beersheba that Jacob had fled to Haran (28:10). Now he was leaving the land, and he stopped in this historic place to offer sacrifices to "the God of his father Isaac" (v. 1). The altar may have been termed this way because he used the same altar that his father had built there.

While Israel was worshipping at the altar he might have been asking God for some confirmation that he was doing the right thing. Maybe his mind went back to the promise God made to his father there, that his descendants would be multiplied (26:23-25).

When the sacrifice was consumed and the encampment had settled down for the night, Jacob might have wondered if God's words to Abraham about his descendants living as strangers in a foreign land were going to be fulfilled in *Egypt* (15:13).

God Speaks to Jacob at Beersheba (vv. 2-4)

God spoke to Jacob in "visions of the night" (v. 2). Many years before, God had appeared to Jacob in a dream when he was on the point of leaving the land in search of a bride (28:13-15). It is interesting to note several similarities between both occasions and revelations.

Notice the names of Jacob that God used here and their possible significance. When God called his name, he answered as his grandfather Abraham had when God called him on Mount Moriah—"Here I am"—to indicate a humble willingness to listen and obey. This was the seventh and last time that God revealed Himself directly to Jacob.

It is significant that God spoke to all three of the patriarchs at Beersheba. It was there He spoke to Abraham when He called him to sacrifice Isaac (21:33-22:2). It was there He spoke to Isaac when He promised him the blessing of His presence and that his descendants would be greatly multiplied (26:23-24). Now, in this chapter, God said to Jacob at Beersheba, "I am God [El, the Mighty One], the God [Elohim] of your father Isaac." By revealing Himself as the God of Isaac God was assuring him that the promises He was about to give were in line with the ones given earlier to his father. God then told him plainly not to fear going down to Egypt (v. 3) On hearing that, the last of Jacob's doubts about leaving Canaan evaporated.

Four Promises

The first promise was *"I will make you a great nation there."* If they stayed in Canaan, they probably would have intermarried with the Canaanites and perhaps lost their identity as a people. In Egypt they would be protected as a group for a long time with the result that they could multiply freely. The fact that they would be shunned because they were shepherds would guarantee their separation. The next 250 years for the Canaanites were to be the filling up of their "cup of iniquity" (15:16), so it would have been difficult for the family to live in Canaan as a God-fearing people. God knew that, and He protected them by directing them to Egypt. It was "there" in Egypt that God was going to make them a great nation.

The second promise was *"I will go down with you to Egypt."* God had promised His continuing presence with Jacob, just one man, when he left the land for Haran; this time He assured Jacob and his whole family that He would be with them all in Egypt.

The third promise was, *"I will also surely bring you up again."* God was guaranteeing Jacob's descendants safe return to the Promised Land. It was fulfilled 215 years later when Moses led them out from Egypt, across the wilderness, and back to Canaan. The Israelites in the wilderness facing various trials would be encouraged by this promise.

The fourth and final promise to Jacob was a personal one: *"And Joseph will put his hand on your eyes."* That is, Joseph would be with him when he died and perform the ritual of closing his eyes. Jacob would be comforted to learn from God that the details of his burial would be properly taken care of by his own son.

The Journey to Egypt (vv. 5-7)

Having made his final offering in the land and received God's assurances through the vision, Jacob arose to lead all his descendants from Beersheba in the south of Canaan to Goshen in the northeast of Egypt. They used the transport (carts) that Pharaoh had provided for them. It must have been a sizeable group: not only Jacob, his sons and their wives and families, his daughters and their families, but servants and other God-fearing people would have increased the size of the company (vv. 5-7).

Seventy Founders of the Embryonic Nation (vv. 8-27)

Egypt was to be the "womb" of the nation Israel. Seventy direct descendants of Abraham became the foundation members of this embryonic nation. The names of the original seventy are all listed here in chapter 46 in the order of their relationship to Jacob's wives. From this point on, the Old Testament focuses on the history of Israel as a nation and God's dealings with her for the next twelve hundred years. Seventy became a number often associated with the nation of Israel. There were seventy elders appointed in Moses' day (Num. 11:16). The nation of Israel was in captivity for seventy years (2 Chron. 26:21). Daniel spoke of seventy weeks to "finish the transgression" (Dan. 9:24). The Lord Jesus sent out seventy disciples to witness to the nation about the good news of the Kingdom (Luke 10:1).

The Sons and Daughters of Leah and Zilpah

The first section in the list of names deals with the sons and grandsons of Leah, Jacob's first wife (vv. 8-15). Her six sons, twenty-three grandsons and two great-grandsons are listed together with her daughter Dinah. Two of Judah's sons died in Canaan and therefore did not go to Egypt. The names listed total thirty-two, so the total of thirty-three probably includes an unnamed daughter (cf. v. 15). The wives of Jacob's sons are not named because they were not descended from Jacob ("from his body," v. 26). These wives, except for one, probably came from the other descendants of Abraham through Ishmael and Esau. The only apparent exception is Simeon's Canaanite wife (v. 10). Following the list of Leah's sons, daughters and grandsons, those of her maid Zilpah are named listed (vv. 16-18). These include two sons, thirteen grandsons, and one daughter. They total sixteen.

The Sons of Rachel and Bilhah

The second section lists the names of the sons and grandsons of Rachel, Jacob's second and most loved wife. These include Joseph and his two sons and Benjamin with his ten sons, making fourteen in all (vv. 19-22). Added to these were the descendants of Rachel's maid Bilhah and her two sons and five grandsons. The descendants of Rachel and Bilhah total twenty-one in all (vv. 22, 25). Of the total number named as the founders of Israel, three were already in Egypt (Joseph and his two sons).

Summary of Jacob's Family

As Benjamin was still only a young man when they left Canaan, it is unlikely that all ten of his sons were born prior to arriving in Egypt. This may be true of others named in this section also (for example, Perez, v. 12, born to Judah and Tamar, could only have been an infant by this time, so had not yet fathered Hezron and Hamul). It may help us to see that the people listed are defined as coming "from Jacob's body," literally "his loins." Therefore, they may not all have been born before leaving Canaan. They did, however, *potentially* comprise "the house of Jacob" in Egypt.

Reunion in Egypt (vv. 28-30)

As Israel and his whole entourage neared Egypt, he sent Judah, now the established leader, on ahead to tell Joseph they had arrived and to arrange their meeting. The company stopped in the land of Goshen, which was on the eastern side of the Nile delta. They were waiting for confirmation that they could settle there. Joseph had already intimated that Goshen was the best place for them (45:10) but he needed Pharaoh's approval. When Joseph and Jacob met, the text says that Joseph "fell on his neck and wept on his neck a good while." Jacob's embrace with Joseph, his long lost son, is one of the most beautiful moments in all of Scripture. At last, after twenty-two years, Israel's family was united. When Israel finally regained his composure he said to Joseph, "Now let me die, since I have seen your face, because you are still alive." He could die in peace because the greatest heartbreak of his life had been transformed into the greatest joy.

Joseph Counsels His Brothers (vv. 31-34)

After Joseph had greeted his father, he told the whole household how he was going to prepare the way for their audience with Pharaoh (vv. 31-32). He then gave them very wise advice as to what they should say when they met him. Pharaoh had promised them the "best of the land" (45:18) and would likely offer a location close to Joseph in the capital, Heleopolis. But Joseph knew that if they lived in Goshen on the northeastern fringe of Egypt they would be far enough away from Egyptian culture to maintain a separate Hebrew identity and lifestyle in keeping with God's truth. Goshen would provide them with excellent pastureland for their flocks and herds and was large enough to allow room for them to multiply as a people. Joseph had a long range vision in view: he was probably aware of God's revelation to Abraham, that his descendants' stay "in a land that is not theirs" (15:13) was destined to last much longer than the remaining five years of the famine.

Goshen's distance from the center of Egypt would be to the Egyptian peoples' advantage too, because shepherding livestock was an occupation that offended their sophisticated culture. Joseph would have known that Pharaoh would gladly hire foreigners to manage his own vast flocks in view of his own peoples' aversion to shepherding (v. 34). With all this in mind, Joseph wisely counseled his brothers to lay heavy emphasis on their livelihood and expertise when they talked to Pharaoh, and he would lay the groundwork for Pharaoh's reception of them too (v. 32).

In Conclusion

One of the lessons in this chapter is that there is often a combination of factors in God's providence. God did His part in making it possible for Jacob's family to live in a very favorable environment to grow into a nation. But on the practical side, Joseph gave very down-to-earth advice to his brothers about what to say to Pharaoh so that he would give them the area that would suit them best. The combinations of God's clear providence and common sense often work together for the best interests of God's people. Most of us can observe from our own experience how well the mind of God and wise planning contribute to a good outcome. We should all adopt that godly pattern (Prov. 21:31).

Jacob Blesses Pharaoh

After being reunited with his father, Joseph went back to the capital and announced to Pharaoh that his family had arrived in Goshen. Joseph may have held a powerful position, and Pharaoh may have already made an earlier generous offer (45:18), but Joseph showed wisdom in observing due protocol and applying for official permission to settle his family there (v. 1). Joseph planned to formally introduce some of his brothers to Pharaoh, so he prepared Pharaoh for the interview by specifically mentioning that his family had brought with them all their flocks and herds. Joseph wanted Pharaoh to take that fact into account when he decided which area of Egypt he would give them to live in.

The first section of this chapter covers the family's visit to Pharaoh's court (vv. 1-12). The central part of the chapter explains Joseph's management of Egypt's economy (vv. 13-26). The last part records Joseph's vow to his father to bury him in the land of Canaan (vv. 27-31).

Joseph's Brothers Meet Pharaoh (vv. 1-6)

Following his own audience with Pharaoh, Joseph presented five of his brothers to him (v. 2). They answered just as Joseph had counseled them and added that they were in Egypt because of the lack of pastureland in Canaan due to the famine. They placed themselves in the graces of Pharaoh and made a specific, formal request: "Please let your servants dwell in the land of Goshen" (v. 4; cf. 46:34).

Pharaoh immediately gave Joseph approval to their request. In addition, as Joseph must have anticipated, he offered positions as chief herdsmen to any of them who were particularly skilled in handling and managing livestock. In making this offer, he paid a high compliment to Joseph, whose work and loyalty he appreciated so much. In this way, the Israelites started to live and prosper in Egypt and became "strangers in a land that was not theirs," as God had told Abraham (15:14). Joseph's wisdom gained them "the best of the land" (vv. 6, 11), where they would be isolated enough from the worst attractions of pagan culture and together enough to be able maintain their spiritual commitment and worship to God. The tension between the attraction of the world and their obligation to God would be a continuing reality for them in Egypt. It parallels the tension in the life of believers today. *We* are strangers in a hostile world as well (Heb. 11:13; 13:14). We live *"in the world"* as worshippers and witnesses for God, but we are to be sufficiently not *"of the world"* to remain faithful to God because we have been chosen *"out of the world"* and set apart for Him (John 13:1; 15:19).

God's Prince Meets Egypt's Pharaoh (vv. 7-12)

Joseph also brought his father to meet Pharaoh (v. 7). Jacob was old and frail, and he walked with a cane. The old pilgrim must have looked out of place surrounded by the splendor of the Egyptian palace and the regal dignity of Pharaoh. Imagine the contrast—the weather-beaten sheep rancher leaning on Joseph and limping slowly toward the Pharaoh seated on his royal throne!

However incongruous his outward appearance might have appeared, Jacob approached Pharaoh as the representative of Almighty God. As Joseph "set him before Pharaoh," his father showed no sign of embarrassment or humility. Instead, he assumed the position of a priest with spiritual authority and opened the dialogue by pronouncing a priestly blessing on Pharaoh (v. 7). The simple record is striking: "And Jacob blessed Pharaoh." Normally Pharaoh would have opened the conversation, but he deferred to the old patriarch. By blessing Pharaoh, Jacob took the high ground. In referring to the time when Melchizedek blessed Abraham (14:19), the New Testament commentator said, "Beyond all contradiction the lesser is blessed by the better" (Heb. 7:7). So here, Pharaoh was blessed by the "better," or greater—Jacob. His blessing was probably a prayer for God to prosper Pharaoh. No doubt Pharaoh sensed his spiritual greatness and perception as a "prince with God."

The meeting between these two men illustrates the character of true greatness in God's eyes. Representing the Lord of the universe before the world's most powerful ruler was one of the high points in Jacob's spiritual life. How feeble and false are the standards by which the world often judges people!

Pharaoh responded to the blessing and asked Jacob how old he was (v. 8). Jacob replied, "The days of the years of my pilgrimage are one hundred and thirty years." Note that he described his life as a pilgrimage. A pilgrim can be described as one who journeys in foreign lands or one who travels to a holy place as a devotee. Both could be said of Jacob (Heb. 11:13-14). He went on to describe those years in two ways: "Few and evil have been the days of the years of my life, and they have not attained to the days of the years of the life of my fathers in the days of their pilgrimage" (v. 9). First, he described his one hundred thirty years as being short and compared them to Isaac's 180 years and Abraham's 175 years. However, just as Isaac had been premature in thinking he was about to die, so was Jacob (cf. 27:1; 35:29). He actually lived another seventeen years.

The second way he described his life was as "evil" or unpleasant, difficult (v. 7). And they *had* been difficult: he had grown up in a family divided by favoritism; he had run from Esau's anger; he had been forced to work and wait for Rachel, only to be tricked by Laban into marrying Leah; he had endured bitter rivalry at home between his wives; he had suffered the rigors of the shepherding life; he had been unfairly treated by Laban as to his wages; he had lost sleep over fear of meeting Esau again; he had been left physically handicapped after wrestling with the Angel; he had been humiliated by his sons' barbarism at Shechem; he had lost his beloved wife Rachel in childbirth; he had grieved for many years over the supposed violent death of his favorite son Joseph; he had felt the burden of the welfare of his large household due to the famine in the land; he had feared for Benjamin's safety in Egypt; he had sorrowed over his sons' betrayal of their brother twenty-two years earlier—these were the "evil" days he had endured.

Through it all, however, he had come to know God better and had been spiritually enriched. Many years later, he summed up his life by acknowledging that God had cared for him during all those hard times (48:15), but he did not give God the glory for it at this time before a pagan king. Perhaps this is the reason the name Jacob, rather than the name Israel, is used five times in this section.

How often we, too, fail to take advantage of opportunities to testify to unbelievers of God's goodness to us! In another way, we can identify with Jacob as well, in that our lives, too, are marked by brevity and difficulty. But it is also true that as long as God keeps us on earth, He will take care of us so that His will is accomplished through us (Ps. 138:7-8).

Goshen, where Jacob's family settled, was also called the land of Rameses (v. 11; cf. Ex. 12:37). The family received "a possession" there, that is, a formal ownership. They also received food from Joseph's storehouses, rationed out to them according to family size for the remaining years of the famine. They evidently had the right to obtain property which they did as they were able when the drought eased. As a community of shepherds, they began to prosper, largely living apart from the Egyptians.

Joseph's Management of Egypt's Economy (vv. 13-26)

Not only did Joseph demonstrate wise policy toward his own family, but he continued to show wisdom in managing the economy of the Egyptians. During the remaining years of the famine, he sold grain to the people at a fair price. After a time, the Egyptians had spent all their available cash buying food from Joseph, and the whole economy of Egypt was under Joseph's direction. When their money was gone, the people sold their livestock in exchange for additional food (v. 17). Soon all the livestock became Pharaoh's. Presumably the increase of Pharaoh's livestock demanded highly skilled animal management, which the Hebrews were able to provide. Thus, they were able to enrich themselves and prosper in Egypt. Three times Moses emphasizes that the land of Canaan was suffering the hardships of the famine throughout this time too (vv. 13-15). He may have been impressing on his readers that if Jacob's family had stayed in Canaan, they would never have survived.

Joseph's Imperial Farm Policy

Later in the drought, with no more livestock to sell, the Egyptians sold their land to Joseph and became Pharaoh's crown tenants. This social system was not slavery as we tend to think of it, but rather like feudal service. The tenant farmers would be allowed to keep four-fifths of the produce and return one-fifth to Pharaoh as a payment for the use of crown land. It was not cruel exploitation, for the people expressed their appreciation and gratitude to Joseph for his management of the famine conditions and willingness to be a part of it. They said, "You have saved our lives; let us find favor in the sight of my lord, and we will be Pharaoh's servants" (v. 25).

During the famine, Joseph moved many of the rural-dwelling people nearer to the cities so they could be served better and the stores of grain handled more efficiently (v. 21). The priests of Egypt's pagan temples were a powerful group with special privileges. Not only did they not have to sell their land, but they also received a free allotment from the central stores during the famine (v. 22). When the famine began to ease, Joseph gave seed grain to the Egyptian farmers for their crops and received one-fifth of the produce as payment (vv. 23-24). Joseph's law for the tenant farmers to pay one fifth to use the state land continued on in Egypt at least until the time of Moses (vv. 25-26). The priests, however, were able to hold their lands and became an elite class of people.

Israel's Final Years (vv. 27-31)

The land of Goshen now became home to *Israel the patriarch* and *Israel the embryonic nation*. The family of Israel prospered there and began to multiply rapidly. Their company numbered approximately one hundred when they first moved to Egypt. If they multiplied at an annual rate of five percent (a conservative estimate for the times and conditions), it would increase to become two million people in two hundred and fifteen years, which is about the length of time they lived there. Numbers 1:46 records the number of fighting men as 600,000 men, so the figure of two million for the whole nation is plausible.

The details of Jacob's final years are much more fully described than those of either Abraham or Isaac (cf. 25:8; 35:29). We conclude from this that what he said and did during this time was important in the mind of Moses, the author writing under the supervision of the Spirit of God. Certainly, his last words to his individual sons recorded in chapter 49 would have great meaning for later generations.

The setting changes to some point near the end of Jacob's seventeen years in Egypt. When he knew he was about to die, he called Joseph to come to Goshen. He put Joseph under solemn oath to swear that he would not bury him in Egypt. The custom was for the one making the oath to put his hand under the thigh of the person to whom he was swearing. It was the same form of oath that Abraham required of his servant when he sent him to obtain a bride for Isaac (see comment on 24:1-9). Jacob wanted to be sure that he would be buried in the cave Machpelah, near Hebron, where both Abraham and Isaac were buried with their wives, along with Jacob's own wife Leah, who must have preceded Jacob in death, presumably before they left Canaan. Machpelah was the first tiny piece of property legally held in the Promised Land, and Jacob wanted to be sure he would be buried there. His eye was not on the present, but on the future, when God would give their descendants the whole land as He had promised Abraham. The destiny of Jacob's people was not in the land of Egypt. Joseph fully understood and solemnly promised his father saying, "I will do as you have said."

Israel Bows and Worships

After Joseph swore that he would buy his father in Hebron, the old man "bowed himself on the head of the bed." What he did was to assume a posture of worship, although exactly what that posture was has been a matter of debate. It may simply be that he turned from sitting up in bed, put his feet on the floor and steadied himself with his hand on the head of the bed. The action marked another high point in his life of faith. Note that he is called "Israel" again here. When he had secured Joseph's promise, he bowed in worship to his promise-keeping God. He had feared that his gray hair would be brought down in sorrow to the grave (42:38). Instead, his heart now looked up to God in the assurance of faith. Joseph was alive; the family was united; and Joseph had promised him that he would bury him in Canaan, which he was well able to do. Thus, to Jacob bowing in worship, the evidence of God's promises looked brighter than ever.

In Conclusion

It is interesting that Jacob cared for Joseph during the first seventeen years of *his* life and that Joseph cared for Jacob in his last seventeen years (cf. 37:2; 47:9). In their care for each other, they illustrate the roles of parents and children at both extremities of life and set an example for us.

We can see at least three other practical lessons in this chapter. Joseph's wise and respectful handling of the introduction and relations between his family and the king of Egypt is a model for Christians as they relate to non-Christian authorities. He used his considerable influence for them but was forthright and honest in what he told Pharaoh (vv. 1-6). Second, Joseph conducted himself so well in his administration of the famine for the good of the general population that they lauded him as their savior, even as they were losing their lands and property (v. 25). He illustrates those godly persons prominent in society who use their positions and influence for the good of all society. The third lesson we can learn is that Israel kept his sights on the future till the end of his life when he made Joseph promise to bury him in Canaan (vv. 29-31). Every believer should strive to maintain a clear view the promises of God for the future and to make choices that are based on them.

Jacob Blesses Joseph's Sons

The story of Jacob's final years and days really began in the previous chapter in which he settled in Goshen with his family and "multiplied exceedingly" in number (47:27). This chapter and the next describe what happened at Jacob's deathbed about seventeen years later. Before blessing each of own sons (recorded in chapter 49), he adopted Joseph's two sons as his own and blessed them. This remarkable act of faith gained him a place among the heroes of faith in Hebrews 11.

The famine in Egypt had been over for twelve years, and life had resumed a more normal routine. Joseph seems to have stayed in the capital as the Prime Minister of Egypt. Presumably he visited his father from time to time. We read no more of Joseph's wife Asenath, whom he married when he first came to power and who bore him two sons (41:35, 50; 46:20). Each time she is mentioned, she is referred to as the daughter of Potiphera the priest of On, or Heleopolis, which was ten miles northeast of modern Cairo and was the center of Egyptian worship of the sun god, Ra. Joseph raised his sons in this environment, but as a follower of Jehovah, he would have done his best to shield them from those pagan influences. In this chapter, Joseph's sons are taken under the umbrella of the covenant blessings.

Joseph Comes to Jacob (vv. 1-2)

The old patriarch, now 147 years old (47:28), became ill and realized that his time on earth was short. Upon hearing this, Joseph went to visit him, taking along his two sons Manasseh and Ephraim. By this time they would have been young men between twenty and twenty-five years old. Joseph was about fifty-six. When Jacob received word that Joseph was nearly there, he mustered all his strength to sit up on the side of the bed. This was an important family occasion. He was so focused on it that he set aside usual greetings when they arrived and abruptly began to tell Joseph what was uppermost on his mind.

Jacob Rehearses the Promises of God (vv. 3-4)

Jacob reminded Joseph of the time when God Almighty appeared to him at Luz (Bethel) and blessed him. Joseph probably remembered (being in his mid-teens at the time) how Jacob had prepared his family for the occasion by commanding them to put away their foreign gods. Jacob recited the two key features of God's blessing. First, God had promised that He would multiply Jacob to become "a multitude of people" and second, that He would give the land of Canaan to his descendants as "an everlasting possession" (v. 4). The multiplied "seed" and the inherited "land" are the twin foundation stones of God's often-repeated covenant to all three of the patriarchs. The twin promises were given by direct revelation to the patriarchs a total of eleven times: seven times to Abraham (12:1-3; 12:7; 13:14-17; 15:5; 17:1-21; 21:12-13; 22:17-18), twice to Isaac (26:1-5; 26:24), and twice to Jacob (28:12-19; 35:6-12). We can see from this not only their importance but that God responds compassionately to the human need for reminder and assurance.

The specific occasion of this appearance of God to Jacob at Bethel (v. 3) was on his second visit there (35:1-15). After he had been back in the land with his family for ten years, God had commanded him to build an altar at Bethel where he had previously encountered "El Shaddai" in his dream of the staircase (28:12). After having made his offerings to God at that altar, God confirmed his name change from Jacob to Israel. Then, God renewed the covenant promises (35:11-12). In reminding Joseph of what God had told Jacob at Bethel, we must understand that, although Jacob himself was dying in Egypt, he was claiming God's promise that the land of Canaan would be an "everlasting possession" for his descendants.

The words "fruitful and multiply" are instructive because they were God's commandments at creation to the living animals and to Adam and Eve in the Garden of Eden (v. 4; cf. 1:22, 28). God issued the same command again to Noah's family after the Flood (9:1, 7). The same phrase is used to describe the growth of the Israelites in Egypt (Ex. 1:7). How appropriate that Jacob remembers the importance of the promise on his deathbed in the context of God's commands from the beginning of time!

Jacob Adopts Manasseh and Ephraim as His Sons (vv. 5-7)

Having rehearsed God's promises, Jacob formally adopted Joseph's two sons as his own. In doing this, he was elevating Manasseh and Ephraim to be equal heirs with Joseph's eleven brothers. "He said, "Your two sons Ephraim and Manasseh … are mine; as Reuben and Simeon, they shall be mine."

The effect of adopting them was that Joseph received a double portion of the family inheritance. The double portion usually went to the eldest son, although the father could change the custom if he chose. Reuben had shown he was unworthy of the privilege because he had committed incest with Bilhah. The writer of First Chronicles makes this clear: "Because he defiled his father's bed, his birthright was given to the sons of Joseph, the son of Israel" (1 Chron. 5:1).

The inclusion of Manasseh and Ephraim in the family would be significant when it came to dividing up the inheritance in the land of Canaan. At that time, the descendants of Joseph's two sons would each receive a portion when the land was divided among the twelve tribes. Thus, the inheritance would be divided thirteen ways to include Ephraim and Manasseh. Jacob was astute enough to take into account that Joseph might father other sons beside Manasseh and Ephraim, although there is no record that he ever did. If he were to have more sons, they would not be considered "sons" of Jacob like Ephraim and Manasseh but would simply share in their inheritance and become a part of one of those two tribes.

Jacob then reminisced about the death of Rachel, his favorite wife and the mother of Joseph. To his great sorrow, she had died near Bethlehem while giving birth to Benjamin. In his mind, Joseph was his firstborn son because Rachel had the preeminent place in his heart, so he comforted himself now by ensuring that Joseph would receive a double portion of inheritance in the land.

Jacob Blesses Manasseh and Ephraim (vv. 8-16)

Israel's poor eyesight prevented him from realizing that the two people with Joseph were actually the ones he had been talking about. He knew there were two other people in the room, though, because he asked, "Who are these?" to which Joseph replied, "They are my sons, whom God has given me in this place." It seemed to dawn on the old man how fitting and providential it was that they were there. He was still fully in control of what he was doing, and he called for Joseph to bring them forward so that he could bless them (v. 9). Having kissed and embraced his grandsons, he expressed gratitude to God. He had never expected to ever see Joseph alive again, but not only had he done that, here he was, embracing Joseph's two sons (vv. 10-11)!

Joseph then bowed down and knelt before his father who was sitting on the side of the bed. In doing so, he expressed his love and respect for him (v. 12). Joseph has left us a wonderful example here. Even though he held one of the highest positions in the world of his day, it was appropriate for him to bow in reverence before his father. Joseph then stood up and presented his sons to his father again. He deliberately positioned Manasseh, the eldest son, in front of his father's right hand and Ephraim, the younger one, in front of his father's left hand. They probably knelt down. Joseph positioned them in this way so that Israel's right hand would be placed on the eldest son Manasseh and his left hand would be placed on Ephraim, the younger (v. 13).

The author of Genesis describes what happened: "Then Israel stretched out his right hand and laid it on Ephraim's head, who was the younger, and his left hand on Manasseh's head *guiding his hands knowingly,* for Manasseh was the firstborn" (v. 14, emphasis added). His hands were guided by the inner prompting of the Spirit of God. His sight was too poor to discern which son was which, but he knew how Joseph would place them according to custom. Israel deliberately crossed his hands and put his right hand on Ephraim and his left hand on Manasseh. At this point, Joseph did not notice what he was doing.

The Blessing is Pronounced

Israel, with his hands on the heads of Joseph's two sons, pronounced a remarkable blessing. It begins "And he blessed Joseph" because Joseph was the collective name for his two sons. In blessing him, he was blessing them. They were represented in him. In pronouncing the blessing, he used poetic language:

> God, before whom my fathers Abraham and Isaac walked,
> The God who has fed me all my life long to this day,
> The Angel who has redeemed me from all evil,
> Bless the lads;
> Let my name be named upon them, and the name of my fathers,
>   Abraham and Isaac;
> And let them grow into a multitude in the midst of the earth.

It was a general blessing on Joseph and both his sons, no doubt inspired by the Spirit of God. Many believe that the threefold description of God in the first three lines reflects His triune character. The first line describes God the Father: the covenant God who gave the promises to Abraham and his seed. The second line speaks of God who has "fed me all my life" and answers to the ministry of the Holy Spirit. The third line refers to the redemptive work of the Angel and quite certainly speaks of the second Person of the Trinity, God the Son, who appeared to Abraham on Mount Moriah (22:11, 15) and to Jacob at Peniel (32:24, 28, 30).

Our Shepherd and Our Redeemer

There are some interesting sidelights on two of the words in the description of Israel's God. The word for "fed" in verse 15 is equally well translated "shepherded" and is the first reference in the Bible to God as our Shepherd. It is significant that Jacob, who was a shepherd himself, calls God *his* Shepherd. The theme is expanded in many passages, the most well-known of which is David's declaration in Psalm 23: "The Lord is my Shepherd." The other significant Old Testament word used here for the first time is translated "redeemed" in verse 16. The Hebrew word is *goel,* meaning "kinsman redeemer" (see Lev. 25:25; Ruth 4:4). In God's wisdom, He included in the Law the opportunity for an Israelite to "purchase" or redeem a relative along with their property if unfortunate circumstances forced the relative into the bond service of others. The purpose was to ensure continued family ownership of the land. The act of redeeming (buying back) a relative who had become a bond slave is seen as a portrayal of Christ who purchased us for Himself at the cost of His own blood (1 Pet. 1:18). Note that the "Redeemer" is the "Angel" of the Lord as noted above. Jacob stated that the Angel redeemed him from all evil, which brings to mind his earlier confession before Pharaoh that his days were few and "evil" (47:9).

The Nature of the Blessing on the Boys

Israel's specific blessing from God was then focused on Ephraim and Manasseh: "God.... Bless the lads" (vv. 15-16). Nothing was said in the blessing here about money, cattle, or other physical inheritance. The emphasis of the legacy that Jacob left to his grandsons was a life lived by faith and prayer for God's favor on them. That is the greatest legacy any parent can give. He went on to pray that his *name* be named upon them. It was by the name "Israel" (prince with God) that he placed his hands on them and blessed them (v. 14). His name stood for his character at the high point of his life of faith. It stood for his dependence on God, not on himself, and his worship of God. To his own name he added the names of his forebears, Abraham and Isaac, who were also giants in faith (v. 16). Both of them exercised faith in following God's command to give their inheritance not to the firstborn sons but to their younger sons. Israel ended his blessing on Ephraim and Manasseh with the phrase, "And let them grow into a multitude in the midst of the earth" (v. 16). He envisaged the descendants of the sons of Joseph becoming a multitude, which in fact they did. The combined tribes of Ephraim and Manasseh became more numerous than any other tribe of Israel.

Joseph Protests Jacob's Action (vv. 17-20)

It was at this point that Joseph noticed his father's hands crossed over his sons' heads. He thought his father had made a mistake, and he objected strongly. He physically took hold of his father's right hand and tried to remove it from Ephraim's head to place it on Manasseh's, saying, "Not so my father, for this one is the firstborn; put your right hand on his head." He interrupted the blessing to tell his father how to place his hands. It was a natural reaction, but Israel knew what he was doing. In responding to reassure Joseph, he also expressed his own confidence that what he was doing was right. In speaking of the tribe of Manasseh, he said, "I know my son, I know, he also shall become a people, and he also shall be great." Israel went on to say, however, that Ephraim's tribe would be "greater than he." As their history unfolded, Ephraim did become the dominant tribe in the northern kingdom when Israel split into two nations (1 Kings 12:19, 25). In this way, Ephraim the younger was blessed to a greater degree than his older brother, Manasseh.

The privilege of the birthright did not follow the customary or natural order in this instance. It is another example of the truth that God's ways are not always our ways. They are based on His sovereign purposes and not on culture or convention. Jacob himself had received both the birthright and the blessing even though he was Esau's younger brother. Abraham's older son, Ishmael, was bypassed for his younger brother, Isaac. Jacob's oldest son, Reuben, was bypassed for Judah and Joseph. Now Joseph's eldest son, Manasseh, was bypassed for Ephraim. Israel also predicted that in the future the words of blessing in the nation of Israel would be "May God make you as Ephraim and as Manasseh!" (v. 20). The order in which their names would be spoken by future generations indicated that Ephraim would be greater than Manasseh. The fact that Joseph made no further objections may show that he now perceived how this divine pattern had been working out in his family ancestry, and he therefore accepted it in his own family's case. He himself had benefited from a change in the natural order.

"Jacob . . . worshipped, leaning on the top of his staff"

We should not neglect the New Testament commentary on this incident in Hebrews 11, the chapter that lists the high points in the lives of the heroes of faith in the Old Testament. The Spirit of God inspired the author to include this particular incident about Jacob. "By faith Jacob, when he was dying, blessed each of the sons of Joseph, and worshipped, leaning on the top of his staff" (Heb. 11:21). What was it about this act of faith that made it outstanding? It was this: Jacob perceived that Ephraim was God's choice for the future on the basis of His grace, not right or merit, and he honored God's choice without question. It was a supreme act of faith in which the old patriarch accepted God's will over his own will and over the objection of his favorite son. He leaned forward on the edge of the bed putting his weight on his staff. With his head bowed low before Almighty God, he worshipped Him. This was the highest point in Jacob's life of faith. It is a wonderful testimony to God's life-changing work in him. He began as a conniving contender for all the selfish advantages he could obtain, but he grew in faith step by step and climaxed his life in a grand act of worship. His physical sight, like his father Isaac's in his old age, was dim, but his spiritual sight, unlike Isaac's at this stage, was sharp and clear. In this incident, Jacob demonstrated the fact that he was one of the outstanding spiritual giants of Scripture.

Some Final Words from Father to Son (vv. 21-22)

The final words of Israel to Joseph in this chapter are remarkable for he was still looking to the future. He assured Joseph and his sons that God's presence would remain with them after he died. God would bring Joseph and his people back to the promised land of Canaan where Abraham, Isaac, and Jacob had lived (v. 21). To his dying day, he never lost faith in the promise of God to give his descendants the land as their inheritance.

Israel also promised Joseph's descendants an extra portion in the land over and above the twelve divisions that were parceled in the days of Joshua. This extra "portion" was described as one which Jacob took from the Amorites with the sword (v. 22). This may be the land purchased by Jacob near Shechem, or it may be the area mentioned by the apostle John close to Sychar (cf. 33:19; John 4:5). We might surmise that after Jacob purchased the land surrounding "Jacob's well" it was later taken over by Amorites and still later recovered by Jacob. There is no biblical record of this, however.

In Conclusion

The chapter leaves us with some excellent examples from the last days of Jacob. First, that he did not lose sight of God's promise even in old age. We, like Jacob, should grow in faith and confidence for the future based on the faithfulness of God that we observe in the past. We have seen him witnessing to the next generation of God's good dealings with him (Ps. 145:4). We have noted, too, the superiority of a spiritual legacy over a material one that parents may leave their children. Another example we see here is Jacob's yielding to the principle that God's ways are not our ways, as when he followed the Spirit's leading instead of the customary practice when he bestowed the blessing on Joseph's two sons.

Finally, and most importantly, we see Jacob reaching the high point of his whole life in submitting to God's sovereign will and bowing in worship. How many of God's people slip backward in the final years of their lives. May we, like Jacob, persevere to the end and reach ever higher until the Lord takes us home.

Jacob Prophesies Concerning His Sons

Jacob spent the final hour of his life pronouncing blessings on his sons and prophesying about the future of their descendants. These oracles have both intrigued and confused many Bible scholars. Some of the statements are *characteristic* in nature, as when Jacob noted certain prominent traits in his sons and predicted them characterizing their tribes in coming generations. Other statements are purely *prophetic.* These looked forward to the invasion and conquest of their new land. Still others are *messianic* in that they looked further into the future to the "last days," that is, events leading up to or related to the reign of Messiah.

Jacob's last words to his sons may be helpfully compared with Moses' last words to the twelve tribes shortly before *his* death (Deuteronomy 33). Jacob's sons were not, as a group, either great or godly men, but because of the importance of the family as a whole, God allowed them to have a prophetic glimpse into their future. The 3600 years since then have proved many of these prophecies true. From the twelve men standing around Jacob's bed came influential leaders like Moses, far-seeing prophets like Isaiah, great kings like David, and brilliant scholars like Paul.

A Great and Solemn Occasion (vv. 1-2)

It was probably immediately after he finished blessing Ephraim and Manasseh that Jacob pronounced these blessings on his sons, though the timing is not specifically stated. Joseph had been called to Jacob's side because of his deteriorating health, so it is likely that his other sons were summoned at that time as well. Perhaps they were arriving as Jacob was speaking to Joseph's sons. With all of them gathered around him, Jacob called for their attention: "Gather together, that I may tell you what shall befall you in the last days." It was one of the great and solemn occasions of biblical history. In voicing these prophecies, Jacob was speaking under the inspiration of the Holy Spirit. The words are in poetic form and include a great deal of symbolism. Jacob's careful attention to the spiritual well being of his family at the end of his life is an example that many of us as believers could follow. We should pay more attention to approaching death and prepare to leave our loved ones advice and admonition suited to their individual spiritual condition and progress.

Jacob knew that God was calling him to look into the future. The expression "in the days to come" or "last days" is a common expression in Scripture connected with some aspect of Messiah's coming and reign on the earth. In studying these prophecies, we shall look for references to the far future as well as to those that were fulfilled in the relative short term. Many of the Old Testament prophets moved from the near future to the far without distinguishing which was which, and we shall observe that same feature in these prophecies.

In verse 2, Jacob appealed to his sons to "hear" and to "listen." He was stressing the importance of his last words. Note that Jacob used both of his names in referring to himself. He called them to "hear" as the sons of Jacob because there was much of the flesh (which had also characterized Jacob himself) in his sons. But he also said they should "listen to Israel [their] father." Just as God changed his name from Jacob to Israel as he grew spiritually, they had the same opportunity to be changed if they chose to yield to God's will in their lives.

The sequence in which Jacob addressed his sons was not in their birth order. All six sons of Leah were spoken to first, then the four sons of his concubines (although not in any particular order), and finally Joseph and Benjamin, the sons of his beloved Rachel.

The Prophecy Concerning Reuben (vv. 3-4)

Reuben, his oldest son, was probably standing closest to him. Like all firstborn children, he had been his father's pride and joy. But Reuben already knew he had forfeited the right to the position of authority in the family. Now he stood as a pathetic figure in the presence of his aged father. Jacob praised him at first by calling him "My might and the beginning of my strength." This phrase was used of other firstborn sons (cf. Deut. 21:17) as fathers expect great things from their firstborn. Jacob called Reuben "the excellency of dignity and the excellency of power."

But Reuben fell from the standard of excellence when he committed incest. Notice the complete reversal of language in the next verse: Jacob prophesied that he would "*not* excel." Sadly, he did not live up to his father's hopes. Reuben turned out to be a weak character with ungoverned impulses. Jacob called him "unstable as water," or literally "a boiling over of water." What an apt metaphor for unstable emotions! Reuben did not follow through on his intentions to rescue Joseph from the pit. He was not even present when the others sold him to the Midianites. As a man of no firm principles, he committed one of the worst forms of immorality—incest (35:22; cf. Deut. 27:20). After all these years, it still pained Jacob to think about it. It appears that Jacob turned from speaking to Reuben and said to his brothers in what must have been a horrified tone, "He went up to my couch." The language may indicate that he was making this public for the first time. Jacob made it clear that it was for this reason that Reuben had forfeited his natural birthright. He said emphatically, "You shall not excel" (v. 4; cf. 1 Chron. 5:1). Like Esau, he lost his birthright by indulging the flesh. Many of God's children have followed in Reuben's footsteps and lost their future usefulness by giving in to the flesh.

As history unfolded, the tribe of Reuben never provided a single leader for the nation. Reuben was the first tribe that was satisfied to not cross over into the Promised Land but to stay on the east side of the Jordan. They asked and received approval from Moses to settle there (Numbers 32). Later, they did fight under Joshua and helped their brother Israelites to conquer Canaan. However, in the days of Deborah and Barak, the tribe of Reuben failed to answer the call to arms (Judges 5:15-16). Over time, the Bible has only confirmed that Reuben never made a positive contribution to the people of Israel. Was Judas Iscariot from Reuben? We do not know definitively, but "Iscariot" indicates he was from Kerioth that was in the land of Reuben.

Concerning Simeon and Levi (vv. 5-7)

Simeon and Levi were Jacob's second and third-born sons. After Reuben, they would have been next in line for the natural birthright, but like Reuben, they were disqualified. Reuben's weakness had been lust. Simeon and Levi's weakness was an aggressive spirit that expressed itself in cruelty. We have considered the historical background of this prophecy found in Genesis 34 where these two brothers slaughtered the men of Shechem by treachery and deceit after their sister Dinah had been raped. They were known for their hotheaded, vengeful spirit. Jacob said that "instruments of cruelty are in their habitation." This phrase means that they "lived" in the realm of cruelty; they were "at home" with violence.

Jacob judged them here for their inner character that expressed itself in anarchy. He stated plainly that he was distancing himself from their motives and actions (v. 6). Jacob gave two examples of their ruthlessness: they killed a man in their self-will, and they hamstrung an ox. There is a textual question here, but they apparently murdered a man then cruelly hamstrung the oxen they did not want for themselves so no one else could use them. Jacob did not want to be associated with such senseless behavior.

Jacob cursed their angry ways. He then prophesied, "I will divide them in Jacob and scatter them in Israel." It would be to their benefit (and the welfare of others) that their descendants would not be allowed to join forces as they had done at Shechem. They would do less harm if they were spread throughout the land. God did scatter them when they received their inheritance in the land. In the case of Simeon, he was given an inheritance "within the inheritance of the children of Judah" (Josh. 19:1-9). That is, the tribe of Simeon was given a number of scattered cities within the land designated to Judah, but not a separate land area of its own. It was the weakest tribe numerically (Num. 26:14). Some Simeonites were captured and lived outside Canaan in the lands of the Edomites and Amalekites (1 Chron. 4:39-43). Later on, some God-fearing people from the tribe of Simeon left their homes in the northern kingdom to join Judah (2 Chron. 15:9). Eventually, most were either assimilated into Judah or scattered outside of the land.

In the case of Levi, his descendants, like Simeon's, were not given a separate inheritance when they came into the land. They were given forty-eight cities scattered among the other tribes (Josh. 21:1-3). Unlike the Simeonites, the Levites regained a good reputation when they chose to channel their zeal for a good purpose and stood firmly for God's honor in the wilderness. After the people sinned by worshipping the golden calf at Mount Sinai, Moses said, "'Whoever is on the LORD's side, let him come to me,' and all the sons of Levi gathered themselves together to him" (Ex. 32:26). Moses himself was a Levite, and following that incident, God chose the Levites to serve Him as the priestly tribe of Israel in place of all the firstborn (Num. 3:5-10). They were to be the teachers and instructors of the Law. Jeremiah, Ezekiel, and John the Baptist were Levites whom God was pleased to use. The restoration of the Levites to a position of service and worship reminds us that, like Paul, we can put our past behind us having "obtained mercy" in Christ. He has given each of us areas of ministry and has enabled us to serve Him (1 Tim. 1:12-17). May He count *us* faithful too.

Concerning Judah (vv. 8-12)

Jacob did not have anything positive to say about Leah's first three sons, but with Judah it was different. Judah's name means "praise." With a play on the meaning of this word, Jacob predicted that his brethren would praise him, indicating that he would be respected as a worthy leader among them. His descendants would also defeat their enemies (v. 8). Judah did prove to be successful in warfare (cf. Num. 2:9, 10:14; Judges 1:2). Jacob predicted that Judah's "father's children," that is, his brothers, would bow down and submit to his leadership.

Jacob called Judah a "lion's whelp," that is, a young lion. As the tribe of Judah matured, it would become the leader of the tribes in the way that the lion is "king of the beasts." He described Judah's strength and victory in picturing him seizing and killing his prey, then resting after eating his fill. In comparing him to a sleeping lioness (the second use of "lion" is feminine), he foresaw how other the tribes would be in awe of him and would not dare "disturb" or challenge him. The other tribes would submit to Judah. In this way, Judah received the patriarchal authority and the responsibility of the firstborn which Reuben had forfeited.

In the biblical record, Judah did become the leading tribe, but apart from Jacob's prophecy in this passage it would not become evident for a long time. Early leaders of the nation did not rise from the tribe of Judah. Moses came from the tribe of Levi, Joshua from Ephraim, Gideon from Manasseh, Samuel from Ephraim, and Saul from Benjamin. The patriarch Jacob could only tell of the coming prominence of Judah by inspiration from God. When David began to reign over Israel, Judah became the dominant tribe and remained so (v. 10). The "lion" theme extends to the Lord Jesus Christ. Judah was the "lion" of Israel, and his noblest son, the Lord Jesus, is rightly called "The Lion of the tribe of Judah" (Rev. 5:1-14).

The Scepter in the Tribe of Judah

The scepter is mentioned in verse 10 for the first time in the Bible. The scepter was an ornamental staff held by kings when seated on the throne that symbolized their power and authority. The king usually held its base between his feet and its top in his right hand. When the king granted favor to one seeking an audience with him, he would extend the top of the scepter toward the petitioner (cf. Esther 4:11; 5:2; 8:4). Balaam prophesied of the scepter that would come from Israel (Num. 24:14-17). There are three other passages that refer to Messiah's scepter: Psalm 45:6, Psalm 110:2, and Hebrews 1:8. In many Bible translations, Psalm 108:8 and Psalm 60:7 also refer to Judah as God's scepter. This passage in Genesis 49 is highly significant in that it predicts not only that the kings of Israel would come from the tribe of Judah but that the scepter of kingship would remain with Judah until Shiloh came.

The Identity of Shiloh

Judah would retain the kingly rule over the twelve tribes "until Shiloh comes; and to Him shall be the obedience of the people." The word "Shiloh" is possibly related to *shalom,* which means "peace." There was a town in Israel called Shiloh between Bethel and Shechem. During the time of the Judges, the tabernacle was set up there, and it became the worship center of the Israelites. It was never an influential town and was later destroyed by the Philistines. This prophecy, however, is directed to a person ("Him"), not a place, so it cannot refer to the long destroyed town of Shiloh. The word Shiloh may mean the *One who brings peace*, but there is a better interpretation.

Both ancient Jewish commentators and early church fathers considered this to be a prophecy about the promised Messiah. In light of the fact that Jacob was looking forward to "days to come" or latter days, Shiloh as another name for Messiah is very appropriate. Another reading of the phrase "until Shiloh comes" that is favored by some commentators is "until he comes, whose right it is" or "to whom it belongs." Ezekiel seemed to pick up this theme when, in the context of messianic times, he spoke to the last king of Judah saying, "Take off the crown ... until he comes whose right it is, and I will give it to Him" (Ezek. 21:27). When He—Shiloh—comes, the obedience of the peoples shall be toward Him.

Judah in the Line of Messiah

We can imagine that Israel would want to make it clear to his sons who of the twelve would transmit the promised Seed of the woman, the Redeemer from sin first promised in Eden (3:15). Through this prophecy, the identity of Messiah was beginning to narrow. In Genesis 3, Adam and Eve were told He was to be a human being, implied by the word "Seed." In Noah's prophecy, we learned that He was to come from the family of Shem (see comments on 9:26). In Genesis 12:3, it was revealed that "all the families of the earth shall be blessed" through a descendant of Abraham. Now, here in Genesis 49, we learn that He was to be from the tribe of Judah. Jesus Christ came through the tribe of Judah legally through his adoptive father Joseph's line (by David's son Nathan) and by blood through Mary's line (by David's son Solomon). See the genealogies in Matthew 1 and Luke 3 for further study. It is, therefore, reasonable to infer that God was revealing through Jacob that Judah was the vehicle of the lineage of Messiah or Shiloh.

Jacob concluded the prophecy by saying of Shiloh that "to Him shall be the obedience of the people." He would claim His right to rule all people. When Christ came the first time "unto His own" (the Jews), they rejected and crucified Him, but one day He will come again in power and great glory to rule the whole world. The "obedience [gathering] of the people" to Him corresponds to God's great promise to all three of the patriarchs that the scope of Messiah's blessing would extend to "all the families of the earth" (12:3, 22:18, 26:4, 28:14 etc.). At that future time, people from every tribe and nation will gather to Him and acknowledge Him to be the King of kings and Lord of lords (cf. Isa. 52:13; 1 Cor. 15:24).

The Lion of Judah

As a result of this prophecy, the lion became the emblem on the standard of tribe of Judah and is so to this day. The scepter of David's dynasty never departed from Judah until Christ came. Even during the captivity, Daniel of the tribe of Judah stood out as a leader. After the captivity, it was largely the people of Judah and Benjamin who returned and re-established the worship of Jehovah in Palestine until the coming and rejection of Jesus. Up until that time, they were still faithfully recording their family genealogies. Because of these records, Christ will need no further identification when He comes in power and glory. In AD 70, Jerusalem was destroyed, and the Jews (a name derived from "Judah") were dispersed among the nations. At that point, they lost most of their tribal distinctives and family records. However, the role of the tribe of Judah will one day be revived and enlarged; a coming scene in heaven shows Messiah on the throne distinguished as the "Lion of the tribe of Judah" (Rev. 5:5).

Jacob went on to describe Judah's bountiful productivity: vines so strong that donkeys can be tethered to them; grapes so plentiful that everyone's garments appear to be washed in their juice; people so healthy that their eyes are dark from the abundance of wine and their teeth white from the abundance of milk. Isaiah spoke of messianic times when wine and milk will be so plentiful that people won't need to pay for them (Isa. 55:1). Judah was, and will be, a tribe greatly blessed and used by God.

Concerning Zebulon and Issachar (vv. 13-15)

Jacob then turned to Leah's fifth and sixth sons. There is nothing distinctive about these two men in the rest of the Genesis record. Only here do we learn anything of them at all. We learn that Zebulon would dwell at (or towards) the seashore. He would be a haven for ships, and his border would be Sidon. Joshua 19:10-16 describes Zebulon's borders, but they are difficult to define because nothing there indicates that they touched the Mediterranean coast. Maps usually place Zebulon between Mt. Carmel and the Sea of Galilee where there is no seacoast. Zebulon's inheritance may have included Capernaum, as indicated in Matthew 4:13. It certainly was in the region of Galilee where much of Christ's public ministry took place (Matt. 4:15-16). Zebulon's territory was on an important trade route from the Mediterranean Sea to the East.

Jacob described Issachar as "a strong donkey lying down between two burdens" or, as other versions put it, "sheepfolds" (v. 14). The description pictures Issachar as strong, but docile and lazy. He preferred the easy life. Eventually, his rich lands of the lower Galilee region would attract enemies from the north. Without the will to defend himself, his tribe became "a band of slaves" to the surrounding Canaanites. Issachar did produce some noteworthy warriors who are mentioned in Judges (Judges 5:14, 15, 18).

Concerning Dan and Gad (vv. 16-19)

Next in line for Jacob's blessing were the four sons of Bilhah and Zilpah. Jacob may have dealt with them in the order in which they were standing around him. The only specific reference to them in Genesis is of the time Joseph had brought a bad report about them to his father in relation to their caring for the livestock under their charge (37:2). In regard to Dan, Jacob said that he would "judge his people." Samson, who lived in the days of the Judges, was probably the best known of Dan's descendants (Judges 13:2). Dan was also called a "serpent by the way" that bites the heels of horses and causes their riders to fall (v. 17). The people of Dan had the dubious distinction of being the ones who introduced idolatry into Israel (Judges 18:30-31). It was in the city of Dan that Jeroboam, the first king of the northern kingdom, set up one of his golden calves for worship (1 Kings 12:28-30). This may be the reason why Dan is omitted from the list of the tribes in Revelation 7:4-8. This omission has prompted some to think that the Antichrist will come from Dan.

After pronouncing this prophecy about Dan as the "serpent," it is as if Jacob sighed, saying "I have waited for your salvation, O LORD!" (v. 18). Maybe in his mind Jacob linked the thought of a "serpent" with Genesis 3 and the promise of the coming Seed who would crush the head of the serpent after being bitten on His heel. The Seed was the one destined to bring the long awaited salvation. Jacob had already spoken of the "last days" when the people will submit to the Messiah (v. 10). Now, he sighed in anticipation of Messiah's coming (cf. Isa. 25:9). The word for salvation in Hebrew is *yeshuah,* which is also the Hebrew name for Jesus. It may be significant that this is the first occurrence of the word "salvation" in Scripture.

Gad, whose name means "troop," was one of Zilpah's sons. Jacob said that a "troop" of invading raiders would assault his home but that he would "triumph at last." The tribe of Gad chose an inheritance east of Jordan. They were constantly harassed by invading bands from the East but consistently fought back (1Chron 5:18; 12:8-15).

Concerning Asher and Naphtali (vv. 20-21)

The prophecy about Asher was associated with the fertility of the land. They would produce rich food and "royal dainties," probably specialty foods suited for the king's table. Their tribal inheritance was in the north along the seacoast from Mount Carmel to Tyre, known for its olive oil and wheat that Solomon gave to King Hiram (1 Kings 5:11). Unfortunately, they failed to take full possession of their inheritance and were eventually dominated by the lifestyle and people of neighboring Phoenecia (see Deut. 33:24-25). The prophetess Anna, who hailed the coming of Jesus, was from Asher (Luke 2:36-38).

Naphtali was described as a "deer let loose," conveying the idea of swiftness in carrying messages. They would be fast runners in war, and they would compose "goodly" or "beautiful" words. This probably means that they carried messages of victory. One of Naphtali's descendants was Barak, who won a victory over the Canaanites (Judges 4:6, 15). Barak acted on Deborah's word from the Lord like a "doe let loose," and the "beautiful words" were at least partially fulfilled in their victory song (Judges 5:1-31). Later, it was in the land of Naphtali that people would "see a great light," the Light of the world (Isa. 9:1-2, 6-7). Naphtali was part of Galilee, where the Lord Jesus grew up and carried out most of His ministry. Thus, the "beautiful words" can be taken to be the words of the good news of the Kingdom that He proclaimed there (Mark 1:14-15).

Concerning Joseph (vv. 22-26)

The prophecy and blessing of Jacob concerning Joseph was the longest. First, Joseph is pictured as a fruitful grapevine in a vineyard: strong, prosperous, and numerous (v. 22). Second, he is portrayed as an archer viciously attacked by his enemies yet keeping his bow steady. A good archer has to have very strong arms. The arms of Joseph's hands were made strong or supple "by the hands of the Mighty God of Jacob" (v. 24). The imagery is of Joseph, as an archer under a withering attack, being helped or supported by God to strengthen him in the "battle." This was probably a reference to Joseph's personal experiences of betrayal and slavery and his eventual triumph over his brothers, but it is also prophetic of the two tribes, Ephraim and Manasseh, who were his inheritance. In addition, it is an illustration of the helping hand that God gives every believer who trusts in Him (Ps. 28:7).

It was the Mighty God of Jacob who would strengthen Joseph's hand. He is called the "Shepherd, the Stone of Israel" (v. 24). This is the first time that God is directly called either the Shepherd or the Stone, although Jacob earlier alluded to God's shepherding work (48:15). As the Shepherd, God would guide, feed, and protect Israel (Isa. 40:11). As the Stone, in the person of Messiah, He would become a solid foundation for His people, although He would initially be rejected as such (Ps. 118; 22; Isa. 28:16; 1 Peter 2:6-7). Both the Shepherd and the Stone were called the Mighty God of Jacob. Isaiah uses the title "Mighty One" for the one who redeems (Isa. 1:24-27). Jacob said that God would also bless Joseph with blessings from heaven (rain) and from the deep (springs of water). Joseph's descendants would multiply with the blessings of the "breasts" and "womb," picturing an increase in both people and livestock (v. 25).

Blessings Excelling

As he addressed Joseph, Jacob seemed to realize the great extent to which God had blessed him—more than He had blessed either Abraham or Isaac. Jacob had more children and heirs, and presumably more wealth in livestock. Joseph would inherit these blessings "up to the utmost bound of the everlasting hills" (v. 26). This phrase may refer to the hills as places of agricultural and pastoral prosperity, as in other passages (cf. Deut 33:15; Isa. 5:1). Thus, Joseph's descendants could look forward to great prosperity. *Everlasting* in Hebrew can mean either "ancient" or "eternal." The hills around Ephraim and Manasseh were ancient and provided confidence for the future. These blessings were to be "on the head of Joseph" as one distinguished or "separate from his brothers." The word *separate* is the same Hebrew word later used for a Nazarite, a person marked out for special distinction. Many great leaders in biblical history came from Joseph's sons including Joshua, Deborah, and Samuel from Ephraim, and Gideon and Jephthah from Manasseh.

It is prophetically significant that Jacob's prophecies focused particularly on two of the twelve, Judah and Joseph. The descendants of these two men eventually became the two dominant divisions of Israel: Judah in the south and Ephraim in the north. Note that, in the case of Joseph, the promised blessings were largely material, but that, in the case of Judah, the promised blessings to his descendants were spiritual in addition to physical and political.

Concerning Benjamin (v. 27)

The prophecy concerning Jacob's youngest son, Benjamin, is rather strange. Benjamin was the focus of his special love because he was one of Rachel's sons. He was described as a "ravenous wolf" that would devour the prey and divide the spoil. As a wolf, he would overcome his prey skillfully. On the other hand, as a ravenous animal, he would be also cruel and voracious. The Benjaminites became expert archers and slingers (Judges 20:16; 1 Chron. 8:40; 12:2). Their excessive cruelty was demonstrated in the war they fought against their brother Israelites recorded in Judges 20, both in relation to the cause and in the war itself. Saul, the first king of Israel, was from Benjamin and was a man of war. For many years, he hunted David like a wolf hunts its prey. Jonathan, Saul's son, was a skilled warrior (1 Sam. 14:1-23). Queen Esther was also from the tribe of Benjamin. These two showed the nobler side of this prophecy. In New Testament times, the apostle Paul boasted of his lineage from the tribe of Benjamin (Rom. 11:1; Phil. 3:5).

"He Blessed Each One" (v. 28)

After commenting on Benjamin, Moses added an editorial note that "all these [the twelve sons of Jacob] are the twelve tribes of Israel," a description that was used of them throughout the writings of the Scriptures. Moses did not call them the tribes of *Jacob*, but the tribes of *Israel,* the name that God gave to Jacob to mark his spiritual progress. It states that "he blessed them; he blessed each one according to his own blessing." As we have seen, these blessings were both prophetic statements of good and bad things to come and warnings of negative characteristics.

It may seem odd that the oracles of Jacob are termed "blessings." In a very real sense, however, all twelve of Jacob's sons were richly blessed as the founders of the tribes of Israel and the bearers of the promises of the covenant with Abraham. All twelve tribes eventually left Egypt under Moses, and all twelve received an inheritance in the land. But, it is also true that the results of their sinful tendencies followed some of them into succeeding generations. Jacob's prophetic words showed that their present character would have an effect on the nature and usefulness of future generations. This is a most sobering principle that has application for us all.

Jacob's Final Charge (vv. 29-33)

Jacob's final words were a charge to his twelve sons to bury him back in Canaan in the cave of Machpelah at Hebron. He had previously made Joseph vow to do this. Now, he spoke to them all about it. He described the exact place and how Abraham had purchased it from Ephron the Hittite. Jacob never knew his grandmother Sarah, but he was probably present when Isaac buried Abraham there. His mother, Rebekah, had died when he was in Haran, but he and Esau had buried their father in that cave. Jacob went on to say reflectively, "And there I buried Leah." Whatever happened, Jacob wanted to be certain that he would be buried beside her there with his father and grandfather in the land of God's covenant.

Jacob had been sitting on the side of the bed while he spoke his final prophetic words. With his last ounce of strength, he pulled his feet back up into his bed and "breathed his last." And with that, one of history's great men of God departed this life. Jacob died at the very peak of his spiritual experience. His 147 years were marked by struggle, disappointment, and sorrow. His plea for blessing in Genesis 32:26 epitomized his life. He learned through adversity that God was the source of all blessing. His deep longing was to pass it on to his sons. Having done that, "he was gathered to his people" (v. 33). In death, he found what all dying believers find: that it is the doorway to eternal fellowship with God and His people.

In Conclusion

The triumphant end to Jacob's life should encourage all God's people to move on from the set backs and disappointments of life. From the beginning, Jacob had sought the things of God, but he was prone to scheme to accomplish them. Slowly over the course of his life God disciplined him to let go of his scheming, and he submitted himself increasingly to God. The climax was when he allowed Benjamin to go to Egypt with his brothers saying, "And may God Almighty give you mercy" (43:14). God rewarded his submissive spirit by restoring not only Benjamin and Simeon to him, but Joseph. His faith rose to its highest point when he followed God's inner urging to break from custom and reverse the blessing on his grandsons and when he boldly voiced prophetic blessings on each of his twelve sons. He breathed his last as a worshipper, leaning on his staff. May we all keep pressing on so that our last breath is the expression of our highest worship.

The Deaths of Jacob and Joseph

The final chapter of Genesis focuses on Joseph during the remainder of his life in Egypt after the death of Jacob. It describes *the burial of Joseph's father* with his ancestors in the cave of Machpelah. It also describes *the fear of Joseph's brothers,* who thought that he might take revenge on them after their father's death. Finally, the chapter records *the instruction about Joseph's bones,* that they be transported to the Promised Land.

Joseph's Grief (v. 1)

When Jacob died, Joseph grieved deeply as they had been very close. He "fell on his father's face, and wept over him, and kissed him." It is natural for a believer to show his sense of loss and bereavement when a loved one dies, although if the person who has died is also a believer, they do not sorrow as those who have no hope (1 Thess. 4:13). As one of the "strangers and pilgrims on the earth" who "desire a better, that is, heavenly country," Joseph believed he would see his father again in "the city which has foundations, whose builder and maker is God" (Heb. 11:10; 13-16), but he still felt the deep human side of sorrow. Jacob died believing that although the far reaching promises of God to him had only just begun to be fulfilled, every one of them would come to pass (Heb. 11:13). Thus, he died a satisfied man. Joseph fulfilled God's promise that he would "close" his father's eyes in death (46:4). We have no record of how Joseph's brothers reacted, but no doubt they were grieving as well.

Mourning for Jacob (vv. 2-3)

Joseph immediately took charge of all the arrangements concerning Jacob's burial. Egyptian custom dictated that important people be embalmed, and many of them were mummified. Joseph asked his own personal physicians to embalm his father. The whole process took forty days. It was usually accompanied by religious ceremonies in which the favor of the gods would be sought to ensure the afterlife of the deceased. Joseph was probably able to dispense with these because of his high influence and the strong faith in the true God that both he and his father shared.

Pharaoh proclaimed seventy days of national mourning over the death of Jacob—only two days less than the period of mourning for pharaohs. This shows the high respect and honor that Jacob the patriarch had earned since coming to Egypt. He was revered not only by his family but also by the Egyptians, for even Pharaoh had been blessed by Jacob.

Joseph Asks Permission to Go and Bury Jacob in Canaan (vv. 4-6)

When the period of mourning was complete, Joseph made a special request to Pharaoh that he be allowed to bury his father in the cave of Machpelah in Canaan. The request held some risk for Pharaoh, because Jacob's family might be tempted to return to Canaan as the famine was now long past. The Egyptians had come to depend on them for their herding skills and certainly for Joseph's leadership in the country. Pharaoh might have been understandably reluctant to allow them to leave. Diplomatically, Joseph first spoke to the officers in the "household of Pharaoh." He asked them to take the request to Pharaoh and to point out that his father had made him solemnly swear to bury him in his own burial place. He had "dug" the grave for himself, meaning that he had chiseled out the stone indentation where his body would be placed into the side of the cave. He may have done this when he buried Leah there. Joseph also promised Pharaoh that he would return to Egypt.

Jacob is Buried (vv. 7-14)

Pharaoh seemed to fully understand the request and granted his permission, going so far as to order an official state funeral with much pomp and ceremony accompanied by the "servants of Pharaoh, the elders of his house and all the elders of the land of Egypt." The whole procession was protected by the Egyptian army ("chariots and horsemen"). The only members of Jacob's family who stayed behind were their young children. All told, it was "a very great gathering" that made its way eastward through the Wilderness of Shur and the Wilderness of Zin, then northwards on the east side of the Dead Sea (vv. 9-10). Their journey back to Canaan with Jacob's body was a miniature rehearsal for the homecoming of the whole nation of Israel led by Moses and Joshua two hundred years later.

They came to a place just east of the Jordan River called the threshing floor of Atad (v. 10). They stopped there for an official seven-day period of mourning which the local Canaanites remarked was unusually somber (v. 11). The event made such an impression on the Canaanites that they named the place Abel-Mizraim, meaning "meadow of the Egyptians." When the mourning days were over, it seems from the wording of verses 12 and 13 that the Egyptians did not accompany the family across the Jordan. The sons of Jacob faithfully carried out their father's instructions and laid him in the cave at Machpelah near Hebron with Abraham and Sarah, Isaac and Rebekah, and Jacob's first wife, Leah. That burial place, apart from the parcel of land near Shechem, was their only claim in the land at the time. It has been highly revered by Jews, Muslims, and Christians to this day, 3800 years later, as one of the most celebrated graves in the entire world.

When Joseph and his brothers were finished with the funeral formalities, they returned to the camp on the other side of the Jordan, and from there, the whole entourage returned to Egypt. Assuming that they were familiar with God's revelation to Abraham that his descendants would be strangers in another country for several hundred years, they would have known that it was not yet time for them to return to the land of Canaan (15:13-16). With this in mind, they settled back in Egypt, awaiting their return according to God's timing.

Joseph Reassures His Brothers (vv. 15-21)

With the death of Jacob and the resumption of their family life in Egypt, Joseph's ten older brothers realized they were in a vulnerable situation with respect to their powerful brother. They feared that he might take revenge on them for betraying him many years before. It seemed natural to them that, with their father gone, Joseph would use his power to "even the score" or "actually repay [them] for all the evil [they] did to him" (v. 15). For his part, Joseph had long ago proved that he held nothing against them by the way he had shown them grace and provided for them. He believed that God had ordained him to go to Egypt to provide for them for both the near and far future (45:7). But they were still plagued by guilt, and they found it hard to believe that Joseph had completely and finally forgiven them.

The ten brothers decided to send messengers (perhaps Judah and Benjamin) to Joseph to communicate their dying father's plea to forgive them. There is no record in Genesis of Jacob telling his sons to do this, which has led some commentators to suggest that they were trying to deceive Joseph into thinking that their father had made such a request. However, it seems more likely that Jacob wanted to ensure complete harmony among all his sons and was confident that Joseph would honor his request. After relating Jacob's words, the brothers pleaded with Joseph directly: "Now, please, forgive the trespass of the servants of the God of your father" (v. 17). The messengers made a clear confession and asked for Joseph's forgiveness. They had already admitted their sin to him unwittingly (42:21-22), but now they did it openly before him.

It was their first full confession to Joseph, and it is a model confession for God's people because they expressed sorrow for what happened, they admitted doing wrong, and they specifically asked to be forgiven. When we sin against someone, we should make full confession to God first and then to those who have been hurt by the offence. Finally, we should ask for forgiveness so that that the offended party may say, "We forgive you" (cf. 1 John 1:9).

Joseph was deeply touched by his brothers' confession and wept before them. He had forgiven them in his heart long ago. His tears may have been an expression of pity or grief because they had either not understood or not accepted that he *had* forgiven them. Alternatively, he may have wept because he was thankful that they had fully confessed their sin and could now fully enjoy his forgiveness. His brothers fell down before him and stated, "We are your servants." They were now deeply grateful for his forgiving them and would humbly do anything that he asked them to do out of gratitude to him. The fellowship between Joseph and his brothers was completely restored.

Joseph then explained that they had no reason to fear for their future and every reason to enjoy their status as forgiven sinners. There were three reasons why they did not need to fear. The first was that God the Judge would make all things right in His own way. Joseph said, "Do not be afraid, for am I in the place of God?" (v. 19). Clearly the answer was a rhetorical "No." It was not Joseph's right to take vengeance. God will judge all sins in His own way. He says, "Vengeance is Mine, I will repay" (Lev. 19:18; Rom. 12:19; cf. 1 Thess. 5:15; 1 Pet. 4:19).

The second reason was that God providentially controls everything, even seemingly evil things like their betrayal of Joseph. "You meant evil against me; but God meant it for good" (v. 20; cf. 45:5). On the human side, they sinned and betrayed him. On the divine side, God "sent" Joseph to Egypt to preserve life as part of His program for providing for His covenant people. Though God is not the Author of evil, He sovereignly incorporates evil into His purposes. The classic example of this principle is how God used the wickedness of people in crucifying His Son to accomplish our redemption. His ways are past finding out (Rom 11:33). How comforting for believers that they can rest confidently in God, knowing that nothing man can do will thwart His purposes!

The third reason why Joseph's brothers did not need to fear was because their evil was being repaid by forgiveness and love. We read that Joseph said, "Do not be afraid; I will provide for you and your little ones." Then it says that "he comforted them and spoke kindly to them" (literally, to their hearts v. 21). Years before, in order to bring about their confession, he had spoken "roughly" to them (42:7). Now, not only did he forgive them, but he provided for all their needs. What Joseph did here teaches us that forgiveness goes beyond words— it acts, as well.

When it comes to Christian forgiveness, we all should remember what this incident teaches: our God is *just* in taking care of sinful actions; He is *sovereign* in bringing good out of bad situations; and He is *gracious* in returning His love when we deserve His wrath. How often, though, we are slow to accept God's forgiveness, even when we have confessed our sin and know intellectually that He has forgiven us. Like Joseph's brothers, we are still afraid that God will make us "pay" for our sin. We need to accept forgiveness for the spiritual blessing that it is, live in the freedom that it brings, and demonstrate our appreciation for it in our service for Him.

The Death of Joseph (vv. 22-26)

Joseph continued as prime minister in the capital while his brothers returned to working with their herds and raising their families in the land of Goshen.

We do not know how long Joseph remained an official in Egypt. We know that Jacob died when Joseph was fifty-six years old (by computing the information in 41:46, 53, 45:6, and 47:28), and we also know that he died at the age of 110 (v. 22). Thus, there are fifty-four years of his life about which there is no biblical record. The information we *do* have is what the Holy Spirit determined was sufficient to be "profitable for doctrine, for reproof, for correction, for instruction in righteousness" (2 Tim. 3:16), a principle that holds true for all the biblical characters and events about which we sometimes wish we had more details. Joseph did not live as long as his forbears. Abraham lived 175 years, Isaac 180, and Jacob 147. Joseph did live long enough to see some of his descendants. He "saw Ephraim's children to the third generation." This may either mean the third generation from himself (his grandchildren) or the third generation from Ephraim (his great-grandchildren).

Manasseh, his older son, seems to have had just one son called Machir (1 Chron. 7:14) whose son was Gilead, the father of the Gileadites (Num. 26:29). Joseph had opportunity to see his family growing as part of the fulfillment of Jacob's blessing on him and them. Joseph's family must eventually have moved to Goshen with the other tribes of Israel. Eventually a king came to power in Egypt who did not know Joseph (Ex. 1:8). This Pharaoh was a native Egyptian as opposed to one of the Hyksos rulers who had conquered and were reigning during Joseph's lifetime.

How many of Joseph's brothers were still alive when he died is not known, but there were enough to call them together for some final words. Joseph reassured them that "God will surely visit you and bring you out of this land, to the land of which he swore to Abraham, to Isaac and to Jacob." The word *visit* meant there would be divine intervention on their behalf. God did indeed deliver them under Moses. Hundreds of years later in Israel's history, Jeremiah prophesied of the Jews in exile that God would "visit" them and bring them back to their country (Jer. 29:10). God brought them back to their land under Zerubbabel. Just before Jesus was born, Zacharias, the father of John the Baptist, spoke of the birth of Jesus as the long awaited "visitation" from on high (Luke 1:68).

Joseph's Last Request

Joseph, like his father, wanted to be buried in Canaan, but he chose to defer his burial there until God brought them out of Egypt (v. 25). He took an oath from his brothers, saying, "You shall carry my bones up from here." He knew the time would come when all children of Israel would return to the land. He demonstrated in his request that he had great faith in the prophetic revelation of God to Abraham concerning the land, and for that reason, he wanted to be buried there. It was this great confidence that gained Joseph a place among the heroes of faith in Hebrews 11 (Heb. 11:22). His faith was rewarded, for when Moses led the people out of Egypt they carried the coffin containing the bones of Joseph with them (Ex. 13:19). There is no record of where Joseph's body was eventually interred.

In Conclusion

The Genesis story ends with the death of Joseph and the embalming of his body (v. 26) which was then placed in a coffin awaiting the exodus of the people of Israel. The story of Genesis began when God placed His crowning act of creation, Adam and Eve, in the Garden of Eden. When man sinned, having been tempted by the serpent, God gave fallen man a promise of a coming deliverer, the Seed of the woman, who would defeat the evil one and provide salvation from the effects of sin. When depravity reached a pinnacle, God destroyed the world of that time with a great flood. We have seen how the remainder of Genesis traced the early development of the promised Seed. By God's pre-determined plan it had come initially through Adam's son, Seth. After Noah, God chose the Shemites, then the family of Terah, then Terah's son Abraham, then Isaac, then Jacob, until by the end of the history covered in Genesis, God revealed that the Seed would be carried through Jacob's son, Judah. Meanwhile, he, along with all his brothers, were growing their families into a nation in Egypt.

God's purpose was not going to end with the body of Joseph in a coffin. That coffin (or mummy case), while it awaited transport to Canaan, would have been kept in a public place in the growing community of the children of Israel. It would have served as a continual reminder to them that their return to the land was still a future prospect. They would have been assured that the promise of God was certain to be fulfilled in a coming day. It would have given them hope.

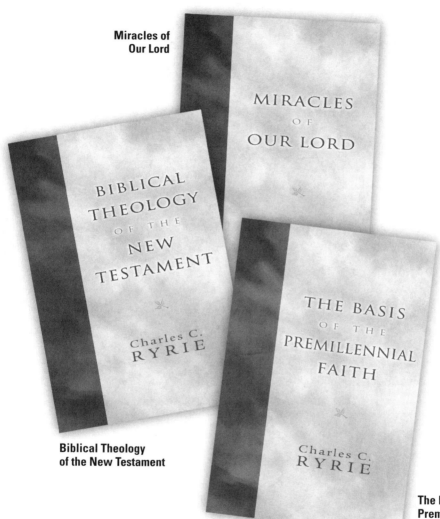

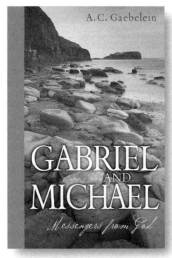
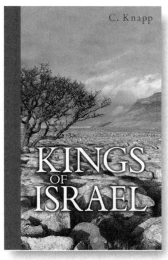
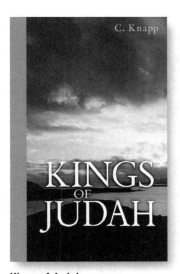
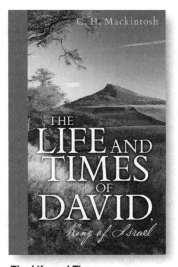

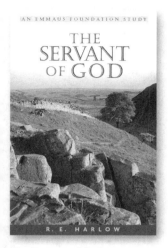
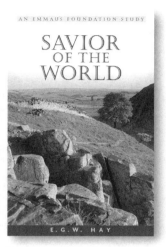
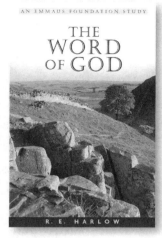
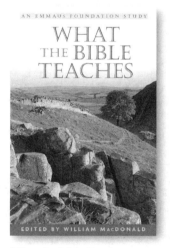
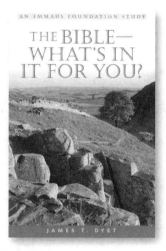

$$
2 \overline{)\,131.53\,} = 65.76
$$

$$
\begin{array}{r}
65.76 \\
2\,\overline{)\,131.53} \\
12 \\
\hline
10 \\
13 \\
14/3
\end{array}
$$

$$
\begin{array}{r}
54.98 \\
146.08 \\
\hline
188.80 \\
+69.28 \\
\hline
49.62
\end{array}
$$